The Oral Interpretation of Literature

McGRAW-HILL SERIES IN SPEECH
Clarence T. Simon, Consulting Editor

THE ORAL INTERPRETATION OF LITERATURE

CHLOE ARMSTRONG *Baylor University*

PAUL D. BRANDES *Ohio University*

McGRAW-HILL BOOK COMPANY

New York San Francisco Toronto London

35188

The Oral Interpretation of Literature

Preface

The Oral Interpretation of Literature is based on two concepts: oral reading of literature vitalizes the experience of literature for the student, and oral interpretation makes a fundamental contribution to the area of oral communication. Therefore, this text is intended to assist the student in the development of his understanding, his sensitivity, and his own reactions. Actual participation in the oral performance results in a more active response on the part of the student. This process should broaden the scope of the student's awareness, deepen his appreciation, and, consequently, add to the enrichment of his total life. Second, the reading from manuscripts of both literary and nonliterary material is becoming increasingly popular in the field of communication. In view of this fact, the ability to understand the printed page and the skill to communicate this understanding to an audience have become more important considerations in the total area of speech training.

Although we recognize there are those students who will be reading aloud to groups outside the classroom and a few who may become professional readers, nevertheless we have emphasized the personal development of the individual in experiencing literature and communicating his experience. We are concerned primarily with the student's reading—in a meaningful manner—worthwhile literature to his classmates, to a group of friends, or to his family circle.

The volume is organized into four parts and the appendix. Part I considers the nature and function of literature with emphasis on the experience of literature. It also considers oral interpretation as it is related to literature and to the field of speech in general. Part II is concerned with selecting, preparing, and presenting literary material. Part III discusses the problem of evaluating the oral-reading process. Part IV covers the different modes of literature: nonfiction prose, prose fiction, drama, and poetry. The appendix offers suggestions for staged reading and the reading of Biblical literature.

v

Throughout the book we have tried to make suggestions specific enough to be meaningful to the teacher and the student, but we have not endeavored to formulate a set of rules.

Literary selections and portions of literary selections have been used to illustrate the discussion, but there is no attempt to include an anthology of readings. There are many excellent anthologies of literature available that can be used with the textbook. In Part II, six literary selections have been included to serve as a common denominator for the discussions in Chapters 5 and 6.

Exercises have been included at the close of each chapter to serve as suggestions for further study and class discussion. It is expected that each teacher who uses the text will have assignments of his own design to supplement or supplant those offered here.

We are aware of our indebtedness to so many friends and colleagues that it would be impossible to name them all. We owe a special thanks to the speech facilities of Baylor University, Wayne State University, and Ohio University for the encouragement and help given us. To our former professors, we recognize our indebtedness. We would acknowledge in particular Gertrude Johnson, Professor Emeritus, University of Wisconsin; Pearl Buchanan, Associate Professor of English at Eastern Kentucky State College; and the late Ralph Dennis, Dean of the School of Speech, Northwestern University. We are thankful to our students who have by their questions and suggestions made a valuable contribution. It was in the classroom with the students that the application of the theory presented was tested. We should like to express our appreciation to Melba Brandes for her assistance in reading and correcting the manuscript and to Catherine Nelson of the Reference Department of Chubb Library of Ohio University for her efforts to help us in documentation.

Chloe Armstrong
Paul D. Brandes

Contents

IV   *How can the oral reader prepare himself to modify audience behavior using specific types as stimuli?*

How does oral reading affect human behavior?

I

I

The function and nature of literature

1

> There is no conceivable way in which the
> experience communicated by an artist in a
> work of art can be "told" by any one person
> to any other person except by pointing
> silently to that work of art in which the
> experience is embodied.

Harold Osborne [1]

In today's world of television commercials, billboard advertisements, high-pressure salesmen, and movie spectaculars, we may not encounter the simple presentation of a work of art of which Osborne speaks. We are being nudged and needled at every turn. Television is shouting at us, "Smoke! Chew! Powder! Grease!" The motion picture is loudly "better than ever." The pages of our magazines say noisily to us over the waves, "You too can have a vacation in Jamaica and you too can look like this and be tanned like this and be sleek like this, if only...."

The din of the hawkers for our time is so immense that we may not even hear Osborne's man pointing silently to the work of an artist. But once we do *hear* this silent fellow, his very silence becomes deafening. This book is concerned with pointing silently to the art that is embodied in literature. It is not in competition with the nudgers and needlers, the budgers and wheedlers that offer so much for so little, for in order to appreciate literature, we must put forth energy on our own part to learn something of the function and nature of the art of composition. Such a task is not to be approached lightly and presupposes a strong motivation on our part. All this book can do is to point silently to literature and ask the question, "What place in our lives should the oral interpretation of literature enjoy?"

---

[1] Harold Osborne, *Aesthetics and Criticism*, Routledge & Kegan Paul, Ltd., London, 1955, p. 156.

The function of literature

Even for the confirmed artist, life must be something of a business. Much of our time is consumed by eating or sleeping or performing menial tasks. What remains to us must be distributed wisely. A goodly portion must be spent in earning our daily bread, and even if we have planned carefully so that our vocation is not only productive but also enjoyable, even then we cannot be at the same time accomplished violinists, psychiatric social workers, travel agents, geologists, and automobile mechanics. As versatile a man as Albert Schweitzer must experience frustrating limitations on how much he can accomplish within a lifetime. Therefore, if we depend upon personal experience alone to enable us to dip deeply into life, our dipping must be confined to one seashore or one lagoon or one sea or, at best, one ocean, while the rest of the waters go untouched. We should give a place in our lives to an appreciation of literature as one means by which we can expand our personal experiences by participating in the experiences of the author.

Second, personal experiences are not only limited, but learning by personal experience may also be costly. The swimmer who, in his efforts to dip deeply into life, is swallowed by the shark, may learn from trial and error; but the knowledge is gained at more cost than he would like. We cannot risk learning everything firsthand. An appreciation of the experiences of literature provides a means by which we can learn from the successes and failures of others.

Third, there are limits to our creativity. We cannot all hope to experience the phenomenon of artistic creation in all areas. If we are to enjoy the riches of arts other than those in which we are proficient, we must find a means of translating the creativity of others into a medium which is meaningful to us. Thus the swimmer may be awkward in his own backstroke, but he can train himself to enjoy watching the Olympic swimmers with their efficient and effortless movements.

The nature of literature

Therefore, a book in the oral interpretation of literature must demonstrate how reading, and particularly oral reading, may help man in his quest for ever-widening experience. The nature of literature enables us to broaden our scope of knowledge by drawing on the *realistic* experiences of the author, on the *imaginative* experiences of the author, and on the *vicarious* experiences of the author. Unless we enjoy the experiences that we borrow from others, our horizons must be narrow.

Participating in the realistic experiences of the artist

There have been times when all of us have come into contact with something of great beauty. In an attempt to share this beauty with a friend, we may have said, "This is beautiful," or "This is awesome," or "This is wonderful." On the other hand, we may have witnessed an automobile accident which provoked us to say, "This is terrible" or "This is frightening" or "This is an experience I shall never forget." It is difficult to sense the totality of the experience in either instance without expressing what is being felt. As people stand watching the Grand Canyon, something happens to them. They must respond. The response demands a mode of expression, which may take the form of a prolonged silence, or it may be vocal, as it was when the woman said, "Golly, what a gully!" Such a response is not literature just because it stems from an experience, but a similar reaction did give rise to the artistic musical expression by Ferde Grofé called the *Grand Canyon Suite*.

Literature preserves for us the experiences of the artist when he is forced to respond. Charles Dickens in *David Copperfield*, Jane Austen in *Pride and Prejudice*, and Thomas Wolfe in *You Can't Go Home Again*, by sharing their lives with us, enable us to do what our personal experiences may never afford, i.e., to travel to London or to live in a country house or to return home after an extended leave. In his poem "To a Contemporary Bunkshooter," Carl Sandburg is recounting for the most part his reactions to Billy Sunday, the religious revivalist of the late nineteenth and early twentieth centuries whom Sandburg had observed preaching at mass meetings and in churches. Such artists have presented their personal experiences for us in art form, permitting us to expand our knowledge judiciously even though we lack the creative ability to write such literature ourselves.

Participating in the imaginative experiences of the artist

Even in the most realistic writing, authors may use imaginative experiences intermingled with their realistic experiences. Sandburg draws from his life in and around the Windy City in his poem "Chicago," but he uses his imagination as well when he says: "Flinging magnetic curses amid the toil of piling job on job, here is a tall bold slugger set vivid against the little soft cities...." Mark Twain combines his actual experiences with his imaginative ones in such works as *Life on the Mississippi* and *Roughing It*. The following passage from *The Adventures of Huckleberry Finn* illustrates how Clemens combines the realistic with the imaginative. Of course, Twain had

had prayers and scripture read to him at his home in Hannibal, Missouri, and had known old maids such as Miss Watson and rapscallions like Huck. Watch how he puts them all together with an imaginative touch for cement:

After supper she [the Widow Douglas] got out her book and learned me about Moses and the Bullrushers, and I was in a sweat to find out all about him; but by and by she let it out that Moses had been dead a considerable long time; so then I didn't care no more about him, because I don't take no stock in dead people.

Pretty soon I wanted to smoke, and asked the widow to let me. But she wouldn't. She said it was a mean practice and wasn't clean, and I must try to not do it any more. That is just the way with some people. They get down on a thing when they don't know nothing about it. Here she was a-bothering about Moses, which was no kin to her, and no use to anybody, being gone, you see, yet finding a power of fault with me for doing a thing that had some good in it. And she took snuff, too; of course that was all right, because she done it herself.[2]

Persons of all ages who have missed experiencing the way Mark Twain imagined Huck to be are poorer than they need to be.

Participating in the vicarious experiences of the artist

Kenneth Burke says: "We do not have to be drug addicts to respond to the guilt of a drug addict."[3] Whereas De Quincey writes of his realistic experiences in his essays *Confessions of an English Opium Eater,* other writers have dealt with drug addiction without being addicts themselves. They have experienced other emotional and physical struggles and are able to substitute these real experiences for the experience of narcotics, thus gaining an understanding of opium by simulation. Such simulated experiences are termed *vicarious.*

In the fall of 1961, a member of the Peace Corps, Margery Michelmore, lost a postcard she had written describing conditions in Nigeria, where she was stationed. The postcard was found by a Nigerian, duplicated, and made public; such a reaction occurred that Miss Michelmore was relieved of her duties in Africa and returned to Washington. Upon hearing that she had offered her resignation to the Peace Corps, President John F. Kennedy wrote as follows:

[2] Mark Twain, *The Adventures of Huckleberry Finn,* Harper & Brothers, New York, 1923, p. 2. Reprinted by permission of Harper & Row, Publishers, Incorporated.
[3] Kenneth Burke, *The Philosophy of Literary Form,* Vintage Press, New York, 1957, p. 22. Permission granted by the author.

Dear Miss Michelmore:
I want you to know that we are most appreciative of your steadfastness in recent days. We are strongly behind you and hope that you will continue to serve in the Peace Corps.
Sincerely,
John F. Kennedy

How could President Kennedy have known about Miss Michelmore's steadfastness? He knew how difficult it was for him to be steadfast in his "recent days" and he was able to transfer this experience so that he could gain an appreciation of Miss Michelmore's difficulty. By empathizing and putting himself in her place, the President was able to comprehend a matter that lay outside the periphery of his immediate experience.

Compositions treating of mythology often illustrate how literature may rest on a combination of real, imaginative, and vicarious experiences. When the goddesses Pallas Athene, Aphrodite, and Hera chose the foundling boy Paris as judge of the most beautiful woman in the world, they began a series of events that led not only to the Trojan War, but also to a long series of compositions, including Tennyson's poem "Œnone," a portion of which is reproduced below:

O mother Ida, many fountain'd Ida,
Dear mother Ida, harken ere I die.
Hear me O Earth, hear me O Hills, O Caves
That house the cold crown'd snake! O mountain brooks,
I am the daughter of a River-God,
Hear me, for I will speak, and build up all
My sorrow with my song, as yonder walls
Rose slowly to a music slowly breathed,
A cloud that gather'd shape: for it may be
That, while I speak of it, a little while
My heart may wander from its deeper woe.

How did Tennyson feel himself capable of writing about this nymph, Œnone, who had lived happily with Paris on Mount Ida and then found herself deserted by her husband when the attractions of Troy took him from her? Tennyson bridged from his own real experiences in love and grief to the fear and desolation of others. Although he could not experience himself what had happened on Mount Ida, he projected his own experiences into those of the nymph and by empathizing, gained an understanding of her grief. Then he mingled his real and vicarious experiences in his imagination to portray a girl lost and forlorn in an ancient world.

The position of the interpreter

Although the writer may use any of the types of experience to create his literary selection, all of the artist's experiences become vicarious for the interpreter. By his association with literature, the student experiences vicariously many things outside the realm of his daily life. We do not mean to imply that vicarious living is a substitute for real living, but only that, for the reasons pointed out previously, our personal experiences have their limitations. The vicarious experiences gained by reading literature can help the student to be aware of the potentialities of his surroundings and to understand his reaction to his environment. Thus literature offers a humanizing influence on its readers and is therefore one of the chief contributors to education and to society.

The responsibilities of the interpreter

The interpreter should understand that, just as scientific investigations may produce unfortunate results, such as poison gases, bacteriological warfare, and atomic bombs, artistic endeavor may also be destructive. There is nothing inherently altruistic or benevolent in the poet's creative experiences. The artist communicates what he feels. There may be desirable and pleasant aspects to the experience, but there may be undesirable and unpleasant aspects as well. The student who is subjecting himself to the humanizing influence of literature must learn to expose himself to a wide variety of experiences. He must not shy away from the stark realities of life that the artist may create.

Although all literature results from an experience, not every experience results in literature or in any other significant creative form. Just as each tourist who visits the Grand Canyon does not produce a painting or music from the inspiration he receives there, so every major emotional experience we have cannot in itself produce a poem or a novel. An artist with creative ability must use his knowledge and skill to translate the sensation into an art form. Art, says DeWitt Parker, "is [an] experience held in a delightful, highly organized sensuous medium, and objectified there for communication and reflection." [4] It is this experience and its highly organized literary style that the interpreter must take into consideration.

An appreciation and understanding of literature cannot be easily achieved by a reliance upon faith, hope, and charity. It is not enough

[4] DeWitt H. Parker, *The Principles of Aesthetics*, 2d ed., Appleton-Century-Crofts, Inc., New York, 1947, p. 42. Copyright, 1920, 1946, F. S. Crofts & Company, Inc. Reprinted by permission of Appleton-Century-Crofts, Inc.

just to feel deeply. In order to understand literature, the reader must know the medium in all its aspects, blending what he knows of the artist with what he knows of the art. Burke points out that the motivation out of which the author writes is symbolic of the structure and values of the writer, or "if you look for a man's *burden,* you will find the principle that reveals the structure of his unburdening; or, in attenuated form, if you look for his problem, you will find the lead that explains the structure of his solution." [5] Therefore, the student of interpretation must investigate the artist to understand fully the art. If the reader is to bring from the printed page a literary experience, he must have sufficient knowledge to comprehend the burden and the unburdening. If he is to know and to evaluate his own reactions to the selection, he must be keenly aware of the total artistic creation. Such an awareness can only come through close contact and study of the selection and its environment. It has too often been considered *unartistic* to probe into the structure of literature. It was thought that to do so would in some way destroy the beauty of its creativity. Appreciation and understanding cannot be achieved by striving to feel deeply, while ignoring a proper study of how and why a selection comes into being. However, in making his evaluation of literature, the student must keep a balance of the emotional and the intellectual. As Langfeld points out, the attainment of perfect balance "must remain a guiding principle for the healthy development of a lasting art." [6] If this balance is disturbed in favor of analysis at the expense of synthesis, then those who say that a study of the medium destroys the beauty of the selection have some justification for their position.

Summary

Literature is the most complicated of all forms of art. Moreover, the positive principles of a logical coherence have yet to be established. Perhaps such principles do exist. If they do, it may be that we shall never find them. In the meantime, although the tasks are not easy, the aesthetic approach is not beyond the understanding of the student. The effort to achieve such an understanding is more than worthwhile, for it will help the student to a fuller appreciation of his own real experiences. It is well for the reader to remember that, by its very nature as an art, literature will develop in him the habitude of change. The reader who explores literature will continue to search and to build. This is one of the greatest values of the art form.

[5] Burke, *op. cit.,* p. 78.
[6] Herbert S. Langfeld, *The Aesthetic Attitude,* Harcourt, Brace and Company, Inc., New York, 1920, p. 5.

Amid the din of the hawkers stands the interpreter, pointing silently to a work of art. An appreciation of his position and a knowledge of his skills are the goals of this book.

Exercises

1. Recall a specific time when you experienced a particular work of art. You may choose a painting, sculpture, concert, play, or any other art form. Recall your reaction. Was your vicarious reaction based upon the response to realistic, imaginative, or vicarious experiences on the part of the artist? Have you thought of this experience often since the time it occurred?
2. What novel or short story have you read that has taken you vicariously into other countries. How vividly were the foreign scenes created for you? Was the scenery or the action predominant?
3. Recall a poem, drama, or short story which provided for you both an emotional and an intellectual adventure. How well can you differentiate between the emotional component and the intellectual component?
4. Read a short story such as "The Open Window" by H. H. Munro or a portion of a novel such as *Roughing It* by Mark Twain. Try to distinguish which of the author's experiences were personal and which imaginative. How did you as the reader react vicariously? Read the selection aloud to yourself and try to follow the blending of the artist's realistic, imaginative, and vicarious experiences.
5. Select a report of a murder from a daily newspaper. Then read Ernest Hemingway's short story "The Killers." Distinguish between the two experiences. Examine other newspaper and magazine reports, searching for the same theme that you have discovered in a reputable short story. What makes for the difference between the two vicarious experiences that you receive?

The unique values of oral interpretation

2

Human knowledge for Aristotle exists in the full sense only in the enunciation, either interior or exteriorized in language; the saying of something about something, the uttering of a statement, the expression of a judgment....

Walter J. Ong [1]

Chapter 1 established in general the function and nature of literature. Chapter 2 will point out the particular values of learning to read literature aloud by analyzing the aural component in meaning and then by demonstrating how this aural component enhances the study of literature.

The aural component of meaning

People are in the habit of saying, "It just doesn't *sound* right to me" or "I didn't mean it to *sound* that way, but when I said it, it *sounded* all wrong." Such people are acknowledging that the words they *see* are affected by the words they *hear*. When we use language to express our thoughts, we must accept the inevitability that words have both a *visual* and an *aural* connotation. The ancient and medieval scholars recognized the importance of sounding an idea. Socrates taught by conversation; Plato wrote down his thoughts in dialogue form so that the interpersonal relationships could be retained; Aristotle attempted to continue the tradition by treating knowledge as basically oral. Rome recognized the gestalt of the visual and the aural, while medieval universities continued to encourage disputations in class and to examine scholars orally on their *theses* or points of view.

When the age of science arrived, scholars came to distrust the

---

[1] Walter J. Ong, *Ramus: Method, and the Decay of Dialogue; from the Art of Discourse to the Art of Reason,* Harvard University Press, Cambridge, Mass., 1958, p. 108.

spoken word because of its complexities and uncertainties. The written word was unwieldy enough for the scientist without adding the unpredictable factor of sound. The laws of the spoken word, from the time of the Renaissance until comparatively recent years, were allowed to remain in the subjective state of development which they enjoyed in the ancient world. Logic in the sixteenth and seventeenth centuries therefore progressed rapidly toward the visual, and the attempt of modern philosophy to perfect a symbolic logic devoid of oral concepts by substituting mathematical symbols for words demonstrates the continued efforts of some phases of science to circumvent the complexities of words.

The curriculum of the modern university demonstrates the schism between the visual and the aural. There are separate courses in English and in speech, with departments of English and speech both offering courses in drama. However, an effort to reunite the visual with the aural has contributed to the development of several modern disciplines. Sociology and psychology, semantics and communication have not hesitated to join a study of the visual with a study of the aural. College catalogues now feature courses in human relations, public relations, industrial relations, industrial sociology, labor relations, social psychology, and group dynamics. These developments represent new disciplines created to effect a reunion of a divided curriculum.

This book will assume that the emphasis on the aural in classical learning was not misguided and that the development of new academic disciplines which recognize the aural demonstrates that the pendulum of knowledge caught in the web of the scientific method has begun to loosen itself from the behavioristic emphasis on the visual. This chapter will show the particular way in which oral interpretation, by combining a study of the visual with a study of the aural, can assist in the study of literature.

The importance of the aural component in literature

Suppose for a moment that a law is passed stipulating that sellers of sheet music must warn their customers that under no condition is the music to be played, but only read silently. How much sheet music would be sold? Or suppose at the next dance the orchestra sat quietly in their chairs, reading sheet music silently, while the couples on the floor had copies of the music and read it silently over their shoulders as they danced. Utterly ridiculous? But are we certain that we are not already involved in situations just as incongruous? It is not at all unusual for college students to be told to *read* a play for the next day's assignment or to *read* Wordsworth's lyrical poetry for an examination. Yet, here go the dancers with their sheet music in front of them, and if the professor may be said to be the orchestra, he reads his Wordsworth silently at home while the students read it silently in their dormitories. The amazing thing is that we are puzzled as to why some students resist literature, when we confine their experience with it to the visual.

The uniqueness of the oral presentation of literature lies in its communication of sound from one person to another. Therefore, all the strengths that are derived from sharing what we have with others by the medium of the spoken word are the unique strengths of oral interpretation. These strengths lie first in the additive component of sound, and second, in the interaction this sound creates between the reader and his audience.

The additive component of sound [2]

How many times do we feel the urge to read to someone a particularly effective passage that we have just enjoyed reading silently. How many times has someone said to us, "Sit down. I have something I want you to hear." Man likes to *hear* his thoughts as well as to *see* them. Reading some literature silently makes it as innocuous as a silent merry-go-round, or a noiseless ocean, or a muzzled football crowd. At least two literary forms are by nature oral. All poetry and all drama must sound better when read aloud than when read silently, or the poetry and the drama are, to that extent, defective. Therefore Dylan Thomas's *Under Milk Wood* is good poetry because it improves with oral reading, whereas Shelley's play *The Cenci* is bad drama because it suffers from oral presentation. Recall that the poet has his origins as an itinerant minstrel who accompanied his selections on a musical instrument and that early drama combined music and words very skillfully. Poetry and drama must suffer from incompleteness until they are freed from the restraints of the visual and allowed the freedom of the aural.

In order to clarify why this freedom will develop, let us discuss the properties of sound as they contribute to a fuller understanding of A. E. Housman's poem the "Lancer."

Lancer [3]

I 'listed at home for a lancer,
  Oh who would not sleep with the brave?

[2] Cf. Joseph F. Smith and James R. Linn, *Skill in Reading Aloud,* Harper & Row, Publishers, Incorporated, New York, 1960, chap. 9.
[3] From A. E. Housman, *Complete Poems,* pp. 9–10. Copyright 1922 by Holt, Rinehart and Winston, Inc. Copyright renewed 1950 by Barclays Bank Ltd. Reprinted by permission of Holt, Rinehart and Winston, Inc.

I 'listed at home for a lancer
    To ride on a horse to my grave.

And over the seas we were bidden
    A country to take and to keep;
And far with the brave I have ridden,
    And now with the brave I shall sleep.

For round me the men will be lying
    That learned me the way to behave,
And showed me my business of dying:
    Oh who would not sleep with the brave?

They ask, and there is not an answer;
Says I, I will 'list for a lancer,
    Oh who would not sleep with the brave?

And I with the brave shall be sleeping
    At ease on my mattress of loam,
When back from their taking and keeping
    The squadron is riding at home.

The wind with the plumes will be playing,
    The girls will stand watching them wave,
And eyeing my comrades and saying
    Oh who would not sleep with the brave?

They ask and there is not an answer;
Says you, I will 'list for a lancer,
    Oh who would not sleep with the brave?

The contribution of tempo to the aural component of meaning.
We will begin with the most specific element of tempo—rhyme—and
proceed from this to the most indefinite of its elements—rhythm.

Although one may *think* of how Housman's words "brave" and
"grave" rhyme, one can get only an imperfect conception in comparison with the richness he feels when he actually utters these words
himself or hears them uttered effectively. It may be true that the poor
oral reader will "fuzz" the thrill of the rhyme with an ineffectual reading, but if oral reading is to be discouraged on this basis, then all
student chemistry experiments must be curtailed because student
chemists do not perform with the proficiency of professional chemists.

Not only the *rhyme* but also the *meter* is enhanced by oral reading. The regularity of the beat almost imitates the martial air of Housman's soldierdom. A sounding of the words will permit the reader and
his audiences to *feel* the shadows of the troops bumping against the

fence posts and splashing down into the puddles as the early morning sun stretches the horses and their riders into giant shadows on the wet grass.

Some literature has neither rhyme nor meter. In such instances, an oral reading exposes the basic rhythm of the style, which may remain concealed altogether in a silent reading. The most obvious tribute to rhythm in the "Lancer" is the refrain, whose regular form placed irregularly throughout the selection demonstrates the rhythm of the reality of death versus the rhythm of the unreality of soldierdom.

Latter portions of this book will treat rhythm, meter, and rhyme in detail. The point to be established here is that an effective oral reading of "Lancer" will allow the student to join in the experiences of Housman in a full and rich way. That there may be some who can read the poem silently with immense satisfaction does not detract from the propositions that (1) many others could not respond as deeply without the assistance of an oral stimulus and (2) even the pleased silent reader will be more satisfied with an effective oral reading.

The contribution of pitch, volume, and quality to the aural component of meaning. Not only does *tempo* have much to add to the meaning of Housman's "Lancer," but the three other properties of sound—*pitch, volume,* and *quality*—are necessary to complete the meaning of the poem. The "Lancer" is, like all poetry, a dissertation addressed to the reader. Housman even goes so far in the last stanza as to address his audience directly: "Says you, I will 'list for a lancer...." Not only is he talking to us, but he puts words in our mouths and causes us to point back. Such a poetic conversation cannot be completely meaningful unless it is imbued with the properties of pitch, volume, and quality. Without such additions, the poem becomes not a conversation but rather a bushel basket full of words.

In order to demonstrate how much pitch amplifies meaning, try reading the poem silently or orally with a constant pitch level.[4] Then, in order to demonstrate how an oral reading may differ from a silent reading, plot the pitch pattern as the poem is read silently, using any simple device to note the rise and fall of the pitch. Afterwards, read the same poem orally and plot the pitch pattern. Compare the two to see if the actual hearing of the words affected the imaginary hearing of the poem. Examine in detail the line "The wind with the plumes will be playing." How much of the meaning of the word "wind" is dependent upon the pitch, the volume, and the quality with which it

---

[4] See Appendix C for a note on the interaction of oral reading and silent reading skills.

is uttered? Is not the vicarious experience heightened by hearing the wind play in the plumes? Wind has a pitch, a volume, and a quality. Without their addition, we leave incomplete the strange motivation that the soldier feels to enlist in an army which may lead to his death.

The particular ways in which the properties of sound—tempo, volume, pitch, and quality—enhance literature will be discussed in detail in subsequent chapters. The point to be made here is that these properties of sound so contribute to the comprehension of literature that their omission often results in an incomplete communication of the art form.

The contribution of diction to the aural component of meaning. Authors choose their words carefully, watching for the interactions of sound. A pronunciation of his words re-creates what the author had intended his meaning to be. For example, Housman uses alliteration in his phrase " 'list for a lancer." He has striven rather hard to get his effect, dropping the prefix *en-* in deference to dialectal usage so that the *l* sounds are both initial. When this phrase is spoken orally, the alliteration emerges with strength. The repetition of the sounds is representative of the lulling of the intellect which encourages a man to risk his life for a slogan. The phrase " 'list for a lancer" is the keystone to the whole poem. Its sounding will force the oral reader to struggle to keep the phrase from absorbing the poem and thereby he will sense its strange attraction for the lancer.

At times we are so accustomed to a word that we do not hear its sound at all. It may take a person who is learning English to point out to us relationships which we should have been hearing all along. A French engineer, striving to pick up English from his American military associates, confused the two words "sweetheart" and "sweatshirt." The American soldiers spoke often of both, and the Frenchman, who was listening for the sound of the words, found the pressure patterns, the rhythm, and the sound repetitions similar. The poet wants us to abandon our customary concept of words in order that we may actually hear their sounds, almost as if the words were being said for the first time. The combinations may be jolting and impelling, or quiet and soothing. One foreigner found the words "cellar door" beautiful. Could not a native-born Englishman or American discover similar pleasures even in familiar words if he trained himself to *hear* rather than just to *see?*

The contribution of dialect to the aural component of meaning. An American couple stood in amazement outside a motion-picture house in Paris featuring "Woody Woodpecker" with French subtitles.

How could Woody speak French? His personality seems so interwoven with American English that a French woodpecker would not be Woody at all.

So it is that literature is written in a particular language with connotations all its own. These connotations are more aural than visual. A poet who tries to preserve dialect in a poem must resort to an improvised usage of punctuation and spelling to achieve even a semblance of what he hears as the flavor of the speech of the area. Thus Housman, who had heard the *en-* of "enlist" slighted in the dialect of his area, chose to drop the prefix and substitute an apostrophe. Yet he was powerless to convey to his readers the flavor of the pronoun "I" as it was pronounced in his area. Only an oral reading could make such a contribution.

At times a word appears in one language which is absent from another. The word "home," the sound of which contributes so much to the folk music of England and America, is absent in French. The sounds "home" and "chez lui" are quite different and emphasize the inadequacy of the French phrase to achieve the meaning of the English word. Again, we like the sound of a foreign word rather than our own because of the freshness it provides. The French like to speak of "les girls" because they find the meaning refreshing and distinctive from "les filles" or "les femmes." It is not surprising that the word "girls" has an individualistic sound, for it is part of our heritage from Old English. Housman chose it deliberately for his poem, putting the girls on the sidelines, waving the lancers to their death. He also employs the word "lancer" which is highly English in its implications in spite of its Norman antecedents. These words, "girls" and "lancer" as well as others such as "grave" and "loam," need to be sounded in English to be fully appreciated.

Oral interpretation has as one of its unique values the restoration of the aural component to literature—permitting pitch, tempo, volume, quality, diction, and dialect to reassume their proper roles.

The interaction between the reader and his audience resulting from the additive component of sound

Not only does the oral interpretation of literature assist in re-creating the stimulus as it was intended by the author, but it also permits the more complete stimulus to initiate an interaction between the poet and his audience, to the mutual benefit of both.

The oral interpreter has the distinct advantage of sharing literature with an audience. The impulse to share what we read is universal. The thwarting of such a natural urge is as frustrating as its gratification is rewarding. When a reader is permitted to join with a class in appreciating literature, the feedback that occurs between the reader and his listeners results in at least three advantages.

First, the reader brings to his interpretation a significant contribution to the understanding of literature. It is almost as if he had written a critical essay, proposing to his audience that after due deliberation he had reached the conclusions that result in his interpretation. If an interpreter is to share his selection with others and knows that they will react to what he says, he cannot permit other than a thorough examination of his material. Thus the feedback motivates the interpreter to grasp his material firmly, while, at the same time, it offers the audience a dynamic stimulus which, by its detail, provokes a heightened response. The impetus offered to the interpreter to prepare his material thoroughly results in benefits to both interpreter and listener.

Second, the role of the interpreter is not limited. He is largely free to adopt such methods as will carry the meaning most effectively. At times, the interpreter may become casual with his audience, assuming the role of the conversational public speaker or talking intimately as he explains or narrates, as the case demands. By his informal manner, he can prepare the listener for what is to follow, using a shrug of the shoulder or a lifted eyebrow or a change in tone of voice to say to his audience, "Let this fellow I am reading about enjoy a few moments of boasting, for it cannot last long." At other times, the reader approaches the dramatic. This does not mean that he will "give a performance," but it does permit him to take on the role of the actor. How could one interpret "My Last Duchess" by Robert Browning and omit the dramatic intensity of the character of the duke? How could the dramatic situation in Robert Frost's poem "Wild Grapes" do other than put the reader to a degree in the role of the actor? At still other times, the interpreter assumes for the audience the part of the critic. Each time he reads a selection he is actually saying that, according to his study, this is what the author's work of art signifies. Therefore, the interpreter has a broad spectrum in which he can present literature and a practically unlimited field from which to choose his material. As interpreter, as speaker, as actor, and as critic, the oral reader has a unique role to play. He provides the medium by which the experiences of the author may become the experiences of the audience. His listeners are fortunate, for the reader not only chooses materials which he thinks are suitable to his particular talents, but the fact that he has the opportunity of sharing encourages him to draw freely from any style of presentation he chooses to impart his interpretation to his audience. Without such motivation, the interpreter might never achieve the variety of style of presentation that the selection requires.

Third, the reader and his audience inspire each other to accomplishments which neither might achieve without the other. It is an unusual reader who does not experience during his reading an increased comprehension of his literature. At first glance, it may appear that something is being manufactured from nothing. But new ingredients have been added. In the first place, the reader is expending increased energy in his effort to impart his interpretation. His senses are quickened. His search for perception is heightened. Moreover, his audience is expending energy also, and the feedback of their energy to the reader gives him added strength and encouragement. If this were not so, poets would require no appreciative readers, dramatists no first-night audiences, and baseball players would perform as well in empty parks as before crowded stands. The impetus that his own striving plus the striving of his audience gives to the reader is destined to achieve results for both.

Summary

In presenting contributions and values for any subject, writers are sometimes caught up in their own enthusiasms and thus overstate their case. We do not maintain that oral interpretation is the answer to all educational problems. A course in oral interpretation will not make great readers of all students. It would be foolish to believe that all students who come into courses in oral interpretation go out devoted lovers of literature. Such an appreciation may only be in the process of developing and will reach fruition later on.

Moreover, the advantages of silent reading are in no way to be disparaged. Silent reading is to be highly encouraged. Indeed, who could propose that there are sufficient audiences for all of us to whom we could read our experiences with literature aloud? Even if we wished to do so, what bores we would make of ourselves.

However, there are unique values gained by the student who seriously studies how to read literature aloud. Naturally, he improves his grasp of the art. Don Geiger says: "... the literary person, writer or reader, though he may be in his fulfillment merely a prodigal son come to some home or another, nevertheless knows better what kind of a home it is than all those sons and daughters who have never been away." [5] Reading literature aloud intensifies the feeling of *being away* by adding the aural component which intensifies the stimulus and therefore intensifies the feedback that results from sharing literature with an audience.

[5] From Don Geiger, *Oral Interpretation and Literary Study*, p. 21. Copyright © 1958 by Scott, Foresman and Company, Chicago.

Exercises

1. In your college classes, you have been assigned literature to read. At times you were asked to read this literature silently and at other times orally. Was there any difference in your response to the two assignments?

2. Have you been reading a poem silently and had a strong compulsion to read a portion of it aloud? Can you explain why?

3. Read one of the following poems silently and write a paraphrase of the poem:

   "Song To Celia" by Ben Jonson
   "Elegy Written in a Country Churchyard" by Thomas Gray
   "Sea Fever" by John Masefield

   Then read the poem aloud. Were any of the aural elements of the poem changed following the oral reading? If so, did these changes contribute to a change in your interpretation of the poem?

4. Choose any one of the following selections and explain how the interpreter acts the role of the critic in reading the selection to others:

   "The Garden of Proserpine" by A. C. Swinburne
   "Fern Hill" by Dylan Thomas
   "Musée des Beaux Arts" by W. H. Auden
   "The Lottery" by Shirley Jackson
   "The Fly" by Katherine Mansfield
   "Araby" by James Joyce

5. Make a list of five selections not included in question 4 above which require the interpreter to assume an active role as the critic.

6. Select a short story and discuss the roles you would assume if you were interpreting it to a friend. To what extent would you be the actor? the public speaker? the casual conversationalist? the critic?

7. State briefly in your own words the value of reading literature aloud. Point out where you agree and disagree with the discussion in this chapter.

8. Choose a lyrical poem by William Wordsworth and point out how tempo, pitch, volume, quality, diction, and dialect are important to its meaning.

The contribution
of oral interpretation
to its allied areas

3

Chapters 1 and 2 have shown that literature is a vital source for enlarging the realm of human experience and that oral interpretation has unique values which assist us in appreciating these experiences. Chapter 3 will further annotate the purposes of studying interpretation by showing the contribution that oral reading makes to its allied areas of drama, radio-television, speech and hearing therapy, public speaking, and communication.[1]

It has been said that a course in the oral interpretation of literature is more *fundamental* to the field of speech than courses labeled "fundamentals of speech." An examination of the way in which oral reading contributes to the various aspects of communication, while it may not justify such a broad assertion, will at least point out how basic are the skills of oral interpretation to effective communication.

The contribution of oral interpretation to drama

The association between oral interpretation and drama is obvious. The recent emphasis on staged reading has illustrated again how many shades there are between acting and oral interpretation. It is true that the actor is accustomed to move about the stage, to play to and with other characters, and to add costume and makeup to his performance. Still, the most vital part of acting, the uttering of lines, is very similar to what would be expected of that same actor were he to become an oral interpreter. The actor and the interpreter are both saying, "Through my study and by my understanding of this role, this is what the character is experiencing." Effective staging, lighting, and costume are important factors to drama, but they are meaningless if the actor does not portray his lines properly.

It is a tribute to oral interpretation that some actors, when moving from the stage to platform reading, are surprised at how mean-

---

[1] See note in Appendix C for comments on communication theory.

ingful a restrained presentation can be. It is almost as if they were afraid to let the literature speak for itself, so accustomed have they been to helping it with staging. When the actress Lynn Fontaine read "The White Cliffs of Dover" on her tour of the United States shortly after World War II, she began her reading as she removed a pair of long white gloves. Was such a prop necessary? Successful training in the art of oral interpretation will assist in the development of a sense of how a minimal stimulus may be used to achieve a maximum amount of response.

The contribution of oral interpretation to radio-television

The importance of oral interpretation to the student of radio-television should be as obvious as it is to the student of drama. Although there are occasions for off-the-cuff speaking when a person finds it necessary to ad-lib, most radio-television programs today center around the reading of a manuscript. Written scripts accompany the radio performer, while scripts and the teleprompter dominate much of television. Both media require participants to give life and meaning to the printed page.[2] Such skill requires much more than just pronouncing words clearly and distinctly. The superior radio-television performer does not give the sponsor's commercial, the latest scientific discoveries, and the current international crisis all in the same tone and manner. The speaker may not involve himself emotionally in each situation, but he does learn to give a specific meaning to the words and sentences of his script. Much of the material for radio-television cannot be termed of superior literary value, and therefore, because of its quality, it may be difficult to read meaningfully. However, the reader must, by his bodily participation and his vocal skills, breathe life into the words.

The exigencies of the radio-television industry often require the reporter or announcer to read a script intelligently with little or no advanced preparation. In such instances, the reader must be able to grasp the meaning of his material quickly. He must be skilled in understanding word phrasing at a glance. Courses in oral interpretation are of much assistance in improving impromptu reading.

With the growth and expansion of the radio-television industry have come increasing opportunities for the oral interpreter to accelerate his contribution to society by disseminating good literature to a degree never before possible. Programs featuring readings of a wide variety of material from religious literature to short stories are now becom-

[2] See Richard A. Norman, "Reading Aloud and Extemporaneous Speaking on the Radio," unpublished doctoral dissertation, Columbia University, New York, 1957, abstracted in *Speech Monographs*, vol. 25, no. 2, pp. 93–94, June, 1958.

ing a regular part of radio-television programming. Increased cooperation between radio-television departments and teachers of oral interpretation has come with the advent of reading programs over the educational broadcasting and telecasting facilities of our colleges and universities.

Students in radio-television have been known to ask, "How can I learn truly professional skills here in college, where I get so little opportunity to work with the latest equipment?" It is true that many colleges can offer only simulated technical conditions. But, for the most part, these skills can be mastered in a short period of time in on-the-job training. What the college can offer that the school of hard knocks cannot provide are skills and knowledge that can seldom be learned in the rush and hurry of the commercial station. If the student does not acquire the ability to read meaningfully and individualistically from the printed page while he is in college, he may never do so.

Therefore, the oral interpretation of literature, not only by achieving the goals of Chapters 1 and 2, but also by providing one of the specific skills which is invaluable to the mass communicator, is a core part of training in radio-television education.

The contribution of oral interpretation to public address

Some public speakers who are very fluent extemporaneously and who communicate effectively in ordinary speaking have considerable difficulty in reading to an audience. All of us have witnessed a speaker who does quite well in presenting his own ideas in his own words, but who suddenly ceases to communicate when he finds it necessary to read a document to his audience to clinch an idea. His volume drops. His tempo speeds up without reason. His articulation becomes cloudy. His eye contact disappears. The speaker gives the impression that the material he is reading is something to get through rather than to emphasize, for he feels so inadequate in reading that he unconsciously speeds up to get the reading over with. This speaker cannot interpret the printed page with meaning. In this age of the availability of evidence, when documentation is expected to shift audience attitudes, public speakers more and more turn to a script to read a statement of authority. Moreover, a speaker may wish to read a particular portion of his speech that has been meticulously prepared to avoid the risks inherent in extemporizing.[3] Such situations are not limited to public speaking, but may occur in any form of group communication—discussion, the conference, the semiformal conversation, the court of law, the pulpit, the scientific colloquy, and so on.

[3] See The Professional Paper and the Manuscript Speech in Chap. 8.

The chairman of the board of directors reads the annual report; the businessman at lunch with a colleague cites sales in a given area; the lawyer refers to a case which he feels supports his point of view; the gynecologist presents a paper to the medical convention.

Not only is the end product of interpretative reading valuable to the public speaker, but the disciplines learned by the reader in the preparation of his selection plus the knowledge of literature gained in such intensive study are both valuable in speaking. The interpreter must learn to analyze the diversified elements that contribute to his selection and then to see the whole again in a unified and organized form. The student of interpretation learns to read and reread and to probe all possible avenues of study to obtain a fuller and more accurate understanding of literature. Such analytical training is basic to instruction in public speaking.

Moreover, the interpreter develops an awareness, a sensitiveness to situations in the literature he studies, which prepares him to respond effectively to the various audience atmospheres he encounters in public speaking. The vast storehouse of quotations acquired by the reader and so necessary to the public speaker help to provide a key sentence by which the speaker can let his audience know that he understands their mood. As was pointed out in Chapter 1, most of us are not creative enough to be able to find just the words we need on all occasions. We seek a quotation for guidance. But it is too late, in the middle of an impromptu speech or even in speech preparation, to seek many quotations. Such literature must already be a part of the repertoire of the public speaker so that he can choose from these commonplaces or fund of knowledge the one quotation that will help him to respond to his audience in just the right way.

The contribution of oral interpretation to speech and hearing therapy

Oral reading makes a twofold contribution to speech and hearing therapy. First, it offers the therapist many experiences and much knowledge of human behavior, permitting him to come in contact with many complex emotional problems described in literature. This added awareness and insight into emotional conflict can be helpful to the clinician in understanding complex problems that have resulted in a speech and hearing defect.[4]

Second, the speech therapist may read a story or a jingle to stimulate an appropriate reaction from his patient. Not only does he wish to read the material effectively, but he also wishes to secure the best

[4] See the note in Appendix C on the relationship between personality and speech.

selections possible. Although books do furnish ready-made suggestions for therapy, the clinician must often organize his own procedures to fit the individual needs of his patient. His knowledge of how to read literature aloud plus his knowledge of a wide range of materials will be most helpful to him.[5]

Excerpts from a method of therapy suggested by Bryngelson and Mikalson are given below. Of particular interest here are the instructions that the teachers should make "an effort to read with dramatic interest and inflection" in order to improve the effectiveness of the therapy.

Getting acquainted with sounds [6]

This chapter is composed of sound stories—stories to be read aloud many times during the retraining steps. They help give personalities to the troublesome sounds and are designed to give the children many opportunities to hear their sounds correctly and incorrectly made in an interesting and often emotionally satisfying context.

There are seven such stories, one for each of the most troublesome sounds (SSS, RRR, LA, THA, GA, and KA) and a final one covering some less common sound difficulties (JA, SH, CH, FFF, VVV, ZZZ, and so on).

In these stories, the critical sounds are presented in isolated form and also in words. Specific directions for using the stories in each retraining step are given at the beginning of each chapter. Ideally, the sound stories should be read aloud to the group early in the retraining program, so that the children will become familiar with the personalities of the various sounds. Depending on the number of speech difficulties the teacher has in her group, she may read two, three, or all seven of the sound stories—one (or part of one) a day until all the necessary sounds are personalized. The reading of the stories may be done any time during the school day, since even those children who do not need speech therapy will enjoy hearing the stories and will profit from listening to a repetition of correct speech sounds.

The children need to understand, of course, that it is their active, concentrated listening that makes the ear-training steps a success. The teacher who makes an effort to read with dramatic interest and inflection is likely to raise the listening quotient of all the youngsters in her class.

Sammy, the mountain garter snake
There once was a small snake named Sammy, who admired beautiful things. He liked to look at the sky, the trees—or a bright yellow bird. Whenever something was lovely, Sammy took time to gaze at it.

---

[5] See also Sara Lowrey, "Interpretative Reading as an Aid to Speech Correction, Acting, and Radio," *The Quarterly Journal of Speech*, vol. 31, no. 4, pp. 460–461, December, 1945.

[6] Bryng Bryngelson and Elaine Mikalson, *Speech Correction through Listening*, pp. 17–18. Copyright © 1959 by Scott, Foresman and Company, Chicago.

He lived near a brook high in the Rocky Mountains of Montana. He and his twenty-three brothers and sisters used to gather behind the rocks and bushes to sing and talk. There they sang, "Oh, Say Can You See a Snake," and said "sss sss" over and over again. When they all talked at once, you could hear "sss" all the way down the mountainside. . . .

Summary

The student of oral interpretation is not in an isolated area where a few learn to read a few selections to a few. He is participating in an integral part of the cultural and educational life of the student. The discipline of oral interpretation brings an added contribution to the understanding and appreciation of literature. Reading aloud offers excellent possibilities for social and psychological growth of the individual and allows him to participate more fully in any of the areas of oral communication. Speech training is built on the understanding of material and on the ability to communicate this understanding to an audience. Oral interpretation is fundamental to this concept.

Exercises

1. For one week, keep a record of the number of times you observe the use of oral reading. Pay particular attention to church services, the college classroom, club meetings, and radio-television programs. For each instance, give the situation which motivated the reading, the type of material read, and your evaluation of the results.

2. Write for the program schedule of three educational television stations. In your letter, ask the program director to encircle the programs which feature oral reading.

3. Consult *Vital Speeches* in your college library and choose a speech which features at least three sizable quotations. Copy these quotations with the material which immediately precedes and immediately follows, and prepare yourself to read your excerpts to the class.

4. Read the excerpt from the radio script at the conclusion of this chapter. Then suppose you are preparing yourself to read this script in two different places: first, over the college radio station, second, to your class in interpretation. Make two lists of comments, one including the steps in preparation that would be the same in both instances and another designating the steps which would vary for each.

5. Select a classical speech, from the works of Emerson, William Jennings Bryan, Charles Fox, Burke, Pitt, Robert Ingersoll, Calhoun, Clay, Webster, Lincoln, Cicero, or from the Athenian era, which employs two or more quotations from literature. Name the selections used, discuss why you think they were inserted, and be prepared to read portions of the speech aloud to show how you think the quotation could be read most effectively.

6. Choose a conversational excerpt from a play and prepare to read the selection in class in two different ways, both of which are effectively done but one of which emphasizes the techniques of drama and the other emphasizes the techniques of oral interpretation. You may use whatever assistance from theatrical devices that you choose. Remember that the purpose of this assignment is to clarify what you would do differently in each instance—to see what, if any, variations exist and what their nature is.

Biography in sound [7]

"They Knew Bernard Shaw"

7:55 P.M. *Est*   *March 27, 1955*   *Sunday*

Announcer: "Let me introduce myself . . . Bernard Shaw." The National Broadcasting Company presents another in the transcribed series of biographies in sound, THEY KNEW BERNARD SHAW. In the next 55 minutes you will hear from Sir Cedric Hardwick, Rebecca West, Bertrand Russell, John Mason Brown, Lady Astor, Norman Thomas, Lili Palmer, and others who knew George Bernard Shaw. Now to guide this study into the personality of the Irish playwright, here is NBC's critic-at-large, Leon Pearson. Mr. Pearson.

Pearson: Ever since the turn of the century we in the United States have been influenced by the wit and wisdom of George Bernard Shaw. For most of the 94 years of his life, Shaw shaped the minds of America—feminism, socialism, militarism, politics,—every sort of human behavior capable of being punctured by satire. For some 60 years we have adored him, scorned, rejected him, and paid him a million dollars. Very few were unaffected by him. And if he were here today, he would look around and say: "Now where did you all come from, and what did you come to see? An old man . . . who was once a famous playwright? Well, here is what is left of him . . . not much to look at, is it? It's pleasant to find that I have so many friends. It's almost the only thing that a man of letters, a writer and playwright, artist, it's almost the only thing he has left. And when I look round you, ah . . . I see two Americans there. I have friends everywhere. And one man, a very famous man in his way, used to say that I had friends everywhere, that I hadn't an enemy in the world, and that none of my friends liked me." Like him? Shaw was a man beyond ordinary likes and dislikes. He evoked extremes of adoration and abomination, and people gathered here run the gamut of those feelings.

(Montage of voices): . . . He had a big heart. . . . All intellect and no heart. . . . All children adored him. . . . He succeeded in offending almost everybody. . . . He was an event. . . . Who the hell was Bernard Shaw. . . .

Pearson: Who was he? Well, for one thing—he was one of the two most important playwrights of all time. The number of actors—British and Ameri-

[7] Reprinted by permission of the National Broadcasting Company.

can—who have risen to fame with Shaw would make a Who's Who in the Theatre. Sir Cedric Hardwick.

Hardwick: He was my godfather in the theatre in many ways because it was owing to Shaw's personal interest in me that I really got my big opportunities in the theatre. I recall Shaw saying to me once at the conclusion of a rehearsal, "You know," he said, "you're my fourth favorite actor." And I said, naturally, who were the other three, and he said the three Marx brothers. And I think that both, both in his writing and in our relationship, the thing that impressed me and pleased me more than anything else was his devotion to the profession of acting. And I don't think many actors realize that but for a handful of men that . . . of course Bernard Shaw is an outstanding example, Shakespeare is another . . . but for these men, actors would never have obtained the recognition that they have today, and I think they'd be little more than vagabonds . . . performing clowns. But a good deal of what these men have written and done for us has rubbed off on us and today we are a recognized profession, and, with a few outstanding exceptions, considered a respectable people. And Bernard Shaw as a director was, of course, very much more concerned perhaps with the meaning and significance of his plays than he was with the actor's performances. But his one passion, of course, was clarity of speaking, and he would say on occasion, "What do you mean by a live horse? I have written no line about a live horse. I suppose you're trying to say light force." Shaw was not the school master who taught his actors how to act. He always thought that the actors should give him as much as he could give them. I remember frequently Shaw interrupting actors, including myself, and saying, "You know, the trouble is that you are following my direction" and you'd say, "Well, Mr. Shaw, isn't that what you want?" and he'd say "No. These directions are put in, not for the actor, they are put in for the reader, and I expect my actors to give me something very much better than I can give them."

Pearson: Lili Palmer went to Shaw to read for Cleopatra. . . .

Palmer: He was very insulting and very rude, and I got terribly angry. I was told not to stand up to him, because once you get intimidated then you are finished. He doesn't like it. And then afterwards he made me laugh so much. Two weeks later an old friend of his saw him and that's what he told him. He said, "I made her angry, and I made her laugh, and I wanted to see what she looked like. She's all right. She'll pass."

*How does the oral reader
prepare himself to modify
human behavior?*

II

How does the oral reader choose the proper stimulus?

4

The appreciation of any art implies discrimination. The ability to discern between the worthwhile and the worthless, the good and the poor, and the great and the inferior is fundamental to successful oral interpretation. The student of literature is always faced with a dilemma involving time because, although he must understand his material to appreciate it, nevertheless, the student must make some type of choice before he begins an intensive study. The means by which the student of literature reaches a pragmatic solution to this dilemma vary. Some students prefer that the instructor make the decision for them, telling them what selections to read; other students are tenacious about their prior concepts and develop the habitude to change slowly; still others are overly eager to pursue new paths of endeavor and vacillate without purpose. The good student must learn to pursue, not only in college, but during the rest of his life, the cautious development of the ability to discriminate by admitting change with circumspection. Naturally, the searcher may lose many battles in search of a final victory, whereas the "leaner," the "standpatter," and the "switcher" will win initial battles with no hope of gaining success in the war. At the conclusion of this chapter are several paired comparisons of selections. The student should read them carefully and then make an effort to evaluate which is the superior literature.

Although there is disagreement, and probably always will be and always should be, as to the measurement of greatness in literature, the quest must be an honest one. The student should not be afraid to acknowledge his liking for a selection even if *they* do not consider the selection favorably. There is an inscription over a Scotch university which reads: "They say. What say they? Let them say." [1] The student should remember that he is in the process of improving his taste and judgment. If he has a fondness for a particular writer, he should not be disturbed if, in a few years, he finds the liking is waning. The matter of taste and judgment is one of growth and development which come from study and experience. Growth often means change.

[1] "Thai half said. Quhat say thai? Let thame say." The family motto of George Keith, Fifth Earl Marischal, on Mitchell Tower, Marischal College, Aberdeen, Scotland.

A student should not have to wait until he becomes a scholarly critic to have an opinion on the merit of literature. However, although he should not be afraid to form preliminary judgments, he should not feel that he must maintain forever his initial decisions. Although one may prefer the latest dance craze at twenty, one may resolve happily into the two-step at forty. Broader experiences and intensive study should cause the student to change his first evaluations. Often the difference in literary merit is a matter of degree rather than a sharp distinction between the good and the poor. It is the task of the reader to continue his study and to keep an open, inquiring mind to allow change and growth in his appreciation.

The aesthetic and educational obligations that the reader has to his audience could be discussed under a variety of headings. This chapter will first discuss the general philosophy of choosing a selection and second, certain specific problems of policy as they apply to the general philosophy.

A perspective on the philosophy of choosing a selection

Everyone's life is composed of only so much time. As was pointed out in Chapter 1, even though one begins with enthusiasm for doing a wide variety of things, soon the affairs of living begin to crowd in and the process of selection takes place. Therefore, even though the oral reader would like to show his interest for the broad spectrum of literature by reading everything that is worthwhile, expediency requires that he prepare himself on a relatively small number of selections. On what basis should he make his choice?

The answer to such a question is not easy, and the pitfalls for anyone brave enough to respond are frightening. Any philosopher who proposes a theory immediately exposes himself to attack, and the objections may have considerable merit. The question, however, should not be avoided, nor should it be treated didactically. Therefore, this chapter offers four postulates, presenting arguments which support and refute each proposition. It will be the obligation of the reader to review the material presented and decide for himself whether the postulates have merit and whether he chooses to support the postulate or to place himself among the opposition.

Postulate 1: Literature which has withstood the tests of time and maintained status over a period of years is preferable to contemporary or obscure literature

Arguments supporting this postulate may be divided into three main headings. First, the problem of maintaining a proper perspective on contemporary literature is difficult. Much that seems important and appears immortal now may be forgotten in twenty to fifty years. Bulwer-Lytton, Fanny Burney, James Fenimore Cooper, and William Congreve were very popular in their day, but are now seldom read. William Faulkner seems destined for posterity, but how are we to know? The nineteenth century would have said that Herman Melville had been relegated to obscurity, whereas the twentieth century has revived Melville with lyrical enthusiasm. Therefore, even a reader who passes over the latest novel in deference to the more respected contemporary authors is not certain that posterity will vindicate his decision.

T. S. Eliot, in his article "On Teaching the Appreciation of Poetry," says: "The study of contemporary poetry, while it might be an immediate stimulant, may encourage a provincialism of taste." [2] Eliot, a contemporary poet himself, does not hesitate to question his own status. It is possible to assume that Aeschylus, Sophocles, Euripides, Goethe, Shakespeare, and Ibsen are not provincial, that the themes of their plays are universally applicable, and that succeeding generations will find a kindredship between the problems presented by the classical dramatists and their own problems. Time tends to reject the provincial and promote the universal. Futhermore, provincialism in taste may assume vast proportions. It took a Wordsworth and a Coleridge to shake loose the poets of nineteenth-century England from a provincialism that was stifling poetry.

The postulate may also be supported by a third contention, namely, that much more research is available on classical literature than on contemporary selections. Assuming that biographies and critical analyses are valuable to the oral reader, the interpreter may find himself making serious mistakes in interpreting contemporary authors because their works have yet to be clarified. Eudora Welty, whose selections are found in this text, has yet to merit a biography. Students who prepare her literature for reading are faced with a realistic handicap of a shortage of information.

Vigorous arguments are also proposed to question postulate 1. The most obvious obstacle to unqualified support of the preference for classical literature is found in the need for continual additions to what we consider classical. If new and unknown works are to be avoided, how are they to become old and known? The dilemma is similar to that faced by a job applicant who has to have experience to get a position, but must get the position to have experience. If Faulkner is

---

[2] T. S. Eliot, "On Teaching the Appreciation of Poetry," *Teachers College Record*, vol. 62, no. 3, p. 220, December, 1960. Eliot's discussion is applicable to postulate 1, for he gives the advantages and disadvantages of studying contemporary literature.

not read, if Eudora Welty is not read, then how are we to know whether or not they deserve continued attention? Each generation has its own standards and tastes and therefore can evaluate the literature of its time if it seeks diligently enough for the proper criteria. Contemporary literature is neither good nor bad because it is contemporary. It must be judged by standards of literary merit and good taste.

Supporters of the postulate counter by saying, "The proposition only says that literature which has withstood the tests of time is *preferable*—this does not mean that in all circumstances the reader will have a choice between something classical and something contemporary. Perhaps only contemporary literature will say what has to be said for a particular audience by a particular reader on a particular occasion." Such an interpretation of the postulate offers a functional compromise. But more than a little doubt needs to be cast as to whether all supporters of the postulate adhere to the compromise.

As we said earlier in this chapter, the development of the ability to make value judgments is fundamental to successful interpretation. Those hesitant to accept the postulate say, "Perhaps the easiest and the safest approach is to choose literature which has withstood the tests of time. But such a policy does not offer personal growth to the student. The expansion of the intellect requires the development of individual tastes, not merely a reliance upon the standards and tastes of others." There is merit in the student's testing his own strength to see, not necessarily what he likes and dislikes, but what is meaningful and purposeful to his more discriminate listeners.

Selections from both contemporary and classical authors are included in this text on the basis that the arguments in support of the postulate are not always diametrically opposed to the arguments against the postulate to preclude a utilization of both philosophies. Additional variables must be considered along with postulate 1 before a decision can be reached.

Postulate 2: Literature which continues to stimulate and to reveal fuller meanings with repeated readings is preferable to literature which reveals itself entirely with initial readings

There is only one valid point of opposition to postulate 2. Many will grant that although Joyce Kilmer's poems will offer a temporary feeling of pleasure, Rupert Brooke's poetry provides a feeling of sharing the experience of war that continues to develop. But, they say, do we always need to tax audiences with a heavy load? Do the supporters of postulate 2 deplore Strauss waltzes, because they are not as profound as Beethoven's *Ninth Symphony*? If they do, they must answer to all the lovers of folk, hillbilly, western, mountain, American Negro, and calypso music who find a pleasurable relief from the pressures of the world in relaxing and untaxing enjoyment. Alfred Lunt and Lynn Fontaine presented frivolous plays in London under the threat of the buzz bombs in World War II. Such a war-weary audience might have responded well to *Macbeth,* but it also gained relief with the comedies of Terence Rattigan. Few would propose that Rattigan will survive the whips and scorns of time. But he fulfilled a need, and, it is asked, why demand more?

Proponents of the postulate argue on the other hand that profoundness does not imply complexity and that the Lord's Prayer and the Gettysburg Address can be read many times, providing a new idea or a different concept each time they are read. Neither of these selections "reveals all" to the reader on the very first acquaintance. The experience in each selection is profound even though the language with which the experience is expressed is simple.

A reader should conclude that a presentation of one of Robert Service's poems such as "The Shooting of Dan McGrew" or "The Cremation of Sam McGee" may be appropriate on certain occasions, but that such readings should not be offered for more than they are worth. Readers who take such literature seriously and who give no indication, by a twinkling eye or the tone of voice, that they understand the frivolity of what they are reading open themselves to justifiable derogatory criticism. Their reading may be compared to a philharmonic orchestra playing a Strauss waltz as a concerto with four pianos and contrapuntal violin orchestration. Of course, a reader should be aware that too steady a diet of light literature will result in a paucity of support for profound thinking and that the needed strength to fathom life's more complicated experiences may not be forthcoming when the reader needs it the most.

Actually, the task of applying postulate 2 is one of selectivity. Readers should use their time judiciously, surrounding themselves with literature which grows with repeated readings. Just as students come to like certain chairs in a classroom because they are accustomed to sit in one place for several semesters, so do readers become attached to the literature which is familiar to them. Students who memorize thought-provoking literature in high school are building themselves rich storehouses of strength. Although memorizing poetry in high school may have its disadvantages, old "grads" gathered for reunions still thrill to recitations of Bryant's "Thanatopsis," and even the most dignified alumni raise their voices lustily "to the songs we love so well." William James, the psychologist, tells us that we like what we attend to and we attend to what we like. Whatever literature we attend to, that is the literature we will like; and because we like it, we will attend to it. If we attend to literature which is sufficiently complex so that it can continue to offer new thoughts and new concepts as the reader and the selection grow old together and learn to like one another more and more, then we have achieved the maximum amount of experience from our labors.

Postulate 3:   The popularity of a selection is a questionable yardstick for measuring the value of literature

The fate of those voted most likely to succeed is problematic. Anyone who frequents secondhand bookstores has experienced the pathos of seeing shelf upon shelf of the best sellers of ten to twenty years ago now available under the sign "Your Pick of Any—Five for $1.49." Although it is fun to thumb through old school annuals, it is disturbing to find how frequently the comments arise, "How did they ever think those hair styles were attractive?" or "Look at the funny way the men's suits were cut in the old days!" So much of what one generation produces is not basic, but only fleeting—the product of existing fads. The proponents of postulate 3 would caution the student to find something, perhaps contemporary, perhaps classical, which has not achieved the popularity (or even the notoriety) of the biggest hit on Broadway. Proponents would advocate that the student stay ahead of his time in that he should distinguish the chaff from the wheat during the harvest itself and prevent the noise made by the harvest celebration from stifling the sound of the true wheat drifting quietly into the bin.

Others would say, however, that the chief pitfall in postulate 3 is the possibility of avoiding the vulgate when the vulgate is worthwhile. There are those who assume that because a work of art is popular, it must be of inferior quality. Such judgments lead inevitably to a criterion of art divorced from general applicability. Dickens was as widely proclaimed in his own day as he is now. A prestige class which insists that what is good in art cannot be what is generally appreciated is in error.

A reconciliation of the arguments in support of and in opposition to postulate 3 is possible. If a reader chooses a popular selection, he should ask himself why. If it is because everyone else is impressed with the material and that he thinks he will also be popular by siding with a popular cause, then his motives should give him pause; if, however, he has chosen the selection almost in spite of its popularity in the sense that its popularity made him hesitate but that he persisted because he felt the selection had desirable qualities which many were trying to appreciate, then his motives appear sound.

Postulate 4:   Literature which is difficult to interpret is preferable to literature which is easy to interpret

The thrill of accomplishment is one of the most rewarding sensations in life. The more difficult the task, the more rewarding the sensation. But the oral interpreter must distinguish between the gymnastics of reading which cause difficulty and the meaning of the selection which causes difficulty. In other words, certain vocal feats of Italian opera of the nineteenth century may have been difficult, but did the difficulty contribute to the meaning of the opera or was it an end in itself?

When one selection is said to be more difficult than another because its theme is more elevated and the emotions which support that theme are more basic, it is not difficult to find considerable support for postulate 4. A shallow theme, lightly treated, should usually be avoided, whether it is difficult to read or not. The real problem arises when two selections have themes of comparatively equal stature and equal emotional support. Such a situation exists in comparing Alfred Noyes's poem "The Highwayman" with Robert Browning's selection "How They Brought the Good News from Ghent to Aix." Both poems deal with the theme of bravery in a romantic mood. Both are content to present broad heroism without pretense of greatness. The differences between these two poems, if they do exist, lie in the complexity of the imagery, the diction, and the composition that support the theme and its mood. If these three elements of style are superior in one poem, then to that extent they amplify the idea and its accompanying emotion and therefore elevate one poem over the other, *not because of the stylistic devices themselves,* but because of what the devices do for the theme and its mood.

Let us examine the first two stanzas of both poems:

How They Brought the Good News from Ghent to Aix	The Highwayman *
I sprang to the stirrup, and Joris, and he;	The wind was a torrent of darkness among the gusty trees,
I galloped, Dirck galloped, we galloped all three;	The moon was a ghostly galleon tossed upon cloudy seas,
"Good speed!" cried the watch, as the gatebolts undrew;	The road was a ribbon of moonlight over the purple moor,
"Speed!" echoed the wall to us galloping through;	And the highwayman came riding, Riding, riding,
Behind shut the postern, the lights sank to rest,	The highwayman came riding, up to the old inn-door.

* Alfred Noyes, "The Highwayman," *Collected Poems*, vol. 1. Copyright 1906–1934 by Alfred Noyes. Published by J. B. Lippincott Company.

How They Brought the Good News from Ghent to Aix (continued)

And into the midnight we galloped abreast.

Not a word to each other; we kept the great pace
Neck by neck, stride by stride, never changing our place;
I turned in my saddle and made its girth tight,
Then shortened each stirrup, and set the pique right,
Rebuckled the cheet-strap, chained slacker the bit,
Nor galloped less steadily Roland a whit.

The Highwayman (continued)

He'd a French cocked-hat on his fore-head, a bunch of lace at his chin,
A coat of the claret velvet, and breeches of brown doe-skin;
They fitted with never a wrinkle: his boots were up to the thigh!
And he rode with a jeweled twinkle,
His pistol butts a-twinkle,
His rapier hilt a-twinkle, under the jeweled sky.

Is the imagery of the Browning poem superior? If so, why? Note that Noyes depends upon *direct* description and employs the third-person narrator, while Browning uses *indirect* description, woven into the story by the first-person narrator. The eye-witness account seems less sentimental and more an integral part of the action than does the third-person narrator.

The manner in which word choice supports the imagery clarifies the difference. The adjective count in the Browning poem is considerably less than that in the Noyes selection. Browning clarifies his imagery with verb metaphors, such as "echoed the wall," "the lights sank," and "cried the watch," while Noyes employs the more obvious adjectival and noun metaphors of "The moon was a ghostly galleon tossed" and "under the jeweled sky." Browning's images are unobtrusive and are therefore less ornamental, providing more realistic imagery to support his theme.

The composition into which the imagery is woven is not merely more intricate in the Browning poem. Intricacy in itself would not make the Browning poem superior. However, the complexity of the Browning poem is not an end in itself, but rather a means for clarifying the mood of the poem and thus enhancing the theme. For example, the sound pattern of both poems imitates the galloping of horses. The Noyes poem maintains a very steady beat, almost unrealistic in its intensity, whereas the Browning poem varies the rhythm with just a sufficient amount of *enjambment* [4] to break the beat real-

---

[4] "The device of continuing the sense and grammatical construction of a *verse* or a *couplet* on into the next." See William F. Thrall and Addison Hibbard, in C. Hugh Holman (ed.), *A Handbook to Literature*, The Odyssey Press, Inc., New York, 1960, p. 174.

istically and provide much needed relief. Browning spaces his run-on lines randomly. Some stanzas have none, while one has as many as three. Such interruptions in the rhythm intensify the uncertainty of the Browning race, thereby enhancing the mood and amplifying the theme. The reader of the Noyes poem and his listeners can relax and allow the rhythm of the poem to carry them along, whereas the reader of the Browning selection and his audience must be more alert to the variety of rhythm which in turn reflects the theme. What is the example of enjambment in the two Browning stanzas reproduced here?

The first-person narrator employs more abrupt changes in pace than does the third-person narrator in the Noyes poem. How, for example, is the reader to simulate the cry of the watch and then indicate almost immediately the echo bounding off the wall as the horses gallop through? The insertion of the conversational element between the rider and the watch breaks the rhythm, causing a fast change from the excitement of the beginning of the ride to the quiet desolation once the postern is shut and the lights of the town are left behind. The Browning poem begins, not quietly and romantically as does the Noyes poem, but in the middle of an action that ceases only with the last lines of the poem.

There are other items of imagery, diction, and composition which differentiate the two selections. The more technical and more exacting vocabulary of the Browning poem vivifies the imagery. But enough has been said in support of the contention that the theme and the emotion of the Browning selection are superior to those of the Noyes poem because of the manner in which they are supported by imagery, diction, and composition.

Supporters of postulate 4, therefore, would say that the Browning poem is superior because the elements which challenge the reader are elements which are not ornaments, but rather integral parts of the theme and the mood of the poem.

Others, although they might accept the judgment that the Browning poem is superior, would caution that the beginning reader is enjoying his first thrill of literature in reading "The Highwayman," "Annabel Lee," "Gunga Din," and other frequently employed selections that offer a steady, rhythmical beat and that only a critic without perspective would discourage a student from using these as stepping stones to higher levels of appreciation.

The student, it must be said, is obligated to make the most of his abilities. If a student is repeatedly choosing simple selections with mediocre imagery, uncomplicated diction, and overly structured rhythm because they are easy, then he should admit his laggardlike qualities and approach more complex material which uses its complexity, not as an end in itself, but as a means of amplifying its theme and emotion. On the other hand, if a student is choosing material which is difficult to read, not because the difficulty adds to the idea and its mood, but because it offers a more difficult feat to perform, then he should admit his pedantry and approach simpler material with good spirit.

Summary

Naturally, the limited discussion presented here of the philosophy of choosing a selection for oral interpretation cannot be comprehensive. The four postulates are offered as a basis for discussion to provoke further comments and assist the interpreter in building his own philosophy of reading. Such a discussion, together with the more specific comments below, should assist the student in developing criteria for choosing his material.

Suggestions for solutions to specific problems involved in choosing a selection

The following discussion will attempt to give the oral interpreter guidance in dealing with the practical problems that arise when the reader must decide what material he will read to a given audience on a given occasion. Many students of oral interpretation will be choosing reading material primarily for class assignments in speech or English. In such a situation, the student may erroneously feel that an analysis of his class and the occasion on which he will read is not necessary. The interpreter should be aware of what stimuli have already been offered to his listeners by way of class discussion, previous readings, and outside associations so that he can choose selections that will be interesting and challenging to his fellow students. In addition to reading to his class, the oral interpreter is often asked to read to civic, social, or church groups. Reading hours are regularly scheduled programs at many colleges and universities, requiring the student of oral interpretation to assume the role of the communicator and thereby entailing audience analysis. All oral interpreters, whether they read inside or outside the classroom, must be sensitive to the audience and the occasion.

Analyzing the audience and the occasion

A practical way to approach the problem of audience analysis is to ask three questions:

Who are the people who compose the audience?
Why are they meeting?
Why are you, the reader, appearing before this audience at this time?

By making a few inquiries of those responsible for arranging the presentation, the reader can gain much helpful information. The age, sex, size, educational level, and cultural background of the audience are among the more important factors to be determined. The time element involved also requires consideration. If only reading is to be done, the interpreter needs to know the exact amount of time allotted to him; if the reader is sharing the program with others, he should consider what will precede, what will follow, and how much time has been allotted to each person. *Readers should be particularly careful to stay within their time limits.*

The sex of the audience must be considered. If, in presenting the more formal type of program, a woman reader insists upon reading only somewhat arty poetry to the parent-teacher association when the wives have persuaded reluctant husbands to come to the school for the evening, she may seriously reduce attendance at the next meeting. A male reader who prefers Rudyard Kipling may bore a ladies' literary club with the outdoors and readers in general if he insists upon inflicting his tastes upon an unwilling and perhaps unsympathetic audience.

Who the audience is depends in part on the time of day. Just as Hitler was careful to adapt his style of speechmaking to morning, afternoon, and evening hours, realizing that the temperament of people differs at different times of the day, so must the reader watch how the hour fits the selection. The contemporary novelist Elizabeth Spencer entitled her first novel *Fire in the Morning* because of the strange affect that a catastrophe has on people in the early hours. A reader who hurls a Medea about to murder her children upon an unsuspecting audience assembled in a church basement at ten o'clock in the morning should not be surprised if he is greeted with wonder and an occasional snicker, rather than a sympathetic reaction to the tragedy. The master craftsman Euripides was careful to prepare his audience for infanticide. Moreover, he was writing for an open-air theater where intense emotions are more easily dissipated. Infanticide is a terrible crime. An audience faced with the burden of such a crime must either laugh or cry. When it has not been properly prepared to weep, it must laugh instead. To prepare an audience to weep early in the morning entails considerable subtlety of effort.

In the less formal type of reading, where the interpreter is sharing literature with his family or presenting excerpts from a book for a radio or television audience, the problem of adaptation must be approached differently. A family reader should ask for suggestions and be willing to forego his personal preferences for the desires of the group. He should sense when the point of saturation of his audience has been reached and curtail his reading until another time. Of course, the major problem with the radio and television reader is the lack of an audience to give him feedback. Many performers prefer a studio audience to help them adjust, but the desired effect may not be achieved if the performer succeeds in appealing to the more particular tastes of the studio audience and not of the general public. Radio and television programs originating in California have too often been uproariously received by studio audiences while the remainder of the country has remained largely unaffected.

Because of the introduction given the reader or inclement weather conditions or a wide range of factors, the audience may suddenly change its mood. Such factors may be unknown to the reader at the time he selects his material. He may be required to make last-minute changes in his plans. He must either shuffle the material he has already prepared or substitute new selections. To prepare himself for such emergencies, the reader must have a sufficiently varied repertoire to permit change. Some of the more skillful readers will keep their programming very loose until they see how the audience reacts to the first one or two selections; then they will proceed to structure the remainder of the program. The actress Agnes Moorehead appears to follow this technique in her public readings.

Who are the people in the audience?   The reader should know. Experience will give him confidence in audience analysis, but research and much preparation will help him to gain this confidence more quickly.

The occasion for the gathering is another factor to be considered. Why the people have gathered—whether they be one or two or many hundreds—should be influential in determining the attitude of the audience. A literary study club, meeting for its annual gala banquet, will be in a different mood from the same club assembled for the final business meeting. The local Lion's club which has just finished with a hassle about how to spend the funds derived from a recent charity drive will have a different demeanor from the same club meeting to hear a speaker discuss international affairs. A family gathered after supper on a winter evening is different from a family gathered for an annual reunion. Despite the obvious significance of the occasion, the oral reader, particularly the inexperienced one, too often overlooks the *why* of the audience in selecting his material.

There are so many possibilities as to why you, the reader, have been selected to read to a particular audience at a particular time that our comments on this subject must be limited to a few generalizations. Readers should remember that there are usually others who could have done as well for the particular occasion. They should hope that they have been chosen because the audience wants an emphasis on the selection and not on the reader. Readers should not assume that any occasion is appropriate for revealing their particular talents. It should be the author's talents that are revealed. Therefore, if after a reading in which he senses he has done well, the reader receives no approbation for himself but hears praises for the selections and their authors, he should consider his job well done. He should be wary of his presentation if he is told what a fine voice he has and how beautifully he has performed.

Summary

With an awareness of the audience and the occasion, the oral reader is ready to begin applying his general philosophy in his search for suitable material. The interpreter now begins to feel his obligation even more deeply, for he is responsible for determining the taste and the level of significance of his material. To a degree any audience on any occasion is a captive one. It is true that its members usually had the choice of attending or not attending, but once present they usually have little choice as to what they will hear. The type of material read, whether it be good or mediocre, dull or interesting, stimulating or apathetic, is largely the decision of the reader. With such responsibilities, the oral interpreter must be careful to select material that is not only suitable to the audience and the occasion, but that is also good, acceptable literature.

Locating suitable material

In Chapters 1 and 2, the nature and value of literature has been discussed. Earlier in this chapter, the philosophy of choosing selections was presented. Now it is necessary to point out, insofar as possible, how the student may find material which meets these qualifications.

Personal reading habits

The student of interpretation must depend to a considerable extent upon his own knowledge of literature in choosing his material. If the student finds his knowledge limited, he should begin by taking inventory. Suppose the student lists as one of his assets an acquaintance with some of Robert Frost's poetry. What poems does he know and how thoroughly has he studied them? Perhaps the student's reading is limited to the more familiar selections such as "Stopping by Woods on a Snowy Evening," "Death of the Hired Man," and "Wild Grapes." As a first step, this much progress is encouraging. But it is not enough.

An excellent paperback edition of Frost's poems is available. The student can easily enlarge his knowledge of Frost by enjoying such narrative poems as "Brown's Descent," "Two Tramps in Mud Time," and "Paul's Wife."

Such a process should be followed for other authors in which the student has already evinced some interest. Many persons limit their knowledge of Robert Browning to a few isolated poems and never enjoy the fun and wit of such lesser known narratives as "Up at a Villa—Down in the City," "An Epistle," and all the intricacies of "The Ring and the Book." Lovers of Charles Dickens may have missed *Hard Times;* Shakespeare fans may have avoided *King Lear;* T. S. Eliot admirers may be familiar with his poetry, but not his essays. A more extensive reading of our existing interests can be the first step in improving our personal reading habits.

The perspective of the student may be limited in another way. Some students have confined their reading to one type or one period of literature. Although there are advantages in specialization and although it is true that intensive reading is necessary for understanding and appreciation, it is equally true that a reader must have a broad background if he is to be able to understand how his specialization fits into the broad spectrum of literature. Moreover, a reader must have a wide knowledge of literature if he is to match the selection to audience and occasion. A choice must be made, therefore, as to what selections will be included before a thorough study of these selections can begin. It is one thing to acclaim a poet or a playwright as a favorite if he is the only one with which the student is acquainted and quite another thing to have studied a group of authors seriously and then have established preferences. If the student has developed a proclivity for English Victorian poetry, let him turn to another age or another type of literature to broaden the scope of his knowledge. New discoveries will not lessen the appreciation of the English Victorians. One age will support another, and no one country has a monopoly on producing good literature.

Some interpreters limit themselves by confining their reading to one or two forms of literature. Poetry and drama are often the most popular. The short story, the essay, the diary, or the literary letter also offer excellent material for oral interpretation. Many novels, with careful and judicious cutting and arranging, provide good sources of material for the oral reader.

But all of the above advice is idle talk unless the student has interests of his own that motivate him to extend his reading. Earlier chapters have pointed out repeatedly that literature is an experience and that many experiences are universal. The student may discover in his reading, experiences which relate to the questions that arise all around him. For example, students are interested in people and in the future of the world. So are the Russian novelists. If a student wants to know why Khrushchev beat on the table with his shoe at the United Nations, let him expend his curiosity in reading the Russian novels of Dostoevski and Tolstoi and the plays of Chekov. The answers to Russian gesturing lie there. Indeed, a student might present a series of readings from Russian novels to the international club entitled, "Dostoevski and Tolstoi Tell All about Khrushchev!"

All students have interests. They may be interested in the traditions and life of the Old South or in a trip by boat to the South Seas. The activities of college life, such as sports, student government, and courtship, lead directly to the fundamental themes in literature. The reader will want to build upon his interests and not accept his existing perspectives as set standards for evaluation. If the student is already set in his tastes, a course in the oral interpretation of literature will have difficulty in being of value to him. Rather, the student's special likes should lead him to other likes, pricking his interest to find out what goes on in the lives of people so that he understands the underlying motivations of situation and circumstance. Provincial taste is often an acquired quality that must be amended. In the process of his reading, the student should ask himself, "Why do I like this particular selection and why do I not respond to that one?" In answering these questions and in making comparisons, the student's taste and judgment of literature will improve.

One particular problem deserves mention. Some students find it difficult to extend their reading to include materials with ideas conflicting with their own. It is not necessary to agree with an idea expressed or implied by an author in order to read his material. No good writer insists upon immediate agreement. But to confine literary reading to a supplementation of existing biases is too narrowing. There is no room to expand to new ideas or to test and redefine old ones. Understanding and appreciation come from an awareness of the full context of literature. Without a cross-fertilization of ideas, a reader will become stagnant and didactic.

Library research to locate selections

Thus far, the student has been encouraged to begin with his existing interests and work from there. However, a reader should also wish to locate material which is new to him or which concerns a theme with which he has had little personal experience. Or perhaps the reader vaguely recalls a first line or a title or an author's name and needs to know how to follow up on his lead. Or again, the student may just be browsing in the library to establish new interests and to develop new contacts which will prove invaluable later in his work. The next several pages list indexes to various literary forms, making a selection relatively easy to locate, provided one knows the title or the author or the first line. For example, suppose a student remembers the title "My Last Duchess" but remembers nothing else except, of course, that he would like to consult a copy of the poem. If he looks in the supplement to the fourth edition of *Granger's Index to Poetry and Recitations*, he will find on page 176 the following entry:

My Last Duchess. Robert Browning. ATP; BrAP; CaFP. . . .

In the front of the index is a list of anthologies to which the initials after the poem correspond. For example, ATP stands for the anthology *Approaches to Poetry* by Walter Blair and W. K. Chandler, published by the Appleton-Century Company, Inc., in 1935. Many libraries mark the list of anthologies in the front of *Granger's Index* to designate which of the collections catalogued by Granger are available in their collection. Some libraries even put the call numbers of the anthologies beside each entry so that the student can go directly to the bookshelves rather than detouring by the card catalogue.

If a student has only one particular subject in mind and wishes to locate relevant material, his task is more difficult, but not formidable. The list of indexes at the end of this chapter shows that many of the more comprehensive indexes carry subject listings. However, the headings are not always satisfactory and a rather ingenious use of the subject listings is often necessary for successful results.

There is much to be said for browsing to supplement the help provided by the indexes and to gain a wider acquaintance with selections available. If the library stacks are open, the student may ask for the call number under which anthologies of American and English literature are classified and then consult the volumes shelved under these call numbers. If such a general number does not include collections of ballads, textbooks used in college English classes, and similar fringe material, the student may wish to request these call numbers also. If the stacks to the library are closed, the student will be forced to use the card catalogue to request anthologies which look promising.

Other sources

Many of the anthologies and special collections are now available in paperback editions. A selected bibliography of promising paperbacks is appended to this chapter. If a student wishes to inquire whether a given book is available in a paperback edition, all he need do is ask his library or his bookseller to consult the latest edition of *Paperbound Books in Print*, published by R. R. Bowker Company of New York

four times annually, with an accumulative index in the December issue. Subject, author, and title listings are given.

In their quest for material for interpretation, many students demonstrate an attitude similar to the one held by Katharine Brush's heroine
in the short story "Night Club" who found herself in the midst of vivid
action and dramatic situations which could have furnished a writer
of fiction sufficient material to develop several novels. But the woman
saw or heard nothing. The evening was dull and uneventful to her.
She only wanted it to end so she could experience some exciting
action from her true story magazine. Material suitable for oral interpretation for all types of audiences is available all around us. It
only requires a discerning person to know how and where to find it.

Programming

With the audience and the occasion in mind, the reader has selected
material that is interesting and that is worthy of being shared with
his listeners. The next step is the arrangement of the material into a
program so that each part will receive the most favorable response
from the audience. There are four major problems in arranging a
sequence of material: the opening selection, the transition from one
selection to another, the climactic selection, and the concluding selection.

The opening selection

The first stimulus offered by a reader has a very special set of obligations. Like the introduction to a speech, it must catch the attention of
the audience and polarize its interest. The skeptics must be convinced;
the converts must be further inspired. It may be more difficult to
please the literary enthusiasts with the first selection than to please
the skeptics because the enthusiasts are expecting so much (perhaps
too much). Therefore, the first selection should often be brief. For example, in an hour of reading, the first selection should last from three
to six minutes. It should be something with an impelling human interest flavor—with a touch of humor (if possible). Narrative prose is
a wise choice because it allows an audience to orient itself quickly
and does not require the listeners to adapt too quickly to strange or
unfamiliar forms.[5]

The classroom teacher of literature, therefore, should pay particular
attention to the type of material assigned first in a series. A parent

[5] See also Sara Lowrey and Gertrude Johnson, *Interpretative Reading*, Appleton-
Century-Crofts, Inc., New York, 1953, pp. 234–253, and Faye L. Hedges, "Select-
ing, Abridging, and Arranging Humorous Prose for Oral Interpretation by High
School Students," unpublished master's thesis, State University of Iowa, Iowa City,
Iowa, 1959.

who wishes to organize a reading hour for his family one night a week after supper should choose the opening material carefully to gain a maximum of rapport with his audience. An elementary school teacher should introduce oral reading to her students with premeditation, making certain that the initial stimulus is as favorably received as possible.

Transitory material

Although contrast and variety are important, an abrupt change or too great a change will often unsettle an audience. It takes a very skillful reader to move an audience quickly from tragedy to comedy, from sadness to joy, from the light to the dark, or from the sublime to the ridiculous. Shakespeare injects humor to relieve tension, e.g., the gravedigging scene in *Hamlet* and the drunken porter in *Macbeth*. But Shakespeare is infinitely skilled and places his abrupt changes of mood to build and then to relieve tension. Most readers should not expect the audience to laugh heartily one minute and to weep the next. It is better to arrange the selections to provide a gradual change of mood, letting each number lead into and blend with the next.

Two problems in particular arise in establishing transitions. The first concerns the degree to which literary forms may change from selection to selection, and the second involves the (extemporaneous) material which the reader introduces between the selections.

Variety can add interest to any program. There is no particular reason why ballads, lyrics, short stories, and drama cannot be offered together, provided the sequence has been carefully arranged. If a reader has planned to vary the type of literature he will read, he should, however, plan his transitions carefully. Not only must he watch the effect of one selection upon its successor, but he must heighten or diminish the contrast, as he so desires, with remarks of his own. Even within a selection, a reader may wish to make a transition in his own words instead of using the words of the author, perhaps to save time or perhaps to point out a particular factor in the reading that needs emphasis.

Interpreters, then, must be good extemporaneous and impromptu speakers as well as good manuscript readers. They must be able to lead an audience from one type of selection to another, changing the mood of the audience to make it receptive to what follows.

The climactic selection

The question is often asked, "Where should the most difficult or the most emotional selection be placed in the sequence of selections?"

Such material may vary from a highly dramatic or tragic selection to a particularly effective excerpt from sophisticated comedy. There are, of course, no hard and fast rules on what selection should be placed at the climax. Individual differences must be taken into account, and readers have varied styles which permit multiple approaches. In general, it is more customary to place the climactic selection near the close of the program, or at least in the second half. The psychology of arrangement in oral-reading programs has yet to receive quantitative investigation. Experimental evidence using other forms of communication is contradictory as to what conditions favor the law of primacy and what conditions favor the law of recency. The psychology of climax, however, appears to favor recency in the placement of the major selection in a series of oral readings, resulting in part from the fact that, if humorous or light selections are presented early and serious selections later, an audience can replace a relative absence of emotion during the humorous and light readings with a more identifiable emotion during the serious readings. The reverse appears less easy to achieve. If an audience develops identifiable emotions early and then is asked to forsake these emotions for a status of neutralism, the force of the stronger emotions carries over to subdue the effect of the humor. The tendency to place the climactic selection toward the conclusion of the program may also be in part caused by a desire for prolonging a favorable sensation. Talking about what we are going to get for Christmas is often more attractive than opening the packages themselves. The longer we can postpone the anticipated desirable event, up to a certain point, the greater the satisfaction derived from the delay. Composers of songs obey this principle when they place one climactic high note near the conclusion of a melody.

The reader should be cautioned against letting one selection dominate a series of selections to the point of imbalance. Even the best audience is something of a clock watcher. The attention span of the group must be kept in mind. One long selection may tire an audience and unbalance a sequence to the detriment of both the long and the short selections.

The concluding selection

Concluding numbers are often short and should offer the audience a measure of the sense of satisfaction of finality. Concluding material need not be light and humorous, but, after the intensive climactic material has been read, the high point of the program is over. The audience will want to "let down." It cannot offer another strong reaction either to tragedy or to comedy because it is too absorbed with enjoying what it has already taken to heart. The conclusion of a program should therefore be a selection that will unify what has gone before and will give the listeners a feeling that the reading is complete.

Summary

Many readers choose their selections around a theme, such as "The Tall Tale," "Go West, Young Man," or "New York, Day or Night." There is much to be said for establishing a unifying element to which a series of selections may be related. Considerable variety both in mood and of literary type is still possible when a central theme is employed. Such themes are often advisable when the reader is preparing for a particular occasion. The historian is turning more and more to writing history in terms of movements rather than in terms of kings and battles. There are trends which show that literature may be treated likewise. The oral interpreter can make a contribution toward clarifying perspectives for his audience if he adopts a theme for his selections and thus allows each selection to contribute to the other.

These suggestions for programming are rather general. They can be applied to one reader who is arranging an entire program, or to several readers in a class, each of whom is to read his own material. It is hoped that the following examples of programs may answer other questions which have not been specifically discussed and will suggest possibilities for variety in programming.

Sample programs for oral interpretation

Understanding women ? ? ?

1. James Thurber, *The Case against Women* [6]
2. a. Andrew Marvell, *To His Coy Mistress*
   b. John Crowe Ransom, *Blue Girls*
3. Richard Brinsley Sheridan, *The School for Scandal*, Act II, Scene 1
4. Eudora Welty, *Why I Live at the P.O.*
5. Robert P. Tristram Coffin, *Departure*

Character study

1. James Thurber, *The Secret Life of Walter Mitty*
2. a. Edwin Arlington Robinson, *Mr. Flood's Party*
   b. A. E. Housman, *Is My Team Plowing?*
3. Tennessee Williams, *The Last of My Solid Gold Watches*

[6] From *Let Your Mind Alone.*

A Christmas program

1.   Selma Lagerlöf, *The Holy Night* [7]
2.   a.   Gerard Manley Hopkins, *God's Grandeur*
     b.   Edna St. Vincent Millay, *To Jesus on His Birthday*
3.   Truman Capote, *A Christmas Memory*

Exercises

1.   It has been suggested that you broaden your knowledge of literature by further reading in the areas in which you have already evinced an interest. Choose the subject from the following list which is closest to you, and locate literary selections which deal with the same subject. Consult the indexes suggested in this chapter.

     a.   The sportsman
     b.   The dog lover (or the horse lover)
     c.   A strong feeling for the great outdoors
     d.   God as He is revealed in the beauty of nature
     e.   The traditions of the South (or New England or the West)
     f.   The psychology of personality
     g.   Classical music
     h.   Stoicism
     i.   The world of fashion
     j.   The painter (or the sculptor)
     k.   Abraham Lincoln
     l.   The atomic age
     m.   The fight against disease
     n.   Atheism
     o.   Life after death
     p.   Parental love

2.   Ask permission to attend a meeting of a local civic club. Then assume that you have been asked to deliver a twenty-minute reading program at the next meeting. Write an analysis of the audience and the occasion, concluding your paper with the names and authors of the selections you intend to read, with time limits marked for each.

3.   Build a reading program around any one of the suggestions below:

     a.   A program constructed around a theme
     b.   A program for a special day, such as Christmas, Easter, or Thanksgiving
     c.   A program for a special audience, such as a high school assembly, a class reunion, the faculty club, or a group of visiting parents
     d.   A program of the works of one author

[7] From *Christ Legends.*

4. Choose any one of the pairs of poems presented below, and make a value judgment as to which is the better poem of the pair. Divide your comments into the following areas:

   a. Which poem has the superior theme?
   b. Which poem supports the theme with more basic emotion?
   c. Which poem supports the theme and its emotion with more vivid imagery?
   d. Which poem has superior diction?
   e. Which poem has superior composition, i.e., rhythm, meter, rhyme, or any other form of unifying element?

Exercise in Discrimination

Pair I

Poem 1

It takes a heap o' livin' in a house t'
   make it home,
A heap o' sun an' shadder, an' ye some-
   times have t' roam
Afore ye really 'preciate the things ye
   lef' behind,
An' hunger fer 'em somehow, with 'em
   allus on yer mind.
It don't make any differunce how rich
   ye get t' be,
How much yer chairs an' tables cost,
   How great yer luxury;
It ain't home t'ye, though it be the
   palace of a king,
Until somehow yer soul is sort o'
   wrapped 'round everything.

Home ain't a place that gold can buy
   or get up in a minute;
Afore it's home there's got t' be a
   heap o' livin' in it;
Within the walls there's got t' be some
   babies born, and then
Right there ye've got t'bring 'em up t'
   women good, an' men;
And gradjerly, as time goes on, ye find
   ye wouldn't part
With anything they ever used—they've
   grown into yer heart:
The old high chairs, the playthings,
   too, the little shoes they wore
Ye hoard; an' if ye could ye'd keep
   the thumbmarks on the door.

Poem 2

Oh, to be in England
Now that April's there,
And whoever wakes in England
Sees, some morning, unaware,
That the lowest boughs and the brush-
   wood sheaf
Round the elm-tree bole are in tiny
   leaf,
While the chaffinch sings on the or-
   chard bough
In England—now!

And after April, when May follows,
And the whitethroat builds, and all the
   swallows!
Hark, where my blossomed pear-tree in
   the hedge
Leans to the field and scatters on the
   clover
Blossoms and dewdrops—at the bent
   spray's edge—
That's the wise thrush; he sings each
   song twice over,
Lest you should think he never could
   recapture
The first fine careless rapture!
And though the fields look rough with
   hoary dew,
All will be gay when noontide awakes
   anew
The buttercups, the little children's
   dower
—Far brighter than this gaudy melon-
   flower!

Pair II

Poem 3

Death, be not proud, though some have
  calléd thee
Mighty and dreadful, for thou art not
  so;
For those whom thou think'st thou dost
  overthrow
Die not, poor Death; nor yet canst thou
  kill me.
From rest and sleep, which but thy picture be,
Much pleasure; then from thee much
  more must flow;
And soonest our best men with thee
  do go—

Rest of their bones and souls' delivery!
Thou 'rt slave to fate, chance, kings,
  and desperate men,
And dost with poison, war, and sick-
  ness dwell;
And poppy or charms can make us
  sleep as well
And better than thy stroke. Why swell'st
  thou then?
One short sleep past, we wake eternally,
And Death shall be no more: Death,
  thou shalt die!

Poem 4

There is no flock, however watched
  and tended,
  But one dead lamb is there!
There is no fireside, howsoe'er de-
  fended,
  But has one vacant chair!

The air is full of farewells to the dying,
  And mournings for the dead;
The heart of Rachel, for her children
  crying,
  Will not be comforted!

Let us be patient! These severe af-
  flictions
  Not from the ground arise,
But oftentimes celestial benedictions
  Assume this dark disguise.

We see but dimly through the mists
  and vapors;
  Amid these earthly damps
What seem to us but sad, funereal
  tapers
  May be heaven's distant lamps.

There is no Death! What seems so is
  transition;
  This life of mortal breath
Is but a suburb of the life elysian,
  Whose portal we call Death.

Pair III

Poem 5

New Year, I look straight in your eyes,
Our ways and our interests blend,
You may be a foe in disguise
But I shall believe you a friend.
We get what we give in our measure,
We cannot give pain and get pleasure,
I give you good will and good cheer
And you must return it, New Year.

We get what we give in this life,
Though often the giver indeed
Waits long upon doubting and strife
Ere proving the truth of my Creed.
But somewhere, someway, and forever

Poem 6

The snow that never drifts—
The transient, fragrant snow
That comes a single time a year—
Is softly driving now;

So thorough in the tree
At night beneath the star
That it was February's self
Experience would swear;

Like Winter as a face
We stern and former knew
Repaired of all but loneliness
By nature's alibi.

Poem 5 (continued)

Reward is the meed of endeavor—
And if I am really worth while,
New Year, you will give me your smile.

Poem 6 (continued)

Were every storm, so spice,
The value could not be;
We buy with contrast—pang is good
As near as memory.

Pair IV

Poem 7

We've fought with many men acrost
    the seas,
  An' some of 'em was brave an' some
    was not:
The Paythan an' the Zulu an' Burmese;
  But the Fuzzy was the finest o' the
    lot.
We never got a ha'porth's change of
    'im:
  'E squatted in the scrub an' 'ocked
    our 'orses,
'E cut our sentries up at Sua*kim*,
  An' 'e played the cat an' banjo with
    our forces.
    So 'ere's to you, Fuzzy-Wuzzy, at
      your 'ome in the Soudan;
    You're a pore benighted 'eathen
      but a first-class fightin' man;
    We gives you your certificate, an'
      if you want it signed
    We'll come an' 'ave a romp with
    you whenever you're inclined.

Poem 8

You may talk o' your lutes and your
    dulcimers fine,
Your harps and your tabors and cym-
    bals and a',
But here in the trenches jist gie me for
    mine
The wee penny whistle o' Sandy Mc-
    Graw.
Oh, it's: "Sandy, ma lad, will you lilt
    us a tune?"
And Sandy is willin' and trillin' like
    mad;
Sae silvery sweet that we a' throng
    aroun',
And some o' it's gay, but the maist o'
    it's sad.
Jist the wee simple airs that sink intae
    your hert,
And grup ye wi' love and wi' longin'
    for hame;
And ye glour like an owl till you're
    feelin' the stert
O' a tear, and you blink wi' a feelin'
    o' shame.
For his song's o' the heather, and here
    in the dirt
You listen and dream o' a land that's
    sae braw,
And he mak's you forget a' the harm
    and the hurt,
For he pipes like a laverock, does
    Sandy McGraw.

Pair V

Poem 9

1

The woman named Tomorrow
sits with a hairpin in her teeth
and takes her time
and does her hair the way she wants it
and fastens at last the last braid and
    coil
and puts the hairpin where it belongs
and turns and drawls: Well, what of it?

Poem 10

The Man with the Broken Fingers
    throws a shadow.
Down from the spruce and evergreen
    mountain timbers of Norway—
And across Europe and the Mediter-
    ranean to the oasis palms of Libya—
He lives and speaks a sign language of
    lost fingers.

Poem 9 (continued)

My grandmother, Yesterday, is gone.
What of it? Let the dead be dead.

2

The doors were cedar
and the panels strips of gold
and the girls were golden girls
and the panels read and the girls
    chanted:
    We are the greatest city,
    the greatest nation:
    nothing like us ever was.
The doors are twisted on broken hinges.
Sheets of rain swish through on the
    wind
        where the golden girls ran and the
        panels read:
    We are the greatest city,
    the greatest nation,
    nothing like us ever was.

Poem 10 (continued)

From a son of Norway who slipped the
    Gestapo nets, the Nazi patrols,
The story comes as told among those
    now in Norway.

Shrines in their hearts they have for
    this nameless man
Who refused to remember names
    names names the Gestapo wanted.
"Tell us these names. Who are they?
    Talk! We want those names!"
And the man faced them, looked them
    in the eye, and hours passed and no
    names came—hours on hours and
    no names for the Gestapo.
They told him they would break him
    as they had broken others.
The rubber hose slammed around face
    and neck,
The truncheon handing pain with no
    telltale marks,
Or the distinction of the firing squad
    and death in a split second—
The Gestapo considered these and de-
    cided for him something else again.
"Tell us those names. Who were they?
    Talk! Names now—or else!"
And no names came—over and over
    and no names.

Poem 1: From Edgar A. Guest, "Home," *A Heap o' Livin'*, Reilly & Lee Company, Chicago, 1916.
Poem 2: From Robert Browning, "Home Thoughts from Abroad."
Poem 3: John Donne, "Death."
Poem 4: From Henry Wadsworth Longfellow, "Resignation," *By the Fireside*.
Poem 5: From Ella Wheeler Wilcox, "New Year," *Poems of Sentiment*, W. B. Conkey Company, Chicago, 1892, p. 159.
Poem 6: From *Bolts of Melody:* New Poems of Emily Dickinson, edited by Mabel Loomis Todd and Millicent Todd Bingham. Copyright 1945 by Millicent Todd Bingham. Reprinted by permission of Harper & Row, Publishers, Incorporated.
Poem 7: From Rudyard Kipling, "Fuzzy-Wuzzy," *Rudyard Kipling's Verse, Inclusive Edition, 1885–1926*, Doubleday, Doran & Company, Inc., New York, 1931, pp. 458–459. Reprinted by permission of Doubleday & Company, Inc.
Poem 8: From Robert Service, "The Whistle of Sandy McGraw," *The Complete Poems of Robert Service*, Dodd, Mead & Company, New York, 1950, pp. 385–388. Reprinted by permission of Dodd, Mead & Company from *The Complete Poems of Robert Service*.
Poem 9: From Carl Sandburg, "Four Preludes on Playthings with the Wind," *Smoke and Steel*, copyright, 1920, by Harcourt, Brace & World, Inc.; copyright, 1948, by Carl Sandburg. Reprinted by permission of the publishers.
Poem 10: From Carl Sandburg, "The Man with the Broken Fingers," *Home Front*

Memo, copyright, 1943, by Carl Sandburg. Reprinted by permission of Harcourt, Brace & World, Inc.

Indexes useful in locating selections [8]

Poetry

Granger's Index to Poetry and Recitations, 3rd ed., ed. H. H. Bessey, Chicago, McClurg, 1940.

Indexes standard and popular collections of poetry, recitations, orations, drills, dialogues, selections from drama, etc. by title, author, and first line.

Granger's Index to Poetry and Recitations, 4th ed., ed. Raymond J. Dixon, New York, Columbia University Press, 1953.

Index divided into three parts: (1) title and first line index; (2) author index; (3) subject index. See also the supplement which brings the anthologies indexed up to and including December 31, 1955.

Short Stories

Short Story Index, eds. D. E. Cook and I. S. Monro, New York, H. W. Wilson, 1953.

An index to 60,000 stories in 4,320 collections, indexed by author, title, and, in many cases, by subject, to stories published in 1949 or earlier. See also the supplement which indexes 9,575 stories in 549 collections through 1954.

Short Story Index, eds. E. A. Fidell and E. V. Flory, New York, H. W. Wilson, 1960.

A supplement to the above, indexing 6,392 stories in 376 collections, indexed under author, title, and often subject.

Essays

Essay and General Literature Index, eds. M. E. Sears and M. Shaw, New York, H. W. Wilson, 1934.

Lists essays and miscellaneous articles by author, subject, and sometimes title. See also supplements which keep the index right up to date.

Speeches

Speech Index, ed. Roberta Briggs Sutton, New York, H. W. Wilson, 1935.

An index to sixty-four collections of world-famous orations and speeches for various occasions. A dictionary catalogue with entries for each oration under author, subject, and type of speech.

Speech Index, ed. Roberta Briggs Sutton, New Brunswick, Scarecrow Press, 1956.

Supplement to above, the same indexing.

Songs

Song Index, ed. M. E. Sears, New York, H. W. Wilson, 1926.

An index to more than 12,000 songs in 177 song collections compris-

---

[8] Reprinted from *Building Better Speech* by Paul D. Brandes and William S. Smith, by permission of Noble and Noble Publishers, Inc.

ing 262 volumes. Contains titles, first lines, authors' names and composers' names in one alphabetized listing. See also supplement indexing more than 7,000 songs in 104 collections comprising 124 volumes, with similar indexing.

Drama

Index to Plays, 1800–1926, ed. Ina Ten Eyck Firkins, New York, H. W. Wilson, 1927.

Indexes available editions of plays by 19th and 20th century authors, 7,872 in number by 2,203 authors. The author index gives complete bibliographical information for each play and indicates type. There is also a combined title and subject index. See also the supplement for the years 1927–1934.

Play Index: 1949–1952, eds. D. H. West and D. M. Peake, New York, H. W. Wilson, 1953.

Combined author, title, and subject index of 2,616 plays in 1,138 volumes.

An Index to One-act Plays, eds. H. Logasa and W. Ver Nooy, Boston, Faxon, 1924.

Plays listed by title, with an author list and a subject index. See also three supplements listing plays through 1957.

Index to Plays in Collections, ed. J. H. Ottemiller, New York, The Scarecrow Press, 1957.

Indexes plays from ancient times to 1956. An author and title index to plays appearing in collections published between 1900 and 1956.

For other indexes available, see C. M. Winchell, *Guide to Reference Books,* Chicago, American Library Association, 1951, and three supplements.

A selected bibliography of paperbound books in print suitable for oral interpretation [9]

Biography

Addams, Jane: *Twenty Years at Hull House,* Signet Classics.
Bligh, William: *Mutiny on Board H.M.S. Bounty,* Signet Classics.
Chesterton, G. K.: *St. Francis of Assisi,* Image Books.
Darrow, Clarence: *Story of My Life,* Universal.
Dooley, Thomas A.: *Doctor Tom Dooley, My Story,* Popular.
Frank, Anne: *Diary of a Young Girl,* Pocket.
Ghandi, Mohandas K.: *The Story of My Experiments with Truth,* Beacon Press.
Gibson, Althea: *I Always Wanted to Be Somebody,* Ed Fitzgerald (ed.), Pyramid Books.
Goodspeed, Edgar J.: *Life of Jesus,* Harper Torchbooks.

[9] All entries are taken from the Winter 1961–1962 issue of *Paperbound Books in Print* published by the R. R. Bowker Company, 62 West 45th St., New York 36, N.Y.

Grant, Ulysses S.: *Personal Memoirs of Ulysses S. Grant*, Premier Books.
Gunther, John: *Death Be Not Proud*, Pyramid Books.
Harkness, Georgia: *John Calvin: The Man and His Ethics*, Apex Books.
Keller, Helen: *Story of My Life*, Dell.
Kennedy, John F.: *Profiles in Courage*, Pocket.
Letters of Sacco and Vanzetti, M. D. Frankfurte and Gardner Jackson (eds.), Dutton Everyman Paperbacks.
Schweitzer, Albert: *Out of My Life and Thought*, New American Library.
Sister Mary Francis: *Right to be Merry*, All Saints Press.
Thurber, James: *My Life and Hard Times*, Bantam.
Washington, Booker T.: *Up from Slavery*, Bantam.

Collections and Anthologies

Faulkner, William: *Portable Faulkner*, Malcolm Cowley (ed.), Viking.
Millay, Edna St. Vincent: *Letters*, A. F. Macdougall (ed.), Universal.
Saroyan, William: *Daring Young Man on the Flying Trapeze*, Bantam.
Twain, Mark: *Portable Mark Twain*, Benard De Voto (ed.), Viking.

Drama

Anderson, Maxwell: *Four Verse Plays*, Harvest Books.
Chekov, Anton: *Nine Plays*, Universal.
Contemporary Drama, E. B. Watson and B. Pressey (eds.), Scribner. There are three other volumes in the same series.
Eight Great Comedies, S. Barnet, M. Berman and W. Burto (eds.), Mentor Books.
Eight Great Tragedies, S. Barnet, M. Berman and W. Burto (eds.), Mentor Books.
Famous American Plays of the 1940's, Henry Hewes (ed.), Dell.
Four Contemporary American Plays (*The Tenth Man, A Raisin in the Sun, Toys in the Attic,* and *The Anderson Trial*), Bennett Cerf (ed.), Vintage Books.
Four Modern Plays, Series I: *Hedda Gabler, Pygmalion, Emperor Jones, and Death of A Salesman*, Holt.
Four Modern Plays, Series II (Ibsen, *Rosmersholm;* Rostand, *Cyrano de Bergerac;* Wilde, *The Importance of Being Earnest;* and Gorki, *The Lower Depths*), Henry Popkin (ed.), Holt.
Ibsen, Henrik: *Four Great Plays*, Bantam.
Literature for Interpretation, Wallace Bacon and Robert Breen (eds.), Holt.
Molière, Jean Baptiste: *Eight Plays*, Modern Library.
Shakespeare, William: *Four Great Tragedies*, Washington Square Press.
Sheridan, Richard Brinsley: *Six Plays*, Louis Kronenberger (ed.), Dramabooks, Hill and Wang.
Ten Greek Plays in Contemporary Translations, L. R. Lind (ed.), Riverside Editions.
Thomas, Dylan: "Under Milk Wood," New Directions.
Three Distinctive Plays about Abraham Lincoln, Willard Swire (ed.), Washington Square Press.
Wilde, Oscar: *Plays*, Penguin.
Wilder, Thornton: *Three Plays*, Bantam.
World's Great Plays, George-Jean Nathan (ed.), Universal.

Literature

Carroll, Lewis: *Alice's Adventures in Wonderland* and *Through the Looking Glass*, New American Library.

Faulkner, William: *The Unvanquished*, New American Library.

Harte, Bret: *Outcasts of Poker Flat and Other Tales*, Signet Classics.

London, Jack: *Call of the Wild and Selected Stories*, New American Library.

Rawlings, Marjorie Kinnan: *The Yearling*, Scribners.

Tolstoi, Leo: *Short Stories*, A. Mendel and B. Makanowitzky (trans.), Bantam.

Twain, Mark: *Adventures of Huckleberry Finn*, Wallace Stegner (ed.), Dell.

Poetry

Browning, Robert: *Men and Women*, Dolphin Books.

——— *The Ring and the Book*, Norton.

Dickinson, Emily: *Selected Poems and Letters*, Robert N. Linscott (ed.), Anchor Books.

Frost, Robert: *A Pocket Book of Robert Frost's Poems*, Louis Untermeyer (ed.), Washington Square Press.

Keats, John: *Selected Poems and Letters*, Douglas Bush (ed.), Riverside Editions.

Masefield, John: *Salt-water Poems and Ballads*, Macmillan.

Millay, Edna St. Vincent: *Collected Lyrics*, Washington Square Press.

Parker, Dorothy: *The Portable Dorothy Parker*, Viking.

Pocket Book of Modern Verse, Oscar Williams (ed.), Washington Square Press.

Poe, Edgar Allan: *Selected Poetry and Prose*, T. O. Mabbott (ed.), Modern Library.

Sandburg, Carl: *Harvest Poems: 1910–1960*, Harvest Books.

Six Centuries of Great Poetry, Robert Penn Warren and Albert Erskine (eds.), Dell.

Story Poems: An Anthology of Narrative Verse, Louis Untermeyer (ed.), Pocket.

Stuart, Jesse: *Man with a Bull-tongue Plow*, ab. and rev., Dutton Everyman Paperbacks.

Tennyson, Lord Alfred: *Poems*, J. H. Buckley (ed.), Riverside Editions.

Victorian Poetry: Clough to Kipling, A. J. Carr (ed.), Holt.

Wordsworth, William: *Poetical Works*, T. Hutchinson (ed.), rev. by E. De Selincourt, Oxford University Press.

Short Stories and Essays

American Short Stories, Ray B. West (ed.), Crowell.

Beerbohm, Max: *And Even Now & a Christmas Garland*, Everyman Paperbacks.

Book of English Essays, W. E. Williams (ed.), Penguin.

Chekhov, Anton: *Early Stories*, N. Gottlieb (trans.), Anchor Books.

Daudet, Alphonse: *Letters from My Mill*, Dolphin Books.

Great English and American Essays, D. S. Mead (ed.), rev. ed., Holt.

Hearn, Lafcadio: *Tales and Essays from Old Japan*, Henry Regnery Co.

Henry, O.: *Pocket Book of O. Henry Stories,* H. Hansen (ed.), Washington Square Press.

James, Henry: *Fifteen Short Stories,* Bantam.

Lamb, Charles: *Essays of Elia* and *The Last Essays of Elia,* Dolphin Books.

Lardner, Ring: *Haircut and Other Stories,* Scribner.

Lawrence, D. H.: *Complete Short Stories of D. H. Lawrence,* Viking, 3 vols.

Mansfield, Katherine: *Stories,* Elizabeth Bowen (ed.), Vintage Books.

Orwell, George: *Collection of Essays,* Anchor Books.

Russell, Bertrand: *Unpopular Essays,* Simon and Schuster.

Short Story Masterpieces, Robert Penn Warren and Albert Erskine (eds.), Dell.

Stevenson, Robert Louis: *Selected Essays,* Henry Regnery Co.

Tate, Allen: *Man of Letters in the Modern World,* New World Publishing Co.

Thomas, Dylan: *Adventures in the Skin Trade and Other Stories,* New American Library.

Twain, Mark: *Complete Short Stories,* Charles Neider (ed.), Bantam.

Williams, William Carlos: *Farmers' Daughters: The Collected Stories of William Carlos Williams,* New Directions.

Prefatory readings for chapters 5 and 6

Poetry

Matthew Arnold, *Dover Beach*
Robert Frost, *Stopping by Woods on a Snowy Evening*
Robert Frost, *Wild Grapes*
Robert Browning, *My Last Duchess*

Prose

Eudora Welty, *Lily Daw and the Three Ladies*
James Michener, *The Landing on Kuralei*

Dover Beach

The sea is calm tonight,
The tide is full, the moon lies fair
Upon the Straits;—on the French coast, the light
Gleams, and is gone; the cliffs of England stand,
Glimmering and vast, out in the tranquil bay.
Come to the window, sweet is the night air!
Only, from the long line of spray
Where the ebb meets the moon-blanch'd sand,
Listen! you hear the grating roar
Of pebbles which the waves suck back, and fling,
At their return, up the high strand,
Begin, and cease, and then again begin,
With tremulous cadence slow, and bring
The eternal note of sadness in.

Sophocles long ago
Heard it on the Aegean, and it brought
Into his mind the turbid ebb and flow
Of human misery; we
Find also in the sound a thought,
Hearing it by this distant northern sea.
The sea of faith
Was once, too, at the full, and round earth's shore
Lay like the folds of a bright girdle furl'd;
But now I only hear
Its melancholy, long, withdrawing roar,
Retreating to the breath
Of the night-wind down the vast edges drear
And naked shingles of the world.

Ah, love, let us be true
To one another! for the world, which seems
To lie before us like a land of dreams,
So various, so beautiful, so new,
Hath really neither joy, nor love, nor light,
Nor certitude, nor peace, nor help for pain;
And we are here as on a darkling plain
Swept with confused alarms of struggle and flight,
Where ignorant armies clash by night.

Matthew Arnold

Stopping by Woods on a Snowy Evening [1]

Whose woods these are I think I know.
His house is in the village though;
He will not see me stopping here
To watch his woods fill up with snow.

My little horse must think it queer
To stop without a farmhouse near
Between the woods and frozen lake
The darkest evening of the year.

He gives his harness bells a shake
To ask if there is some mistake.
The only other sound's the sweep
Of easy wind and downy flake.

The woods are lovely, dark and deep.
But I have promises to keep,
And miles to go before I sleep,
And miles to go before I sleep.

Robert Frost

Wild Grapes [2]

What tree may not the fig be gathered from?
The grape may not be gathered from the birch?
It's all you know the grape, or know the birch.
As a girl gathered from the birch myself
Equally with my weight in grapes, one autumn,
I ought to know what tree the grape is fruit of.
I was born, I suppose, like anyone.
And grew to be a little boyish girl
My Brother could not always leave at home.
But that beginning was wiped out in fear
The day I swung suspended with the grapes,
And was come after like Eurydice
And brought down safely from the upper regions;
And the life I live now's an extra life
I can waste as I please on whom I please.
So if you see me celebrate two birthdays,

And give myself out as two different ages,
One of them five years younger than I look—

One day my brother led me to a glade
Where a white birch he knew of stood alone,
Wearing a thin head-dress of pointed leaves,
And heavy on her heavy hair behind,
Against her neck, an ornament of grapes.
Grapes, I knew grapes from having seen them last year
One bunch of them, and there began to be
Bunches all round me growing in white birches,
The way they grew round Lief the Lucky's German;
Mostly as much beyond my lifted hands, though,
As the moon used to seem when I was younger,
And only freely to be had for climbing.

My brother did the climbing; and at first
Threw me down grapes to miss and scatter
And have to hunt for in sweet fern and hardhack;
Which gave him some time to himself to eat,
But not so much, perhaps, as a boy needed.
So then, to make me wholly self-supporting,
He climbed still higher and bent the tree to earth,
And put it in my hands to pick my own grapes.
"Here, take a tree-top, I'll get down another.
Hold on with all your might when I let go."
I said I had the tree. It wasn't true.
The opposite was true. The tree had me.
The minute it was left with me alone
It caught me up as if I were the fish
And it the fishpole. So I was translated
To loud cries from my brother of "Let go!
Don't you know anything, you girl? Let go!"
But I, with something of the baby grip
Acquired ancestrally in just such trees
When wilder mothers than our wildest now
Hung babies out on branches by the hands
To dry or wash or tan, I don't know which
(You'll have to ask an evolutionist)—
I held on uncomplainingly for life.
My brother tried to make me laugh to help me.
"What are you doing up there in those grapes?
Don't be afraid. A few of them won't hurt you.
I mean, they won't pick you if you don't them."
Much danger of my picking anything!
By that time I was pretty well reduced
To a philosophy of hang-and-let-hang.
"Now you know how it feels," my brother said,

"To be a bunch of fox-grapes, as they call them,
That when it thinks it has escaped the fox
By growing where it shouldn't—on a birch,
Where a fox wouldn't think to look for it—
And if he looked and found it, couldn't reach it—
Just then come you and I to gather it.
Only you have the advantage of the grapes
In one way: you have one more stem to cling by,
And promise more resistance to the picker."

One by one I lost off my hat and shoes,
And still I clung. I let my head fall back,
And shut my eyes against the sun, my ears
Against my brother's nonsense. "Drop," he said,
"I'll catch you in my arms. It isn't far."
(Stated in lengths of him it might not be.)
"Drop or I'll shake the tree and shake you down."
Grim silence on my part as I sank lower,
My small wrists stretching till they showed the banjo strings.
"Why, if she isn't serious about it!
Hold tight awhile till I think what to do.
I'll bend the tree down and let you down by it."
I don't know much about the letting down;
But once I felt ground with my stocking feet
And the world came revolving back to me,
I know I looked long at my curled-up fingers,
Before I straightened them and brushed the bark off.
My brother said: "Don't you weigh anything?
Try to weigh something next time, so you won't
Be run off with by birch trees into space."

It wasn't my not weighing anything
So much as my not knowing anything—
My brother had been nearer right before.
I had not taken the first step in knowledge;
I had not learned to let go with the hands,
As still I have not learned to with the heart,
And have no wish to with the heart—nor need,
That I can see. The mind—is not the heart.
I may yet live, as I know others live,
To wish in vain to let go with the mind—
Of cares, at night, to sleep; but nothing tells me
That I need learn to let go with the heart.

Robert Frost

My Last Duchess

That's my last Duchess painted on the wall,
Looking as if she were alive; I call

That piece a wonder, now: Frà Pandolf's hands
Worked busily a day, and there she stands.
Will't please you sit and look at her? I said
"Frà Pandolf" by design, for never read
Strangers like you that pictured countenance,
The depth and passion of its earnest glance,
But to myself they turned (since none puts by
The curtain I have drawn for you, but I)
And seemed as they would ask me, if they durst,
How such a glance came there; so, not the first
Are you to turn and ask thus. Sir, 'twas not
Her husband's presence only, called that spot
Of joy into the Duchess' cheek: perhaps
Frà Pandolf chanced to say "Her mantle laps
Over my Lady's wrist too much," or "Paint
Must never hope to reproduce the faint
Half-flush that dies along her throat"; such stuff
Was courtesy, she thought, and cause enough
For calling up that spot of joy. She had
A heart . . . how shall I say? . . . too soon made glad,
Too easily impressed; she liked whate'er
She looked on, and her looks went everywhere.
Sir, 'twas all one! My favour at her breast,
The dropping of the daylight in the West,
The bough of cherries some officious fool
Broke in the orchard for her, the white mule
She rode with round the terrace—all and each
Would draw from her alike the approving speech,
Or blush, at least. She thanked men,—good; but thanked
Somehow . . . I know not how . . . as if she ranked
My gift of a nine-hundred-years-old name
With anybody's gift. Who'd stoop to blame
This sort of trifling? Even had you skill
In speech—(which I have not)—to make your will
Quite clear to such an one, and say "Just this
Or that in you disgusts me; here you miss,
Or there exceed the mark"—and if she let
Herself be lessoned so, nor plainly set
Her wits to yours, forsooth, and made excuse,
—E'en then would be some stooping, and I choose
Never to stoop. Oh, Sir, she smiled, no doubt,
Whene'er I passed her; but who passed without
Much the same smile? This grew; I gave commands;
Then all smiles stopped together. There she stands
As if alive. Will't please you rise? We'll meet
The company below, then. I repeat,
The Count your Master's known munificence
Is ample warrant that no just pretence
Of mine for dowry will be disallowed;

Though his fair daughter's self, as I avowed
At starting, is my object. Nay, we'll go
Together down, Sir! Notice Neptune, though,
Taming a sea-horse, thought a rarity,
Which Claus of Innsbruck cast in bronze for me.

Robert Browning

Lily Daw and the Three Ladies [3]

Eudora Welty

Mrs. Watts and Mrs. Carson were both in the post office in Victory when the letter came from the Ellisville Institute for the Feeble-Minded of Mississippi. Aimee Slocum, with her hand still full of mail, ran out in front and handed it straight to Mrs. Watts, and they all three read it together. Mrs. Watts held it taut beween her pink hands, and Mrs. Carson underscored each line slowly with her thimbled finger. Everybody else in the post office wondered what was up now.

"What will Lily say," beamed Mrs. Carson at last, "when we tell her we're sending her to Ellisville!"

"She'll be tickled to death," said Mrs. Watts, and added in a guttural voice to a deaf lady, "Lily Daw's getting in at Ellisville!"

"Don't you all dare go off and tell Lily without me!" called Aimee Slocum, trotting back to finish putting up the mail.

"Do you suppose they'll look after her down there?" Mrs. Carson began to carry on a conversation with a group of Baptist ladies waiting in the post office. She was the Baptist preacher's wife.

"I've always heard it was lovely down there, but crowded," said one.

"Lily lets people walk over her so," said another.

"Last night at the tent show—" said another, and then popped her hand over her mouth.

"Don't mind me, I know there are such things in the world," said Mrs. Carson, looking down and fingering the tape measure which hung over her bosom.

"Oh, Mrs. Carson. Well, anyway, last night at the tent show, why, the man was just before making Lily buy a ticket to get in."

"A ticket!"

"Till my husband went up and explained she wasn't bright, and so did everybody else."

The ladies all clucked their tongues.

"Oh, it was a very nice show," said the lady who had gone. "And Lily acted so nice. She was a perfect lady—just set in her seat and stared."

"Oh, she can be a lady—she can be," said Mrs. Carson, shaking her head and turning her eyes up. "That's just what breaks your heart."

[3] Eudora Welty, "Lily Daw and the Three Ladies," in *A Curtain of Green*, Harcourt, Brace and World, Inc., New York, 1941, pp. 3–20. Copyright, 1938, by Eudora Welty. Reprinted by permission of Harcourt, Brace & World, Inc.

"Yes'm, she kept her eyes on—what's that thing makes all the commotion?—the xylophone," said the lady. "Didn't turn her head to the right or to the left the whole time. Set in front of me."

"The point is, what did she do after the show?" asked Mrs. Watts practically. "Lily has gotten so she is very mature for her age."

"Oh, Etta!" protested Mrs. Carson, looking at her wildly for a moment.

"And that's how come we are sending her to Ellisville," finished Mrs. Watts.

"I'm ready, you all," said Aimee Slocum, running out with white powder all over her face. "Mail's up. I don't know how good it's up."

"Well, of course, I do hope it's for the best," said several of the other ladies. They did not go at once to take their mail out of their boxes; they felt a little left out.

The three women stood at the foot of the water tank.

"To find Lily is a different thing," said Aimee Slocum.

"Where in the wide world do you suppose she'd be?" It was Mrs. Watts who was carrying the letter.

"I don't see a sign of her either on this side of the street or on the other side," Mrs. Carson declared as they walked along.

Ed Newton was stringing Redbird school tablets on the wire across the store.

"If you're after Lily, she come in here while ago and tole me she was fixin' to git married," he said.

"Ed Newton!" cried the ladies all together, clutching one another. Mrs. Watts began to fan herself at once with the letter from Ellisville. She wore widow's black, and the least thing made her hot.

"Why she is not. She's going to Ellisville, Ed," said Mrs. Carson gently. "Mrs. Watts and I and Aimee Slocum are paying her way out of our own pockets. Besides, the boys of Victory are on their honor. Lily's not going to get married, that's just an idea she's got in her head."

"More power to you, ladies," said Ed Newton, spanking himself with a tablet.

When they came to the bridge over the railroad tracks, there was Estelle Mabers, sitting on a rail. She was slowly drinking an orange Ne-Hi.

"Have you seen Lily?" they asked her.

"I'm supposed to be out here watching for her now," said the Mabers girl, as though she weren't there yet. "But for Jewel—Jewel says Lily come in the store while ago and picked out a two-ninety-eight hat and wore it off. Jewel wants to swap her something else for it."

"Oh, Estelle, Lily says she's going to get married!" cried Aimee Slocum.

"Well, I declare," said Estelle; she never understood anything.

Loralee Adkins came riding by in her Willys-Knight, tooting the horn to find out what they were talking about.

Aimee threw up her hands and ran out into the street. "Loralee, Loralee, you got to ride us up to Lily Daws'. She's up yonder fixing to get married!"

"Hop in, my land!"

"Well, that just goes to show you right now," said Mrs. Watts, groaning as she was helped into the back seat. "What we've got to do is persuade Lily it will be nicer to go to Ellisville."

"Just to think!"

While they rode around the corner Mrs. Carson was going on in her sad voice, sad as the soft noises in the hen house at twilight. "We buried Lily's poor defenseless mother. We gave Lily all her food and kindling and every stitch she had on. Sent her to Sunday school to learn the Lord's teachings, had her baptized a Baptist. And when her old father commenced beating her and tried to cut her head off with the butcher knife, why, we went and took her away from him and gave her a place to stay."

The paintless frame house with all the weather vanes was three stories high in places and had yellow and violet stained-glass windows in front and gingerbread around the porch. It leaned steeply to one side, toward the railroad, and the front steps were gone. The car full of ladies drew up under the cedar tree.

"Now Lily's almost grown up," Mrs. Carson continued. "In fact, she's grown," she concluded, getting out.

"Talking about getting married," said Mrs. Watts disgustedly. "Thanks, Loralee, you run on home."

They climbed over the dusty zinnias onto the porch and walked through the open door without knocking.

"There certainly is always a funny smell in this house. I say it every time I come," said Aimee Slocum.

Lily was there, in the dark of the hall, kneeling on the floor by a small open trunk.

When she saw them she put a zinnia in her mouth, and held still.

"Hello, Lily," said Mrs. Carson reproachfully.

"Hello," said Lily. In a minute she gave a suck on the zinnia stem that sounded exactly like a jay bird. There she sat, wearing a petticoat for a dress, one of the things Mrs. Carson kept after her about. Her milky-yellow hair streamed freely down from under a new hat. You could see the wavy scar on her throat if you knew it was there.

Mrs. Carson and Mrs. Watts, the two fattest, sat in the double rocker. Aimee Slocum sat on the wire chair donated from the drugstore that burned.

"Well, what are you doing, Lily?" asked Mrs. Watts, who led the rocking.

Lily smiled.

The trunk was old and lined with yellow and brown paper, with an asterisk pattern showing in darker circles and rings. Mutely the ladies indicated to each other that they did not know where in the world it had come from. It was empty except for two bars of soap and a green washcloth, which Lily was now trying to arrange in the bottom.

"Go on and tell us what you're doing, Lily," said Aimee Slocum.

"Packing, silly," said Lily.

"Where are you going?"

"Going to get married, and I bet you wish you was me now," said Lily. But shyness overcame her suddenly, and she popped the zinnia back into her mouth.

"Talk to me, dear," said Mrs. Carson. "Tell old Mrs. Carson why you want to get married."

"No," said Lily, after a moment's hesitation.

"Well, we've thought of something that will be so much nicer," said Mrs. Carson, "Why don't you go to Ellisville!"

"Won't that be lovely?" said Mrs. Watts. "Goodness, yes."

"It's a lovely place," said Aimee Slocum uncertainly.

"You've got bumps on your face," said Lily.

"Aimee, dear, you stay out of this, if you don't mind," said Mrs. Carson anxiously. "I don't know what it is comes over Lily when you come around her."

Lily stared at Aimee Slocum meditatively.

"There! Wouldn't you like to go to Ellisville now?" asked Mrs. Carson.

"No'm," said Lily.

"Why not?" All the ladies leaned down toward her in impressive astonishment.

" 'Cause I'm goin' to get married," said Lily.

"Well, and who are you going to marry, dear?" asked Mrs. Watts. She knew how to pin people down and make them deny what they'd already said.

Lily bit her lip and began to smile. She reached into the trunk and held up both cakes of soap and wagged them.

"Tell us," challenged Mrs. Watts. "Who you're going to marry, now."

"A man last night."

There was a gasp from each lady. The possible reality of a lover descended suddenly like a summer hail over their heads. Mrs. Watts stood up and balanced herself.

"One of those show fellows! A musician!" she cried.

Lily looked up in admiration.

"Did he—did he do anything to you?" In the long run, it was still only Mrs. Watts who could take charge.

"Oh, yes'm," said Lily. She patted the cakes of soap fastidiously with the tips of her small fingers and tucked them in with the washcloth.

"What?" demanded Aimee Slocum, rising up and tottering before her scream. "What?" she called out in the hall.

"Don't ask her what," said Mrs. Carson, coming up behind. "Tell me, Lily—just yes or no—are you the same as you were?"

"He had a red coat," said Lily graciously. "He took little sticks and went *ping-pong! ding-dong!*"

"Oh, I think I'm going to faint," said Aimee Slocum, but they said, "No, you're not."

"The xylophone!" cried Mrs. Watts. "The xylophone player! Why, the coward, he ought to be run out of town on a rail!"

"Out of town? He is out of town, by now," cried Aimee. "Can't you read? —the sign in the café—Victory on the ninth, Como on the tenth? He's in Como. Como!"

"All right! We'll bring him back!" cried Mrs. Watts. "He can't get away from me!"

"Hush," said Mrs. Carson. "I don't think it's any use following that line of reasoning at all. It's better in the long run for him to be gone out of our lives for good and all. That kind of a man. He was after Lily's body alone and he wouldn't ever in this world make the poor little thing happy, even if we went out and forced him to marry her like he ought—at the point of a gun."

"Still—" began Aimee, her eyes widening.

"Shut up," said Mrs. Watts. "Mrs. Carson, you're right, I expect."

"This is my hope chest—see?" said Lily politely in the pause that followed. "You haven't even looked at it. I've already got soap and a washrag. And I have my hat—on. What are you all going to give me?"

"Lily," said Mrs. Watts, starting over, "we'll give you lots of gorgeous things if you'll only go to Ellisville instead of getting married."

"What will you give me?" asked Lily.

"I'll give you a pair of hemstitched pillow cases," said Mrs. Carson.

"I'll give you a big caramel cake," said Mrs. Watts.

"I'll give you a souvenir from Jackson—a little toy bank," said Aimee Slocum. "Now will you go?"

"No," said Lily.

"I'll give you a pretty little Bible with your name on it in real gold," said Mrs. Carson.

"What if I was to give you a pink crêpe de Chine brassière with adjustable shoulder straps?" asked Mrs. Watts grimly.

"Oh, Etta."

"Well, she needs it," said Mrs. Watts. "What would they think if she ran all over Ellisville in a petticoat looking like a Fiji?"

"I wish *I* could go to Ellisville," said Aimee Slocum luringly.

"What will they have for me down there?" asked Lily softly.

"Oh! Lots of things. You'll have baskets to weave, I expect...." Mrs. Carson looked vaguely at the others.

"Oh, yes indeed, they will let you make all sorts of baskets," said Mrs. Watts; then her voice too trailed off.

"No'm, I'd rather get married," said Lily.

"Lily Daw! Now that's just plain stubbornness!" cried Mrs. Watts. "You almost said you'd go and then you took it back!"

"We've all asked God, Lily," said Mrs. Carson finally, "and God seemed to tell us—Mr. Carson, too—that the place where you ought to be, so as to be happy, was Ellisville."

Lily looked reverent, but still stubborn.

"We've really just got to get her there—now!" screamed Aimee Slocum all at once. "Suppose—! She can't stay here!"

"Oh, no, no, no," said Mrs. Carson hurriedly. "We mustn't think that." They sat sunken in despair.

"Could I take my hope chest—to go to Ellisville?" asked Lily shyly, looking at them sidewise.

"Why, yes," said Mrs. Carson blankly.

Silently they rose once more to their feet.

"Oh, if I could just take my hope chest!"

"All the time it was just her hope chest," Aimee whispered.

Mrs. Watts struck her palms together. "It's settled!"

"Praise the fathers," murmured Mrs. Carson.

Lily looked up at them, and her eyes gleamed. She cocked her head and spoke out in a proud imitation of someone—someone utterly unknown. "O.K.—Toots!"

The ladies had been nodding and smiling and backing away toward the door.

"I think I'd better stay," said Mrs. Carson, stopping in her tracks. "Where —where could she have learned that terrible expression?"

"Pack up," said Mrs. Watts. "Lily Daw is leaving for Ellisville on Number One."

In the station the train was puffing. Nearly everyone in Victory was hanging around waiting for it to leave. The Victory Civic Band had assembled without any orders and was scattered through the crowd. Ed Newton gave false signals to start on his bass horn. A crate full of baby chickens got loose on the platform. Everybody wanted to see Lily all dressed up, but Mrs. Carson and Mrs. Watts had sneaked her into the train from the other side of the tracks.

The two ladies were going to travel as far as Jackson to help Lily change trains and be sure she went in the right direction.

Lily sat between them on the plush seat with her hair combed and pinned up into a knot under a small blue hat which was Jewel's exchange for the pretty one. She wore a traveling dress made out of part of Mrs. Watt's last summer's mourning. Pink straps glowed through. She had a purse and a Bible and a warm cake in a box, all in her lap.

Aimee Slocum had been getting the outgoing mail stamped and bundled. She stood in the aisle of the coach now, tears shaking from her eyes.

"Good-bye, Lily," she said. She was the one who felt things.

"Good-bye, silly," said Lily.

"Oh, dear, I hope they get our telegram to meet her in Ellisville!" Aimee cried sorrowfully, as she thought how far away it was. "And it was so hard to get it all in ten words, too."

"Get off, Aimee, before the train starts and you break your neck," said Mrs. Watts, all settled and waving her dressy fan gaily. "I declare, it's so hot, as soon as we get a few miles out of town I'm going to slip my corset down."

"Oh, Lily, don't cry down there. Just be good and do what they tell you —it's all because they love you." Aimee drew her mouth down. She was backing away, down the aisle.

Lily laughed. She pointed across Mrs. Carson's bosom out the window toward a man. He had stepped off the train and just stood there, by himself. He was a stranger and wore a cap.

"Look," she said, laughing softly through her fingers.

"Don't—look," said Mrs. Carson, very distinctly, as if, out of all she had ever spoken, she would impress these two solemn words upon Lily's soft little brain. She added, "Don't look at anything till you get to Ellisville."

Outside, Aimee Slocum was crying so hard she almost ran into the stranger. He wore a cap and was short and seemed to have on perfume, if such a thing could be.

"Could you tell me, madam," he said, "where a little lady lives in this burg name of Miss Lily Daw?" He lifted his cap—and he had red hair.

"What do you want to know for?" Aimee asked before she knew it.

"Talk louder," said the stranger. He almost whispered, himself.

"She's gone away—she's gone to Ellisville!"

"Gone?"

"Gone to Ellisville!"

"Well, I like that!" The man stuck out his bottom lip and puffed till his hair jumped.

"What business did you have with Lily?" cried Aimee suddenly.

"We was only going to get married, that's all," said the man.

Aimee Slocum started to scream in front of all those people. She almost pointed to the long black box she saw lying on the ground at the man's feet. Then she jumped back in fright.

"The xylophone! The xylophone!" she cried, looking back and forth from the man to the hissing train. Which was more terrible? The bell began to ring hollowly, and the man was talking.

"Did you say Ellisville? That in the state of Mississippi?" Like lightning he had pulled out a red notebook entitled, "Permanent Facts & Data." He wrote down something. "I don't hear well."

Aimee nodded her head up and down, and circled around him.

Under "Ellis-Ville Miss" he was drawing a line; now he was flicking it with two little marks. "Maybe she didn't say she would. Maybe she said she wouldn't." He suddenly laughed very loudly after the way he had whispered. Aimee jumped back. "Women!—Well, if we play anywheres near Ellisville, Miss., in the future I may look her up and I may not," he said.

The bass horn sounded the true signal for the band to begin. White steam rushed out of the engine. Usually the train stopped for only a minute in Victory, but the engineer knew Lily from waving at her, and he knew this was her big day.

"Wait!" Aimee Slocum did scream. "Wait, mister! I can get her for you. Wait, Mister Engineer! Don't go!"

Then there she was back on the train, screaming in Mrs. Carson's and Mrs. Watts's faces.

"The xylophone player! The xylophone player to marry her! Yonder he is!"

"Nonsense," murmured Mrs. Watts, peering over the others to look where Aimee pointed. "If he's there I don't see him. Where is he? You're looking at One-Eye Beasley."

"The little man with the cap—no, with the red hair! Hurry!"

"Is that really him?" Mrs. Carson asked Mrs. Watts in wonder. "Mercy! He's small, isn't he?"

"Never saw him before in my life!" cried Mrs. Watts. But suddenly she shut up her fan.

"Come on! This is a train we're on!" cried Aimee Slocum. Her nerves were all unstrung.

"All right, don't have a conniption fit, girl," said Mrs. Watts. "Come on," she said thickly to Mrs. Carson.

"Where are we going now?" asked Lily as they struggled down the aisle.

"We're taking you to get married," said Mrs. Watts. "Mrs. Carson, you'd better phone up your husband right there in the station."

"But I don't want to git married," said Lily, beginning to whimper. "I'm going to Ellisville."

"Hush, and we'll all have some ice-cream cones later," whispered Mrs. Carson.

Just as they climbed down the steps at the back end of the train, the band went into "Independence March."

The xylophone player was still there, patting his foot. He came up and said, "Hello, Toots. What's up—tricks?" and kissed Lily with a smack, after which she hung her head.

"So you're the young man we've heard so much about," said Mrs. Watts. Her smile was brilliant. "Here's your little Lily."

"What say?" asked the xylophone player.

"My husband happens to be the Baptist preacher of Victory," said Mrs. Carson in a loud, clear voice. "Isn't that lucky? I can get him here in five minutes: I know exactly where he is."

They were in a circle around the xylophone player, all going into the white waiting room.

"Oh, I feel just like crying, at a time like this," said Aimee Slocum. She looked back and saw the train moving slowly away, going under the bridge at Main Street. Then it disappeared around the curve.

"Oh, the hope chest!" Aimee cried in a stricken voice.

"And whom have we the pleasure of addressing?" Mrs. Watts was shouting, while Mrs. Carson was ringing up the telephone.

The band went on playing. Some of the people thought Lily was on the train, and some swore she wasn't. Everybody cheered, though, and a straw hat was thrown into the telephone wires.

From the Landing on Kuralei [4]

James Michener

Meanwhile power has been building up on Green Beach. At 1544, with the sun dropping lower toward the ocean, they tried the first row of coconut trees again. They were driven back. This time, however, not quite to the coral. They held onto some good positions fifteen or twenty yards inland.

At 1557 Admiral Kester pulled them back onto the coral. For the last

---

[4] James Michener, "The Landing on Kuralei," *Tales of the South Pacific,* The Macmillan Company, New York, 1952, pp. 309–315. Reprinted with permission of The Macmillan Company. Copyright 1947 by James Michener.

time that day. He sent the planes in to rout out that first trench. This time, with noses almost in the coconut stumps, our fliers roared up and down the trenches. They kept their powerful .50's aimed at the narrow slits like a woman guiding a sewing machine along a pre-determined line. But the .50's stitched death.

At 1607 the planes withdrew. At a signal, every man on that beach, every one, rose and dashed for the first trench. The Japs knew they were coming, and met them with an enfilading fire. But the Green Beach boys piled on. Some fell wounded. Others died standing up and took a ghostly step toward the trench. Some dropped from fright and lay like dead men. But most went on, grunting as they met the Japs with bayonets. There was a muddled fight in the trench. Then things were quiet. Some Americans started crawling back to pick up their wounded. That meant our side had won.

Japs from the second trench tried to lead a charge against the exhausted Americans. But some foolhardy gunners from a cruiser laid down a pinpoint barrage of heavy shells. Just beyond the first trench. It was dangerous, but it worked. The Japs were blown into small pieces. Our men had time to reorganize. They were no longer on coral. They were inland. On Kuralei's earth.

At 1618 Admiral Kester made his decision. Green Beach was our main chance. To hell with Red. Hang on, Red! But everything we had was thrown at Green. It was our main chance. "Any word from the tanks?" "Beating down the peninsula, sir." It was no use banging the table. If the tanks could get through, they would.

At 1629 about a hundred amphibs sped for Green Beach. They were accompanied by a tremendous barrage that raked the western end of the beach toward the cliffs. Thirty planes strafed the Jap part of the promontory. A man beside me started yelling frantically. A Jap gun, hidden somewhere in that wreckage, was raking our amphibs. "Get that gun!" he shouted. "It's right over there!" He jumped up and down and had to urinate against the bulkhead. "Get that gun!" Two amphibs were destroyed by the gun. But more than ninety made the beach. Now, no matter how many Japs counter-attacked, we had a chance to hold the first trench.

"A tank!" our lookout shouted. I looked, but saw none. Then, yes! There was a tank! But it was a Jap tank. Three of them! The Jap general had finally conceded Lt. Col. Hyaichi's point. He was rushing all moveable gear to the promontory. And our own tanks were still bogged down in the jungle.

"LCS-108! Beach yourself and use rockets!" The order came from the flagship. With crisp command the young skipper got up as much speed as possible. He drove his small craft as near the battle lines as the sea would take it. We braced ourselves and soon felt a grinding shock as we hit coral. We were beached, and our bow was pointed at the Jap tanks.

Our first round of rockets went off with a low swish and headed for the tanks. "Too high!" the skipper groaned. The barrage shot into the cacao trees. The Jap tanks bore down on our men in the first ditch. Our next round of rockets gave a long hissss. The first tank exploded loudly and blocked the way of the second Jap.

At this moment a Jap five-incher hit the 108. We heeled over to port. The men at the rocket-launching ramps raised their sights and let go with another volley. The second tank exploded. Japs climbed out of the manhole. Two of them dived into the cacaos. Two others were hit by rifle fire and hung head downward across the burning tank.

The third Jap tank stopped firing at our men in the first trench and started lobbing shells at LCS-108. Two hit us, and we lay far over on the coral. The same foolhardy gunners on the cruiser again ignored our men in the first trench. Accurately they plastered the third tank. We breathed deeply. The Japs probably had more tanks coming, but the first three were taken care of.

Our skipper surveyed his ship. It was lost. It would either be hauled off the reef and sunk or left there to rot. He felt strange. His first command! What kind of war was this? You bring a ship all the way from Norfolk to stop two tanks. On land. You purposely run your ship on a coral reef. It's crazy. He damned himself when he thought of that Jap plane flashing by. It had killed two of his men. Not one of our bullets hit that plane. It all happened so fast. "So fast!" he muttered. "This is a hell of a war!"

At 1655 the Marines in trench one, fortified by new strength from the amphibs, unpredictably dashed from the far western end of their trench and overwhelmed the Japs in the opposite part of trench two. Then ensued a terrible, hidden battle as the Marines stolidly swept down the Jap trench. We could see arms swinging above the trench, and bayonets. Finally, the men in the eastern end of trench one could stand the suspense no longer. Against the bitterest kind of enemy fire, they rushed past the second row of coconut stumps and joined their comrades. Not one Jap survived that brutal, silent, hidden struggle. Trench two was ours.

At 1659 more than a thousand Jap reinforcements arrived in the area. Not yet certain that we had committed all our strength to Green Beach, about half the Japs were sent to Red. Lt. Col. Hyaichi, tight-lipped and sweating, properly evaluated our plan. He begged his commanding officer to leave only a token force at Red Beach and to throw every ounce of man and steel against Green. This was done. But as the reserves moved through the coconut grove, the skipper of the LCS-108 poured five rounds of rockets right into their middle. Results passed belief. Our men in trench two stared in frank astonishment at what the rockets accomplished. Then, shouting, they swamped the third Jap trench before it could be reinforced.

At 1722, when the sun was beginning to eat into the treetops of Kuralei, our tanks broke loose along the shore of the promontory. Sixty sweating footslogging axmen dragged themselves after the tanks. But ahead lay an unsurmountable barrier of rock. The commanding officer of the tanks appraised the situation correctly. He led his ménage back into the jungle. The Japs also foresaw what would happen next. They moved tank destroyers up. Ship fire destroyed them. We heard firing in the jungle.

At 1740 our position looked very uncertain. We were still six rows from Line Albany. And the Japs had their blockhouse right at the edge of the cacaos. Our chances of attaining a reasonably safe position seemed slight when a fine shout went up. One of our tanks had broken through! Alone, it dashed right for the heart of the Jap position. Two enemy tanks, hidden up to now, swept out from the coconut emplacements and engaged our tank. Bracketed by shells from each side, our tank exploded. Not one man escaped.

But we soon forgot the first tank. For slowly crawling out of the jungle came the other three. Their treads were damaged. But they struggled on. When the gloating Jap tanks saw them coming, they hesitated. Then, perceiving the damage we had suffered, the Japs charged. Our tanks stood fast and fired fast. The Japs were ripped up and down. One quit the fight. Its occupants fled. The other came on to its doom. Converging fire from our three tanks caught it. Still it came. Then, with a fiery gasp, it burned up. Its crew did not even try to escape.

At 1742 eleven more of our tanks landed on Sonova Beach. You would have thought their day was just beginning. But the sun was on their tails as they grunted into the jungle like wild pigs hunting food.

An endless stream of barges hit Green Beach. How changed things were! On one wave not a single shot from shore molested them. Eight hundred Yanks on Kuralei without a casualty. How different that was! We got Admiral Kester's message: "Forty-eight minutes of daylight. A supreme effort."

At 1749 the Japs launched their big counter-attack. They swept from their blockhouse in wild assault. Our rockets sped among them, but did not stop them. It was the men in trench three that stopped them.

How they did so, I don't know. Japs swarmed upon them, screaming madly. With grenades and bayonets the banzai boys did devilish work. Eighty of our men died in that grim assault. Twelve had their heads completely severed.

But in the midst of the melee, two of our three tanks broke away from the burning Jap tanks and rumbled down between trench three and trench four. Up and down that tight areaway they growled. A Jap suicide squad stopped one by setting it afire. Their torches were their own gasoline-soaked bodies. Our tankmen, caught in an inferno, tried to escape. From trench three, fifty men leaped voluntarily to help them. Our men surrounded the flaming tank. The crewmen leaped to safety. In confusion, they ran not to our lines but into trench four. Our men, seeing them cut down, went mad. They raged into trench four and killed every Jap. In a wild spontaneous sweep they swamped trench five as well!

Aboard the LSC-108 we could not believe what we had seen. For in their rear were at least a hundred and twenty Japs still fighting. At this moment reinforcements from the amphibs arrived. The Japs were caught between heavy fire. Not a man escaped. The banzai charge from the blockhouse had ended in complete rout.

At 1803 Admiral Kester sent his message: "You can do it. Twenty-seven minutes to Line Albany!" We were then four rows from the blockhouse. But we were sure that beyond trench seven no trenches had been dug. But we also knew that trenches six and seven were tougher than anything we had yet tackled. So for the last time Admiral Kester sent his beloved planes in to soften up the trenches. In the glowering dusk they roared up and down between the charred trees, hiccupping vitriol. The grim, terrible planes withdrew. There was a moment of waiting. We waited for our next assault. We waited for new tanks to stumble out of the promontory. We waited in itching dismay for that tropic night. We were so far from the blockhouse! The sun was almost sunk into the sea.

What we waited for did not come. Something else did. From our left flank, toward the cliffs, a large concentration of Jap reinforcements broke from heavy cover and attacked the space between trenches one and two. It was seen in a flash that we had inadequate troops at that point. LCS-108 and several other ships made an instantaneous decision. We threw all our fire power at the point of invasion. Rockets, five-inchers, eight-inchers and intermediate fire hit the Japs. They were stopped cold. Our lines held.

But I can still see one flight of rockets we launched that day at dusk. When the men in trench two saw the surprise attack coming on their flank, they turned sideways to face the new threat. Three Americans nearest the Japs never hesitated. Without waiting for a command to duty they leaped out of their trench to meet the enemy head on. Our rockets crashed into the advancing Japs. The three voluntary fighters were killed. By their own friends.

There was no possible escape from this tragedy. To be saved, all those men needed was less courage. It was nobody's fault but their own. Like war, rockets once launched cannot be stopped.

It was 1807. The sun was gone. The giant clouds hanging over Kuralei turned gold and crimson. Night birds started coming into the cacao grove. New Japs reported to the blockhouse for a last stand. Our own reinforcements shuddered as they stepped on dead Japs. Night hurried on.

At 1809, with guns spluttering, eight of our tanks from Sonova Beach burst out of the jungle. Four of them headed for the blockhouse. Four tore right down the alleyway between trenches five and six. These took a Jap reinforcement party head on. The fight was foul and unequal. Three Japs set fire to themselves and tried to immolate the tank crews. They were actually shot into pieces. The tanks rumbled on.

At the blockhouse it was a different story. Tank traps had been well built in that area. Our heavies could not get close to the walls. They stood off and hammered the resilient structure with shells.

"Move in the flame-throwers. Everything you have. Get the blockhouse." The orders were crisp. They reached the Marines in trench five just as the evening star became visible. Eight husky young men with nearly a hundred pounds of gear apiece climbed out of the trench. Making an exceptional target, they blazed their way across six and seven with hundreds of protectors. They drew a slanting hailstorm of enemy fire. But if one man was killed, somebody else grabbed the cumbersome machinery. In the gathering darkness they made a weird procession.

A sergeant threw up his hands and jumped. "No trenches after row seven!" A tank whirled on its right tread and rumbled over. Now, with tanks on their right and riflemen on their left, the flame-throwers advanced. From every position shells hit the blockhouse. It stood. But its defenders were driven momentarily away from the portholes. This was the moment!

With hoarse cries our flame-throwers rushed forward. Some died and fell into their own conflagration. But three flame-throwers reached the portholes. There they held their spuming fire. They burned away the oxygen of the blockhouse. They seared eyes, lips, and more than lungs. When they stepped back from the portholes, the blockhouse was ours.

Now it was night! From all sides Japs tried to infiltrate our lines. When they were successful, our men died. We would find them in the morning with their throats cut. When you found them so, all thought of sorrow for the Japs burned alive in the blockhouse was erased. They were the enemy, the cruel, remorseless, bitter enemy. And they would remain so, every man of them, until their own red sun sank like the tired sun of Kuralei.

How does the oral reader prepare the selection?   5

Between nature and ourselves, nay, between ourselves and our own consciousness a veil is interposed: a veil that is dense and opaque for the common herd,—thin, almost transparent, for the artist and the poet.

Henri Bergson [1]

Previous chapters have pointed out how oral interpretation affects human behavior and how the reader chooses the proper selection (or stimulus) for presentation. Chapters 5 and 6 concern themselves with how the stimulus, once chosen, may best be prepared to achieve the desired response. The discussion in these chapters is confined to remarks which are applicable to all forms of literature. Discussions of problems which are unique to one particular type have been reserved for Part II.

The preface to this chapter contains six selections which are used repeatedly as examples in the discussion that follows. This material should be carefully read before study is begun on Chapters 5 and 6.

In his preparation for interpretative reading, the student must first gain a thorough understanding of the literature he is to read. Such preparation must precede any work or drill on the skill of *how to read.* The basis for any of the performing skills that the reader may wish to develop must be founded in the meaning of the selection itself. Otherwise, the reading becomes superficial, shallow, and often exhibitory. The reader cannot give to others an understanding of the selection which he himself does not have.

There are two approaches which lead to a fuller understanding of literature: The first is concerned with areas directly related to the selection, and the second is concerned with an analysis of the selection itself. This text lists four divisions of the related areas, namely, the

---

[1] Henri Bergson, "Laughter," in Wylie Sypher (ed.), *Comedy,* Doubleday & Company, Inc., Garden City, 1956, p. 158. Reprinted by permission of Doubleday & Company, Inc.

life and times of the author, other works by the same author, the appraisal of the critics, and the medium. The discussion of the analysis of the selection itself is divided into two parts: the selection and the style of the selection.

A study of the related areas

The life and times of the author

Behind each piece of art is the artist or the creator. The artist is, or was, a person, an individual living in a society during a given period of history. How significant is a knowledge of the author's life to the understanding of the artist's work? Does a knowledge of the historical background of the selection give insight into the meaning of literature?

Should not the student of interpretation *wish* to know something about the personality of the creator of the literature he is about to read and should he not wish to know something about the times in which the literature was written? If for no other reason than to satisfy his intellectual curiosity, he should gather information on the artist, the times, and the conditions under which he worked.

The second approach lies in showing that there is usually much that the reader can learn from studying the life and times of the author which will make him better prepared to read the author's works to others. There are exceptions, of course, and perhaps biographical study has at times been overstressed as an approach to literary study. However, knowing something of the solitary life of Emily Dickinson would certainly add to an understanding of much of her poetry. For example, it would be difficult to imagine a reader who could successfully interpret the following poem without a knowledge of Miss Dickinson's life.

I Was the Slightest in the House [2]

I was the slightest in the house,
I took the smallest room,
At night, my little lamp and book
And one geranium,

So stationed I could catch the mint
That never ceased to fall,
And just my basket, let me think,
I'm sure that this was all.

[2] From *Bolts of Melody: New Poems of Emily Dickinson,* edited by Mabel Loomis Todd and Millicent Todd Bingham. Copyright 1945 by Millicent Todd Bingham. Reprinted by permission of Harper & Row, Publishers, Incorporated.

I never spoke unless addressed,
And then 'twas brief and low,
I could not bear to live aloud
The racket shamed me so.

And if it had not been so far,
And anyone I knew
Were going, I had often thought
How noteless I could die.

Emily Dickinson

Also, in the case of such subjective writers as the Romantic poets—
Byron, Shelley, Keats, Coleridge, and Wordsworth—biographical
knowledge would be of great value to the reader. These men and
many others have written about themselves and their deepest feelings.
The reader who has not read the journals of Dorothy Wordsworth
cannot hope to read her brother's poetry with much more than surface
comprehension. A knowledge of the author's life will also make clear
many of the references and allusions in the selection which are the
result of his associations and experiences. Willa Cather said that she
was not successful as a writer until she stopped trying to write and
began to remember. The things which Miss Cather remembered, of
course, were the events in her own life.

On the other hand, the artist may write as if a large gulf existed
between his life and his work, in which case the reader should develop
a sense of the degree of the discrepancy. Wellek and Warren point
out: "A work of art may rather embody the 'dream' of an author than
his actual life, or it may be the 'mask,' the 'anti-self' behind which his
real person is hiding, or it may be a picture of the life from which
the author wants to escape." [3] Therefore, it must not be assumed that
every piece of literature is a direct reflection of the author's life or
that the life and the work must show a simple cause and effect relationship. A biographical study would be of little aid in gaining a
fuller meaning of the works of Alexander Pope. Furthermore, the
interpretative reader could not rely on the biographical approach in
a study of Shakespeare. In fact, very little information about the life
of this great poet and dramatist is available. Much study has been
done and will continue to be done on the meaning of Shakespearean
poetry, but this study will be undertaken without the benefits of
biographical material.

As a case in point, how much should a reader know about the life
of Eudora Welty before he can read her short story about Victory, Mis-

[3] René Wellek and Austin Warren, *Theory of Literature,* Harcourt, Brace and Company, Inc., New York, p. 72.

sissippi? Unfortunately, there are as yet no biographies of Miss Welty. Helpful essays, however, are available. From jackets on the covers of her books, introductions to her works, and newspaper and magazine articles, the student can put together a rather accurate account of the author's life. Would it be helpful for the reader to know that Miss Welty attended Mississippi State College for Women? Would it be of value for him to know that Miss Welty lives in Jackson, Mississippi, where Mrs. Carson and Mrs. Watts were going to help Lily change trains? Would it be helpful for him to know that Miss Welty has had a comparatively easy time in selling her stories? Because of the strong autobiographical thread in many of the Welty stories and because of Miss Welty's own admission that *place* is of significance in her work,[4] the authors of this text conclude that it would be wise for the interpreter to gather as much biographical data on the author as possible before trying to interpret "Lily Daw and the Three Ladies."

Other works by the same author

The second of the related areas concerns other works by the same writer, particularly those that are akin to the selection he has chosen. The interpreter must comb his selection searching for similarities, differences, and relationships in not just one but several other works by the same author.

Suppose the reader has chosen as his selection the poem "Dover Beach" by Matthew Arnold. In his biographical study, the reader would already have learned pertinent facts about the poet. He would have become aware that this Victorian lived during a period of English history when there was intellectual and social conflict. He would have discovered that new knowledge and a renewed interest in the scientific had a strong effect on Arnold who thought that with the surge toward the scientific approach science could possibly supercede religion and that literature would take its place "to interpret life for us, to console us, to sustain us."[5]

Knowing all this and much more, the reader should turn to a second poem by Matthew Arnold, "The Scholar Gipsy," parts of which are reproduced below:

For what wears out the life of mortal men?
  'Tis that from change to change their being rolls:

---

[4] See Eudora Welty, "How I Write," *Virginia Quarterly Review*, vol. 31, pp. 240–251, Spring, 1955.
[5] Matthew Arnold, "Introduction," in T. H. Ward (ed.), *The English Poets*, The Macmillan Company, New York, 1880, vol. 1, pp. xviii. Reprinted by permission of The Macmillan Company.

'Tis that repeated shocks, again, again,
  Exhaust the energy of strongest souls,
    And numb the elastic powers.
Till having us'd our nerves with bliss and teen,
  And tir'd upon a thousand schemes our wit,
  To the just-pausing Genius we remit
    Our worn-out life, and are—what we have been. . . .

                          . . . and we others pine,
And wish the long unhappy dream would end,
  And waive all claim to bliss, and try to bear
With close-lipp'd Patience for our only friend,
  Sad Patience, too near neighbour to Despair:
    But none has hope like thine.
Thou through the fields and through the woods dost stray,
  Roaming the country side, a truant boy,
  Nursing thy project in unclouded joy,
    And every doubt long blown by time away.

O born in days when wits were fresh and clear,
  And life ran gaily as the sparkling Thames;
    Before this strange disease of modern life,
  With its sick hurry, its divided aims,
    Its heads o'ertax'd, it palsied hearts, was rife—
      Fly hence, our contact fear!
Still fly, plunge deeper in the bowering wood!
  Averse, as Dido did with gesture stern
  From her false friend's approach in Hades turn,
    Wave us away, and keep thy solitude.

The similarity of philosophies in these two poems is at once evident. In "Dover Beach," Arnold recommends a refuge from the confusing modern world in the love and affection of two of its lost people;
in "The Scholar Gipsy," Arnold uses an old story about an impover-
ished student at Oxford University to advise us not to live in reality
but to bury ourselves in rural seclusion. Yet another poem by the same
author, "The Forsaken Merman," while using mythical characters
and a mythical setting, contrasts the detached life with the material
world, without disparaging either.

The interpreter, now armed with some knowledge of the philosophy
of Arnold by reading other of his poems, can return to his own selection "Dover Beach" with renewed vigor and understanding.

Perhaps instead of "Dover Beach" the reader has chosen the poem
"Wild Grapes" by Robert Frost. He has read of the New England
background of this Vermont poet, whose sense of humor and box-
ing match with life led him boldly into some eighty years of crea-

tive living. The reader has examined prefaces, scholarly articles, and book reviews to discover Frost's keen and sympathetic insight into the thinking and feeling of the American people. He has learned of Frost's answer to Matthew Arnold's question of where the world can gain peace—that a calm life can be found anywhere if one is really seeking it, whether it be in rural Vermont or at 32 Bank Street in Greenwich Village, where Frost's daughter once lived and still visits.

There are many poems that the reader might choose to broaden his concept of Frost's poetry. He could begin by digesting thoroughly "Stopping by Woods on a Snowy Evening," one of Frost's more famous poems. As he reads, the interpreter will become aware of rural Vermont, its simplicity—woods, snow, a little horse, and the last two lines of philosophy. He then sees Vermont in the winter, as he saw it in the summer in "Wild Grapes." He notes that in both poems the concluding passage provokes thought.

"The Road Not Taken" [6] is another description of the woods in New England with a strong similarity to "Wild Grapes" because both require that a decision be reached.

Two roads diverged in a yellow wood,
And sorry I could not travel both
And be one traveler, long I stood
And looked down one as far as I could
To where it bent in the undergrowth;

Then took the other, as just as fair,
And having perhaps the better claim,
Because it was grassy and wanted wear;
Though as for that the passing there
Had worn them really about the same,

And both that morning equally lay
In leaves no step had trodden black.
Oh, I kept the first for another day!
Yet knowing how way leads on to way,
I doubted if I should ever come back.

I shall be telling this with a sigh
Somewhere ages and ages hence:
Two roads diverged in a wood, and I—
I took the one less traveled by,
And that has made all the difference.

The reader will need to become acquainted with many other Frost selections, such as "The Runaway" and "The Tuft of Flowers" before he can say that he has gained sufficient understanding of "Wild Grapes" to permit him to interpret it successfully.

Literary Criticism

In addition to studying the life of the author and his other works, the interpreter must also consult the critics for additional help to comprehend his selection. Scholars have made extensive inquiries, asking questions as to what a selection means and why it was written. The interpreter has no more right to read a poem without consulting the students of that poem than he has to stage a debate on atomic energy without having informed himself of the opinions of the leading physicists of the day. Let us consider briefly the comments of the critics on the work of Eudora Welty and, to the extent that they are available, the comments on "Lily Daw and the Three Ladies."

The first question that many students ask when they are told to consult the critics is: Where does a reader go to locate criticism? He would do well be begin with the *Social Sciences and Humanities Index* since it indexes articles in such scholarly publications as *The Kenyon Review*, the *Sewanee Review*, and the *Virginia Quarterly Review*. Second, he can consult the *Book Review Digest*, select the reviews which seem most promising, and then locate the original reviews in the sources indicated in the index. Third, he can follow up on the footnotes he finds in the articles cited in the *Social Sciences and Humanities Index* and the *Book Review Digest*.

Here is an example of how a student would use these three steps to develop a bibliography of criticism for "Lily Daw and the Three Ladies."

There are six articles on Eudora Welty in the *Social Sciences and Humanities Index:*

Hardy, J. E.: "Delta Wedding as Region and Symbol," *Sewanee Review,* vol. 60, pp. 397–417, July, 1952.
Jones, W. M.: "Eudora Welty's Use of Myth in 'Death of a Traveling Salesman,'" *Journal of American Folklore,* vol. 73, pp. 18–23, January, 1960.
Jones, W. M.: "Growth of a Symbol: the Sun in Lawrence and Eudora Welty," *University of Kansas City Review,* vol. 26, pp. 68–73, October, 1959.
Jones, W. M.: "Name and Symbol in the Prose of Eudora Welty," *Southeastern Folklore Quarterly,* vol. 22, pp. 173–185, December, 1958.
Welty, Eudora: "Place in Fiction," *South Atlantic Quarterly,* vol. 55, pp. 57–72, January, 1956.
Welty, Eudora: "How I Write," *Virginia Quarterly Review,* vol. 31, pp. 240–251, Spring, 1955.

Two of the articles by Jones were marked in the *Social Sciences and Humanities Index* as including bibliographies. From these articles, the following two leads were obtained:

Porter, Katherine Anne: "Introduction" to Eudora Welty's *A Curtain of Green and Other Stories,* Harcourt, Brace & World, Inc., New York, 1941, pp. xi–xxiii.
Welty, Eudora: "The Reading and Writing of Short Stories," *Atlantic Monthly,* vol. 183, pp. 46–49, March, 1949.

The *Book Review Digest* notes briefly the comments of several newspaper and periodical reviews of *A Curtain of Green and Other Stories* in which "Lily Daw and the Three Ladies" appears. These two were chosen to follow up:

New Yorker, Nov. 15, 1941.
Saturday Review, Nov. 22, 1941.

The comments of the former were so terse that it was discarded as a major source of criticism. The more extensive remarks in the *Saturday Review* were noted for further reference.

Such a bibliography, although not extensive or pretentious, would permit the reader to examine the self-criticism that Miss Welty has issued on herself and to sample the criticism given her work by others. What in particular should the student look for in reading the criticism? Four of the many areas of interest will be mentioned here, which, if explored, should materially increase the comprehension of the selection for the interpreter.

The allusion.   It is safe to assume that most writers are also persons who are well read themselves. If literature is the powerful medium that we propose it to be, it is inevitable that what a writer has read will make its mark on his writing. Indeed, a writer uses his knowledge of history and literature to help him say as much as possible with a minimum amount of effort. If a writer says, "This man is a Hercules" or "The flames reminded her of the burning of Joan of Arc," he hopes that his own experiences with mythology in the case of Hercules and history in the case of Joan of Arc will arouse in his reader similar experiences and so enhance the meaning of his words enormously. By the simple introduction of the word "Hercules," the author hopes to bring to mind the whole Greek legend and asks the reader to visualize the twelve labors, including the cleansing of the Aegean stables and the seizure of the golden apples of Hesperides.

His hopes are sometimes in vain. Students often resist a critical analysis of the allusions of the author. Bacon and Breen point out one of the reasons why students approach such analytical study with hesitation:

Unfortunately for our older writers, readers nowadays are frequently empty of such knowledge [the knowledge of history and literature]. That is why textbooks containing literature from earlier periods are so full of notes! It is not very pleasant constantly to be looking at footnotes in order to comprehend a text, and it is no wonder that students resist them; how much pleasanter if all of us read widely enough so that the allusions found us already prepared to respond! [7]

What are the results of such a breakdown in communication? Bacon and Breen add: "We find ourselves growing impatient with a writer whose references are all to such private experiences that we *cannot* respond; is it not quite proper that a writer should be impatient with a reader who has so small a store of knowledge that he *will not* respond?" [8]

It is the obligation of the critic to assist the reader in enhancing his response. The critic is particularly sensitive to allusions. He has trained himself to see what others may miss. Although he may at times exceed the mark and become overanalytical, he will many more times reveal associations between the selection and other literature and historical events that were meaningful to the author which may completely escape the less trained person. It falls to the lot of the interpreter to so train himself that he can distinguish good from poor criticism. This he cannot do unless he studies the critics and their critical analyses. [9]

[7] Wallace A. Bacon and Robert S. Breen, *Literature as Experience*, p. 137. Copyright 1959 McGraw-Hill Book Company, Inc., New York. Used by permission.
[8] *Ibid.*
[9] For example, both Hardy and Jones find considerable symbolism in the stories of Eudora Welty. Hardy speaks of the symbolic meaning of Robbie Reid and Troy Flavin in Eudora Welty's novel *Delta Wedding*, while Jones speaks of the symbolism of the sun, a symbol which he proposes that Welty adopted from Lawrence (note that Welty refers at length to Lawrence in her own article in *The Atlantic Monthly*). Is the search for symbolism in the Welty stories profitable or is it meaningless pedantry? For some, the search for symbolism in the characterizations in "Lily Daw and the Three Ladies" might prove most provocative. Could Lily become a symbol of normality rather than a representation of abnormality, the label which her surrounding society has placed upon her? Is the symbolism of the sun apparent in "Lily Daw and the Three Ladies"? Perhaps because the author seems to be brushing her strokes lightly as she creates Lily, her symbolism is more subdued, for there is no reference to the sun as such. But a student who found the search for symbolism provocative could point to the inevitable presence of the heat of the sun. Mrs. Watts is hot and fanning, Lily is in the dark of the hall where we presume it is cooler, Estelle Mabers is drinking an orange Ne-Hi, and

Bacon and Breen have pointed out one reason why students resist searching for the allusions pointed out by the critics. There are additional causes for hesitation. We are often disappointed that we did not notice such relationships ourselves and are resentful that our more shallow comprehension is shattered by a critic who shows us what we should have been intelligent enough to see for ourselves. This is a very human reaction. It is why we resent all forms of criticism. For when the critic reveals allusions which we did not see, he is not only criticizing the writer, but the reader as well. When we as interpreters realize that we are resisting criticism because we ourselves have been wounded, the resistance is more easily overcome.

Third, the student may say, as many writers themselves say, "All this discussion of allusions and symbolism is too involved. The critics are reading too much into the selection." Authors often state that they intended no such subtleties. The poet Robert Frost was wont to do this in his public lectures and took to task one of his analysts, John Ciardi, of the *Saturday Review*.[10] Yet, from the "deep well" of experience so adequately described by John Livingston Lowes [11] can come thoughts that the poet himself did not know existed within him. It does not surprise us that a teacher of voice who cannot sing well can detect the faults of an opera aspirant and direct him to fame, nor does it seem untoward that a track coach, in observing his prize sprinter, can point out to newspaper reporters why his star can run faster than his nearest competitor, when the star himself does not know. But we do seem surprised when a highly skilled critic can detect in a poet things of which the poet himself is unaware.

There is yet a fourth reason why the student may be reluctant to admit the critic. Lowes says: "I know full well that this reluctance springs, with most of us, from the staunch conviction that to follow the evolution of a thing of beauty is to shatter its integrity and irretrievably to mar its charm." [12] Is this necessarily the case? Lowes does not think so: "... there are those of us who cherish the invincible belief that the glory of poetry will gain, not lose, through a recognition of the

---

the possibility of a lover "descended suddenly like a summer hail over their heads." The student who searched for symbolism could support his findings by pointing to the following statement by Jones in his article in the *University of Kansas City Review*: "Eudora Welty ... buries her sun symbol deep in her work and hopes that those who are not completely lost in the materialistic world will respond to the age-old symbol that Lawrence advocated so strongly and used so ineffectively."

[10] Strangely enough, Frost proposed that the great joy in learning is the conscious thrill of making associations. Yet he often resented the attempts of the critics to reconstruct unconscious associations that have given rise to his own poetry.

[11] John Livingston Lowes, *The Road to Xanadu*, Houghton Mifflin Company, Boston, 1927, pp. 3–63.

[12] *Ibid.*, p. 428.

fact that the imagination works its wonders through the exercise, in the main, of normal and intelligible powers." [13] Those who agree with Lowes propose that once the initial shock of finding that there may be some measure of system in creativity is over, the resulting appreciation of the intricacies of the system become far richer than before.

Not that the critic intends to say that by his analyzations the mystery of creativity can be solved. His purpose is rather to point out where order does exist so that the reader is free to appreciate the intricacies of the imagination and to wonder at the creative spirit that has made more out of two plus two than four.

Therefore a study of the criticism of a work may reveal allusions and symbolism used by the author to enhance the meaning of his writing. If the interpreter is aware of these factors, he is in a more informed position and can communicate more richly to his audience. If he feels his audience would also profit from a knowledge of certain subtleties of the literature, he may wish to call attention to them in his introduction.

It should be repeated here that not all criticism is good criticism. The student of oral interpretation must read enough of the works of the critic to develop a sense of what is constructive criticism and what is overanalytical nonsense. Not that he will ever be sure in all cases. But by delving into criticism with vigor and enthusiasm, he will make progress toward a selective sense of values.

Themes. In addition to allusions, the critic may reveal certain motifs that reappear throughout the work of an author. For example, one critic of Eudora Welty's work comments how often the author concerns herself with the unusual and the grotesque. Miss Porter comments that "many of the characters are of the sort that caused a Bostonian to remark that he could not care to meet them socially." [14] The *Saturday Review* concurs: "Miss Welty turns instinctively, it seems, to the odd, grotesque, or sardonic. It is encouraging to find a young writer eschewing the first personal introspective and turning to the world around her for people and for plot." [15] Such comment should motivate the reader to reexamine his story, to look again, with wiser eyes, at the xylophonist who "wore a cap and was short and seemed to have on perfume, if such a thing could be."

[13] *Ibid.*, pp. 428–429.

[14] Katherine Anne Porter, "Introduction" to Eudora Welty's *A Curtain of Green*, Harcourt, Brace & World, Inc., New York, 1941, p. xix. Copyright 1941 by Eudora Welty. Reprinted by permission of Harcourt, Brace & World, Inc.

[15] Gladys Graham Bates, "Two Southerners," *Saturday Review*, vol. 24, p. 10, November 22, 1941.

Places of importance. Critics often reveal the surroundings which were inspirational to a writer. In studying his bibliography for "Lily Daw and the Three Ladies," the reader would note Miss Welty's own comment: "...I am myself touched off by place. The place where I am and the place I know, and other places that familiarity with and love for my own make strange and lovely and enlightening to look into, are what set me to writing my stories."[16] Katherine Anne Porter observes that the scene of the Welty stories "is limited to a town the author knows well; the farthest reaches of that scene never go beyond the boundaries of her own state...."[17] Such observations by the critics would provoke the student to return to the story to see what "strange and lovely and enlightening" facets that Victory, Mississippi, had for the author. He might then make a list of the items of local color which he had missed before:

The water tank (What town does not have a unique atmosphere around its water tank?)

The bridge over the railroad tracks (Such a bridge often plays a prominent role in a small town.)

The trunk with the "asterisk pattern showing in darker circles and rings" (Are not similar remnants with an atmosphere of the past found in every reader's attic or in his aunt's or his grandmother's attic?)

The crate full of baby chickens loose on the platform (What are the symbols of comfortable confusion in other towns?)

The interpreter may have noted these items before, but he cannot help letting them gain additional significance after he has read the comments of Welty and Porter.

Evaluations. A fourth item that the interpreter can seek in the comments of the critics is evaluative comment. The interpreter of the work of Eudora Welty would gain strength from the general approval that the critics give to the author and even to the particular selection that he has chosen. Hardy notes that Welty has arrived;[18] Porter says of this first set of stories, "splendid beginning that this is, it is only the beginning";[19] the *Saturday Review* finds her first work "distinctive and, in most cases, engrossing."[20] The reader can note with satisfaction that his own short story is referred to as Miss Welty's "typical best."[21] Such reinforcements of his choice cannot

[16] Welty, *Virginia Quarterly Review*, pp. 240–241.
[17] Porter, *op. cit.*, p. xix.
[18] J. E. Hardy, "Delta Wedding as Region and Symbol," *Sewanee Review*, vol. 60, p. 397, July, 1952.
[19] Porter, *op. cit.*, p. xxiii.
[20] Bates, *op. cit.*, p. 10.
[21] *Ibid.*

but inspire the reader to work harder to find the way in which Miss Welty uses this story to order "her view of the present by constantly manipulating the parallel between past and present." [22]

The medium

There is yet one other area with which the reader must become familiar before he concentrates on the selection itself, namely, the medium or the literary type into which the piece is cast. To illustrate the importance of knowledge of the form of the selection, consider the old favorite, "My Last Duchess," by Robert Browning. This poem does not reflect the philosophy of its author, nor does it come from the life of his times. The knowledge of the biographical details of Browning, although very interesting to read, is of much less value to the interpreter in preparing to read "My Last Duchess" than is a study of the medium used by the author to present his story, namely, the dramatic monologue. Such a study should include not only a thorough acquaintance with the literary form of the monologue, but also an investigation into the history of the period in which the setting for the monologue is placed. Since Part IV specializes in literary types, the reader is referred to this section for additional information to aid him in understanding how he may best prepare himself to interpret the various forms of literature.

The selection itself

Now that the reader has given himself adequate background material, he must understand the selection itself. For the remainder of this chapter, the student will have his attention focused on an analysis of the chosen material.

The first readings

To ensure acquaintance with the selection, the interpreter should begin his intensive study by reading his material several times, silently and orally. The number of readings required will vary with the selection and the interpreter. The reader must be *receptive* as he reads, letting the literature *talk to him*. He must think and feel with the literature, and most important, this thinking and feeling should result in enjoyment. The reader who is in the process of introducing himself to literature through the process of oral reading should remember that, as William James points out, we are interested in what we attend

---

[22] W. M. Jones, "Eudora Welty's Use of Myth in 'Death of a Traveling Salesman,' " *Journal of American Folklore*, vol. 73, pp. 18–19, January, 1960.

to. The only way to become interested and therefore to enjoy literature is to associate with literature. Through this association, enjoyment will inevitably result.

As he reads, the interpreter should become aware of the over-all impact of the selection. Much of literature was not written to convey logical facts or to give a list of events. When we are studying literature, we are associating with a creative art. Perrine points out that short stories, plays, and poems have as their purpose not just to communicate information, but also to share an experience.[23] If the reader is to participate in this creative experience, he must allow sufficient time for the literature to permeate his thinking. The sympathy of thought, feelings, and reaction may be present in the reader, but they are latent and unintelligible. Horace says: "If you wish me to weep, you must first grieve yourself."[24] The grief may take time to develop. The reader should not expect a good poem or a good drama to reveal all at the first or second reading any more than he would expect to understand a plate from the Hogarth series of paintings "A Rake's Progress" at first exposure. When Queen Victoria told the Polish pianist Paderewski that he was a genius, the artist replied that perhaps he was, but that before he was ever a genius, he was a drudge. Paderewski knew, as did Wordsworth when he spoke of the poet as a man who had thought long and deep, that what appears to be the product of pure inspiration is mostly the product of hard work.

In order to reveal the deepest meanings of his selection, the reader must analyze it in detail. However, it is important that after each bit of insight the interpreter return to the whole selection. Such returns will remind the student of the unity of the selection and make him aware of the total composition. Literature is a gestalt. It cannot be taken apart piece by piece and then put back together in the same manner that a trained technician can assemble an engine. Edgar Allan Poe's essay "The Philosophy of Composition" to the contrary,[25] a piece of literature cannot be built from its parts into the whole. Frost would say of such a composition: "It has been worried into existence." This does not preclude a probing of the parts to gain a comprehension of thought and feeling. Many of the details will require provocative study. Nevertheless, each time the reader must remember to put the piece back and be prepared for the reaction that it will no longer

[23] Laurence Perrine, *Sound and Sense*, Harcourt, Brace & World, Inc., New York, 1956, p. 4.

[24] Horace, "Epistle to the Pisos, or The Art of Poetry," James Harry Smith and Sara Carron Smith (trans.), in James Harry Smith and Edd Winfield Parks (eds.), *The Great Critics*, W. W. Norton & Company, Inc., New York, 1939, p. 117.

[25] Edgar Allan Poe, "The Philosophy of Composition," *Graham's Magazine*, vol. 28, no. 4, pp. 163–167, April, 1846.

be just that piece, but will become something larger and greater by its association with the whole.

The nature of the content

What is the student hoping to find in the excitement of exploring the details of his selection? The archaeologist, in sifting through ton after ton of dirt, is attempting to restore the pieces of a lost civilization; the scientist, in controlling all but one of the variables of an experiment, is attempting to show how his one variable, be it a drug, treatment, or process, can modify the functioning of a society. The task of the oral reader, if he wishes to share the literature with an audience, is to establish *who* is saying *what* to *whom* and *where*, in order to unify these elements of the selection into a meaningful whole.

The who. In initiating his analysis, the first question for the reader to ask is, "*Who* is speaking?" As Brooks and Warren point out: "In poetry, as in all other discourse, one person is saying something to another person." [26] Such discourse may be put in one of two forms: The author may be speaking directly to his listeners, or the author may be using the device of a third person to speak to his listeners. in many instances, it is impossible, and perhaps unnecessary, to know whether the author is speaking directly or indirectly. Is the man speaking in the poem "Stopping by Woods on a Snowy Evening" Frost himself, or has Frost created a nameless third person who is contemplating the beauty of the scene? Certainly Frost does not tell us. Nor does Eudora Welty in "Lily Daw and the Three Ladies."

The author may have expressly created vehicles for his ideas. In the poem "Wild Grapes" Frost has drawn a woman recalling something that happened to her as a child:

As a girl gathered from the birch myself
Equally with my weight in grapes, one autumn,
I ought to know what tree the grape is fruit of.

In the poem "Dover Beach" Matthew Arnold created a man speaking to his beloved and uses this man as a vehicle to carry Arnold's ideas of the future of the world. In the dramatic monologue "My Last Duchess," Browning has allowed the duke to speak to the count's envoy concerning an oncoming marriage between the duke and the count's daughter. The whole point of Browning's poem is to give us a clear idea of *who* is speaking.

[26] Cleanth Brooks and Robert Penn Warren, *Understanding Poetry*, rev. ed., p. xxxiii. Copyright 1950 by Holt, Rinehart and Winston, Inc., New York.

It may be that one particular selection will provide for both indirect and direct narration. Any prologue or epilogue to a play puts the author in direct conversation with his audience, in contrast to the indirect manner in which he customarily addresses the spectators through his characters, once the action has begun. One of the most perplexing things about Shakespeare is the way in which he conceals his own thoughts and feelings, even when he appears to be speaking most directly to us. Shakespeare has Iago speak the noble lines: "Who steals my purse, steals trash"; and Polonius says: "This above all: to thine own self be true." Yet, neither Iago nor Polonius is to be trusted. Is Shakespeare trying to say, through these undesirable characters, that the wisest of platitudes proceed from the mouths of undesirables who say what they wish they believed?

The what. After the reader has established *who* is speaking, he must ask: what is being said? Why did the author write these words and phrases? As has been pointed out, the narrator of "Stopping by Woods on a Snowy Evening," be it Frost or another, slips into a philosophical observation at the conclusion of the poem which has given the critics much cause for disagreement:

The woods are lovely, dark and deep.
But I have promises to keep,
And miles to go before I sleep,
And miles to go before I sleep.

Is Frost saying to us, "Death is often a welcome refuge, but the road to death is blocked by promises which require us to live out our lives"? What is the purpose of the last stanza? The interpreter must seek an answer. He must have at his disposal, when he makes his decision, the interpretation the critics have made. But the final decision must be his own.

The man speaking in "Dover Beach" is trying to persuade or inspire his beloved with the idea "Ah, love, let us be true to one another!" since the world itself is out of joint. The woman speaking in "Wild Grapes" is giving us an analogy to help us gauge the extent to which a man may let go with his hands but not with his heart. The narrator in "Lily Daw and the Three Ladies" does much more than just relate the events, for although he describes the action in the small town in detail, he editorializes freely. How complacent are the self-satisfied ladies when they recall their acts of charity:

Mrs. Carson was going on in her sad voice: "We buried Lily's poor defenseless mother. We gave Lily her food and kindling and every stitch she had on. Sent her to Sunday school to learn the Lord's teachings. . . .

The narrator is telling us of the strengths and weaknesses of the people of the town, their mores, their beliefs, and their prejudices. Why are these given? What does the author wish us to conclude? We shall want to consider these questions in our study of the story before we share it with an audience.

The to whom. Now that the reader has identified the speaker and what his purpose is, he must explore the question: Who is the audience? *To whom* is the *who* saying his *what?* "Dover Beach," "Wild Grapes," "Lily Daw and the Three Ladies," "Stopping by Woods on a Snowy Evening," and "The Landing at Kuralei" are addressed to mankind in general. The authors have in no way limited the application of their theme to any group. Some selections, however, are directed to a well-defined person or persons. For example, all letters have a primary audience. It may be argued that any letter writer is really addressing all mankind and that many famous letter writers, such as Lord Chesterfield and Benjamin Franklin, were in truth talking to the world when they wrote. But even if this point is granted, for each letter, there is still a primary audience which must be identified.

In complete contrast to the poem or story which is written for the world in general is the journal, which is written to oneself. On December 24, 1801, Dorothy Wordsworth recounts that she took out her last year's journal to reflect on what had happened the year before. The original copies of these journals, as they speak for themselves in a small house near Dove Cottage, Grasmere, England, show that Dorothy was talking to herself as she kept her diary. Internal evidence in the diaries themselves show that Dorothy was not writing for posterity. If she had been, she would have commented on many items that are ignored and she would have left out many items on which she spends considerable time.

The soliloquy raises an interesting point as to who is being addressed. Is Hamlet talking to himself in his famous "To be or not to be" passage, or is he talking to the world? A fuller exposition of this point will be found in Part IV under literary types.

It is not always clear to whom the writer is speaking, but the reader must try to reach a decision. When he fails, the resulting concept of universality or anonymity will become a part of the interpretation.

The where. Finally, the oral interpreter will want to know the *where,* or the conditions, the surroundings, and the circumstances of the speaker when he was saying that something to someone. The narrator in "Lily Daw and the Three Ladies" might be in a rocking chair on a front porch in the cool of the afternoon, peeling peaches on the back steps, or talking to a total stranger on the train to Chicago. Matthew Arnold's narrator must be in a house or a hotel on the beach, looking across the channel from England to France. It is night because the lover can see the lights on the French coast. Robert Frost's woman who knew her wild grapes might be in any of the positions described for the narrator of Lily Daw, or she might be visiting an acquaintance or one of her children where she encountered an acquaintance, probably a younger person, who would be likely to doubt her knowledge of the woods. The speaker in "Stopping by Woods on a Snowy Evening" is out in the country with his horse and the falling snow in December, on the shortest day of the year.

Sometimes the author identifies the place directly and quickly; at other times, the identification is indirect and delayed. Shirley Jackson in her paralyzingly frightening short story "The Lottery"[27] uses the first paragraph to let us know the setting in which the story takes place:

The morning of June 27th was clear and sunny, with the fresh warmth of a full-summer day; the flowers were blossoming profusely and the grass was richly green. The people of the village began to gather in the square, between the post office and the bank, around ten o'clock; in some towns there were so many people that the lottery took two days and had to be started on June 26th, but in this village, where there were only about three hundred people, the whole lottery took only about two hours, so it could begin at ten o'clock in the morning and still be through in time to allow the villagers to get home for noon dinner.

Such a description of the landmarks of the town and its population does not tell us whether the narrator expects us to join him in the square for the horrible events that are to follow or whether he will allow us to retreat a safe distance and observe the unquestioning acceptance of a primitive practice from a spot far enough away to allow us to retain our equilibrium.

In contrast to the frank avowal of the *where* in the Shirley Jackson short story, the *place* in "Wild Grapes" is obscure and left largely up to the reader to create from his own past experiences.

Summary.   As the reader explores the conditions under which the storytelling was done, he can ask himself, "What would I say if I were the narrator? What would my reactions be as I told the story? How would I describe what I saw and felt?" This type of participation and visualization will help the interpreter to delve deeply into his selection so that he knows it through and through.

[27] Shirley Jackson, "The Lottery," Farrar, Straus & Cudahy, Inc., p. 25. Copyright 1948 by the *New Yorker Magazine*, 1949 by Shirley Jackson.

Armed with answers to who said what to whom and where, the interpreter is free to return to his selection and read it again and again, watching for details and innuendos that he may have missed before, when his understanding was more shallow. For example, he may notice for the first time that Mrs. Watts was wearing a thimble when the letter was being read in the post office or that Lily "wagged" the cakes of soap at the ladies when they asked her whom she was going to marry. His explorations of *who* Mrs. Watts and Lily really are have caused him to examine the story more closely.

The style of the selection

The return to the selection allows the reader to put into its proper place the material he gained from the answers to the four preceding questions. It should also serve to call to his attention the *style* that the author has used to express himself in this particular selection. The reader must remember that all literature is someone saying something to somebody at some place. Therefore, there must be a method or a means by which the speaker conveys his thoughts and experiences. An artist has special tools with which he works; the painter has his oils and brushes; the sculptor, his chisel; the architect, his drawing board and pencils. The writer also has his special tools—the words that he uses—to create his art. An additional study of the selection is therefore necessary to examine the literary style of the author.

It is difficult to separate the way a speaker uses words from the thoughts he is trying to express. The style of the artist is an integral part of his thinking. Therefore, style makes no pretense of remaining mutually exclusive to the content of the selection. There are numerous ways to approach the study of style, all of which are in some measure faulty. For he who analyzes style is attempting to probe the mystery of poetry in yet another way, and therefore no simple formula can be found which will expose how a writer has assembled his symbols to achieve the desired effect. The approach of Longinus has been used to give order and direction to these comments on style, which might otherwise be random and disconnected. If following the sequence suggested by Longinus results in some duplication and in questionable stratification, the authors would prefer to err in this direction rather than toward incompleteness and fragmentation.

Longinus recommends to us what he calls the *sublime* or the greatest style that an author can achieve. His treatise endeavors to show how literature may reach its highest peak. In doing so, he has set for us a standard which operates in a manner not unlike the par score in golf. Few are the golfers who reach par, and yet much enjoyment can be had by those who seek it and achieve degrees of success.

Without par, our minor victories would lack luster. Longinus's standards are high. Only occasionally can they be met. But an understanding of them allows us to evaluate the degree to which the writer has approached the best style that can be written. Many writers make no pretense of writing in an unqualified sublime style. Yet their works have considerable merit. This merit can in part be evaluated by the degree to which Longinus's qualifications have been met.

Longinus, in his essay *On the Sublime,* or as Allan H. Gilbert prefers, *On Literary Excellence,*[28] lists five principal sources of elevated language:

The power of forming great conceptions
Vehement and inspired passion
The formation of figures [29]
Noble diction
A dignified and elevated composition

Each of these will be discussed briefly as phases of the author's style which the interpreter must examine before he can say that he thoroughly understands his selection. More detailed discussions of particular facets of style will be reserved for Part IV.

Forming great conceptions

Longinus puts elevation of the mind first, insisting that the stylist should have "a firm grasp of ideas." [30] He quotes himself as saying: "Sublimity is the echo of a great soul." [31] In other words, a man who is less than great cannot write great literature. Emerson gave us a similar thought when he said that what a man is speaks so loudly that his words are eclipsed by his character.[32] Longinus reminds us: "Great accents we expect to fall from the lips of those whose thoughts are deep and grave." Wordsworth has already advised us along similar

[28] Allan H. Gilbert, *Literary Criticism,* American Book Company, Cincinnati, Ohio, 1940, p. 145.
[29] The third and fourth sources of sublime style are not mutually exclusive. For the purposes of this discussion, the third source has been treated as the broader aspect of imagery and the fourth source as the special technique for achieving imagery, even though chaps. xvi–xxix of the treatise discuss figures of speech. See Charles Sears Baldwin, *Ancient Rhetoric and Poetic,* The Macmillan Company, New York, 1924, pp. 122–131.
[30] In Gilbert, *op. cit.,* p. 153.
[31] Longinus, "On the Sublime," W. Rhys Roberts (trans.), in Smith and Parks, *op. cit.,* p. 72.
[32] Ralph Waldo Emerson, "Social Aims," in *Letters and Social Aims,* Houghton Mifflin Company, Boston, 1876, p. 80.

lines. The interpreter must ask, "How noble is the soul who created this composition? How deeply and gravely has he thought?"

Answers to these questions cannot be made hastily. Eudora Welty's story, because of its humor, makes less pretense to greatness than do her more serious works. Humor, by its very nature, is destructive and unbenign, and it therefore reduces to some extent the nobility of its user by convicting him of uncomplimentary deeds. How else is Molière an inferior playwright to Shakespeare, and how else are Shakespeare's tragedies elevated over his comedies? But long and deep thinking have gone into the creation of Lily Daw and her friends. Miss Welty's thought may have been: The simple mind and the simple heart are often nearer the truth than are the sophisticated minds and hearts. If so, this is certainly a noble thought.

The nobility of the thinking of Robert Frost and Matthew Arnold is more easily established. Again Frost's proclivity toward comedy and his grin or wistful smile as he tells his story are said by some to reduce the loftiness of his style. Arnold, completely serious, thinking deeply and gravely about the plight of the world and the effect of war upon the innocent, qualifies more easily for noble thinking.

The Michener essay provokes the most controversial discussion. Does the description of a battle deserve the label of sublime? Is the reporter capable of expressing a noble thought when he is reporting and not interpreting? To what extent does Michener report and not interpret? An interesting study could be made comparing the sublimity of the *Iliad* and the *Odyssey* with contemporary treatments of the theme of war, to see what elements of the sublime in Homer are maintained in contemporary writers.

Vehement and inspired passion

Longinus's second qualification for elevated language is that it spring from vehement and inspired passion. It has been said previously that the factor peculiar to literature is not that it conveys information, but that it shares an experience. Such sharing entails a fusing of the thoughts, feelings, and emotions of the creator and the receptor—the author and his audience. Literature has deep roots in both thought (Longinus's first category) and emotion (Longinus's second category). To understand the selection, the student must be aware not only of the thought involved, but also of the possible emotional reactions of the audience to this thought.

The reader must therefore seek answers to these questions: What motivational factors did the author intend to develop? How does the mood change to respond to these factors?

The interpreter should be able to trace the changes of motivational factors in his selection so that he can share these factors by creating a corresponding mood for the audience. True, many of us will respond differently to the same poem, and therefore what one would establish as *sad,* another would establish as *glad.* The varying reactions of the critics to Eudora Welty's short story "Why I Live at the P.O." illustrate the extreme differences of opinion that can develop from the same stimulus. Some critics, including Katherine Anne Porter, find the heroine of the story "a terrifying case of dementia praecox"; [33] others see in her no more than the narrator of a humorous family squabble among people who enjoy sparring with each other. Therefore, the interpreter does not seek to establish *the* emotions in the selection, but only a legitimate interpretation of what the emotions and their corresponding moods may be. By the time the interpreter has reviewed the life of the author and the criticism of the selection and has examined the thought patterns of the literature, he is in a position to establish a legitimate mood for his audience to experience, with the confidence that his decisions are not snap judgments but are based on as complete an understanding of the material at hand as could be expected of him at this point in the progression of his work.

Not all literature can reach vehement and inspired passion. The Welty story, of course, falls far short of Longinus's requirements. The passions are not vehement and inspired, but rather gentle and even soothing. Miss Welty has preferred to knit up the raveled sleeve of care with laughter, making us more at home in our world by showing us the foibles of others. Frost's emotions in "Stopping by Woods on a Snowy Evening" and "Wild Grapes" again are not vehement, although they may be inspired. Arnold also falls short in "Dover Beach." The passion he creates is too defeatist and too selfish to be inspired. Of the group of selections included in the Prefatory Readings for Chapters 5 and 6, only the Michener selection might qualify. Certainly the Marines, in Michener's descriptions, show the noblest of passions and are determined about them *if we concede that the horrors of war may be sublime.* The unselfishness of the acts of the soldiers who leaped from trench to trench and the bravery of the three Americans in trench two who leaped up to attack the oncoming Japanese certainly exhibit vehement and inspired passion.

In summary, the author of each selection has endeavored to instill in his selection certain emotions which will motivate his audience. The oral reader must determine what these emotions are and decide what mood he wishes to create in order that the audience may grasp the emotional content of the selection. Naturally, readers may respond

[33] Porter, *op. cit.*, p. xx.

differently to a given selection. Furthermore, some readers may wish to plan much more specifically than others for the desired mood. In many situations, the reader will be able to assume that his own reactions and those of his audience will be highly similar; in other instances, he should be reluctant to draw such a conclusion. The reader's task, therefore, is to establish insofar as possible the mood of the selection, without so specifically directing it that possible emotional reactions by the audience are stifled.

Imagery

Longinus's third principal source of the sublime is the image. How does the selection make the listener *see* what he is hearing? How vivid are the pictorializations?

Imagery can be made comprehensible to the student if he remembers the following precepts. First, images may be created *literally* or *figuratively*. A literal image of a star would consist of a description of a star itself; a figurative image of a star might be created with a metaphor or a simile.

Second, the basic senses act as the receptors of the image stimuli. An *image* may be transmitted by *sound* ("Ed Newton gave false signals to start on his bass horn"), by *sight* ("Mrs. Carson and Mrs. Watts, the two fattest, sat in the double rocker"), by *smell* ("'There certainly is always a funny smell in this house. I say it every time I come,' said Aimee Slocum"), by *taste* ("I'll give you a big caramel cake"), and by *touch* ("When she saw them she put a zinnia in her mouth, and held still"). These senses are also known by their technical labels: auditory, visual, olfactory, gustatory, and tactile. Combinations of these may result in additional labels. There have developed such terms as *organic* and *motor* imagery, or as Simon prefers, the "intimate senses" [34]—those of pain, temperature, and the like. The terms *kinetic* imagery and *kinesthetic* imagery are used to refer to the images of motion and to the images of muscle sense, respectively. The former concerns itself with external bodily movement; the latter, with internal responses to the muscles, tendons, and joints. [35]

Third, the purpose of the image is to stir the passions and stimulate elevated thought. Whenever the reader identifies an image, he should seek to explore what possible emotional and thought reactions

[34] Clarence T. Simon, "Appreciation in Reading," in *Studies in the Art of Interpretation*, Gertrude Johnson (ed.), Appleton-Century-Crofts, Inc., New York, 1940, p. 26.
[35] Modern psychology is hesitant to limit the number of senses. Contemporary treatments include such labels as the hunger sense, the static sense, and the vestibular sense.

his prospective audience may have to the stimulus he offers them. The previous discussions of thought and emotion should therefore be read in close conjunction with these remarks on imagery.

More important than the labeling of images is a comprehension of how the images relate to the meaning of the selection. Categorizing images is purposeful only if it helps to clarify the image's contribution to the selection. The reader cannot afford to label the images without considering the wide variability with which the audience may react. When the poem "Sea Fever" by John Masefield is used as the stimulus, the sensory images created in the audience may show considerable range. One person may see a ship; another may hear the roar of the waters; another may taste the salt of the ocean; a fourth may feel a strong *pull* to return to the sea. The type of image called forth by each person in the audience is determined only in part by the selection; of more influence are the past associations, experiences, either real or vicarious, that each listener has had with the sea.

Therefore, although it is true that our awareness of things about us comes to us through our senses, each stimulus given by the reader finds a responder whose reactions will be governed by the complex of his past sensory reactions. In the discussion of images, therefore, the student should remember that it is *the image that the audience creates* which determines the success of the reader. If the reader allows his own vivid images to dictate the responses of his audience, he may be removing the reinforcements to pictorialization that the past experiences of the audience can offer.

The deft strokes with which Eudora Welty moves into the image of Victory, Mississippi, are masterful. There are no long descriptive passages, but the town is exposed with enough detail for the mind to supply the complete picture. The water tank, *the* store, the bridge over the railroad tracks with Estelle Mabers sitting on a rail drinking an orange Ne-Hi *slowly*, Lily's house with its weather vanes, the Victory Civic Band at the railroad station, and the crate full of baby chicks loose on the platform are more than vivid enough to tell us what the small town is like.

The pictures of the women are as clearly drawn as are those of the town. Each reader is given sufficient material to begin his image of Mrs. Carson, Mrs. Watts, and Aimee Slocum, without so constricting the image that the audience must conform to the rigid lines drawn by the author. Mrs. Watts's pink hands and Mrs. Carson's thimbled finger assist in drawing an accurate picture of the charitable ladies of Victory without binding the audience to images that may be foreign to it.

The reader, in making his detailed study of style, must ask himself what pictures the audience will be asked to create. He must make certain that he has exercised his own imagination to the fullest before he is prepared to ask his audience to do the same. In striving to assist his audience in exercising its imagination, the interpreter must remember that he should avoid "clouding the lens" by intruding or stumbling clumsily into the audience's images. Anything that the reader does which attracts attention to himself and away from his selection risks interference with successful imagery. As Longinus says: ". . . art is perfect when it seems to be nature, and nature hits the mark when she contains art hidden within her." [36] An audience cannot be forced to create images. They must come naturally. Only if the art of the reader is natural and unobtrusive will the images come unmolested.

Diction

The progression from the study of the third principle, imagery, to the fourth principle, diction, is marked only by a change in emphasis, for the chief purpose of diction (or the choice of words) is to intensify the image.

Figures of speech. The first phase of diction to be discussed, the formation of figures of speech, has the connotations of technique. It is, of course, used in an effort to intensify the imagery and so to intensify the great concepts and the vehement and inspired passions of Longinus's first and second criteria. But it is a trick of the trade. It is a roundabout way of instruction since a simple exposition would be less ostentatious than a figure of speech. That is why Longinus says: "Wherefore a figure is at its best when the very fact that it is a figure escapes attention." [37] The interpreter must uncover the figures of the author and then ask himself how much they have been made a part of the whole so that they escape attention. Of course, the harder the reader has to look for the figures, the better concealed they have been. Osborne states the threefold relationship between craftsmanship and artistry as follows:

There are in all the arts some constructs judged to be beautiful though they reach no high level of craftsmanship, there are masterpieces of craftsmanship which are antithetical to beauty and there is fine craftsmanship which is contributory to beauty.[38]

[36] Longinus, *op. cit.*, p. 90.
[37] Longinus, *op. cit.*, p. 87.
[38] Harold Osborne, *Aesthetics and Criticism*, Routledge & Kegan Paul, Ltd., London, 1955, p. 267. To illustrate Osborne's three degrees of art, it may be said that the Sacco-Vanzetti letters are an example of a beautiful thing with no high level of craftsmanship, that St. Peter's Cathedral in Rome is a masterpiece of craftsmanship without beauty, and that the Parthenon represents the type of craftsmanship which contributes to beauty.

It must be admitted that the figure of speech entails craftsmanship. Man does not speak naturally in figures. Therefore, the craftsmanship of the figure must contribute to the total effectiveness of the selection and, at the same time, not call attention to itself. The reader, in examining his selection, must decide how to approach the figures only after he has determined their contribution to the literature he is presenting. If he feels they are artificial, he may even go so far as to suppress them.

We often say in our everyday speech, "That was not exactly what he said, but I read the meaning between the lines." The writer wishes to help us read between the lines. He wants to use language that will convey more than just the literal or denotative meaning. What does the common expression "It is as dark as pitch" really mean? We know that it connotes something very, very dark, but the word "dark" alone is not sufficient to convey the dense blackness that must be conveyed; therefore a figure is used, joining the sense of *blackness* to all the connotations of *pitch*.

The following discussion, although limited to only a few of the many aspects of figurative language, endeavors to show how the figure is used to intensify imagery.

The metaphor and the simile.   Both the metaphor and the simile (1) make comparisons (2) of unlike objects (of objects which do not belong to the same class). The metaphor makes a direct or implicit comparison; the simile makes an indirect or explicit comparison which is *softened* by stating that one object is *similar* to another. The metaphor says one thing *is* another; the simile says one thing is *similar* to another. The metaphor, therefore, is more pointed than the simile. Such words as "than," "as," "like," and "similar to" are marks of the simile.

Thomas Hardy's poem "Nature's Questioning" presents a particularly effective use of the simile:

When I look forth at dawning, pool
　Field, flock, and lonely tree
　All seem to gaze at me
Like chastened children sitting silent in a school. . . .

Hardy's comparison of the scenery to "chastened children" establishes a mood and a completeness of thought that might not be gained by a less figurative description. Such a simile helps the interpreter to intensify his own meaning of the dawn and therefore helps him in his preparation to share this same feeling with his audience.

When Eudora Welty wishes her readers to understand just how

Mrs. Carson must sound, she compares her sad voice to "the soft noises in the hen house at twilight." Lily's sucking on the zinnia stem sounds "exactly like a jay bird." Note that when the direct comparison is made between the way Lily says "O.K.—Toots!" and the way the xylophone player says the same words, no figure is intended because here the comparison is between objects or ideas or actions of the same class (two persons saying the same words) and not between objects or ideas or actions of different classes, as is required for a figure. The vividness of the figure lies in its association of two things which previously were not thought to have a resemblance.

Alfred Lord Tennyson, in his poem "The Eagle," uses both metaphor and simile to intensify his thoughts:

He clasps the crag with crooked hands;
Close to the sun in lonely lands,
Ringed with the azure world he stands.

The wrinkled sea beneath him crawls;
He watches from his mountain walls,
And like a thunderbolt he falls.

Note the two metaphors in the line "The wrinkled sea beneath him crawls." First, Tennyson is comparing the sea to something that can be wrinkled, such as silk or linen cloth. He does not say that the sea is *like* wrinkled (cloth) but that the sea *is* wrinkled (cloth). Again, he does not say that the sea resembles a crawling animal or insect, but that the sea crawls. Note also the simile in the last line—"like a thunderbolt he falls."

The metaphors in Eudora Welty's short story appear most often in the verbs. Such verb metaphors are likely to be concealed within the art, and it takes a careful search for even the practiced eye to ferret them out. Some of the metaphors in the short story are listed below:

The ladies all *clucked* their tongues.

The bell began to ring *hollowly.* . . .

"Don't you all dare go off and tell Lily without me!" called Aimee Slocum, *trotting* back to finish putting up the mail.

The author, however, uses the less stringent form of figure to describe the possibility of a lover which descended suddenly *"like* a summer hail" and the manner in which the xylophone player pulled out his notebook *"like* lightning."

Personification.   In the strictest sense, personification is a kind of metaphor. Its distinction is that it gives human or lifelike qualities to inanimate objects. Most uses of personification are obvious and easily identified. Some, however, are obscure. When Miss Welty says, "The three women stood at the foot of the water tank," is the use of "foot" here giving qualities of life to the inanimate tank? Or is the use of "foot" in this respect so customary and widespread that any figurative quality of its use has long since disappeared?

The oral interpreter should note that the nature of personification will tend to remove his selection from reality. He should also be aware of the propensity toward sermonizing that is often characterized by personification.

Apostrophe.   The apostrophe is an extension of personification. Its distinguishing feature is that the inanimate object is actually addressed or spoken to as if it were human. The figure, although rarely used, can be most effective, providing the craft is concealed by the art. Byron offers the famous line "Roll on, thou deep and dark blue Ocean, roll!" as if the ocean could hear what he is saying and abide by his command.

The short stories of Miss Welty are far more realistic than Byron's poetry and therefore do not contain apostrophes. They are also absent from the Frost, Arnold, and Michener selections, largely because the apostrophe would seem stilted and artificial in the more earthy styles of these writers, in the selections given here.

Hyperbole and litotes.   *Hyperbole* and its opposite, *litotes,* are frequently found in colloquial literature. The Welty short story features many hyperboles, which are nothing more than exaggerations not intended to deceive. The large number of them found in "Lily Daw and the Three Ladies" points to the frequent use of hyperbole in ordinary conversation:

"She'll be tickled to death," said Mrs. Watts. . . .

"Till my husband went up and explained she wasn't bright, and so did everybody else."

"Oh, she can be a lady—she can be," said Mrs. Carson, shaking her head and turning her eyes up. "That's just what breaks your heart."

Litotes, the converse of hyperbole, is a purposeful understatement. It is often used to minimize the effect of what otherwise would be a too uncomplimentary remark, as in the expression "That's not half bad" and "She's not as young as she used to be." [39] Litotes is frequently employed to achieve the effect of humor, for its efforts to avoid the unpleasant make it mechanical rather than elastic.[40] Since it is, by design, a crooked yardstick, it is seldom found in scientific writing or in philosophical literature, but is reserved for colloquial conversations and satire, irony, buffoonery, and other forms of comedy.

Eudora Welty uses litotes in an effort to give us a quick but complete picture of the xylophone player:

"What business did you have with Lily?" cried Aimee suddenly.
"We was only going to get married, that's all," said the man.

Lewis Carroll makes frequent use of litotes in *Alice in Wonderland*. When Alice finds the bottle with a paper label saying "Drink Me," she reasons from her past experiences whether she should follow such directions, remembering that "she had never forgotten that, if you drink much from a bottle marked 'poison,' it is almost sure to disagree with you, sooner or later."

A sensitivity to litotes will materially assist the oral reader in analyzing the character of the persons in his selection and will help him to convey the mood of understatement to the audience.

Metonymy. *Metonymy* and its subdivision, *synecdoche,* are often used to make what might otherwise be a commonplace statement into something more palatable. Metonymy, which comes from the Greek word meaning *change of name,* involves substituting one object for another because the two are so closely related. At least five types are distinguishable:

The use of the container for the thing contained: *The kettle boils.* (The kettle is not boiling, but the water which it contains.)
The sign for the thing signified: *He won the crown.* (The crown is only a symbol for the particular achievement made.)
Cause used for effect: *You should read Milton.* (Milton is the cause which created the literature which you should read.)
Effect used for cause: *The wrinkled face deserves our respect.* (The endurance of the cares of the world have resulted in a wrinkled face. What we are paying our respects to is not the wrinkles but the endurance.)

[39] From A. W. Green, D. R. Hutcherson, W. B. Leake, and P. K. McCarter, *Complete College Composition,* Appleton-Century-Crofts, Inc., New York, 1945, p. 273. Copyright 1940, 1945, F. S. Crofts and Co. Adapted by permission of Appleton-Century-Crofts, Inc.
[40] See Bergson, *op. cit.,* pp. 66–74.

Synecdoche (the part for the whole or the whole for the part): "We gave Lily all her food and kindling and every stitch she had on," illustrates the part (the stitch) for the whole (Lily's clothes) and "That's just what breaks your heart" is a similar substitution. College newspapers refer to their school as having defeated another school in football, but the whole is substituted for the part since it is not all of Utah State which defeated Colorado State, but only the teams of each school.

Since the author of the selection has elected to use metonymy to make his style more vivid and thus to communicate his thoughts and emotions more accurately, the oral reader should be able to identify such figures of speech and attempt to assist the author in achieving the desired goals. Much of metonymy begins as slang. Some of the slang expressions migrate into clichés while others gravitate into more acceptable figurative usage. When an author uses metonymy, he may be purposefully employing slang or a cliché or effective figurative language. An awareness of the place of metonymy will allow the interpreter to sharpen the focus of his selection.

Summary. The student of interpretation should keep in mind that, although there are classifications for the types of figures of speech, one figure may deserve more than one label. "That's just what breaks your heart" is an example of both synecdoche and hyperbole. Classifications of figures of speech are important only as they help the interpreter to understand the figures so that he may sense more completely the author's intent.

The preceding examples of figurative language do not comprise a total list. Additional references will be made in Part IV where the several literary types are discussed. This presentation, however, is sufficient to show the importance of figurative language as it is used by the author and the means by which the interpreter can gain a fuller insight into the significance of the language. A knowledge of figurative language will make the reader more cognizant of the need for flexibility and good voice quality in order to communicate his understandings and reactions. An awareness of the figures of speech should be a very strong motivating force in challenging the reader to develop his potential to the utmost, showing him how important vocal and bodily support are to his reading.

Choice of words. Another factor in the author's quest for superior diction is his choice of literal words. A study of the vocabulary of the characters in a selection is an excellent way of understanding the character's mood, thoughts, and attitudes. Abner Snopes in William Faulkner's "Barn Burning" speaks the language of his personality:

His father spoke for the first time, his voice cold and harsh, level, without emphasis: "I aim to. I don't figure to stay in a country among people who . . ." he said something unprintable and vile, addressed to no one.[41]

Faulkner chooses the adjectives "cold," "harsh," "level," and the prepositional phrase "without emphasis" to describe Abner's voice, and then the terse words in Snopes's conversation match the description.

Later in the same selection Abner's son Sarty, whose full name is Colonel Sartoris Snopes, brushes off his mother as she attempts to dress a bruise the boy received in a fight:

"Does hit hurt?" she said.
"Naw," he said. "Hit don't hurt. Lemme be."
"Can't you wipe some of the blood off before hit dries?"
"I'll wash tonight," he said. "Lemme be, I tell you." [42]

The choice of words for the conversation, the colloquialisms, the poor grammar—all give considerable insight into the boy and his mother.

In the dramatic monologue "My Last Duchess" the duke reveals a great deal about himself by the language he uses. Browning provides him with the words which allow him to be cold and calculating and, at the same time, aristocratically dignified:

—E'en then would be some stooping, and I choose
Never to stoop. Oh, Sir, she smiled, no doubt,
Whene'er I passed her; but who passed without
Much the same smile? This grew; I gave commands;
Then all smiles stopped together.

Much of the duke's personality is revealed in the words he chooses to tell of his wife's demise. It would apparently not be in keeping with the duke's social position to confess openly to the murder of his first wife, and yet he feels called upon to make his point. The choice of an indirect statement about her death is in keeping with his disdain for mentioning her failures to her.

Vocabulary. Not only must the reader note carefully the choice of words used by the author, but he must also learn the meaning of any unfamiliar words and phrases. Even well-known words may re-

[41] From William Faulkner, "Barn Burning," p. 5. Copyright 1939 by William Faulkner. Reprinted from *Collected Stories of William Faulkner*, by permission of Random House, Inc., New York.
[42] *Ibid.*, pp. 6–7.

quire investigation (1) if the interpreter has only a general idea of what a word means and cannot express it clearly and (2) if the author has used the words in an archaic or provincial sense. Eudora Welty refers to "the double rocker," "an asterisk pattern," and "a Fiji," while Michener speaks of ".50's," "enfilading," "cacao," "footslogging," "menage," and "immolate."

If an interpreter were unfamiliar with these words or with any others, he should make certain that he has conquered their meaning before he reads the selection. He can only be certain that he has mastered the word after he has taken it from his passive vocabulary and placed it in his active vocabulary. Students of oral interpretation would do well to employ words they are studying in other phases of college life to assist them in making the words their own.

Summary. The reader must therefore note the diction of his selection in three respects: he must observe the figures of speech; he must note the choice of words in the nonfigurative passages; and he must make himself familiar with the vocabulary of the selection. It is through these elements that he will share with his audience his understanding of the selection.

Dignified and elevated composition

Longinus's fifth principal source of sublime style is dignified and elevated composition. Longinus says:

Among the chief causes of the sublime in speech, as in the structure of the human body, is the collocation of members, a single one of which if severed from another possesses in itself nothing remarkable, but all united together make a full and perfect organism. So the constituents of grandeur, when separated from one another, carry with them sublimity in distraction this way and that, but when formed into a body by association and when further encircled in a chain of harmony they become sonorous by their very rotundity....[43]

In this manner Longinus pays his respects to the gestalt of a composition. The reader must ask himself: How does this composition strike the observer as a unit?

Three phases of dignified and elevated composition will be discussed here: rhythm, meter, and rhyme.

Rhythm. One of the chief factors which assists a selection in making an over-all impact on an audience is its rhythm. Osborne says:

---

[43] Longinus, *op. cit.*, pp. 105–106.

"The most important aspect of the adaptation of sound to meaning . . . is that element of literary craftsmanship known as rhythm." [44] Osborne defines rhythm as "a quality of word-groups as conveyors of meanings. . . ." [45] That such a definition still leaves much in doubt is inevitable since rhythm can be compared to vitamins. We do not know what a vitamin is, but we know what its presence and absence can bring. We know that both prose and poetry may or may not have rhythm, and we know what the results are in either instance. If there exists a difference between prose and poetry, it appears to lie in the addition of meter (and perhaps also rhyme) to intensify the rhythm.

Therefore, we may say that although the Eudora Welty short story has no presumptions to either meter or rhyme, it does have considerable rhythm. Its word groups are arranged in a particular way to convey meaning. There is, in the composition of the story, a unity of style, a coherence of ideas, and a sufficiently reoccurring emphasis to give the reader a feeling of completeness. There are no jarring episodes to break the rhythm. That Miss Welty is consciously trying to retain a consistent rhythm is witnessed by the unobtrusive way in which she progresses from the interview with Lily in the old house by the railroad tracks to the train station of Victory, without losing momentum. Some time must have elapsed here, for Miss Welty says that the xylophone player was in Como the day of the interview with Lily. Moreover, the hat had to be exchanged, the brassiere bought, the cake baked, and the telegram sent. But the author wishes to minimize these interruptions to preserve the rhythm she has given to the story, and once the momentum has been established, it is not to be broken.

The rhythm in the Welty story is as apparent to the oral interpreter as is the rhythm in the Michelangelo statue of Moses to the critic of art. Specific evidence in both instances is not flagrant. The statue of Moses, housed in the Church of Saint Peter in Chains on a side street in Rome and surrounded by inferior statuary, emerges immediately as a living, vital thing. The cheap imitations on all sides of it seem lifeless and lacking in vitality. The Welty story emerges much as does the statue. The story is a living, breathing work of art. There is rhythm in all that is living. Miss Welty's characters are alive. All the reader must do is to respond to their vitality and make certain that he has caught their vitality and can convey it satisfactorily to his audience.

Rhythm continues to defy definition. It hides itself in the quality of word groups. When these groupings result in an identifiable momentum, rhythm has been achieved. The reader cannot always find obvious signs which will lead him to the rhythm of the selection. It

[44] Osborne, *op. cit.*, pp. 277–278.
[45] *Ibid.*, p. 278.

may be that only association with the selection over a period of months, or even years, will result in the reader finding himself "in tune" with the rhythm of his literature.

Meter. Wordsworth says: "... it would be a most easy task to prove ... that not only the language of a large portion of every good poem, even of the most elevated character, must necessarily, *except with reference to metre*, in no respect differ from that of good prose, but likewise that some of the most interesting parts of the best poems will be found to be strictly the language of prose when prose is well written." Thus, says Wordsworth, poetry and prose may only be distinguishable by meter. What is this meter of which he speaks?

Meter is nothing more than a regularly reoccurring beat caused by stress on syllables. In the case of "Wild Grapes," there are five *beats* to the line, and the accent is on the second *step* in the beat, making the meter an example of iambic pentameter:

What *tree* may *not* the *fig* be *gath*ered *from?*
The *grape* may *not* be *gath*ered *from* the *birch?*

The meter in this Frost poem is there, but it is so unobtrusive that, as Wordsworth says, Frost's story in meter reads like the finest of prose.

The intricacies of meter will be discussed in Part IV. The point to be made here is that, in analyzing his selection, the reader must make himself aware of the degree of rhythm in his passage, whether it be prose or poetry. If the rhythm is intensified by meter (or beat), the reader must know how and where in order to present his selection to its maximum advantage. Without an awareness of meter, the reader may easily make one of two mistakes:

First, the reader, in his ignorance of the proper position of meter, may *punch* the beats and so fall into what Longinus terms "the worst of it all" by adopting the overrhythmical pattern and thus smothering the feeling of the words by an overabundance of rhythm.[46] The tail must not wag the dog. Meter is present to assist in communicating the style, not to dominate it.

Second, the reader, in his ignorance of what meter is, may fail to respond to the rhythm of the selection and thus rob his material of one of its greater strengths. If he does this, the reader will resemble the couple on the dance floor who appear to have all left feet and who stumble through the music, while other couples are responding to the rhythm.

---

[46] Longinus, *op. cit.*, pp. 106–107.

Rhyme. The first mistake outlined above is even more likely to occur if rhyme is added to meter and rhythm. As Osborne points out, rhyme "may either enhance and intensify rhythm or it may be devoid of rhythm. In general, the more complex and rigid the pattern, the harder the poet's task to infuse it with rhythm." [47] Even if the poet has been successful in enforcing the rhythm of his writing with rhyme, a poor reader can easily undo all the writer has done and, by punching the rhyme, destroy the rhythm completely. The unusual rhyme pattern in Frost's "Stopping by Woods on a Snowy Evening" has already been pointed out. A poor reader, by exposing the mathematical precision in the rhyme, could easily enforce the meter of the poem (iambic tetrameter) to the total destruction of the rhythm that Frost intended. The smooth flow of thoughts that Frost strove for and achieved would be smothered and literally "beat" out of existence with improper emphasis in reading. That Frost succeeded in walking the narrow tightrope between sterile beating and overly flowing rhythm has been well attested to by the critics. However, the poor reader could defeat Frost easily by reading the poem something like this:

Whose WOODS these ARE I THINK I KNOW.
His HOUSE is IN the VILL-age THOUGH;
He WILL not SEE me STOP-ping HERE
To WATCH his WOODS fill UP with SNOW.

Who has not heard the disastrous effects of removing meter and rhythm from their proper perspectives?

Alliteration, assonance, and onomatopoeia. Rhythm, of course, is not the only element in the arrangement of words. There exist the effects of alliteration, assonance, and onomatopoeia. Alliteration, says Donald Davidson, is "the repetition of the same sound at the beginnings of words in pairs or in series; or, more rarely, in a series of stressed syllables within a word." [48] Lily just " 'set in her seat and stared' "; the duke says: "Oh, Sir, she smiled, no doubt, whene'er I passed her." Frost says: "The only other sound's the sweep of easy wind and downy flake."

Assonance provides for the repetition of the same vowel sound in syllables that have different consonants. Davidson observed that it

---

[47] Osborne, *op. cit.*, p. 279.

[48] Donald Davidson, *American Composition and Rhetoric*, 3d ed., Charles Scribner's Sons, New York, 1939, p. 296. Note: When a stressed vowel is repeated in words with differing consonants, as in Frost's "the sweep of easy wind," Davidson's distinction between alliteration and assonance becomes indistinct.

"may be viewed as a form of inexact rhyme, since true rhyme provides for the repetition of vowels in syllables that have the same terminal consonants but different initial consonants." [49] The duke says: "... perhaps Frà Pandolf chanced to say 'Her mantle laps over my Lady's wrist too much"; Arnold refers to the sea's "melancholy, long, withdrawing roar."

Onomatopoeia results when the pronunciation of a word echoes the meaning of the word. A survey once established "murmur" as the English word whose sound most resembled its meaning. Once a search is begun, the reader will find many words exhibiting onomatopoeia. For example, Eudora Welty says that the ladies "clucked" their tongues, an obvious use of "cluck" which not only sounds like the noise that the ladies made, but also adds the metaphor of comparing the women in the post office to a group of hens, thinking about their lost biddy, Lily. Mrs. Watts's "groaning as she was helped into the back seat" shows a choice of the word "groan" with its back *g* sound, its muffled *r* sound, and the diphthong *ou* often used by someone in pain.

The reader should be aware of the refinements in word arrangements. Unless he perceives the method the author has used to strive for sublimity, he cannot hope to help the audience grasp the true meaning of the selection. Further comments on the refinements of word arrangement will be considered in Part IV.

Summary

From the discussion of Longinus's five principles of the sublime style, it can be seen that language is a tool that not only the writer, but also the interpreter must be able to handle. When this tool is used skillfully by both, successful style in oral interpretation results; when this tool is used most artfully by both, the sublime style results. As always, after the reader has made his study of language and style, he should reread the selection, inserting the new findings into the complete composition in order that he may maintain his approach to the selection as a whole, studying each detail only as it relates to the over-all effectiveness of the selection.

The paraphrase

In order to consolidate his gains, the reader may wish to paraphrase his selection; i.e., he may wish to put the selection into words of his own choice. This step, if undertaken, can serve as a means of testing previous study and may excite additional investigation. Concepts

---

[49] *Ibid.*, p. 297.

which may have been vague in previous research will emerge from their shadows and clarify themselves, once the reader forces himself to face in his paraphrase what he has and what he has not understood. Whatever concepts that remain shadowy can then be given further study. The interpreter will come to recognize the genius of the poet when he finds how detailed and clumsy his paraphrase seems when contrasted with the original work.

There are several aspects of composition which can be given attention in the paraphrase. Each writer has selected a certain literary type to house his creation. He has developed within his structure an organization for his ideas. Brooks and Warren point out that "... all poetry, including even short lyrics or descriptive pieces ... involves a dramatic organization." [50] Poetry begins, it moves, it develops, it concludes. The several phrases of structure will be discussed briefly below.

The opening

In order to understand the way a selection unfolds, the interpreter must ask a series of elemental questions, the first of which is: How did the author begin? It is very important that the reader take note of the opening remarks in his preparation. Too often the reader neglects the opening lines and does not allow the audience to get set for the experience that is to follow. For example, Matthew Arnold opens his poem "Dover Beach" with a description:

The sea is calm tonight,
The tide is full, the moon lies fair
Upon the Straits. . . .

The scene is set and the mood established in these first few lines.

In "Lily Daw and the Three Ladies," Miss Welty gets off to a brisk start:

Mrs. Watts and Mrs. Carson were both in the post office in Victory when the letter came from the Ellisville Institute for the Feeble-Minded of Mississippi. Aimee Slocum, with her hands still full of mail, ran out in front and handed it straight to Mrs. Watts, and they all three read it together.

Very quickly, the reader is introduced to the three main characters in the story and his interest is aroused about the contents of the letter. In three more sentences, Miss Welty explains that it is Lily who is to be sent to Ellisville. Already we have the antagonists and the pro-

---

[50] Brooks and Warren, *op. cit.*, p. liv.

tagonist at odds since we assume that "no one in her right mind" wishes to be sent to an institute for the feeble-minded. The first sentence explains the purpose of Ellisville, and since the institution will be subsequently referred to by its location rather than by its full name, the reader must be certain that his audience understands where Lily is to be sent.

The development

In his paraphrase, the interpreter will want to note the steps by which the author unfolds his action. In some instances, the sequence of ideas may be overt; in other instances, the plot may be quite complicated and even indistinct.

In "Dover Beach," it is easy to outline the steps which lead to the climax. The author has the central character tell the entire story in simple but vivid language. The organization of the poem proceeds as the narrator recalls the past and appraises the present, until the climactic point is reached:

Ah, love, let us be true to one another!

The poet and his companion have experienced the sea at night from their window. The experience, melancholy in nature, has reminded the poet of a passage from Sophocles and has forced him to admit that once the world was secure in its faith, but that now those times have passed. The only thing that remains, at that hour, appears to be the kindredship of spirits. Thus the climax.

An inspection of the plot development in Miss Welty's story shows several interesting omissions. For example, the author leaves to our imagination how the women get from the post office to the foot of the water tank. Subtly, she guides us along the main street of Victory until the ladies meet Ed Newton. He reveals how forceful the *protagonist* may be:

"If you're after Lily, she come in here while ago and tole me she was fixin' to git married," he said.

Immediate action is called for. But Lily is apt to be anywhere. The search must continue, except now in earnest. Evidently, the addition of transportation in the form of Loralee Adkin's Willys-Knight provides the motivation to streak off to Lily's house, in the hopes of finding her there.

Miss Welty does not say how far from the main street Lily's house is, or even if it is Lily's house. Evidently, it is where she lives and it has in front the inevitable cedar tree. The fact that it is by the railroad signifies that it is probably in the old part of town, once fashionable, but now decadent. Luckily enough, Lily is at home and the *antagonists* begin their march. This step in the plot is brought to an abrupt close with the lines " 'Pack up . . . Lily Daw is leaving for Ellisville on Number One.' "

We do not know how long it took to ready Lily for the trip, but as we have said before, sufficient time must have elapsed to allow for the promised preparations. An important *plot line* follows: "Everybody wanted to see Lily all dressed up, but Mrs. Carson and Mrs. Watts had sneaked her into the train from the other side of the tracks." We are not told why, but a little thought will show that it was necessary to the plot. The xylophone player has been on the same train and is now getting off to look for Lily. It was not the author's intention for them to meet in front of everyone. The protagonists and the antagonists are all at the station, but Lily and the xylophone player are temporarily divided, while the three ladies find safety in numbers.

The author now has a good setting for suspense. Every reader knows that trains leave, and every reader knows that he would rather have Lily marry the xylophone player than go off to the Institute for the Feeble-Minded of Mississippi, for, by this time, the reader has gained considerable respect for Lily's intelligence at the cost of his respect for the intentions of the three ladies. The suspense is intensified because it is up to Aimee to take the decisive step, and Aimee is the least capable of the three ladies.

The reader is returned frantically to the train, where he gets more than impatient with the procrastination of Mrs. Watts and Mrs. Carson, who find it difficult to be led by Aimee into action when they have been leading her for so long. The author takes his characters down the back stairs of the train, thereby creating a contrast between the actions of the leading characters in the train station and those of the Civic Band and the crowd by the train.

In writing a paraphrase of the development of the story, the reader would observe the gradual buildup of emotion in the three ladies. Their motivation proceeds from concern, to self-satisfaction, to righteousness, to indignation, to fright, and then to relief in a plan of action. If the reader's previous analyses have missed the quick reversal of emotion from excitement to relief, the composing of a paraphrase should clarify the movement for him. Of course, at the close of the story, the women are still dictating what is *good* for Lily, in an oversolicitous manner, as usual, but the reader does gain relief from such pretentiousness in the hopes that the xylophone player will take good care of Lily.

The transitions

It is particularly important for the interpreter to note how the writer has joined one element of his development to another. He must know where the joining takes place so he can assist his audience in making the transfer from one idea to another.

The transition from Lily's house to the train station is very abrupt, involving only one sentence: "In the station the train was puffing." The reader should give special consideration to such a key line and not slight it or hurry by it. Time must be given for the listener to move with the author. In silent reading, if the reader misses a transition, he may go back to search for it, but not in oral reading.

Transitional sentences are very important parts of the structure of literature and can be easily overlooked by the inexperienced reader. The transition, be it a word or a phrase, is a signpost that must be appreciated by both the reader and his audience. It may designate a change of place, a change of time, or a change in situation. The author has provided the transitions to guide the reader through the selection, without losing the thread of thought. They therefore present individualistic delivery problems which will be discussed in Chapter 6.

The conclusion

The conclusion finishes or completes the *something to say* that the author has treated in the development. The author may have a surprise ending, a device for which O. Henry is deservedly famous. He may have a suspense ending, as in Frank Stockton's short story "The Lady, or the Tiger?" Or the climax may be shocking, reserved for and to the last few lines, as in Edwin Arlington Robinson's poem "Richard Cory":

And Richard Cory, one calm summer night,
Went home and put a bullet through his head.[51]

The quizzical philosophy of Robert Frost is often reserved to the last, as in "Stopping by Woods on a Snowy Evening":

But I have promises to keep,
And miles to go before I sleep,
And miles to go before I sleep.

[51] Edwin Arlington Robinson, *The Children of the Night*, Charles Scribner's Sons, New York, 1921.

The conclusion of Matthew Arnold's poem, "Dover Beach," is slow and somewhat drawn out, in keeping with the doleful mood Arnold wishes to create:

And we are here as on a darkling plain
Swept with confused alarms of struggle and flight,
Where ignorant armies clash by night.

The conclusion to "Lily Daw and the Three Ladies" sustains the humor of the story and leaves us wishing that we could learn more of the details of the wedding that is to follow. The five central figures go into the waiting room, while the noise continues outside:

The band went on playing. Some of the people thought Lily was on the train, and some swore she wasn't. Everybody cheered, though, and a straw hat was thrown into the telephone wires.

Summary

Thus, in writing his paraphrase, the reader has asked himself four simple questions:

How does the selection begin?
How does it proceed to its climax?
What transitions are used?
How does it conclude?

When he finishes putting the selection into his own words, the reader would do well to put the following additional questions to himself to see if his summary has accomplished its purpose:

Have I understood why each character does what he does?
Have I understood the relationship of each detail to the whole?
Do I understand the relationship of each character to the plot?
Have I described each place or character adequately and vividly?
Have I understood and followed the organization of the selection?

If the reader is satisfied with his answers to these questions, he is free to muse on his own relationship to the story and to ask himself, "Have I seen or experienced anything similar to what the author is saying which could enhance my understanding of what I have read?"

When the reader is conscious of the structure of the story—the introduction, the lines of the plot, the transitions, and the conclusion—he is further motivated to remove any faulty speech habits which may prevent him from conveying what he has learned. For he knows as never before the limitations of poor speech and a dull voice which prevent him from communicating with his audience. The familiar terms, variety of voice, use of poise, and vocal quality, take on a new meaning for him. A thorough knowledge of the selection will make it much easier for the reader to sustain a mood. In this way, the student may find an answer to the old question: How do I keep from "bogging down" in a twenty- or thirty-minute reading?

Conclusion

In this treatment of background preparation for his reading, the interpreter has been advised to give consideration to the biography of the author, other selections by the author, criticism of the author, and the literary type in which the author has clothed his thoughts. It has been stressed that the selection itself must be the focal point of study and that each part of the analysis must be put back into place and seen as it affects the whole tenor of the selection. To understand literature, the reader must know who is speaking, what he is saying, to whom he is saying it, and under what conditions it is being said. The style of the selection must be thoroughly understood, and the structure of the selection may be clarified by a paraphrase. Once these steps have been completed, the reader is ready to further his study of how to present his selection orally by giving particular attention to delivery.

Exercises

1. Select a poem and note how each figure of speech contributes to the meaning of the poem.
2. Read another short story by Eudora Welty such as "Death of a Traveling Salesman" or "Petrified Man." Note the symbolism used and point out how the symbolism contributed to the theme of the story. Consult the *International Index to Periodicals* and the book *Literature as Experience* by Bacon and Breen for comment on the use of symbolism by Eudora Welty.
3. Read James Joyce's story "Araby," and note the use of irony in the narrative. Name at least one other selection in which the writer has used irony effectively to create the experience.
4. Choose a contemporary novel, set of short stories, or collection of poems, and consult at least five different critical reviews of the publication. Select one of the reviews and tell why you agree or disagree with its evaluation.
5. Choose five selections, the understanding of which presupposes an intimate knowledge of the life and times of the author.

How does the oral reader deliver the selection?

6

A complete understanding of the selection, however basic, is not enough in itself. Just as many persons of a sensitive nature never become poets because they lack the ability to express what they feel, many interpreters read poorly because they lack the ability to deliver what they understand.

The situations in which literature is read aloud vary widely. Members of a family may read to each other on a winter evening; a poet may read his own poems from the lecture platform; a lawyer may quote at length in the presentation of his brief; an actor may tour the country reading excerpts from classical plays to college audiences. Naturally, it is impossible to establish rules of thumb for the delivery of literature which will apply equally well to all steps along such a continuum. Also, the experiences of the reader in interpreting literature and the proficiency of his presentation vary widely. The comments given below, therefore, are in the form of suggestions. The student will need to adapt the discussion to his own purposes and proficiencies.

Limiting the selection

Interpreters often reduce the length of their selection for two main reasons. First, readers, even in the most informal of situations, may be forced to conform to time limits. Poets who have been reluctant to obey the rules of audience fatigue have become bores as oral readers. Alfred Lord Tennyson often had to draft his friends as audiences at his island home at Farrington because he did not know when to stop reading.[1] Such interpreters resemble the contemporary amateur photographers who invite friends in to see a few colored slides and then subject the visitors to three or four hours of pictures.

The amateur photographer also illustrates the second reason why

[1] See Harold Nicolson, *Tennyson*, Houghton Mifflin Company, Boston, 1923, pp. 170–174. As Nicolson points out, comments on Tennyson's reading ability were largely limited to Tennyson's own remarks, which, of course, were complimentary to his verse.

cutting may be necessary. Many of his slides may be uninteresting to anyone other than his own family. Aunt Emma at the beach with little Susie may tickle grandmother, but the Robertsons from up the street will find such a picture only faintly amusing. Also, some of the slides may not have turned out well and are therefore unsuitable for audience viewing, even though they may interest very much the man who took them. The interpreter, therefore, may cut his selection because he feels that certain portions of it are not particularly suitable to his audience or because he feels that it contains passages which read much better silently than aloud. The interpreter should remember that the eye in silent reading can move quickly over passages which the reader feels are inapplicable to him, whereas, in oral reading, each listener must review all that is being read. The interpreter's audience is in this sense a captive one. It has lost the customary avenues of escape of silent reading. Therefore, the interpreter has a responsibility to edit his selection as he feels his readers might, attempting to conform to his time limits and to eliminate inapplicable and "unreadable" passages without distorting the author's intent.

In general, the interpreter may look for three items which are subject to elimination: parenthetical thoughts, descriptive passages, and minor plots.

Parenthetical thoughts

Although the *asides* of the author and his *footnotes* are often among the more interesting of his comments, they are easily deleted and often can be sacrificed without unnecessary distortion of the selection. For example, in Eudora Welty's short story about Lily Daw, the interpreter could cut (with regret) Miss Welty's editorializing on Aimee Slocum's character:

> Aimee Slocum had been getting the outgoing mail stamped and bundled. She stood in the aisle of the coach now, tears shaking from her eyes.
> "Good-bye, Lily," she said. She was the one who felt things.
> "Good-bye, silly," said Lily.

Again, in the same story, Mrs. Watts's *aside* to the deaf lady could be deleted if time limits required:

> "What will Lily say," beamed Mrs. Carson at last, "when we tell her we're sending her to Ellisville!"
> "She'll be tickled to death," said Mrs. Watts, and added in a guttural voice to a deaf lady, "Lily Daw's getting in at Ellisville!"
> "Don't you all dare go off and tell Lily without me!" called Aimee Slocum. . . .

Descriptive passages

Descriptive passages may be cut. However, the Eudora Welty short story is remarkably free from long descriptions. What few passages exist are terse and essential. Such an inherent description as the one below should only be cut after much hesitation, for it reveals much about Lily and the ladies. Yet expediency may require the reader to eliminate much that he knows is valuable, forcing him to choose what he considers essential:

> The paintless frame house with all the weather vanes was three stories high in places and had yellow and violet stained-glass windows in front and gingerbread around the porch. It leaned steeply to one side, toward the railroad, and the front steps were gone. The car full of ladies drew up under the cedar tree.
>   "Now Lily's almost grown up," Mrs. Carson continued. "In fact, she's grown," she concluded, getting out.

The memorable first chapter of Charles Dickens's *A Tale of Two Cities* which begins, "It was the best of times, it was the worst of times . . ." is followed by a sequence of events allowing for the return of Dr. Manette from the Bastille to his refuge in London. Since *A Tale of Two Cities* was first published in serial form, each chapter is complete in itself. Chapter 2 therefore makes excellent reading material. Note how the reader may reduce the chapter's descriptive passages, but at the same time retain the atmosphere that Dickens so skillfully creates:

> It was the Dover road that lay, on a Friday night late in November, before the first of the persons with whom this history has business. The Dover road lay, as to him, beyond the Dover mail, as it lumbered up Shooter's Hill.[2] He walked uphill in the mire by the side of the mail, as the rest of the passengers did; not because they had the least relish for walking exercise, under the circumstances, but because the hill, and the harness, and the mud, and the mail, were all so heavy, that the horses had three times already come to a stop, besides once drawing the coach across the road, with the mutinous intent of taking it back to Blackheath. Reins and ship and coachmen and guard, however, in combination, had read that article of war which forbad a purpose otherwise strongly in favour of the argument, that some brute animals are endued with Reason; and the team had capitulated and returned to their duty.[3]

[2] Assuming an American audience, both references to local place names (Shooter's Hill and Blackheath) have been omitted.
[3] This sentence, a form of aside on the part of Dickens, is easily omitted.

With drooping heads and tremulous tails, they mashed their way through the thick mud, floundering and stumbling between whiles, as if they were falling to pieces at the larger joints. As often as the driver rested them and brought them to a stand, with a wary 'Wo-ho! so-ho then!' the near leader violently shook his head and everything upon it—like an unusually emphatic horse, denying that the coach could be got up the hill. Whenever the leader made this rattle, the passenger started, as a nervous passenger might, and was disturbed in mind.

Minor plots

Minor or counterplots may also be cut. Such additions to the mainstream of thought are not only eliminated without disturbing the momentum of the selection, but their exclusion may help to clarify the sequence of events for an audience which must rely on its ears and not on its eyes for receiving stimuli. In silent reading, if one becomes confused by the counterplot, he may interrupt his trend of thought and return to the last point for clarification, rereading the selection until the ideas become clear. But the audience in oral interpretation does not have this opportunity. Therefore, the central theme of the selection must be given primary consideration.

Many highly compact selections have no minor or counterplots. This is certainly true of Eudora Welty's "Lily Daw and the Three Ladies," the style of which allows for only a few asides and no diversions. The Michener story is also relatively free of counterplot material. However, the reflections of the skipper in the passage below could be eliminated:

The third Jap tank stopped firing at our men in the first trench and started lobbing shells at LCS-108. Two hit us, and we lay far over on the coral. The same foolhardy gunners on the cruiser again ignored our men in the first trench. Accurately they plastered the third tank. We breathed deeply. The Japs probably had more tanks coming, but the first three were taken care of.

Our skipper surveyed his ship. It was lost. It would either be hauled off the reef and sunk or left there to rot. He felt strange. His first command! What kind of war was this? You bring a ship all the way from Norfolk to stop two tanks. On land. You purposely run your ship on a coral reef. It's crazy. He damned himself when he thought of that Jap plane flashing by. It had killed two of his men. Not one of our bullets hit that plane. It all happened so fast. "So fast!" he muttered. "This is a hell of a war!"

Short selections are usually free of counterplot material. Full-length plays and novels often involve one or more subplots. For example, the love affair of Lorenzo and Jessica in *The Merchant of Venice* and the fate of Lady Macduff in *Macbeth* are two Shakespearian counterplots. The reader should examine his selection to see if the elimination of the subsidiary material results in an acceleration and clarification of the author's main purpose and, at the same time, assists the reader in confining himself to the proper time limits.

Cutting poetry involves problems more complex and difficult than cutting prose. The terseness of most poetry makes deleting a real challenge. Brooks, Purser, and Warren point out: "... a poem can give a *comparable* effect, that is, can provoke an appropriate emotional response in the reader, in much fewer words than can usually a story or play; and this fact points to a most important characteristic of the poetic method: it tends toward intensification and concentration."[4] Students should be cautioned that, although in some poems an entire stanza may be omitted, an isolated line cannot be eliminated without considerable reflection for fear of destroying the rhythm and/or meter and/or rhyme. A student who finds a poem too long for the time available should consider choosing a shorter selection rather than cutting the longer poem.[5]

Practicing the selection

Now that the interpreter has chosen an appropriate selection, gained a thorough understanding of its significance, and properly limited his material, he is ready to practice reading.

Naturally, the most experienced reader can do a passable job with a minimum of practice. But a mere passable performance is not desired. The interpreter must strive to do his best at all times because he has an ethical responsibility to represent faithfully the author whose material he is reading. Therefore, extensive preparations are required of both experienced and inexperienced readers. No track star would think of going "cold" into a track meet simply because he had broken the school record the year before. No interpreter, no matter how good his past achievements, should consider reading to a group without deep thought and considerable rehearsing. Wordsworth says: "... all good poetry is the spontaneous overflow of powerful feelings: and though this be true, poems to which any value can be attached were never produced on any variety of subjects but by a man who, being possessed

[4] See Cleanth Brooks, John Thibaut Purser, and Robert Penn Warren, *An Approach to Literature*, Appleton-Century-Crofts, Inc., New York, 1938, p. 420. Copyright, 1936, F. S. Crofts & Co., Inc. Reprinted by permission of Appleton-Century-Crofts, Inc.

[5] Additional advice for cutting selections is available in other textbooks on the oral interpretation of literature, in Part IV of this text, and in the following references: Faye Lois Hedges, "Selecting, Abridging, and Arranging Humorous Prose for Oral Interpretation by High School Students," master's thesis, State University of Iowa, 1959; Edna Gilbert, "Oral Interpretation at Speech Festivals," *The Speech Teacher*, vol. 5, no. 2, pp. 117–120, March, 1956.

of more than usual organic sensibility, had also thought long and deeply." Such long and deep thoughts are also the responsibility of the reinterpreter, who must re-create the author's idea. The reader who expects "the spontaneous overflow of powerful feelings" to develop when he has not thought "long and deeply" is asking for a phenomenon that will not occur.

When the reader begins his practicing, he should keep in mind the study he has made of the selection, letting the analysis of his material form the foundation of his practice. The study and exploration of his literature are not meaningless requirements. The oral reader should strive to make his research, analysis, and practice contribute toward a single goal—the sharing of the printed pages that he has chosen to read.

The reader practicing by himself

There is much that the reader can do to improve his abilities when he is working by himself. He may be sitting in his own study room or out on a hill or working by himself in the classroom where he is to read at a later date. Or the reader may assist himself with a tape recorder, which will give him a mirror in which he can catch a reflection of his abilities. But in any event, the oral reader must read. He must perform. He must practice. He must learn to listen carefully to himself so that he can correct his own mistakes.

The reader's voice.   Since the interpreter's position is that of a catalyst who assists the audience in gaining strength from the selection, since the interpreter is the "man behind the throne," since he performs the duty of the lens, which fixes and focuses the beam of the selection on the receptors of the audience, he should keep himself "out of the act" to the extent that he does not distort the author's purpose or the audience's ability to grasp that purpose. It is common knowledge that the type of lens used in a camera does influence the quality of the picture produced. But there is general discontent when the lens is out of focus, causing the picture to become blurred.

In both body and voice, the interpreter should remain unobtrusive. To define this unobtrusiveness in relation to voice, the student should consult the famous Shakespearian critic, Samuel Johnson, who points out the disadvantages of the two extremes of style and advocates the adoption of a style "to be sought in the common intercourse of life":

If there be, what I believe there is, in every nation, a stile [sic] which never becomes obsolete, a certain mode of phraseology so consonant and congenial to the analogy and principles of its respective language as to remain settled and unaltered; this style is probably to be sought in the common intercourse of life, among those who speak only to be understood, without ambition of elegance. The polite are always catching modish innovations, and the learned depart from established forms of speech, in hope of finding or making better; those who wish for distinction forsake the vulgar, when the vulgar is right; but there is a conversation above grossness and below refinement, where propriety resides. . . ."[6]

The interpreter is advised to style his voice as Johnson advised the writer to style his words, to seek a voice which is above grossness and below refinement, in order that he may not fall into the traps that Johnson lists—of catching modish innovations of enunciation and pronunciation, of departing from the established forms of enunciation and pronunciation in an effort to bring glory on himself, of departing from the vulgar when the vulgar is acceptable.[7] The interpreter is advised to do as Wordsworth recommends in his "Observations Prefixed to 'Lyrical Ballads' " and seek to use the "language really used by men," which, Wordsworth says, is less under the "influence of social vanity" and therefore conveys "feelings and notions in simple and unelaborated expressions."[8] When the philosophies of Johnson and Wordsworth on written style are applied to the use of the voice in oral interpretation, the conclusion is that the reader should strive for a voice which does not call attention to itself either by its substandardisms of enunciation or pronunciation *or* by its *overstandardisms* of enuniciation or pronunciation. Would not Johnson shudder to hear Shakespearian comedy performed by actors whose voices contradict the style he finds so commendable? Would not Wordsworth shudder to hear his lyrical ballads read by a voice which was not "purified indeed from what appear to be its real defects, from all lasting and rational causes of dislike or disgust" without, on the other hand, falling under the "influence of social vanity," the effect which Wordsworth so deplored in the poetry of his day?

The discussion below, then, is based upon this definition: *An effective voice for the oral interpretation of literature is one which supplements the total impact of the selection by avoiding the errors of the vulgar and the pretentious, refraining from calling attention to itself, and achieving grace by performing a maximum amount of work with a minimum amount of energy.* Although some students of interpreta-

[6] Samuel Johnson, "Preface to Shakespeare," in J. H. Smith and E. W. Parks (eds.), *The Great Critics*, W. W. Norton & Company, Inc., New York, 1939, p. 451.
[7] For example, avoiding pronouncing "roof" as "rŏŏf," although *Webster's New Collegiate Dictionary*, 2d ed., G. & C. Merriam Company, Springfield, Mass., 1956, allows for it. See p. xv, n. 85.
[8] In Smith and Parks, *op. cit.*, pp. 500–501.

tion may be able to approximate a voice which meets this definition with a minimum amount of knowledge about how and why the voice functions as it does, others respond noticeably to an accelerated knowledge of why their voices do not measure up to the desired standards. The following discussion offers only that information on voice which is particularly oriented toward the oral interpretation of literature. Students who are able to adjust their voices by ear training (hearing their deviations and adjusting satisfactorily) may find the material below inapplicable to them; others who prefer a more detailed comprehension of the physiology and psychology of voice will find the material insufficient and will wish to consult the more detailed treatments of Kaplan and others.

Volume.   There are two factors relative to volume (or loudness) [9] that the oral interpreter must consider. The first of these is projection, and the second is emphasis.

In order that an audience may focus its attention on the selection, it should be as free of distractions as possible. Nothing blurs the lens more quickly and causes attention to be directed to the reader rather than to the selection than does inadequate projection. A voice that lacks sufficient energy or carrying power to allow the audience to listen with ease is a major distraction. A voice that is too loud is also poor. The interpreter must achieve that degree of projection which, in its sympathy with the content of the selection, provides the greatest focus on the material and the least attention on the reader.

When practicing, the beginning reader should consider using more projection than he is at first inclined to do. The reader should remember that his own ear receives added amplification by the direct conductor his body provides between the resonators of the voice and the organs of the middle and inner ear. An audience, however, must rely only on what sound waves bring through the outer ear. The interpreter may simulate audience reaction by cupping his right hand over his right ear in such a manner as to allow only the sound approaching the ear from behind him to strike the eardrum.

Some interpreters confuse projection with loudness. When they are told to project, they merely get louder. A reader, however, may project satisfactorily at a relatively low volume. Experienced actors and readers learn to simulate a whisper so that it can be heard in the last row of the balcony. Therefore, it is not only the *loudness* of the sounds (that is, the amount of energy by which they are transmitted)

---

[9] Some writers, including Gray and Wise, distinguish between the terms *volume* and *loudness*, associating volume with connotations of fullness and expansiveness and loudness with the energy by which the sound waves move through their medium. This text will use the two terms interchangeably.

but the audience reaction to the sounds (whether they are perceived as loud or soft) which determines whether or not a sound has been satisfactorily projected.

Below are three selections which could call for *quiet projection.* The interpreter may wish to practice these until he feels that he is penetrating every corner of the room with his voice and yet permitting the audience to interpret his projection as subdued.

It Is a Beauteous Evening

It is a beauteous evening, calm and free,
The holy time is quiet as a Nun
Breathless with adoration; the broad sun
Is sinking down in its tranquility;
The gentleness of heaven broods o'er the Sea:
Listen! the mighty Being is awake,
And doth with his eternal motion make
A sound like thunder—everlastingly.
Dear Child! dear Girl! that walkest with me here,
If thou appear untouched by solemn thought,
Thy nature is not therefore less divine:
Thou liest in Abraham's bosom all the year;
And worshipp'st at the Temple's inner shrine,
God being with thee when we know it not.

William Wordsworth

From Flow Gently, Sweet Afton

Flow gently, sweet Afton! among thy green braes,
Flow gently, I'll sing thee a song in thy praise;
My Mary's asleep by thy murmuring stream—
Flow gently, sweet Afton, disturb not her dream.

Thou stock-dove, whose echo resounds thro' the glen;
Ye wind whistling blackbirds in yon thorny den;
Thou green-crested lapwing, thy screaming forbear—
I charge you disturb not my slumbering fair.

Robert Burns

From The Landing on Kuralei

The sun was gone. The giant clouds hanging over Kuralei turned gold and crimson. Night birds started coming into the cacao grove. New Japs reported to the blockhouse for a last stand. Our own reinforcements shuddered as they stepped on dead Japs. Night hurried on.

Not only must the oral interpreter learn to use sufficient volume, but he must also vary the volume of his projection to provide variety.

The refrigerator is heard only when it comes on and then again, when it goes off. What causes attention to be fixed momentarily upon an item which was not in the realm of consciousness just a second ago? It is the *change* in sound which results in sufficient emphasis to cross the threshold of the conscious. Both the silence preceding the coming on of the refrigerator motor and the noise of the motor itself seem much louder than normal. It is only after the lack of variety causes the ear to become accustomed to the motor that the effectiveness of the variety is minimized, and the frequencies set up by the motor of the refrigerator return to the subconscious level.

The stimulus provided by the interpreter's voice is similar to that of the refrigerator, in that attention is renewed when change occurs. A variety of volumes, all of them well projected, will result in effective emphasis. A lack of variety results in a lack of emphasis and boredom. A constant change of volume must also be interpreted as a lack of variety. The radio announcer who is always enthusiastic and always modulating his voice may be well received for the first few minutes, but his very variety becomes monotonous.

Therefore, the interpreter should be able not only to speak both loudly and softly with effective projection, but he must also use loudness and softness to achieve the emphasis and degree of audience attention he desires.

It is difficult to offer positive suggestions to the interpreter without skirting the fringes of dogmatism. The following suggestions on volume are offered, just as all suggestions in this text are offered, for the student's consideration. There is no intent to dictate or to draw definitive concepts of what can or cannot succeed. However, repeated questions by students have provoked the comments in the areas mentioned below.

First, the interpreter should consider very carefully the possible reaction of his audience before he begins his selection with a loud volume. Unless he has prepared the listeners for such an assault, they will be taken aback, and their reactions cannot be predicted accurately. If the selection begins at an intense level of excitement, the introduction should gain sufficient momentum so that the listeners are not startled by the force of the opening lines.

Second, the interpreter should consider simulating all extreme deviations from normal volume levels. It is usually enough to suggest both shouting and whispering. The interpreter cannot hope to shout or whisper as effectively as an audience can imagine a shout or a whisper.

Third, the interpreter should adjust his volume to the occasion and be able to project sufficiently to fill a large auditorium without the assistance of a microphone, the mechanical limitations of which will seriously limit the nuances of his vocal inflections. He should also be able to read effectively in his own living room or in a small seminar room without blasting or losing his ability to gauge his volume properly.

Tempo. There are three factors relating to tempo (or speed of delivery) which the oral reader should consider. The first of these is his over-all rate of delivery; the second concerns variety in tempo; and the third and most important involves adapting the tempo to the mood of the selection.

Some interpreters have a basic rate of delivery which is too fast or too slow. All readers should remember that they are producing a single stimulus that must be grasped by the audience *at the time it is given.* There are no second chances. An audience which becomes frustrated because the reader is going so quickly that the ideas are bumping into each other and cannot be properly sorted and absorbed is an unhappy audience. It can be compared to a child who has been given a beautiful box of chocolates only to have one after the other of them poked into his mouth before he has had time to chew or taste the previous one.

Interpreters should also be aware that the listening abilities of the audience vary widely. For some persons, the speed of reading must be very slow if comprehension is to be achieved; others demand a much more rapid rate of delivery and become islands of discontent when the selection does not move fast enough. It is impossible for the reader to please all groups. His speed cannot be geared to his lowest group. Such a speed will cause the quicker persons to disturb the audience with their restlessness until even the slower responders lose attention. Moreover, the speed should be fast enough to give the audience a sense of achievement. A selection read at too slow a tempo resembles a motion picture run at a speed slightly slower than that at which it was filmed.

Variety in tempo is just as important as is variety in volume and must be planned to fit the selection. A constant rate of speed is an invitation to boredom. Good dance music is often poor concert music, for one of the requisites of good dance music is that it maintain a constant beat. If variety is to be achieved in dance music, it must be gained by varying volume, pitch, and quality. As soon as the tempo changes, the dancers are confused. Therefore, such famous dance tunes as "In the Mood" and "Star Dust" demand a constant rhythm. The dance recordings of "In the Mood" feature abrupt changes in volume and many shifts in instrumentation, but the tempo remains regular. A good concert band can seldom provide good dance music, for its frequent changes in tempo are planned to gain attention through emphasis.

The oral reader should practice until he is able to read quickly and slowly. When the tempo is fast, the reader must be careful to enunciate clearly. Fast tempos should seldom be maintained for long periods of time. Slow tempo, instead of emphasizing the consonants, requires a prolongation of the vowels. It is often awkward to try to prolong a consonant, but the length of vowels is easily varied without artificiality. The tempo may also be slowed down by pauses between the phrases and by pauses between the sentences. There are, therefore, three ways to slow down reading speed:

Prolonging vowels (and, when possible, consonants)
Pausing between phrases
Pausing between sentences

The pause is one of the most effective aids to emphasis available to the oral reader, but the beginning student is apt to shy away from it. The silence that ensues after he pauses seems deafening to him. He has an uncontrollable urge to keep on reading. One second of silence seems like a minute. In order to reassure the student that a pause that he may feel appropriate should be honored, the four purposes of the pause are presented below:

First, the pause gives the listener time to digest what has preceded before more complications are added.

The reader should always consider pausing after difficult phraseology or complex material. If the listener becomes frustrated because he has yet to grasp what has already been said when the reader is busy adding more stimuli, he is not in the proper mood to listen effectively.

Second, the pause gives the audience time to enjoy what it is hearing.

Time to laugh and to grin must be permitted in comedy. Although the speed of comedy is more often quick than not, it must not be so quick that the tempo prevents the audience from enjoying what it is experiencing. Often, in theaters, members of the audience are heard to say, "What was that?" or "What did she say?" The rest of the audience may be laughing, but these persons, for whom the speed of delivery may have been too great, become stumbling blocks to audience attention and possibly destroy what would otherwise have been a highly cohesive situation.

Third, the pause provides emphasis to what precedes and what follows.

The silence allows the preceding thought to ring out and the subsequent thought to enter a rested mind. When the last church bell rings and silence follows, it seems as if the quality of that last bell is sweeter and purer than any of the others. If the bells begin to sound again, we take up their message with renewed enthusiasm and appreciation.

Fourth, the pause provides time for the reader to gain his bearings and move with ease through his selection.

The pause will permit the reader to keep a perspective on his reading and make decisions to change his style of delivery to meet the demands of his audience. A reader must give himself an opportunity to gauge the mood of the audience and permit himself time to respond to that mood.

Although the pause can be very effective, it becomes artificial when it is striven for rather than felt. As effective as the pause may be, it can also result in an artificially delayed tempo and thus destroy the mood of the selection. The beginning reader will probably have to make mistakes in his efforts to gain proper use of tempo before he learns how to move at just the right speed. Such mistakes as may occur in the process of learning are permissible if the goal of the reader is to learn to blend himself, the selection, and the audience into a unity of spirit, but such mistakes may do much harm if the student learns only the mechanics of the pause without understanding how those mechanics must be subordinated to the mood of the selection.

In the preceding discussions of the general rate of delivery and of achieving variation from this rate, it has also been mentioned that changes in tempo must often conform to changes in mood. There are, of course, no rules as to what mood is associated with what tempo, but without fear of serious contradiction, it can be said that a slow tempo is most often associated with somberness, seriousness, and conservatism; a fast tempo is most often linked with frivolity, comedy, and liberalism. The exceptions to these generalizations, such as the deadpan comedian and the fire engine, only prove the rule. How ridiculous it would seem to find a hearse going pell-mell through the streets in a hurry to get to the graveyard. Such a funeral procession, it would be said, is disrespectful. We laugh when we see a motion picture of a high jumper run in slow motion. We would be amused at a minister who prayed at a fast rate of speed. Society has associated these events with certain tempos, and the necessity of adjusting to an unfamiliar speed causes the audience to manifest its insecurity in laughter.

Obviously enough, the interpreter can use changes in tempo to enhance the moods he is trying to create. What tempo would be most suitable to establish the mood of the Christina Rossetti poem "Remember"?

Remember me when I am gone away,
  Gone far away into the silent land;
  When you can no more hold me by the hand,
Nor I half turn to go yet turning stay.
Remember me when no more day by day
  You tell me of our future that you planned:
  Only remember me; you understand
It will be late to counsel then or pray.
Yet if you should forget me for a while
  And afterwards remember, do not grieve:
  For if the darkness and corruption leave
  A vestige of the thoughts that once I had,
Better by far you should forget and smile
  Than that you should remember and be sad.

Fast tempo finds a ready servant in comedy. The brisk speed at which most limericks are read exemplifies the association between a rapid tempo and humor. How fast should the limericks below [10] be read?

I sat next the Duchess at tea.
It was just as I feared it would be:
  Her rumblings internal
  Were simply infernal,
And everyone thought it was me.

There was a young lady of Lynn who was so uncommonly thin that when she essayed to drink lemonade she slipped through the straw and fell in.

A decrepit old gas man named Peter,
While hunting around for the meter,
  Touched a leak with his light.
  He arose out of sight,
And, as anyone can see by reading this, he also destroyed the meter.

The discussion of tempo may be concluded with these supplemental observations:

First, it may be necessary at times for the reader to consider the addition of certain nonfluencies—grunts, exclamations, hesitations—which the author does not mention specifically but only infers from the mood he established. Robert Browning, for example, liked to write

[10] From Laurence Perrine, *Sound and Sense*, Harcourt, Brace & World, Inc., New York, 1956, pp. 189–190. (Stanza form has been modified.)

good conversation. He realized that such conversation is full of non-fluencies, but experienced difficulty in writing these nonfluencies into his poetry. Browning took a chance when he wrote "Soliloquy of the Spanish Cloister" and began the selection with the representative letters "GR-R-R—" which have all too often been literally interpreted. In "The Glove" Browning tries "'Heighho,' yawned one day King Francis, 'Distance all value enhances!'" In "My Last Duchess" Browning discards all efforts to write nonfluencies into the dialogue, employing only an occasional dash, which he hopes will connote to his readers the flavor of conversation.

Second, it can be said that the novice interpreter should make a particular effort to avoid a choppy delivery. In order to achieve variety, he should vary his tempo. If his tempo is not varied, either he is reading atypical or poorly written literature, or he has failed to respond properly to the style of his selection.

Third, the inexperienced reader may, by improper use of the pause, overstress the rhythm in poetry to the extent that he distorts the thought sequence. Not only can the reader *sing* his poetry rather than speak it, but he can also distort the author's intended meaning by this singing. For example, in the Isaac Watts hymn "O God, Our Help in Ages Past," the first stanza could be *sung* with artificial stress on the second syllable of the *iamb,* so that the poetry would jolt along:

o GOD our HELP in A -ges PAST our HOPE for YEARS to COME

Here the pattern of the rhythm is overstressed, resulting in a distortion of the meaning of Watts's line. Note the second line of the same hymn:

Under the shadow of thy throne thy saints have dwelt secure.

This is one sentence, one thought. But how often do we hear choirs pause after the word "throne" so that the whole meaning of the line is lost. The beginning reader is tempted to do as the choir does. He must overcome the temptation to let the rhythm drown the thought and use the pause to emphasize the meaning rather than to subdue it.

Pitch. There are three factors relating to pitch which the oral interpreter must consider. The first concerns achieving sufficient variation in pitch; the second encourages the reader to let his pitch respond to the mood of the selection; and the third cautions the reader to be aware of the pitch patterns he is using.

Variety in pitch is equally as desirable as is variety in volume and tempo. We most often associate the unfavorable connotations of the word "monotone" with inflexibility of pitch. The unfavorable effect that constancy of pitch has upon an audience can be understood if the reader imagines how devastating would be the effect of an orchestra which played a concert involving only two or three closely related notes of the scale. Even carefully arranged variations of volume and tempo would not relieve the boredom of such an orchestra, and the audience would soon disperse. Yet many people carry such a monotonous orchestra with them daily and never give their audiences a rest from a highly limited pitch range. Little wonder that their listeners respond unsatisfactorily!

Many students lack variety in pitch because they are using an unrealistic pitch level. Once a more satisfactory pitch has been adopted, such students must learn how to vary properly from this new level. Variety does not come automatically with a change in pitch any more than normal speech results from cleft-palate repair. A relearning process must be undertaken, for the student with a monotone must unlearn his habits of stability of pitch and assume new habits of variety.

Other students have developed monotone pitch patterns in imitation of a parent or a sib or an influential teacher. The environment of many students has precluded an opportunity to change from a faulty pitch. Such students may respond to reading a selection with a pitch as close to a monotone as possible, followed by a reading of the same selection with as much variety as possible, until they can hear a pronounced difference between the first and second readings. In such an exercise, neither reading will be acceptable, but a sense of the ability to vary pitch will be achieved. The use of the tape recorder during such an exercise should intensify the results.

In his story "Spotted Horses," William Faulkner has pitted the observant traveling salesman, Ratliff, against the scheming, up-and-coming "poor white," Flem Snopes. Flem and a Texan named Buck Hipps have brought a bunch of wild Texas ponies into a small town and intend to auction them off the next day. Ratliff and some other men are sitting along the veranda, discussing the possibilities of tomorrow's auction. The static quality of the dialogue will permit variety, but it must be a subtle variety, so much a part of the mood created that the audience does not detect the changes. What possibilities are there for a successful reading of the selection?

Ratliff was among them now. He had returned just before supper. . . . "So Flem has come home again," he said. "Well, well, well. Will Varner paid to get him to Texas, so I reckon it aint no more than fair for you fellows to pay the freight on him back." From the lot there came a high, thin squeal. One of the animals emerged. It seemed not to gallop but to flow, bodiless, without dimension. Yet there was the rapid light beat of hard hooves on the packed earth.

"He aint said they was his yet," Quick said.

"He aint said they aint neither," Freeman said.

"I see," Ratliff said. "That's what you are holding back on. Until he tells you whether they are his or not. . . . But then, when a man's done got trimmed, I dont reckon he cares who's got the money."

"Maybe if Ratliff would leave here tonight, they wouldn't make him buy one of them ponies tomorrow," a third said.

"That's fact," Ratliff said. "A fellow can dodge a Snopes if he just starts lively enough. . . . You folks aint going to buy them things sho enough, are you?" Nobody answered. They sat on the steps, their backs against the veranda posts, or on the railing itself. Only Ratliff and Quick sat in chairs, so that to them the others were black silhouettes against the dreaming lambence of the moonlight beyond the veranda. The pear tree across the road opposite was now in full and frosty bloom, the twigs and branches springing not outward from the limbs but standing motionless and perpendicular above the horizontal boughs like the separate and upstreaming hair of a drowned woman sleeping upon the uttermost floor of the windless and tideless sea. . . . A bird, a shadow, fleet and dark and swift, curved across the moonlight, upward into the pear tree and began to sing; a mockingbird.

"First one I've noticed this year," Freeman said.

"You can hear them along Whiteleaf every night," the first man said. "I heard one in February. In that snow. Singing in a gum."

"Gum is the first tree to put out," the third said. . . .

"Gum first to put out?" Quick said. "What about willow?"

"Willow aint a tree," Freeman said. "It's a weed."

"Well, I dont know what it is," the fourth said. "But it aint no weed. Because you can grub up a weed and you are done with it. I been grubbing up a clump of willows outen my spring pasture for fifteen years. They are the same size every year. Only difference is, it's just two or three more trees every time."

"And if I was you," Ratliff said, "that's just exactly where I would be come sunup tomorrow. Which of course you aint going to do. I reckon there aint nothing under the sun . . . that can keep you folks from giving Flem Snopes and that Texas man your money." [11]

The selection above is particularly challenging because the mood of stability must be established within which variety moves unobtrusively. The time is the quiet of the evening, and the participants, except for Ratliff, are farmers whose inflection patterns are often as controlled as are their emotions. Only Ratliff stands out as stubbornly resisting the inevitable. The farmers serve as a reference point from

[11] William Faulkner, "Spotted Horses," [originally published as "The Peasants"] *The Hamlet*, Random House, Inc., New York, 1940, pp. 315–317. Copyright 1931, 1940, renewed 1958 by William Faulkner. Reprinted by permission of Random House, Inc.

which Ratliff varies. Without a contrast between the farmers and Ratliff, neither can achieve emphasis, and the all-important mood suffers.

The Faulkner selection also illustrates the third pitch factor important to the interpreter. The pitch must match the mood. In general, high pitches are associated with excitement, instability and merriment; low pitches, with somberness, stability, and sobriety. Music illustrates the direct association between pitch and mood. Weber's "Invitation to the Waltz," intended for dancing and frivolity, features high pitches; Beethoven's famous funeral march from the *Eroica Symphony* (No. 3) features low pitches and slow rhythms.

Abrupt changes in pitch often connote instability; constancy of pitch, whether low or high, often signifies stability. If the reader wishes to build a characterization featuring conservatism and/or irresoluteness, he may find himself using a relatively constant pitch; if he wishes to build a characterization which must indicate impatience with society as it is and a willingness to change, he may find himself using more variety in pitch than is his custom. The extreme lack of variety, the monotone, can indicate senility and obstinacy; the extreme use of variety often indicates nervous instability and weakness of character.

The third and last factor of pitch which is important to the oral reader is pitch pattern. The experienced reader will be aware of when he is reading in a pattern and when he is not reading in a pattern so that he can shift in and out of a set variation in pitch at will.

Pitch patterns are usually acceptable only when they are used deliberately to establish mood or characterization. Otherwise, they should be avoided. A pitch pattern may be defined as a regularly reoccurring sequence of pitches. There are several which are quite common. The first involves a steady pitch which is maintained on each sentence until the last few syllables, when the pitch drops off. It can be nicknamed "the preacher's waltz." In diagram form, it looks like this:

$$\overline{}\smile \quad \overline{}\smile \quad \overline{}\smile$$

In order to recognize this pitch pattern when he hears it or when he uses it himself, the reader should learn to say the following lines with the inflection of the diagram above:

When God began to create the heavens and the earth,
the earth was a desolate waste,
with darkness covering the abyss
and a tempestuous wind ranging over the surface of the waters.
Then God said,
"Let there be light!"

And there was light;
And God saw that the light was good.[12]

The second pitch pattern which is commonly detected among oral readers is the converse of the first. It involves a gradual rise in pitch which is climaxed by an abrupt rising inflection at the end of the sentence. Diagrammed, it resembles the following:

This pitch pattern can be nicknamed the "eternal surprise." It exhausts the listener by leaving him continually on an inflected plane without allowing him to come to rest. The reader should attempt the same passage from Genesis using the pattern of eternal surprise.

The third common pitch pattern is often called the "puncher." It involves a periodical, abrupt rise in pitch, usually on syllables and/or words that are accented. It is also called "over the waves." In diagram form it is:

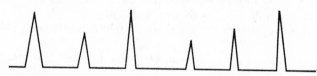

The purpose of the puncher is to stress those things which are important and to unstress those things which are unimportant. Such intentions are commendable. However, it is often used to excess with most undesirable results. Just as ice cream for every course in the meal would become unbearable, so does the pattern of the puncher become annoying.

In order that the student can recognize the symptoms of this pattern in his own reading, he may wish to practice saying the lines below as marked, giving heavy stress to each word set in italics:

When *God* began to create the *heavens* and the *earth*, the *earth* was a desolate *waste*, with *darkness* covering the *abyss* and a *tempestuous* wind ranging over the *surface* of the waters. Then God *said:* "Let there be *light!*" And there *was* light; And God *saw* that the light was good.[13]

Patterns in pitch are often helpful in depicting dialectal differences. What is commonly called the "melody" of a language is, for the most

[12] J. M. P. Smith & E. J. Goodspeed (trans.), *The Bible: An American Translation,* The University of Chicago Press, Chicago, p. 1. Copyright 1935 by the University of Chicago.
[13] *Ibid.* (Italics added.)

part, a resultant of the effect of patterns in pitch, some of which are so subtle as to escape notice of all but the discerning ear. Bertrand Russell, the famous English philosopher, has defended the existence of dialects and deplored the present trend to eliminate them.[14] The melody pattern of the American Cajun in Louisiana, for instance, is sufficiently distinct to distinguish it from other American dialects.

In conclusion, the reader should keep in mind these particular concepts:

First, men should not attempt to imitate women's voices or vice versa. If pitch is used as an indication of sex, it should mildly suggest, rather than imitate. The reader should remember that an audience can determine characterization in ways other than pitch. As a case in point, how much variation in pitch, if any, is necessary to distinguish Ed Newton from the three ladies in the selection below?

> The three women stood at the foot of the water tank.
> "To find Lily is a different thing," said Aimee Slocum.
> "Where in the wide world do you suppose she'd be?" It was Mrs. Watts who was carrying the letter.
> "I don't see a sign of her either on this side of the street or on the other side," Mrs. Carson declared as they walked along.
> Ed Newton was stringing Redbird school tablets on the wire across the store.
> "If you're after Lily, she come in her while ago and tole me she was fixin' to git married," he said.
> "Ed Newton!" cried the ladies all together, clutching one another. Mrs. Watts began to fan herself at once with the letter from Ellisville. She wore widow's black, and the least thing made her hot.
> "Why she is not. She's going to Ellisville, Ed," said Mrs. Carson gently. "Mrs. Watts and I and Aimee Slocum are paying her way out of our own pockets. Besides, the boys of Victory are on their honor. Lily's not going to get married, that's just an idea she's got in her head."
> "More power to you, ladies," said Ed Newton, spanking himself with a tablet.

Second, in reading dialogue, are variations in pitch, together with variations in volume, tempo, and quality, sufficient to allow the reader to delete the "he saids" and "she saids" that often stick in the throat of the reader? In the story of Lily Daw, there are three adult women plus Lily whom the audience must distinguish. Suppose that, in practicing his selection, the reader felt that he had achieved sufficient variety to allow his listeners to establish clear characterizations of all four women. Could he then eliminate the portions of the reading copy below in parentheses?

[14] Bertrand Russell, "The Political and Cultural Influence," *The Impact of America on European Culture*, Beacon Press, Boston, 1951, pp. 13–14.

"Go on and tell us what you're doing, Lily," said Aimee Slocum.

"Packing, silly," said Lily.

"Where are you going?" [15]

"Going to get married, and I bet you wish you was me now," said Lily. But shyness overcame her suddenly, and she popped the zinnia back into her mouth.

"Talk to me, dear," (said Mrs. Carson.) "Tell old Mrs. Carson why you want to get married."

"No," said Lily, after a moment's hesitation.

"Well, we've thought of something that will be so much nicer," (said Mrs. Carson.) "Why don't you go to Ellisville!"

"Won't that be lovely?" said Mrs. Watts. "Goodness, yes."

"It's a lovely place," (said Aimee Slocum uncertainly.)

"You've got bumps on your face," said Lily.

"Aimee, dear, you stay out of this, if you don't mind," (said Mrs. Carson anxiously.) "I don't know what it is comes over Lily when you come around her."

Lily stared at Aimee Slocum meditatively.

"There! Wouldn't you like to go to Ellisville now?" (asked Mrs. Carson.)

"No'm," said Lily.

"Why not?" All the ladies leaned down toward her in impressive astonishment.

" 'Cause I'm goin' to get married," said Lily.[16]

Quality. If volume is associated with loudness, if pitch is associated with frequency, and if tempo is associated with speed, what residual is there to be labeled quality?

Quality is sometimes defined as that component of voice not included in the designations, volume, tempo, and pitch. It is also spoken of as an X factor which is to a large extent undefinable. This text associates the term *quality* with *resonance* and attempts to show that the factor yet to be explored in voice after volume, tempo, and pitch have been discussed lies in the amplification factor or the resonance of the sound wave. The discussion considers the deficiencies in quality that interfere with oral reading, assuming that a voice which is relatively free of these properties has a satisfactory voice quality.

There are three aspects of voice quality which concern the interpreter: first, the interpreter must establish a philosophy of voice quality; second, the interpreter must learn to recognize, produce, and eliminate, when he wishes, certain deviations from *normal* quality; third, the interpreter must learn to use quality to achieve his desired mood.

Samuel Johnson's attitude that the style which never becomes obsolete is the style used by those "who speak only to be understood with-

---

[15] Note the lack of identification which Miss Welty risks for this line only
[16] Parentheses added.

out ambition of elegance" has already been recommended. Wordsworth, in turn, says much the same thing: "Poetry sheds no tears 'such as Angels weep,' but natural and human tears; she can boast of no celestial choir that distinguishes her vital juices from those of prose; the same human blood circulates through the veins of them both." The interpreter should speak in order to have his selection understood, without any ambitions of elegance of quality which will point to him as a polished performer. He should speak with a natural and human quality which boasts of no differences from acceptable speech in any walk of life. His enunciation and resonance are unpretentious and unobtrusive. Whatever techniques of quality the interpreter may develop, these techniques should not be ostentatious. If the interpreter's quality resembles a white carnation which has been tinted blue so that people do not say, "What a beautiful flower!" but rather, "What an unusual color for a carnation," he has exceeded the mark and can be convicted of splitting the ears of the groundlings. If the interpreter's quality makes the audience say, "What a fine selection!" and not, "What a beautiful voice!" the quality has reached the mark and such an interpreter is to be congratulated. If, in progressing down the other end of the scale, the interpreter has not developed sufficient resonance to carry his message so that the audience says, "I somehow feel that I missed the greater part of what the selection had to offer," then the mark has not yet been reached.

With this in mind, the interpreter should have a rudimentary knowledge of the chief defects in voice quality so that he may know at all times the status of the quality of his own voice. The first deviation in resonance that the interpreter must recognize is excessive nasality. Some nasality is helpful to effective resonance, but the interpreter who relies too much on the nasal chamber to project his voice is adding overtones which the English-speaking peoples generally consider unpleasant.[17] Overly nasal voices may be found in all dialects and in all regions. It is such an outstanding characteristic of Yankee English that the caricature of the American on the English stage is a man with a clothespin on his nose.

The interpreter with an excess of nasality is trying to get resonance, but he is developing it in the wrong areas. If the interpreter has not learned to adjust the valve (or sphincter) which separates the mouth and the pharyngeal cavities from the nose cavity during the resonance of vowels, he allows the sound waves to enter the nasal chamber, where they develop a *hollow* overtone which mixes with the tones being resonated in the mouth and pharynx. These overtones add to

[17] There is probably nothing inherently unpleasant in nasal overtones. It is society which has established that they are unpleasant. Nasality in French is acceptable. But, in its extremes, it is taboo in English.

the voice the characteristic hypernasality which we recognize as a twang. Many persons who are hypernasal have learned to depend upon this bottled-up resonating chamber to amplify their sounds to the point where they are slighting the possibilities for resonance in the mouth and pharynx. Such persons are not only

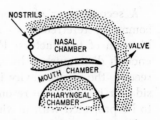

limiting their ability to project, but also adding what English-speaking societies have analyzed as an unpleasant voice quality.

Because of the social stigma placed upon it, *nasal speech* is commonly associated with the less educated and more colloquial. It is often used to depict the general run of persons in rural areas and in big city areas. Because it lacks grace (it uses more energy than is necessary to perform a given amount of work), it tends to be rejected by society by the purifying element of humor.[18]

The interpreter who distinguishes a difference when he reads the lines below with his nostrils open and with his nostrils closed is using nasal resonance on his vowels:

The First Day That I Was a Life [19]

The first day that I was a life
I recollect it—how still!
The last day that I was a life
I recollect it as well.

'Twas stiller, though the first
Was still.
'Twas empty, but the first
Was full.

Emily Dickinson

[18] Occasionally, because of a stoppage in the nasal region, either permanent (caused by such abnormalities as enlarged adenoids) or temporary (caused by swollen nasal passages from hay fever or the common cold), an interpreter may become *denasal*. In this case, he has three defective sounds: *m*, *n*, and *ng*. These sounds, commonly called the nasals, achieve their bottled-up resonance in the mouth. The denasal person has no trouble in generating this resonance in the mouth chamber, which must be closed to the outside air for *m*, *n*, and *ng*, but he experiences difficulty in allowing the airstream to pass freely through the nasal passages which are blocked. Such a person often substitutes other sounds for *m*, *n*, and *ng*, which permit a passage of air out of the mouth. Thus, the denasal persons says he has a cold in his *dose*, simulating the *n* which he cannot pronounce with the *d* which he can.

[19] From *Bolts of Melody: New Poems of Emily Dickinson*, edited by Mabel Loomis Todd and Millicent Todd Bingham. Copyright 1945 by Millicent Todd Bingham. Reprinted by permission of Harper & Row, Publishers, Incorporated.

A second error of resonance which the interpreter must avoid is commonly referred to as *mumbling*. This error is caused by a combination of two factors: First, the sounds themselves are not clearly enough distinguished by accurate positioning of the articulators, and second, the mouth cavity is not permitted sufficient access to the outside air to allow the resonance generated in the mouth and pharynx to be projected with maximum effectiveness.

Since the air pumped up through the larynx by the lungs has no distinguishing qualities of its own and since the sound that is generated at the vocal folds has little more to distinguish it than the property of pitch, the majority of the characteristics of the vowels and the consonants of English are developed by the articulators. If these articulators are not correctly placed to achieve a sound which is easily identifiable, mumbling results. Even if the articulators are properly placed, unless the mouth itself is sufficiently open to allow the sounds to be projected without developing muffled overtones in the mouth region itself, mumbled speech again occurs.

Mumbling, like nasality, is associated with the uneducated. It connotes carelessness, introversion, and self-centeredness. The mumbler is not sufficiently interested in other people to bother to make himself understood. He therefore feels that he can get along by himself.

The converse of mumbling, the overmellow voice, is too often found among persons skilled in speech. For such people, the medicine has been too effective. They have learned their lesson too well. Their own overly developed resonance and clipped articulations thrill them, and they speak, as Johnson said, in the hope of finding or making better, forsaking the vulgar when the vulgar is right. Their attitude toward the average person's voice quality is one of disdain. The error of the ways of such pedants should be apparent to all who examine the artificiality of poetic language in the eighteenth century.

Too many interpreters fall into this overmellow category. Singers experience a similar difficulty, cultivating their voices to such a degree that they can no longer sing the simple folk songs effectively. Therefore, the United States has developed the folk singer to fill a void left by the concert and operatic star. Gladys Swarthout's recording of "Comin' through the Rye" approaches the ludicrous. It is impossible to imagine such a refined, cultured lassie ever wandering in the fields. She might whiz through in a taxi on the way to the opera, but she would not be found kissing a country boy in the rye.

Mahalia Jackson, on the other hand, has doggedly retained her identity with the common man, while developing sufficient articulation to clarify her words.[20] She will occasionally slur a word on pur-

---

[20] See Ralph Ellison, "As the Spirit Moves Mahalia," *Saturday Review*, vol. 41, p. 43, Sept. 27, 1958.

pose, but she carefully avoids developing habits of resonance which will divorce her from Wordsworth's "very language of men." Harry Belafonte has successfully developed such a variety of styles that he can shade from extreme dialect to straight singing with naturalness. Such a variety of voice qualities is indeed remarkable.

The overmellow voice is characterized by a stressing of final consonants, the *rolling* of the vowels, the use of the compromise vowel [a], and an excess of hissing on the sibilant sounds, particularly on the *s*.

In his rehearsing, the interpreter should try to establish a happy medium between the mumbling voice and the overmellow voice. He should strive for adequate resonance without exceeding the mark. If he can read the selection below both as a mumbler and as an over-articulator, he is better able to identify his own position on the continuum between the two:

A tutor who tooted the flute
Tried to tutor two tooters to toot.
  Said the two to the tutor,
  "Is it harder to toot or
To tutor two tooters to toot?"

Oversibilance is a third defect of quality which deserves the particular attention of the oral reader. Persons with this defect are commonly referred to as "hissers." Their speech is characterized by distortions of the *s* sound which add overtones to their quality generally considered annoying. The interpreter may have a hissing *s* sound if he is doing any one or more of the following:

Overemphasizing the *s* sound, which, because of its individuality, needs less stress than other consonants

Smiling during the enunciation of *s*, permitting any air which fans out along the teeth to escape through a narrow aperture, causing the addition of high-frequency *s* sounds

Placing the tongue against the teeth for the *s* sound, forcing the air to fan out instead of escaping through an orifice formed by the tongue and the front teeth

Putting the teeth together for the *s* sound, again forcing the air to fan out to find an opening for escape

While practicing, the interpreter should listen carefully to himself for evidence of hissing. If he detects an overpreciseness of the *s* sound or if he finds he is subject to any one of the categories described above, he should refer to proper sources for special assistance.

The interpreter should be able to get a concept of how much his *s* sounds are hissing by reading the selection below. If he is able to produce a *hollow,* low-frequency s sound, he should not hear much hissing; if his s sounds are populated with high-frequency overtones, he should detect the commonly noted *radiator s* sounds.

Silver [21]

Slowly, silently, now the moon
Walks the night in her silver shoon;
This way, and that, she peers, and sees
Silver fruit upon silver trees;
One by one the casements catch
Her beams beneath the silver thatch;
Couched in his kennel, like a log,
With paws of silver sleeps the dog;
From their shadowy cote the white breasts peep
Of doves in a silver-feathered sleep;
A harvest mouse goes scampering by,
With silver claws, and silver eye;
And moveless fish in the water gleam,
By silver reeds in a silver stream.

Walter de la Mare

Oversibilance in speech is associated with petulance, pedantry, and simpering.

The fourth and last aspect of voice quality to be discussed involves peculiar resonances often caused by an atypical functioning of the vibrators. We employ the words "breathiness," "huskiness," "hoarseness," and "gutturalness" to describe the characteristics of resonances stemming largely from an abnormal functioning of the vocal folds. Breathiness is associated with fear, huskiness with sex appeal, hoarseness with horror and exasperation, and gutturalness with coarseness.

In conclusion, special attention should be called to the following aspects of voice quality in oral interpretation:

First, the good interpreter should possess a variety of voice qualities. Otherwise, he must run the risk of monotony.

Second, the use of voice quality to suggest characterization and mood should not exceed the mark. The interpreter is not an actor, but a lens. If his characterizations are too broad, if his attempts at adopting specific voice qualities are too obvious, he colors the lens and distorts the picture the author intended to portray. The interpreter should remember that what can be suggested should not be etched, that the imagination can create a much more citified or countrified person than the author's voice can ever hope to imitate.

[21] Walter de la Mare, "Silver," *Peacock Pie,* Faber & Faber, Ltd., London, 1946, p. 94. Reprinted by permission of The Literary Trustees of Walter de la Mare and The Society of Authors as their representative.

The reader's bodily movement. The same general philosophy that was established for the use of voice will apply equally well to the use of the body. Any physical response to the selection must be unobtrusive and subordinate to the total impact of the selection. Any eye contact, gestures, bodily tension, bodily movement, and handling of the reading copy that calls attention to itself violates the concept of the lens and distorts the focus.

That suggestion rather than portrayal can achieve the mark is pointed out very forcefully by Wordsworth:

For the human mind is capable of being excited without the application of gross and violent stimulants; and he must have a very faint perception of its beauty and dignity who does not know this, and who does not further know, that one being is elevated above another, in proportion as he possesses this capability.

Just as Wordsworth felt that his poetry did not need "gross and violent stimulants" to move his readers, so must the interpreter learn that his delivery does not require broad gesturing or exciting movements to present a comprehensible and effective reading. He must learn that suggestion in movement can do what attempts at portrayal can never do.

Shakespeare's chronicle plays illustrate this point. These dramas involve battlefields, castles, and splendid courts with costly drapery. But Shakespeare knew that his plays would be produced in a theater which *suggested* all of these things, with no attempt to reproduce them accurately. His audience was asked in *Henry IV*, part I, to imagine the vastness of a rebel camp near Shrewsbury or the lists at Coventry or Kenilworth Castle. It was only during the age of realism and literal staging that the chronicle plays suffered in performance because of their settings. As soon as a more figurative theater returned, and the designs of Appia and Gordon Craig began to revive the idea that scene design should be suggestive rather than realistic, the chronicle plays resumed their position as effective theater. Now the theater has gone so far as to put Shakespeare in theater-in-the-round, where, it has been said, much of his art was actually first produced.[22]

Therefore, the attitude of the discussions below will encourage restraint rather than portrayal. The audience will be asked to use its imagination rather than have its imagination fenced in with literal concepts.

Eye contact. The selection must be the predominant factor in deciding whether the reader will establish a direct or an indirect relation-

[22] Leslie Hotson, "Shakespeare's Arena," *Atlantic Monthly*, vol. 193, no. 2, pp. 62–66, February, 1954.

ship with his audience. One of the famous sonnets in English literature calls for a minimum of direct eye contact. It is not only a famous
sonnet, but it is also an intimate love letter, written, not for publication, but for private consumption. Lovers speak their lines in privacy,
not in public. How can the interpreter simulate an atmosphere of seclusion most effectively?

How Do I Love Thee?

How do I love thee? Let me count the ways.
I love thee to the depth and breadth and height
My soul can reach, when feeling out of sight
For the ends of Being and ideal Grace.
I love thee to the level of everyday's
Most quiet need, by sun and candle-light.
I love thee freely, as men strive for Right;
I love thee purely, as they turn from Praise.
I love thee with the passion put to use
In my old griefs, and with my childhood's faith.
I love thee with a love I seemed to lose
With my lost saints,—I love thee with the breath,
Smiles, tears, of all my life!—and, if God choose,
I shall but love thee better after death.

Elizabeth Barrett Browning

The exact positioning of the eyes when they are not on the audience
should be left to the individual style of the reader. Needless to say,
the eyes may rest on the printed page a part of the time. If the reader
does look up, he should not appear to be purposely avoiding his audience, since this would also be distracting.

There is a second reason why the Browning sonnet should be read
with minimal direct eye contact. It is a very familiar passage. Many
persons will have established previous associations with the selection
which they would prefer to rekindle, instead of lighting a fire under
a new association. The reader's goal, therefore, is to stimulate the audience so that it can re-create its former images and live in its memories and its imagination. There is no more impressive experience than
the first time one hears Patrick Henry's famous oration. But the anti-
climaxes in subsequent exposures are annoying and frustrating. Somehow, the subsequent performances never come up to the thrill that
the subject experienced when he first heard the memorable words
in the fifth grade. Better let the interpreter bring back to mind this
first thrill than smother it with an attempt to out-Herod Herod.

Hollywood has never learned this lesson. It distorts the story of
Ivanhoe to the point where one who thrilled to the escapades of this
heroic Norman in the eighth grade cannot enjoy the film. It takes Dolly

Madison, who every school child learns saved the important documents in the White House from being burned in 1812, and turns her into Ginger Rogers, who spends the picture flirting with Aaron Burr. Such effrontery shows that Hollywood has a very faint perception of the beauty and dignity of the human mind. The work of Cecil B. DeMille illustrates again how Hollywood insists upon splitting the ears of the groundlings. When a foreign producer such as Ingmar Bergman appears, he finds the front door wide open, while Hollywood continues to clamor noisily outside the windows.

Yet the number of selections which profit from direct eye contact far outnumber those with which it is questionable. There are few parts of Eudora Welty's story about Lily Daw which cannot profit from direct eye contact. However, the degree needed for maximum audience comprehension is not so great as to move the reader to memorize the selection, with all the pitfalls that this move entails. Rules of thumb for such concepts as eye contact are dangerous to formulate, for they can always be refuted for given instances. Definitions of how much direct eye contact to use under a given situation is subject to as much controversy as is a definition of poetry itself. T. S. Eliot refused to define the latter, saying: "I have not attempted any definition of poetry, because I can think of none which does not assume that the reader already knows what it is, or which does not falsify by leaving out much more than it can include." [23] We likewise refuse to define the former, for very similar reasons.

Gesturing and bodily movement. Students often ask for guidance on how much gesturing and torso movement they may use without calling too much attention to themselves. The beginning student who wishes to be a successful reader and who is apprehensive lest his audience fall short in its appreciation is likely to want to add emphasis to his reading by physical support. Again, there is no set answer as to how much gesturing and bodily movement results in reinforcement and how much results in distraction. Just as artists develop individual qualities in their styles of painting, so do interpreters in their styles of reading. One reader might deliver the selection below with no movement at all and be effective; another might employ, with good taste, considerable movement. The student may wish to practice the selection below in more than one way to see wherein his own strengths lie.

Aimee Slocum had been getting the outgoing mail stamped and bundled. She stood in the aisle of the coach now, tears shaking from her eyes.

[23] T. S. Eliot, *The Use of Poetry and the Use of Criticism,* Harvard University Press, Cambridge, Mass., 1933, p. 155.

"Good-bye, Lily," she said. She was the one who felt things.

"Good-bye, silly," said Lily. . . .

"Get off, Aimee, before the train starts and you break your neck," said Mrs. Watts, all settled and waving her dressy fan gaily. "I declare, it's so hot, as soon as we get a few miles out of town I'm going to slip my corset down."

"Oh, Lily, don't cry down there. Just be good and do what they tell you you—it's all because they love you." Aimee drew her mouth down. She was backing away, down the aisle.

Lily laughed. She pointed across Mrs. Carson's bosom out the window toward a man. He had stepped off the train and just stood there, by himself. He was a stranger and wore a cap.

"Look," she said, laughing softly through her fingers.

"Don't—look," said Mrs. Carson very distinctly, as if, out of all she had ever spoken, she would impress these two solemn words upon Lily's soft little brain. She added, "Don't look at anything till you get to Ellisville."

Facial movement.   Horace says: "Sad words become the sad face, threatening words the angry one, sportive jests the frolicsome, grave precepts the mien of austerity." [24] To what extent should the interpreter use changes in facial expression to support his stimulus?

In practice readers vary widely in the degree of facial movement during interpretation. All readers respond to a limited degree, but with some the changes are pronounced while with others they are minimal. Wordsworth said that the poet wrote under one restriction only, that of "the necessity of giving immediate pleasure to a human Being possessed of that information which may be expected from him . . . as a Man." The interpreter is under a like obligation. Therefore, he must gauge the amount of facial movement he uses by the amount of pleasure he feels such movement will kindle in his audience. It is not the purpose of this text to recommend the amount or degree of the contribution of facial response. The purpose of the discussion is to offer suggestions to those who may find a need for an intensification of the stimulus of facial movement.

The feelings that facial expressions represent are only simulated by the interpreter at the time that he is reading because, while he is performing, the interpreter must be in complete control of his own emotions if he wishes to direct those of his audience effectively. Wordsworth says: ". . . the Poet is chiefly distinguished from other men by a greater promptness to think and feel without immediate external excitement, and a greater power in expressing such thoughts and feelings as are produced in him in that manner." This certainly describes the position of the interpreter. He must have thought and felt more deeply than his audience. He cannot wait for an immediate external

[24] Horace, "Epistle to the Pisos," in Smith and Parks, *op. cit.*, p. 117.

exciting force to inspire him to action, but he must be his own self-stimulus to action. At the time that he is reading, however, the reader cannot afford to let his own feelings interfere with his ability to communicate effectively with others.

Therefore, just as the poet cannot publish the first impulses that his pen dashes off, the reader cannot subject his audience to his first reactions to a selection. Practice should provide opportunities for the reader to let his facial expression respond to the mood of the selection. Consciously or unconsciously, the reader soon learns what expressions are comfortable to him, and he lets the muscles of his face respond.

This particular phase of bodily reaction can best be illustrated by the problem of how the face should respond to humor. Many beginning readers are disappointed in the audience reaction they receive to their attempts at comedy. In many instances, the lack of audience response is directly proportional to the lack of facial response by the reader. Unless he is a dry comedian, the reader should indicate that he expects a humorous response. One of the ways to offer the proper stimulus to the audience is by a twinkle in the eye or by a sly grin. An audience does not like to offend the reader. In many instances, an audience is afraid to laugh for fear that it has misunderstood the situation and that the reader is not calling for comedy at all.

Suppose the interpreter read the excerpt below with a most serious facial expression. How much of the comedy would be smothered?

I must say that Uncle Rondo has been marvelous to me at various times in the past and I was completely unprepared to be made to jump out of my skin, the way it turned out. Once Stella-Rondo did something perfectly horrible to him—broke a chain letter from Flanders Field—and he took the radio back he had given her and gave it to me. Stella-Rondo was furious! For six months we all had to call her Stella instead of Stella-Rondo, or she wouldn't answer. I always thought Uncle Rondo had all the brains of the entire family. Another time he sent me to Mammoth Cave, with all expenses paid.

But this would be the day he was drinking that prescription, the Fourth of July.

So at supper Stella-Rondo speaks up and says she thinks Uncle Rondo ought to try to eat a little something. So finally Uncle Rondo said he would try a little cold biscuits and ketchup, but that was all. So *she* brought it to him.

"Do you think it wise to disport with ketchup in Stella-Rondo's flesh-colored kimono?" I says. Trying to be considerate! If Stella-Rondo couldn't watch out for her trousseau, somebody had to.

"Any objections?" asked Uncle Rondo, just about to pour out all the ketchup.

"Don't mind what she says, Uncle Rondo," says Stella-Rondo. "Sister has been devoting this solid afternoon to sneering out my bedroom window at the way you look."

"What's that?" says Uncle Rondo. Uncle Rondo has got the most terrible temper in the world. Anything is liable to make him tear the house down if it comes at the wrong time.

So Stella-Rondo says, "Sister says, 'Uncle Rondo certainly does look like a fool in that pink kimono!'"

Do you remember who it was really said that?

Uncle Rondo spills out all of the ketchup and jumps out of his chair and tears off the kimono and throws it down on the dirty floor and puts his foot on it. It had to be sent all the way to Jackson to the cleaners and re-pleated.

"So that's your opinion of your Uncle Rondo, is it?" he says. "I look like a fool, do I?" . . .

"I didn't say any such a thing, Uncle Rondo," I says, "and I'm not saying who did, either. Why, I think you look all right. Just try to take care of yourself and not talk and eat at the same time," I says. "I think you better go lie down."

"Lie down my foot," says Uncle Rondo. I ought to of known by that he was fixing to do something perfectly horrible.

So he didn't do anything that night in the precarious state he was in— just played Casino with Mama and Stella-Rondo and Shirley-T. and gave Shirley-T. a nickel with a head on both sides. It tickled her nearly to death, and she called him "Papa." But at 6:30 A.M. the next morning, he threw a whole five-cent package of some unsold one-inch firecrackers from the store as hard as he could into my bedroom and they every one went off. Not one bad one in the string. Anybody else, there'd be one that wouldn't go off.[25]

Muscular tonus. The reader cannot afford to respond to his selection only from the neck up. His whole body is a sounding board for what he is presenting. The extent to which the reader responds is again governed by the reader and his selection.

If he is reading literature whose aim is to create fear, the interpreter may respond by manifesting some tenseness of muscle which would be reflected in the frame of his body. If the selection calls for humor, the interpreter may wish to relax his muscles, responding by an easier and less rigid posture. Again it is difficult to suggest how the student can practice proper bodily support for a given selection without risking misinterpretation. Some beginning interpreters could follow directions for gestures and bodily movement with intelligent restraint, while others, especially novices, would try to follow the directions implicitly and miss the over-all characterization completely. It seems sufficient

[25] From Eudora Welty, "Why I Live at the P.O.," in *A Curtain of Green*, Harcourt, Brace and Company, Inc., New York, 1941. Copyright, 1941, by Eudora Welty. Reprinted by permission of Harcourt, Brace, & World, Inc.

to say that total bodily response in reading is desirable and to allow the weapon of criticism to develop the proper sympathy between a given reader and a given selection in regard to muscular tonus.

The reader practicing with a partner

The interpreter experiences considerable difficulty in maintaining a perspective on his progress during his period of preparation. After he has worked sufficiently to feel a degree of competence but before he has solidified his approach to where it would require major adjustments to effect any changes, he would do well to read his selection to another person, asking for an evaluation.

Any interpreter—any truthful interpreter, that is—is sensitive about unfavorable criticism. There is an old saying which goes, "Oh, yes, I welcome criticism, BUT...." In the last three-letter word lie our reservations. However, one of the criteria of an educated man is that he can properly evaluate both favorable and unfavorable criticism. Wagner never matured to his full potential as a musician because any unfavorable criticism threw him into a tirade. No one really wants to be told that he has not done as well as he could have. But the successful interpreter overcomes this natural impulse and learns to welcome, with as good grace as possible, the criticism he seeks.

Readers should shy away from criticism which is altogether favorable. Evaluators should not be members of the reader's own family or his intimate friends. They should rather be chosen from personnel available who are not sufficiently close to the reader to avoid suggesting anything which might offend him.

The instructor in a class in oral interpretation is of course an evaluator. But the student should secure an evaluator in advance of his classroom performance so that the instructor does not become a guinea pig, but rather an adviser on the limited problems that remain after the reader has done an effective job in his practice sessions.

Formulating the introduction

Except perhaps for the most informal of audiences, listeners to literature prefer that the interpreter preface his selection with introductory remarks. Aristotle points out that if men were all as intelligent as they should be, introductions would be unnecessary. But since few reach the peaks of which they are capable, the thinking apparatus usually needs to be "warmed up" so that it is ready to receive the central stimulus.

The introduction to a selection is much more important than it may seem at first glance. If it is handled properly, it may add materially to the comprehension and appreciation of the literature; if it is handled clumsily and perfunctorily, it achieves no position and fails in its goals.

Unfortunately, there are very few objective data as to what types of introductions are most successful. The discussion below, with two exceptions, will be confined to generalities, many of which still need to be tested.

The introduction to an oral reading has the same purpose as any other introduction. It aims to divorce the audience from its previous thoughts and proposes to concentrate the energies of the listeners on the selection. This general purpose may be divided into subpurposes: first, the introduction should gain the attention of the audience; second, it should successfully introduce the theme of the literature; third, it should disarm the hostility of the audience toward the selection and establish a favorable atmosphere for the reading.

Gaining the attention of the audience

The introduction should gain and hold the attention of the audience. A provocative quotation from a critic, a direct challenge to the audience, an exposition of an unusual quality of the literature, and many other approaches may be used to focus the attention of the audience on the selection. Below are three introductions to poems by Robert Frost.

Robert Frost told a story about the next poem I am going to read which John Ciardi denies is completely accurate. Frost claimed that he wrote "Stopping by Woods on a Snowy Evening" in one sitting, that he just wrote it off as it came to him without making any changes.

But, says Ciardi, the poetry critic for the *Saturday Review*, "Once . . . I heard him add one very essential piece to the discussion of how it 'just came.' One night, he said, he had sat down after supper to work at a long piece of blank verse. The piece never worked out, but Mr. Frost found himself so absorbed in it that, when next he looked up, dawn was at his window. He rose, crossed to the window, stood looking out for a few minutes, and *then* it was that 'Stopping by Woods' suddenly 'just came,' so that all he had to do was cross the room and write it down." [26]

Ciardi says furthermore that, although there is no way of telling because Frost guarded his wastebaskets carefully, he would stake his life on the fact that the discarded pieces of blank verse that Frost had been working on all night contained the essentials of the poem he just "dashed off" at dawn.

Robert Frost was not a friend of the English teacher. On the lecture platform, he often made fun of them—indirectly, of course—but still he poked fun. He laughed at the merits of literary criticism although most advanced courses in English literature today are grounded on the opinions of the critics.

[26] John Ciardi, "Robert Frost: The Way to the Poem," *Saturday Review*, vol. 41, no. 15, p. 65, Apr. 12, 1958.

Frost was particularly "Frost-like" in ridiculing the critics who find hidden meanings in the poem I shall read next, "Dust of Snow." Frost held that his purpose in this poem was merely to describe a change of mood which he experienced, that the hemlock tree might just as well have been a cedar or a fir and that no sinister implications of poison were intended, that the crow might just as well have been a redbird or a sparrow, only it was not. Frost said he just wrote down a simple incident that happened to him and that made him feel better on a day when he was worrying about some matter.

What do you think? Are the critics right in finding implicatons of tragedy in the hemlock tree and the crow, or is Frost right?

Dust of Snow [27]

The way a crow
Shook down on me
The dust of snow
From a hemlock tree

Has given my heart
A change of mood
And saved some part
Of a day I had rued.

Robert Frost

The poet can also be the mathematician. We should not be surprised that Lewis Carroll, the author of *Alice in Wonderland*, was also Charles Dodgson, the author of *Symbolic Logic*. Therefore, when Frost shows up as a mathematician, we should only glory in his versatility.

The poem "Stopping by Woods on a Snowy Evening" is truly mathematical in its basic concepts of rhyme. It provides that the first, second, and fourth lines of each stanza should rhyme with each other; then, to maintain continuity from stanza to stanza, the third line of the first stanza rhymes with the first, second, and fourth lines of the second stanza. And so on. Thus "here" of the first stanza rhymes with "queer," "near," and "year" in the second stanza.

For a poet less skilled than Frost, such a formula might have resulted in a mechanical poem. But the formula is so subtly used that most listeners are not even aware that the complicated rhyme pattern exists.

I shall read the poem twice.[28] During the first reading, listen only for the thought of the poem; during the second reading, listen for the unusual rhyme pattern.[29]

[27] From *Complete Poems of Robert Frost*. Copyright 1916, 1921, 1923 by Holt, Rinehart and Winston, Inc. Copyright renewed 1944, 1951 by Robert Frost. Reprinted by permission of Holt, Rinehart and Winston, Inc.
[28] It must be repeated here that such a direct allusion to the mechanics of verse would not be suitable for all audiences.
[29] See poem, p. 64.

Introducing the theme of the literature

The second problem that the interpreter faces in formulating his introduction is: How much should the audience be told about the selection before it will be at its maximum preparedness to listen? The discussion will be subdivided into three problem areas, none of which has a "yes" or "no" answer. The material below only offers some guidance to the reader so that he is better able to find his own answers in each particular case. Since there may well be more than one correct approach, the very fact that the reader is sufficiently informed to ask what content he should include in his introduction may be enough to force him to make a suitable choice.

How much of the plot, story, or action should the introduction include? The dilemma here is obvious. If the reader tells too much about the action, the suspense is spoiled; if he does not tell enough, the suspense may never be created, for the audience may miss the plot structure.

This is a genuine dilemma. The extent to which it applies to each selection varies. If the plot of the literature is obvious or very well known, the introduction does not need to supplement and preview the plot to any measurable extent; but if the action is obscure and there is much to contemplate and imagine, a summary of the action seems more appropriate.

A pilot study at Mississippi Southern College in 1957 attempted to "escape between the horns" of the dilemma by formulating an introduction which gave considerable plot material without spoiling the story for the audience. Two introductions were prepared for Robert Browning's monologue "My Last Duchess": the first gave little of the details of the plot, concentrating on the history and the mood of the selection; the second carefully led the audience through much of the action in the poem. Two readers, a man and a woman, were trained to read the selection, using first one introduction and then another. A twenty-question posttest was administered after each reading, including six thought questions, six simple retention questions, and eight attitude questions.

The results indicate that the group hearing the introduction containing the details of the plot scored better on all three types of questions. The difference on factual retention between the two groups was 14.33 per cent, whereas the difference in favor of the plot-revealing introduction on the thought questions was 23.33 per cent. The answers to the thought questions were not given in the poem, but had to be inferred from the information that Browning gives. For example, one question asked, "Does the duke consider himself a good speaker?" The correct answer on the key was, "He says he does not, but he really does." Thus, those who retained the plot details were more prepared to understand the deeper significances of the monologue.[30]

A similar investigation was undertaken at Ohio University in 1961. Similar questions were used. Seven different readers, varying from highly skilled to unskilled, replicated the experiment. The results show a significant difference in favor of the plot-revealing introduction for the content questions, but not for the thought questions, although the difference in the means for the thought questions favored the plot-revealing introduction.[31]

The evidence from these two investigations points to a more satisfactory result for an introduction which gives plot details when a relatively difficult and subtle poem such as Robert Browning's "My Last Duchess" has been chosen as the selection.

The two introductions used in the Ohio University experiment, together with two other sample introductions, appear at the conclusion of this chapter. The prefatory remarks to the Michener essay feature little plot material but rather concentrate on setting the scene; those to the Eudora Welty short story are concerned directly with the plot. Introductions giving considerable attention to plot would be suitable for many of the Frost poems, such as "Wild Grapes," "Blueberries," and "The Witch of Coos."

How much material about the author should be included in the introduction? If the author is well known, a simple mention of his name should be sufficient. However, less known writers should be satisfactorily introduced to the listeners and given the status they merit. Note how the sample introduction to "Lily Daw and the Three Ladies" attempts to acquaint the audience with the contribution Miss Welty is making to American literature.

The interpreter should consider mentioning any specific relationship between the selection and the author which can be brought out in the time allowed. An audience often understands a selection better if it knows why the author composed the work. The reader will have to decide whether the relationship between the author and the selection is of sufficient significance to warrant an explanation. For example, because of the pertinent details of Poe's life which caused him to write "Annabel Lee," the interpreter would be wise to give sufficient

[30] Glen Sweatman, unpublished study, Mississippi Southern College, Hattiesburg, Miss., 1957.
[31] Marie Shepardson and Paul D. Brandes, "The Effect of the Introduction on a Literary Communication," unpublished study, Ohio University, Athens, Ohio, 1960.

background material to let the audience know who Annabel Lee was and under what circumstances she died. Charles Dickens's novels were highly biographical. If the reader has chosen passages from *David Copperfield*, he will have difficulty deciding whether he has time in his introduction to point out the many relationships between Dickens and his novel. One reader might enjoy developing in some detail the way in which David Copperfield resembles Charles Dickens; another might prefer to make only an isolated reference to the similarities; a third might omit any such references whatsoever.

If there is some highly colorful incident in the author's life which an audience should know and could enjoy and which might help impress upon it the significance of the selection, it may also be included in the introduction. It would seem a shame to read material by Ambrose Bierce without commenting on his strange and still unexplained disappearance.[32] An interpreter who was reading from *Treasure Island* might find it appropriate to refer to Robert Louis Stevenson's life on Samoa and the epitaph "Home is the sailor, home from sea, and the hunter home from the hill."

What words or phrases should be explained in the introduction? Any important proper names should be considered for mention in the introduction. An audience becomes easily frustrated if it finds name after name piling up in its mind, without the time to sort them. In a silent reading of a novel or a short story, the student can return to trace down a character whom he has misplaced. But such is not true in oral reading. For example, if the reader has chosen to present Oliver Wendell Holmes's "The One-Hoss Shay," the names "Georgius Secundus," "Braddock," and "Lisbon-town" should be identified in the introduction. "Grave Alice and laughing Allegra and Edith with golden hair" need to be identified as Longfellow's children in his poem "The Children's Hour." Notice how Lily and the three ladies are all mentioned in the sample introduction so that the audience is prepared for them when they appear in the action of the story.

Also any important terms which are unfamiliar should be defined. Alfred Noyes's poem "The Highwayman" includes this passage:

And dark in the dark old inn-yard a stable-wicket creaked
Where Tim the ostler listened. . . .

---

[32] Associating the works of one author with those of another is often interesting. The interpreter of the works of Ambrose Bierce might find it refreshing to read from James Thurber's facetious explanation of what happened to Bierce. See James Thurber, "Casuals of the Keys," *The Middle-aged Man on the Flying Trapeze*, Harper & Brothers, New York, 1935.

A modern audience is no longer familiar with an "ostler" or a "stable-wicket." A brief sentence in the introduction explaining these terms should sharpen the focus on the villain.

A particularly difficult passage might be quoted in the introduction and explained briefly so that the audience can have two opportunities to understand it. The compactness of Robert Browning's monologues make this procedure appropriate in introducing such poems as "Fra Lippo Lippi," "Pictor Ignotus," and "My Last Duchess." In preparing the audience for "My Last Duchess," the reader might say: "The line, 'I repeat, the Count your Master's known munificence is ample warrant that no just pretence of mine for dowry will be disallowed,' reveals how slyly the duke works in his intentions to ask for a large dowry from his prospective father-in-law." Without such an explanation, because of the complicated structure of the line, the audience might miss altogether the significance of this key to the duke's personality.

Removing hostility toward the selection and its author

If the reader himself has prestige with his audience, it may be well for him to clarify his own attitude toward the selection. Perhaps an incident in the life of the reader has made this selection particularly meaningful to him, and a retelling of that incident will also improve the appreciation of the audience for the selection and its author. Or the reader may have chosen the selection because it is unpopular. An audience may have only half-truths about the author and/or the selection. It may be necessary to orient the group properly before it will give the selection an impartial hearing. Although the famous Mississippian William Faulkner won the Nobel Prize for Literature, many persons who are familiar only with his novel *Sanctuary* are prejudiced against his work in general. A wider breadth of knowledge of Faulkner and his works may be necessary before an audience is willing to listen respectfully to the more complicated Faulkner prose.

In concluding the discussion of the introduction, it should be said that there is disagreement as to the mode of presentation of the introductions. Some interpreters memorize their introductory material; others do not. Again, the style of the particular reader should be given consideration. Novice interpreters who memorize introductions are sometimes tempted to seek only enough information to complete their prefatory statement and are therefore at a loss to adapt to their audience. Also, the reader's own prose is almost certain to be inferior to that of the selection itself, and if he memorizes his introductions, he may be interpreted as matching his own prose with that of the outstanding authors of the world. On the other hand, the reader who has memorized his introduction is free to word it carefully and to concentrate on the way it is received by his audience.

Summary

This chapter has dealt with three main issues: the means by which the reader can improve his delivery when practicing by himself, the means by which he can profit most effectively from objective criticism of his delivery, and the way in which he can formulate a satisfactory introduction to his selection.

The student should remember that a book cannot teach an artist how to paint a Rembrandt or a Picasso. This text can do no more than suggest ways in which the reader can strive for effective oral-reading habits. If the reader is able to achieve success in violation of them, neither he nor the authors should be surprised.

Sample introductions

To Eudora Welty's short story "Lily Daw and the Three Ladies"

The beauty that we are given by inheritance is little to be proud of, because we ourselves have little to do with its making. But the beauty that we ourselves create on earth is something else again. We have a right to be proud of it because, without us, it would not have existed.

Eudora Welty is, among other things, an accurate and sympathetic recorder of the beauty of the Mississippi scene. Whatever moralizing she does is so incorporated into her exposition that it is easily digested. Miss Welty has seen and heard more of what went on around her than did most of us who grew up in the same locality. She has the artistry to reproduce it so that its appeal is without the boundaries of a particular region.

The story "Lily Daw and the Three Ladies" makes one observation certainly not original with Miss Welty—that the mentally deficient are often closer to the truth of life than are those of us who are called sane. Lily Daw, a simpleminded girl, has been "taken over" by three of the good ladies of the small town of Victory, Mississippi, who seek her admission to Ellisville, the colloquial name for Mississippi's Institution for the Feeble-Minded.

Although Lily herself has little to say during the story, her few remarks are surprisingly direct in contrast to the machinations of the ladies. Notice the line, "And I have my hat—on," which is difficult to read, even though one can feel the way Lily must have looked as she stopped in the middle of her thought and put her hand up to her head where the two ninety-eight hat proudly sat. That Lily had to give up this jewel for a plain one is an indication of how much Miss Welty feels that convention restrains the carefree and the happy.

Although Victory is an imaginary town, Como, where the xylophone player has gone, is real, with galleries (or balconies) on the stores like the ones seen in the westerns on television. The town of Ellisville, Mississippi, also exists. Its institution, situated on green, expansive lawn, is attractive and inviting.

The respectable widow, Mrs. Watts, the Baptist preacher's wife, Mrs. Carson, and the postmistress, Aimee Slocum, all have counterparts in your own home town. Perhaps the kindly and yet penetrating way in which Miss Welty sees Victory will enable you to enjoy an equally disarming glimpse of your own home environment.

To James Michener's "The Landing on Kuralei"

All of us who slept safely in our beds while the Marines were storming the islands of the South Pacific have something of an obligation to understand what took place there. Perhaps we can recall with pride the status of the Yankees erecting the flag on Iwo Jima. But how much do we know of the less glamorous part of the battles?

James Michener, in his set of essays *Tales of the South Pacific,* which incidentally served as the basis for the famous Broadway musical *South Pacific,* has given us a description of the landing of the Marines on the fictitious island of Kuralei. Michener may have had in mind the island of Kwajalein in the Marshall group which the Marines did capture from the Japanese, but without much opposition.

The storming of these small islands was one of the steps that led directly to the capitulation of Japan. Michener creates a plan formulated by the Americans for capturing the seven Japanese trenches and a strategic block-house on Kuralei. The attack was to begin at 5:27 A.M. and to end at 10:45 A.M., a period of five hours and eighteen minutes. As you will see, it was not until 6:09 P.M. that the attack on the blockhouse even began.

Our action begins after the first Marines had gained a weak foothold on Green Beach at 1544, or 3:44 P.M. As we said before, the first landings had begun very early in the morning. Between that time and the point at which our story begins there had occurred attacks by American planes, softening-up barrages by big American ships, suicide attacks on American ships by Japanese pilots, and an attempt to land American tanks farther up the island. By 3:34 P.M., the Marines were still no farther than the very edge of the coral.

The scene invented by Michener is as follows. Some high cliffs jutted out into the sea at one end of the island. The Americans decided to land on either side of these cliffs and to strike at the rough coral. Beyond the coral, on the Green Beach side, lay nine rows of trees. Beyond the first seven rows, the Japanese had dug slit trenches. On the other side of the coconut trees, in a cacao grove, stood a blockhouse of sod and concrete. Line Albany, the objective for the night, lay on the other side of the blockhouse.

Note the words "banzai boys" and "LCS-108." "Banzai" in Japanese means "forever." As the suicide attacks by the Japanese troops came at the Americans, the Japanese would yell "banzai," meaning that they were willing to give their all for the Emperor. An LCS is a landing-craft supply ship used to land supplies for troops. In this story, the LCS was purposely run up on the beach and wrecked.

To Robert Browning's "My Last Duchess"

A Narrative Introduction

"My Last Duchess" by Robert Browning is a poem about a sixteenth-century duke who is entertaining a representative from a minor count. This representative has been sent to arrange a marriage between the count's daughter and the duke. The duke has been married before and wants to make quite clear beforehand just how his future wife should behave in order to avoid the things that displeased him with his last wife. The last duchess was, among other things, too friendly with persons below the duke's social level and had smiled at others besides the duke. Because of these things, the duke "gave orders," and now is ready to marry again.

You will notice that the duke is a name-dropper, as can be seen when he makes certain that the representative knows that it was Frà Pandolf, a fictitious monk famous for his skill as a painter, who did the portrait of the last duchess and that it was Claus of Innsbruck, a fictitious sculptor, who cast the statue of Neptune which adorns the staircase.

You will also notice that the duke can see beauty only in those things which are culturally artistic. He can see no worth whatsoever in the sunset or in a bough of cherries broken in the orchard. The value which the duke puts on his name is seen not only in the pride with which he mentions it, but also in the fact that he expects a large dowry for marrying the count's daughter.

The passage in which the duke and the envoy leave the upper gallery and return to the guests below can be interpreted in several ways. One interpretation is that the duke's description of how he treated his first wife so alarms the representative that he stands up in horror. The duke, pretending not to notice, merely asks, "Will't please you rise?" He escorts the representative down the stairs. The shocked envoy hurries ahead of him, but the duke calmly puts his hand on the representative's shoulder, saying, "Nay, we'll go together down, Sir." At this point he calls attention to the statue of Neptune taming a seahorse. A more conventional interpretation depicts the duke as inviting the envoy to rise as a sign that the conversation has been concluded. The line "Nay, we'll go together down, Sir" is then interpreted as an act of graciousness on the part of the duke, who permits his inferior to accompany him down the stairs.

The scene of the poem takes place in the upstairs galleries of the duke's palace at Ferrara. The duke and the representative have just been discussing the matter of the duke's marriage when they pass a covered portrait of the last duchess. The duke, who never allows anyone but himself to unveil the portrait, draws the curtain and speaks to the representative.

A Conventional Introduction

The poem "My Last Duchess" is a dramatic monologue. The dramatic monologue is a form of poetry in which the plot, the setting, and the characters are revealed through the voice of one speaker. In this case the speaker is probably Alfonso II, fifth Duke of Ferrara. The poem is "My Last Duchess" by Robert Browning. Browning was one of the major figures in the development of the dramatic monologue as a form of poetry. In Browning's monologues, however, the minor, unspeaking characters play a very important role, as we shall see when we hear the poem. "My Last Duchess" is somewhat unusual in the field of dramatic monologues since it is composed of rhyming couplets rather than the customary blank verse. It illustrates well Browning's method of revealing one of the darker aspects of humanity, which flashes forth in a significant moment. This poem suggests that it is possible to have a highly developed aesthetic sense, but at the same time to have no sense of morality.

"My Last Duchess" was originally published under the title of "Italy" and was a companion poem of one entitled "France," which was renamed "Count Gismond." The purpose of the two poems was to show the difference in the cultures of the two countries, especially concerning the aspects of love and marriage. To accomplish this purpose, Browning went back into the sixteenth-century history of both nations.

Although the duke in the poem is generally thought to be Alfonso II of Ferrara, there have been several other Italian noblemen advanced as the protagonist of the poem. From this it might be assumed that the events described in the poem were not uncommon in sixteenth-century Italy.

When the poem begins, the duke is entertaining a representative from a minor count, who has been sent on some important business by his master. In the beginning we do not know exactly what this business is, but we shall find out before the end of the poem. The representative and the duke have just been discussing this matter while strolling through the spacious upstairs galleries at the palace of Ferrara. These galleries are adorned with the duke's collection of art treasures. The two men pass a covered portrait. The duke stops suddenly and draws the curtain. As the poem begins, the duke is speaking.

Exercises

1. In this chapter we have discussed the importance of voice in oral interpretation, emphasizing the need for the reader to develop all the potentialities of his vocal mechanism. But we have also said that an interpreter should not develop an *affected* or *arty* voice. The first step in any voice-improvement program is for the student to be able to hear his own voice. Make a tape recording of your speech, including both an element of conversation with a friend and a short passage of oral reading, preferably poetry. Play back the recording several times. Write an essay describing your reaction to hearing your own speech. Continue with the exercise, alternating between listening to the tape recording and listening to yourself. A repetition of this exercise will result in *voice objectivity* on your part so that you can hear yourself. Such an achievement will be of great assistance to you in evaluating your oral interpretation, for it will permit you to be your own critic.

2. Read the poem "Stopping by Woods on a Snowy Evening." Note the quality of sound entailed in these phrases:

The only other sound's the sweep
Of easy wind and downy flake.
The woods are lovely, dark and deep. . . .

What opportunities do these and similar words offer the oral reader?

3. Characterization may be achieved in many different ways. Choose a selection from this text which features dialogue. Practice reading it aloud, giving special attention to characterization. Try various methods to achieve characterization, ranging from slight, subtle techniques to the broad, obvious type of character portrayal. How much did you rely on your voice in each characterization? Did you use bodily action and movement to help you in every instance?

4. Choose either "Lily Daw and the Three Ladies" or "The Landing on Kuralei," and inquire as to what actions, movements, or gestures are stated or implied in the story. As the oral interpreter, how will you share the actions, movements, and gestures of the story with your audience?

5. Study any selection in this text until you feel you have understood it fully. Then experiment to see how much of the total experience you can convey to your audience by the use of movement, action, and gesture without the use of voice.

6. Assume that you are going to read one of the following selections:

a. "Dover Beach" by Matthew Arnold
b. "Wild Grapes" by Robert Frost
c. "A Christmas Memory" by Truman Capote

Prepare an introduction for your selection for each of the following audiences:

a. Your class in oral interpretation
b. A local civic club
c. A local literary club
d. A college sorority, fraternity, or club

How can the changes in human behavior produced by oral reading be evaluated?

III

III

The evaluation of the oral reading process

7

In order to improve, an oral interpreter must be aware of his successes and failures. Either he must be observant enough to evaluate himself or he must be fortunate enough and wise enough to be evaluated by others. There is an innate resistance to unfavorable comment and considerable suspicion of favorable comment. Nevertheless, the interpreter must seek constructive criticism.

The evaluation of the communication process of oral reading involves evaluation problems similar to those encountered in measuring any form of communication. However, the difficulties in making evaluations are unique for several reasons.

1. *Objective evaluations* of the degree of response of either the reader or his audience, unless they are carefully planned, may distort the communication process being evaluated. As soon as a reader is told that his reading will be observed and as soon as an audience knows that its reactions will be measured, the dangers of distortion are accelerated. Any awareness of the aesthetic experience tends to destroy the experience itself.

2. *Subjective evaluations* of the degree of response of the reader and his audience are of doubtful accuracy. Readers tend to substitute a wish for a reality, or to depreciate an effective performance and/or to inflate an ineffective performance for compensatory reasons. Audiences who have come to enjoy literature are observed to act similarly to patrons at an art festival who clutch their prestige factors closer than their programs, determined not to be thwarted by poor art into losing what they had expected would be an aesthetic experience.

The following discussion will follow the philosophy that a constant vigilance is needed to improve the means of evaluating oral interpretation. It will attempt to avoid the errors of positivism where exactness is inappropriate and to clarify vagueness where randomly subjective comments on evaluation can be replaced with consistently meaningful philosophies.

The empathic process

A student is reading Michener's "The Landing on Kuralei" to a class in oral interpretation. After his first silent reading of the selection, the student had felt exhausted. He felt as if he had participated in the supreme stress of the invasion. He realized how much of his own energy he had put into the experience of the reading. Now, after considerable additional preparation during which he has become somewhat inured to his original reactions, the student hopes to engender in his audience feelings similar to those he himself had experienced earlier. He also hopes to enhance his own responses to the selection in the process of his reading, but only to the extent that he can improve his audience's response by the acceleration of his own appreciation of the selection.

If the student is successful, he will stimulate his audience to mental and physical responses which will enable it to participate in a new experience. The audience will transpose itself onto an imaginary island, will quicken its heartbeat, will expend energy in increased muscular and neurological tension. It will unconsciously mimic the muscular responses needed to carry the flame-throwing equipment up to the blockhouse. Mentally and physically, the audience will react sympathetically to the student's interpretation of Michener's communication. Such a reaction is termed *empathy*.[1]

The evaluation of oral interpretation can be accurately assessed by an evaluation of the empathy resulting from the oral interpretation. For literature aims to do more than convey information. The transmission of content is important, and the degree to which the information has been transmitted should be known to the interpreter.[2] But emphatic changes are indicative of something more than the transfer of content. They signify the degree to which the reader has himself responded and the degree to which the reader has been able to assist his audience, not just in comprehending, but also in experiencing. Therefore, the discussion here will limit itself largely to the measurement of the two faces of empathy which are involved: the degree to which the reader responds to his selection and the degree to which he can stimulate his audience to respond. The discussions below are meant to apply to both processes even though specific distinctions are not always made.

At least four separate properties of empathy must be recognized before it can be properly evaluated as an instrument of measurement.

The conscious versus the unconscious

Aesthetic empathic responses are largely unconscious responses of the mind and body. With consciousness comes an awareness of our-

---

[1] See Note on Empathy in Appendix C.
[2] Such content can be measured by any of the conventional methods of retention testing.

selves and in general a loss of an aesthetic projection into other persons, places, and things. In salesmanship, in teaching, in preaching, the communicator and his audience may make conscious efforts to transplant themselves. But as soon as an audience realizes that a reader has caused it to react aesthetically, the audience retreats from the empathic response and returns to a concentration on itself.

If a reader who has successfully created empathy exceeds the mark or fails to sustain the mark so that the empathy is replaced with self-centeredness rather than detachment from self, the reader has broken his *aesthetic distance*. Aesthetic distance may be defined as that suspension from self-centeredness which occurs when empathy is operating to a desired degree. The distance therefore refers to the separation that the audience develops between the mechanics of the stimulus and the aesthetics of the stimulus. A reader may break his successfully created aesthetic distance in any number of ways, including any focusing of attention on himself or the mechanics of his reading.

The changing stimulus

Empathy requires adaptation. Muscles and nerves must adjust themselves to a stimulus. Such adjustments result in pleasure. The dancer must respond to his music. If he is to continue achieving pleasure from his responses, the music must change sufficiently to inspire him to react.

The reader must seek variety to keep the muscular and neurological responses of his audience changing. He cannot expect to maintain a given neuromuscular set in his audience for an extended period of time. Relief is necessary. A reader who eliminates all relief from a play he intends to present and offers only the intense passages will find that his audience soon tires and cannot maintain the pace.

Unity

A conflict of interests tends to destroy the empathic response. A harmony of stimuli is necessary for a subject to project himself *out* of his own consciousness and *into* a sphere of detachment. When a conflict of interests occurs, the subject becomes aware of the dissension within himself and transfers his sphere of attention back to himself.

For example, there are few operatic performances where the dance, orchestra, lighting, acting, costumes, scenery, and singing are so united that they all pull together. What an immense task it is for a director of an opera to blend so many different media of communication! Yet unevenness in any one element can spoil the effect of all the others.

Similarly, an oral interpreter must blend his body and his voice with the selection, achieving that degree of unity which will permit his listeners to forget him and the room they are in and the time of day it is in their empathic response to the selection.

Grace

Langfeld says: "The beauty of movement depends on the success of its muscular economy." [3] A graceful movement, therefore, is one which performs a maximum amount of achievement with a minimum amount of energy. Such movements seem pleasing to us because they conserve our energy. When we respond empathically to an awkward or ungainly movement, we experience unconsciously the amount of work it would take to establish ourselves in a position similar to that of the stimulus. Such an expenditure of our psychical energy tires us. However, when we respond empathically to a graceful movement, we experience a sense of pleasure because we recognize what a minimum amount of energy is really necessary to achieve our goal. Instead of being asked to expend more psychical energy than we would like, we are asked to expend less. The result is pleasure.

Let us suppose that a particular member of the class has always felt that Shakespeare was beyond him. The very thought of understanding Shakespeare tires him considerably. Unconsciously, his muscles tighten and his nerves become taut at the very mention of Shakespeare. Then let us suppose that this student hears a reading of Shakespeare which affects him deeply. Without realizing it, he becomes engrossed in the selection, responding to it both mentally and physically. What pleasure this empathy gives him! What he thought was going to require more than he had to give turns out to be within his grasp. The reader gracefully led the class member into expending more energy than the class member had intended, but this energy was so much less than had been anticipated that the result was pleasurable.

A reader who violates the graceful, who works too hard to achieve his effect or does not work hard enough to achieve his effect, will find his empathy suffering. Speech that is too labored or too articulate, bodily movement that is sluggish, an interpretation which reads more into a selection than the author intended—all of these fail to be graceful because they use too little or too much energy and the corresponding response of the audience is unsatisfactory.

Any student who has attended a swimming meet or a track meet grasps this point immediately. He recognizes how pleasing it is to see a swimmer dive gracefully into the water, making a most dif-

[3] Herbert S. Langfeld, *The Aesthetic Attitude*, Harcourt, Brace and Company, Inc., New York, 1920.

ficult movement seem effortless. As a spectator, he was prepared to expend considerable psychical energy to witness such an event. Now he finds his empathic responses pleasing because, although he unconsciously tightens and relaxes his muscles and nerves as the dive progresses, his work is pleasurable because he senses how much he has accomplished in responding to the dive while expending so much less energy than he had originally thought necessary.

Empathy, therefore, is a largely subconscious reaction which is sustained by variety, destroyed by disunity, and pleasurable to the extent that it is provoked by a graceful stimulus. With these factors in mind, let us approach the ways in which a measurement of empathy can help us to evaluate the oral interpretation of literature.

The subjective measurement of empathy [4]

In his book *The Process of Communication,* Berlo proposes four prerequisites for success in projecting ourselves into other people's personalities.[5] The four hypotheses that Berlo develops from his prerequisites will be used as a basis for this discussion of how an oral reader can subjectively evaluate his performance in terms of the empathic responses he creates.

As group size increases, empathic accuracy decreases. The larger the size of the class, the more difficulty the student will have in effecting empathy. The difficulty is caused not so much by the increase in energy required of the reader, for this increase is mechanically rather easy to achieve; the difficulty is rather caused by the heterogeneous quality of the larger audience, making it more difficult to create a common stimulus which will gain a sympathetic response. A small number of unempathized members in a class is sufficient to provide enough disturbance to decrease the ability of other more susceptible members to project themselves into the selection.

Therefore, in evaluating his performance, the reader should keep in mind the following:

First, a student who is reading outside his classroom should be prepared for a proportionate decrease in empathy as the size of the audience increases. Such a decrease is not inevitable. The old saying, "The bigger they come, the harder they fall," is certainly true of audiences. A successful capture of a large audience results in an ac-

---

[4] For a discussion of the objective measurement of empathy, see note in Appendix C.

[5] David K. Berlo, *The Process of Communication,* pp. 134–135. Copyright 1960 by Holt, Rinehart and Winston, Inc., New York. Reprinted by permission of Holt, Rinehart and Winston, Inc.

celeration of the empathic response and gives a reader a sense of the thrill of communication.

Second, the larger the group, the more the reader can interpret minimal movement and noise on the part of the audience as an indication of successfully created empathy. An audience which is projecting itself has become, in a matter of speaking, weightless. It can feel no pain. Therefore, it does not scratch or cough or cross its legs or do any of the other restive movements which are characteristic of groups. To minimize distraction in a large group is indeed a compliment.

Third, the quieter the edges of the group, the greater the empathy. A reader should gain satisfaction from observing that the center of the audience is attentive, but he can be much more proud of concentration by the fringes of the class where the distractions are greater and the pull of the group is less.

Fourth, the larger the group, the more the reader should be prepared for varying degrees of response. If a reader senses that a particular selection has achieved only a minimum amount of empathy from his class, he should not interpret this as a sign that other selections will be received as passively. The dynamics of an audience are highly complex. It is difficult to know why a class responds in one instance and fails to respond in another. If a reader becomes discouraged early in his reading, his discouragement will affect his audience, and the rapport that was to be established later may never materialize.

Fifth, an interpreter should resist the tendency to consider overt audience reactions as the most accurate sign of empathy. Because there is something concrete about a laugh or a sigh, the interpreter tends to covet them as evidences of success. A dedicated, respectful, and energetic silence is as great a compliment as a reader can receive. Overt audience reactions are often the result of successfully aroused empathy, but they are by no means an exclusive measure of success.

When prior communication is minimal, empathic accuracy decreases. A reader should look for increased empathy as the reading progresses. A reader and his audience grow to understand one another. The rapport established leads to an acceleration of empathic responses. An interpreter, therefore, should not expect to establish rapport with his audience from the very beginning. He should be careful to choose his opening lines or his first selection so as to demand less than he intends to require later on. Some readers put humorous passages at the beginning or deliberately choose a humorous selection in order to gain the satisfaction that an overt response will give. Such early laughter again ensures an audience response. Although there is nothing categorically wrong in beginning with humor, there is danger of using it solely to reassure the reader that empathy is possible. Humorous material may not be appropriate, or it may not blend with what is to follow. If so, the reader would do better to evaluate his first appearance before a group by means other than overt audience behavior. He should be satisfied initially with minimal audience responses, contenting himself with the knowledge that the empathic responses will be intensified after he and his audience have grown accustomed to one another.

Just as a skillful playwright delays his more vigorous action until later in the play, so should the reader play his sequence of materials so that he can begin casually, allowing the audience to become accustomed to his voice, to his facial mannerisms, and to its surroundings in general. He should interpret early audience restlessness as normal. After he and his audience have grown used to one another, then they may demand the degree of empathy of one another which can result in vigorous muscular and neurological rapport.

When we are insensitive to the behavior of others, empathic accuracy decreases. In evaluating his reading, the interpreter must evaluate himself. He must know himself frankly and honestly, putting his weaknesses on the table before him and sorting out his strengths into what he hopes is an ever-growing pile. If he can see himself clearly, he has what amounts to a measuring stick for seeing others clearly. For, after all, he *was* the stimulus. He did present the reading. If he can frankly and honestly say that the sense of completeness that he has within him is genuine and without reservation, then he can assume that the stimulus offered was powerful and that the empathic response was likely to be powerful also.

In evaluating his own performance, a reader must ask himself if he was capable of assuming an internal state comparable to the one required in the selection he read. Has he felt deeply enough, dipped deeply enough into experience to deserve an appropriate response? If his answer is no, if he must say that he really does not respond empathically to his own selection, he must be frank in admitting that it is highly unlikely that his audience did either. Not that the reader permits himself to indulge in an unrestrained empathic state during his reading. He responds, but he is more concerned during his reading with securing an appropriate audience response than he is in responding himself. He must know that he has the potential to respond.

It is true that a man may simulate what he has not felt directly. An actress may accurately portray the Medea without having murdered her children. But that actress must understand what it was that made the Medea commit infanticide, or she cannot hope to ask her audience to do the same.

In evaluating his reading, the interpreter must examine his own re-actions impartially, confessing his inadequacies and evaluating his strengths. Without such self-inspection, improvement is impossible.

Second, in evaluating his performance, the reader must evaluate his ability at role playing. He must ask himself the degree to which he is capable of communicating a complex which is something other than himself. If the reader cannot crawl out of himself and approxi-mate, for the moment, someone else, then he may well lack the ability to produce a similar response in others.

It can be argued that we cannot know ourselves until we know others. Without the ability to role play, we can get no perspective on ourselves. Without such a perspective, our keenness in evaluating ourselves is lacking. For example, in reading the Michener tale of the Pacific landings, the reader would need to ask himself to what extent he had actually put himself in the place of the Marine on the beach at Kuralei. Had he heard the explosions of the mortars? Had he smelt the burning flesh of the dead Japanese? Had he gulped in the strange combination of fear and courage that possessed the soldiers on both sides? If he as a reader has not felt this for at least a little while, he can never establish a point from which he can look back at himself and ask what sort of fellow he himself is and how he would have re-acted to the dangers of such a landing. The reader therefore can evaluate his performance in part by the degree to which he has achieved the identification that he is asking his listeners to achieve.

When we are not motivated in the communication situation, em-pathic accuracy decreases. Both the reader and his audience must understand what the rewards are for projecting. Unless both wish to empathize, the phenomenon is difficult to achieve.

In evaluating his reading, the interpreter should ask himself whether his introductory material was sufficiently skillful in motivating the audience to listen. Was sufficient background material given to pique the curiosity of the audience so that it welcomed projecting rather than brushed it aside? If he determines that the motivation was slow in assuming its proper proportions, he may wish to look at his prefatory remarks, revising them so that the audience grasps more fully the consequences of absorbing the material.

The selection itself must be examined to see if its motivating ele-ments are most attractively displayed. Perhaps a more judicious cutting will lead the audience more directly into the emotional drives that underlie the theme. The paraphrasing of certain introductory materials may accelerate the movement and lead the audience and the reader more directly into the impelling drives of the material. Again, the reader must remember that the ear is the audience's sole receptor. Where the eye can speed along, slowing up when motivated to delve more deeply, the ear must obey the rate established by the reader. If the ear becomes bored, it is at the mercy of the interpreter.

The reader must again examine himself to see if he has been motivated. Has the selection been meaningful to him? Does it make a difference to the reader whether or not the idea carries to the group? Does the reader feel his own muscles and nerves responding to the selection?

Summary

The comments above are nothing more than a guide to self-understanding. They are valuable only insofar as the student uses them as signposts to develop a technique for self-evaluation. They are foolish if the student has expected them to tell him just how to measure his performance or if the student rejects them because they are not sufficiently concrete. Just at the first-rate painter may be distinguished from the second-rate painter by the ability of the first-rate painter to know when he is doing good work and when he is doing bad, so is the superior interpreter distinguished from the reader who splits the ears of the groundlings by the ability of the superior interpreter to evaluate his performance. Time and experience may work for or against the development of self-criticism, depending upon whether or not time is helping to develop the necessary detachment. The discussion above has aimed at helping the student to develop that degree of detachment which will result in improved reading skills

How can the oral reader prepare himself to modify audience behavior using specific types as stimuli?

IV

VI

Nonfiction prose

8

The professional paper and the manuscript speech

Some scholars and speechmakers compose an effective manuscript, but do not make any particular preparation to read aloud what they have so painstakingly written. Others are very conscious of their ineptness at reading aloud, but lack the information with which to correct their errors. Since effective oral reading of a professional paper or a manuscript speech employs the same basic principles involved in any type of effective oral reading, it is appropriate to clarify briefly how the techniques of oral interpretation are applicable to the prose of the professional convention and the speaker's rostrum.

Reasons for reading from a manuscript. At times enthusiasts for extemporaneous speaking ask why it is necessary to read a speech or a professional paper. The reasons are several. First, the comments may be of such a nature that their accuracy is imperative. When the President of the United States makes an important policy statement or a physician describes to his colleagues at a medical convention his procedure for performing a new type of surgery, exactness is of prime importance. It does not seem advisable to chance a misstatement or an ambiguous commitment. Second, a more carefully perfected style can result from the development of a manuscript. Some figures of speech may occur to us spontaneously as we deliver an extempore comment, and a crude sort of rhythm may develop. But unless one is unusually gifted, these occur too infrequently or are too crude to achieve an elevated style. Third, professional papers and manuscript speeches are often delivered by persons who are relatively inexperienced in extempore speaking and would hesitate to trust themselves to speaking from an outline. Such persons deserve to be heard, and it seems more plausible to instruct them in proper reading habits than it does to insist that they surrender the security of a manuscript to speak informally.

Naturally, not all manuscripts are effective for oral reading. The professional man or speaker must compose his manuscript so that it can be read effectively. However, it is not the purpose of this chapter to instruct in speech composition. Therefore, we will assume that the manuscript is reasonably suitable for oral reading and concentrate on how the effectively written manuscript may be properly interpreted.

First readings. The preliminary readings of prose manuscripts serve a somewhat different purpose from those of other interpretative situations, for, unless the material has been ghost-written, the reader should be familiar with its content. It is therefore the comprehension of the style and the fixing of the style in the memory that are important in the study of the prose manuscript. Since the *nature of the selection* is a part of the invention of the speech and the *paraphrase* would be highly redundant, our discussion here will concentrate on the preliminary readings of the manuscript and its style, followed by appropriate comments on the delivery techniques involved.

In the initial stages, the reader should approach his manuscript with no intention of perfecting the delivery of a particular passage or of fixing a key phrase in mind. Rather, he should seek a perspective on the material as a whole in the hopes that he will see the composition in its entirety. Although limiting the manuscript will be discussed later on, much cutting may be done during the first readings when the interpreter senses that the over-all tempo is too slow, a particular explanation is too detailed, or a series of figures of speech have exceeded the mark. Readers of manuscripts are more sensitive about cutting their own material than they are the material of others. However, the intelligent reader overcomes his reluctance to admit a mistake. Specific suggestions on how he may cut his manuscript are offered later in the chapter under Limiting the Selection.

A reader should not fear that, just because he makes no special effort to fix particular portions of the manuscript in his mind, he is not making a major step forward in conquering his delivery problems. As in all forms of interpretative reading, the preliminary examinations of the manuscript have a lasting effect, and the words and phrases will begin to make their way inside the reader without any conscious effort on his part.

The style of the manuscript. A reader of a professional paper or a speech must look at his own words and determine what level of idea he is conveying and what mood or tone his emotional content should enjoy. A minister who reads a moderately philosophical sermon as if it were one of the basic tenets of his faith is destroying not only his message but the truly serious concept which he wishes to present in a future sermon. An audience which comes to church expecting to find a sermon manuscript intensely interpreted regardless of the degree of seriousness of the material becomes confused and can no longer distinguish the cry of "Wolf!" from the call for chicken for a church supper. Secretaries who read minutes as if they were Paul Revere and treasurers who present routine financial reports as if the very foundations of the society were at stake have not assessed their material properly. Like all interpreters, the reader of a manuscript must decide upon the proper level of thought which his material deserves and be prepared to respond appropriately.

The mood or tone of his reading must be coordinated with the level of thought he has elected to convey. Readers who are tempted to give witty, impromptu introductions to serious speeches simply because everyone else has been telling jokes are risking a serious error. However, if the composition deals frivolously or facetiously with a theme, the reader must respond appropriately or he may destroy the humor. Audiences are often afraid to laugh or smile unless the reader lets them know by the mood he establishes that such laughing and smiling are acceptable. Many manuscripts which are well written in an ironic style fail when delivered because the reader did not cue his audience appropriately. Similarly, if a manuscript deals earnestly with a serious problem, the reader must accept his responsibilities for establishing an appropriate emotional atmosphere, relinquishing any temptations to dilute his effort toward a major goal with minor triumphs along the way. Moderately serious material must not be overplayed and given an emotional tone that it does not deserve. The reader must assess properly the level of thought he seeks and must imbue that level with the appropriate mood to permit maximum effectiveness.

The imagery, the figures of speech, and the composition of the manuscript are presumably appropriate to its level of idea and intensity of emotion. The imagery of a professional paper or a speech manuscript may have any one of the following characteristics:

1. The imagery may be highly literal, as would be appropriate to a paper at a medical convention or a speech delivered to a gathering of atomic scientists.
2. The imagery may be highly figurative, relying upon metaphors, similes, allusions, personification, and other figures of speech to clarify its concepts. Such a manuscript is atypical.
3. The imagery may be a proper blending of the literal with the figurative so that the reader is required to convey empirical pictures as well as images that can exist only in the imagination.

We have chosen the 1961 inaugural address of President John F. Kennedy to illustrate imagery in a manuscript because it employs both literal and figurative language effectively.[1] Since the theme of an inaugural address aspires to be profound and since the mood aims to be correspondingly dignified, it is not surprising to find that there is almost a symbolic usage of words in the Kennedy address to create a Biblical image which hovers over the speech or that the literal and

---

[1] The concept of diction has been discussed simultaneously with that of imagery.

figurative images compare an abstract concept to a familiar scene which creates a broad and expansive image. The figurative images include a *torch* being passed from generation to generation, the *"ranks of the free,"* the riding on the back of a tiger, the *preying* of hostile powers, and the *engulfing* of humanity, all of which are expansive in nature and require the interpreter to create a feeling of the importance of the theme so that it might be worthy of such breadth of image. The literal images are likewise almost grandiose in nature: The United Nations is compared to a forum; the graves of young Americans surround the globe; the stars, the deserts, disease, and the ocean depths are to be explored. Such references would permit the reader a more extreme variation of voice and bodily movement than less expansive images would encourage.

Therefore, a reader of a manuscript with ideas and moods approaching the seriousness of those of an inaugural address is encouraged to interpret the imagery so that it adds to the breadth of the audience's response. Readers of more commonplace materials, however, should avoid emphasizing or encouraging imagery which is inappropriate to the theme and its tone. For example, the phrase "the ranks of the free" may be delivered in a subdued manner, or it may be delivered expansively, as the interpreter wishes. The words in both instances are the same, but the resulting image is quite different. An interpreter can so deliver the phrase "the master of its own house" so that the image of the extent of the rule is limited or expanded. Naturally, he cannot *control* the thoughts of his audience, but he can direct them sufficiently so that the range of their imagery varies appropriately with the stimuli he offers.

The allusion to Isaiah is carefully worded into the manuscript so that the quotation does not stop the rhythm of the sentence. It is, of course, clumsy to say "quote" and "unquote" before and after such references when an appropriate pause will permit the listeners to isolate the quotation without interrupting the flow of thought.

We observed earlier that there is almost a symbolic use of words to give the entire Kennedy manuscript a Biblical flavor. Such diction is not infrequent in speech manuscripts where the writer has sought an elevation of style. Note the archaic flavor of these phrases:

Holds in his mortal hands
The word go forth from this time and place
The master of its own house
In which its writ may run
Can we forge against these enemies

When a reader finds that his manuscript is in imitation of or holds the flavor of a style which may be familiar to his audience, he must make a decision whether to amplify the similarities or to subdue them. His decision will, of course, depend upon the circumstances surrounding the delivery of the manuscript. Mr. Kennedy's address was preceded by a series of blessings and followed by another. Under such an atmosphere, a reader might be able to emphasize the Biblical style of a manuscript without seeming presumptuous.

Perhaps the most important phase of style to the reader of the manuscript is composition. Awkwardness is seldom effective. Whereas in poetry and the most creative forms of prose, rhythm can be more pointedly created in all but the most auspicious of occasions, the manuscript speech or the professional paper must achieve its rhythm subtly. An ill handling of a subtle rhythm can result in extreme awkwardness and jerkiness so that what might have grace and form becomes a jumbled mass of confusion.

The reader of a manuscript must be aware of the position of the figures of speech in the sentences he is to read. Noun metaphors and all types of similes are more likely to interrupt the rhythm of his reading than are verb and adjectival metaphors. For example, "the hand of mankind's final war" is an obvious figure of speech that calls attention to itself and must be given its proper emphasis, else the audience will be frustrated by its failure to absorb what it senses is an image to be reckoned with. However, the adjectival metaphor "iron tyranny" and the verb metaphor "engulf all humanity" are much less conspicuous and can blend themselves into the general momentum of the selection. Personification in the manuscript speech may break a natural rhythm if it is too obvious because the audience may not be expecting such poetic usage. On the other hand, there are forms of personification which will accelerate rather than break the rhythm. When "allies" are spoken of as "friends" and "history" becomes a final "judge," the momentum is not broken, first, because these uses of personification are familiar and, second, because the imagination is not asked to endow with life objects which are singularly inanimate.

Second, the reader must be aware of the use of all forms of repetition in the manuscript, including anaphora, alliteration, and assonance. A skillfully written manuscript will probably feature repetitions of three and five because, for reasons which we are still investigating, these uneven numbers seem to hold some fascination for the human being. Such series should be noted and a decision made whether to emphasize the series by vocal and bodily support or to subdue the repetition so that the audience does not feel encouraged to respond, but merely responds on its own volition. The content of the selection will, of course, determine such a decision. When Mr. Kennedy says: "*born* in this century, *tempered* by war, *disciplined* by a hard and bitter peace, *proud* of our ancient heritage—and *unwilling* to witness or permit," he has elected to list five adjectives to modify a noun, each adjective being followed by a phrase, four of which are prepositional and the last of which is infinitive. He has not hesitated to use three participles and two simple adjectives in his repetition of five. Because of the dissimilarity of the adjectives themselves and the breaking of the rhythm of the antiphonal prepositional phrases following the fifth adjective, the repetition is not likely to become monotonous and might therefore be somewhat predominantly displayed, with some form of vocal emphasis on each adjective. However, later in the speech, when Mr. Kennedy uses a sequence of five, employing anaphora, in his use of "Let both sides," the device is more obvious and can probably be relied upon to achieve its effect without pointed vocal or bodily support.

When a manuscript speech contains as much repetition as does the Kennedy inaugural, it almost achieves the effect of meter. A reader must exercise the same care in avoiding slighting and overemphasizing such metrical effects in the manuscript. There may also be instances where not only meter but also rhyme is approached. The Kennedy speech includes the following:

Symbolizing an end as well as a beginning
Signifying renewal as well as change
United, there is little we cannot do
Divided, there is little we can do

Again the thoughts and the mood of the selection must determine how much emphasis the reader wishes to give such gestures toward rhyme.

Assonance and alliteration are less likely to appear in a manuscript speech or a professional paper than is anaphora because of their obviously poetic effect. Mr. Kennedy does say "our *f*orebears *f*ought" and "to *f*riend and *f*oe alike," but such mild employment of alliteration is not likely to cause the interpreter any particular difficulty. It is only when he is confronted with more ostentatious and deliberate usages of sound patterns that the reader must make a decision about whether to emphasize or to de-emphasize. For example, the use of *chiasmus*, a form of antithesis "in which the second part is syntactically balanced against the first but with the parts reversed," [2] is showy rhetoric. If not handled properly by the reader, the inversion becomes artificial and the audience rebels, feeling that its drinks are being mixed for it. [3] Mr. Kennedy says:

[2] William F. Thrall and Addison Hibbard, in C. Hugh Holman (ed.), *A Handbook to Literature*, The Odyssey Press, Inc., New York, 1960, p. 820.
[3] Aristotle, *Rhetoric*, Lane Cooper (trans.), D. Appleton-Century Company, Inc., New York, 1932, p. 186.

Let us never negotiate out of fear. But let us never fear to negotiate.

Here "negotiate" and "fear" are balanced in their appearance in the two sentences, but their positions are interchanged, making the phrase a classic example of chiasmus. It is not important that "fear" is a noun in one part and a verb in the second, while "negotiate" is verbal in both. The juxtaposition of the two terms is the rhythmical disturbance that produces the effect. Some writers of manuscripts are often tempted to use the more ostentatious forms of rhythm. William Jennings Bryan liked the feeling of chiasmus and employed it in his "Cross of Gold" speech. An audience which is sympathetic to a reader is likely to respond favorably to such manipulations whereas a hostile audience may feel put upon and handled. Readers may be fooled, therefore, in their audience analysis of the reaction to the more showy forms of rhythm, responding to the feedback of their supporters in such instances, but failing to sense the antagonism of the negative feedback from others.

If it is true that the more rhythmical portions of a manuscript are likely to enhance an emotional effect, a reader should be aware of those passages which require the highest level of concentration on idea so that he may control the rhythm in delivering his more difficult thoughts. He should also be aware of the need for variety in the use of rhythm. The Kennedy speech has its sequences of anaphora carefully spaced with more conventional prose in between so as not to spoil the effect of either.

Summary of style. The reader of a manuscript speech or of a professional paper must be more than usually attentive to keep the stylistic usages subservient to the thought and the mood of the material. The degree to which he should permit the mood to dominate the thought and the thought to dominate the mood depends upon his intent. Professional papers usually stress thought, although some of the ones which are best received are those that make a subtle use of emotion. Scientific and scholarly audiences enjoy the thrill of mood and tone as much as others, provided they feel that the idea of the material has predominated. A manuscript speech may allow a dominance of idea or a dominance of emotion. The reader is warned against an extreme of either, for he should remember that an idea without emotion is static, while emotion without idea may be frantic.

Limiting the selection. We have already pointed out that the situation of cutting is unique in the professional paper or the manuscript speech because the reader is working with his own material. We are more reluctant to delete what we ourselves have created.

Therefore, the reader must be aware of his hesitancy to cut, even where needed, and must continually remind himself that not all of his words are destined for posterity and that he should prefer to read an effective presentation of limited material rather than an ineffective presentation of lengthy material. Consider the following:

Have we held to a minimum side issues which may be our particular hobbies or interests, but which are not essential to the theme of the material?
Have we arranged our manuscript so that the rhythmical passages afford variety to the less rhythmical passages?
Have we deleted the particular words and phrases which are our *pets* of the moment, such as "in which we live," "we see that," or "consequently"?
Have we retained a sufficient amount of descriptive material without going too much into detail?
Is illustrative (or inductive) material in proper proportion to generalizations (the enthymeme), or is our manuscript so crowded with apothegms that we will exhaust our readers at an early stage?

The old adage that "no souls are saved after the first twenty minutes" should perhaps be written as a heading on all paper on which manuscripts are typed. A judicious cutting can turn a mediocre composition into a satisfactory presentation, whereas a timid cutting can relegate to obscurity what might otherwise be forceful thinking.

Practicing the delivery of the manuscript. The first readings of the material should provide the reader with a perspective on his work which, it is hoped, he will not lose during his subsequent study. His final readings will permit him to add a more intensive study with deliberate attempts to plan his presentation.

The reader should take the proper precautions to ensure that his volume is sufficient. If he is to read from a speaker's stand, he must remember that, when his head is pointed down, his voice is also directed down. If possible, he should adjust his speaker's stand so that he can look up from his manuscript with a minimum amount of head movement and still not seem awkward. If the stand is not adjustable, he may even consider holding his manuscript in his hand at an appropriate level so that his voice has its maximum opportunity to project itself. An audience would prefer to see the manuscript and hear it also, rather than not see it and not hear it either. The reader should not hesitate to memorize certain key phrases so that he is certain he can project them with the emphasis they deserve, looking forcefully at his audience as he does so.

The reader should time his manuscript at more than one reading, remembering that he may go faster when he is by himself because he need not consider audience feedback or that he may go slower when he is by himself because he is not as excited as he may be during the final delivery. Both abnormalities can result in an improper advance timing. The reader should consider whether he is diminishing his tempo during the more complicated passages of his reading, whether he has allowed for pauses to achieve the four functions of the pause pointed out in Chapter 6, and whether his tempo makes appropriate use of the rhythm of the manuscript. He may even wish to underline the instances of anaphora that he wishes to emphasize, to remind himself to achieve a more stylized rhythm at such points in his reading.

The pitch of his voice should not be any more monotonous than should his volume or his tempo. Some readers of manuscripts are more sensitive to variations in pitch than to the other elements of voice, fearing that pitch variation may be interpreted as dramatization of what should be expository material. There is, of course, this danger, but there is also the danger of sounding unresponsive by droning on and on with the same pitch pattern. The reader should remember that such an unimaginative reading will also provoke an objectional emotional response in his audience of boredom and ennui, which is as serious a deterrent to his success as would be the unfavorable emotional reaction to what the audience considered a nonscientific approach.

The voice quality of the reader of the manuscript is less under his control than the other elements of voice. He should require himself to keep his resonance under continual vigilance so that it gains an overall effectiveness, rather than an adjustment for a particular occasion.

The reader of the speech or the professional paper must remember that, like all interpreters, he reads with his whole being and not just with his vocal folds and articulators. His whole body should resonate to his words. He should be particularly observant of his muscular tonus during his preparatory readings to see if it is appropriate to his purpose. A limp, unresponsive body cannot help but deter from a forceful message. The gestures of the reader will probably be limited, but they should not necessarily be absent, particularly during passages which the reader has memorized or wherein his script is less critical so that he may vary from it without fear. His eye contact is, however, his chief means of physical support. Although it should not call attention to itself, it should reinforce the ideas and moods appropriately. If an audience feels that it is being looked at purposely, it may respond negatively; if an audience feels that it is not being looked at purposely, it may feel neglected. The ideal situation results if an audience cannot remember what the ratio of eyes up and eyes down has been for a particular occasion. Although there are pitfalls in looking up too much, there are more frequent pitfalls in staring bleakly down at a manuscript. A reader whose head seems to be going up and down too much, as if he were watching a strangely inverted ping-pong match, is equally distracting.

Reading his manuscript to a second party should give the speaker or scholar an objective concept of the status of his eye contact. It will also be of material use to him in all of the phases of vocal reinforcement and should take place, if possible, in the room in which the material is to be delivered. The tape recorder, although a poor substitute for a second party in some ways, is more effective for preparation in that a reader is more likely to face up to his errors if he corrects himself. We sometimes rebel against the unfavorable comments of others, but respond well to self-criticism.

The introduction.   Some readers of manuscripts preface their delivery with extemporaneous or impromptu comments. Although there is nothing wrong per se with such remarks, they are usually more harmful than good, for two reasons: first, they are seldom in keeping with the mood of what follows, and second, they are often apologetic for the manuscript as if the reader was saying that he wished he could speak informally the entire time but that he supposed he had better get around to the manuscript. Unless such off-the-cuff comments are appropriate, they should be avoided. The manuscript should be permitted to speak for itself, without a distracting interlude and without regret.

A summation.   There is a distinct place and a firm need for the manuscript speech and professional paper to be *read* to appropriate audiences, provided the manuscript is effectively composed and the reading is effectively done. The ineptness of many manuscript readers should not discourage effective interpreters from pursuing such a form of delivery. The three reasons offered in this chapter as to why manuscript reading is necessary require no defense. Readers who pursue the directions offered in this chapter should be secure in that their objectives are sound and their goal obtainable. The skills that are basic to the interpretation of other forms of literature are basic to reading the manuscript speech and the professional paper. Proper study will result in satisfactory results.

Exercises

The following exercises refer to the two speeches reprinted below.

1.   Make an analysis of the speech on fluoridation as if you had written it, discussing the several components of style, the limiting of the se-

lection, and the use of vocal and bodily support you would give to the manuscript.

2. Practice reading the Kennedy inaugural address giving full emphasis to its rhythmical effects. Then practice reading the same address giving a minimal emphasis to the rhythmical effects. Avoid exaggerating in either instance so that the readings become ineffective. Be prepared to read portions of the manuscript in class, first stressing rhythm and then subduing it.

3. Make a list of the figures of speech in the Kennedy inaugural, grouping each figure under its appropriate classification.

4. Consider how you would deliver the quoted material in the speech on fluoridation. What vocal and bodily support would you offer during the quoted material that you might not offer in the passages that we assume you have written?

5. If you were to follow the suggestion of memorizing certain sentences in a manuscript so that you were free to give them special emphasis, what sentences in the inaugural address would you choose? What sentences in the speech on fluoridation would you choose? Be prepared, of course, to defend your decision.

The inaugural address of President John F. Kennedy [4]

Vice President Johnson, Mr. Speaker, Mr. Chief Justice, President Eisenhower, Vice President Nixon, President Truman, Reverend Clergy, fellow citizens:

We observe today not a victory of party but a celebration of freedom—symbolizing an end as well as a beginning—signifying renewal as well as change. For I have sworn before you and Almighty God the same solemn oath our forebears prescribed nearly a century and three-quarters ago.

The world is very different now. For man holds in his mortal hands the power to abolish all forms of human poverty and all forms of human life. And yet the same revolutionary beliefs for which our forebears fought are still at issue around the globe—the belief that the rights of man come not from the generosity of the state but from the hand of God.

We dare not forget today that we are the heirs of that first revolution. Let the word go forth from this time and place, to friend and foe alike, that the torch has been passed to a new generation of Americans—born in this century, tempered by war, disciplined by a hard and bitter peace, proud of our ancient heritage—and unwilling to witness or permit the slow undoing of those human rights to which this nation has always been committed, and to which we are committed today at home and around the world.

Let every nation know, whether it wishes us well or ill, that we shall

---

[4] Delivered Jan. 20, 1961. The version is that of the *New York Times* of Jan. 21, 1961, with some deletions, reparagraphing, and modifications in punctuation as reported in *Public Papers of the Presidents of the United States, John F. Kennedy*, U.S. Government Printing Office, 1962, pp. 1–3. Copyright by the New York Times. Reprinted by permission.

pay any price, bear any burden, meet any hardship, support any friend, oppose any foe to assure the survival and the success of liberty.

This much we pledge—and more.

To those old allies whose cultural and spiritual origins we share, we pledge the loyalty of faithful friends. United, there is little we cannot do in a host of new cooperative ventures. Divided, there is little we can do —for we dare not meet a powerful challenge at odds and split asunder.

To those new states whom we welcome to the ranks of the free, we pledge our word that one form of colonial control shall not have passed away merely to be replaced by a far more iron tyranny, We shall not always expect to find them supporting our view. But we shall always hope to find them strongly supporting their own freedom—and to remember that, in the past, those who foolishly sought power by riding the back of the tiger ended up inside.

To those people in the huts and villages of half the globe struggling to break the bonds of mass misery, we pledge our best efforts to help them help themselves, for whatever period is required—not because the communists may be doing it, not because we seek their votes, but because it is right. If a free society cannot help the many who are poor, it cannot save the few who are rich.

To our sister republics south of our border, we offer a special pledge— to convert our good words into good deeds—in a new alliance for progress —to assist free men and free governments in casting off the chains of poverty. But this peaceful revolution of hope cannot become the prey of hostile powers. Let all our neighbors know that we shall join with them to oppose aggression or subversion anywhere in the Americas. And let every other power know that this Hemisphere intends to remain the master of its own house.

To that world assembly of sovereign states, the United Nations, our last best hope in an age where the instruments of war have far outpaced the instruments of peace, we renew our pledge of support—to prevent it from becoming merely a forum for invective—to strengthen its shield of the new and the weak—and to enlarge the area in which its writ may run.

Finally, to those nations who would make themselves our adversary, we offer not a pledge but a request: that both sides begin anew the quest for peace, before the dark powers of destruction unleashed by science engulf all humanity in planned or accidental self-destruction.

We dare not tempt them with weakness. For only when our arms are sufficient beyond doubt can we be certain beyond doubt that they will never be employed.

But neither can two great and powerful groups of nations take comfort from our present course—both sides overburdened by the cost of modern weapons, both rightly alarmed by the steady spread of the deadly atom, yet both racing to alter that uncertain balance of terror that stays the hand of mankind's final war.

So let us begin anew—remembering on both sides that civility is not a sign of weakness, and sincerity is always subject to proof. Let us never negotiate out of fear. But let us never fear to negotiate.

Let both sides explore what problems unite us instead of belaboring those problems which divide us.

Let both sides, for the first time, formulate serious and precise proposals for the inspection and control of arms—and bring the absolute power to destroy other nations under the absolute control of all nations.

Let both sides seek to invoke the wonders of science instead of its terrors. Together let us explore the stars, conquer the deserts, eradicate disease, tap the ocean depths and encourage the arts and commerce.

Let both sides unite to heed in all corners of the earth, the command of Isaiah—to "undo the heavy burdens . . . (and) let the oppressed go free."

And if a beach-head of cooperation may push back the jungles of suspicion, let both sides join in creating a new endeavor—not a new balance of power, but a new world of law, where the strong are just and the weak secure and the peace preserved.

All this will not be finished in the first 100 days. Nor will it be finished in the first 1,000 days, not in the life of this Administration, nor even perhaps in our lifetime on this planet. But let us begin.

In your hands, my fellow citizens, more than mine, will rest the final success or failure of our course. Since this country was founded, each generation of Americans has been summoned to give testimony to its national loyalty. The graves of young Americans who answered the call to service surround the globe.

Now the trumpet summons us again—not as a call to bear arms, though arms we need—not as a call to battle, though embattled we are—but a call to bear the burden of a long twilight struggle, year in and year out, "rejoicing in hope, patient in tribulation"—a struggle against the common enemies of man: tyranny, poverty, disease and war itself.

Can we forge against these enemies a grand and global alliance, North and South, East and West, that can assure a more fruitful life for all mankind? Will you join in that historic effort?

In the long history of the world, only a few generations have been granted the role of defending freedom in its hour of maximum danger. I do not shrink from this responsibility—I welcome it. I do not believe that any of us would exchange places with any other people or any other generation. The energy, the faith, the devotion which we bring to this endeavor will light our country and all who serve it—and the glow from that fire can truly light the world.

And so, my fellow Americans: ask not what your country can do for you—ask what you can do for your country.

My fellow citizens of the world: ask not what America will do for you, but what together we can do for the freedom of man.

Finally, whether you are citizens of America or citizens of the world, ask of us here the same high standards of strength and sacrifice which we ask of you. With a good conscience our only sure reward, with history the final judge of our deeds, let us go forth to lead the land we love, asking His blessing and His help, but knowing that here on earth God's work must truly be our own.

Should fluoride be added to the public water supply? [5]

Good morning, gentlemen. This morning I would like to discuss briefly whether or not fluoride should be added to the public water supply.

I suppose the first thing we should do is to agree exactly on what we mean when we speak of fluoridation. If a compound of fluorine is administered to the teeth in the proper proportions, there is much evidence to prove that the teeth become harder than they were and thus more resistant to tooth decay. What I am discussing today is whether or not a fluorine compound should be added to the *public water supply* in order to prevent tooth decay. I wish to make it clear that I am not discussing the rights of individuals to add fluorine to their own water or to administer fluoride to their teeth in any manner whatsoever. I am concerned here with governmental action affecting the public supply of drinking water.

Many people think that every enlightened person is in favor of adding fluorides to the public water supply. This is definitely not the case. There are many qualified men in the fields of medicine, politics, and education who are definitely opposed to such action. In general, their opposition falls into two major divisions. Some informed persons oppose fluoridation for *medical* reasons; others oppose it for *political* reasons.

To give me some direct insight into this question, I interviewed several prominent physicians in Columbus, Ohio, in October of this year. Each of them gave me a statement of his position which I have now before me, and I will use these statements to support the arguments offered against fluoridating the public water supply.

Let us first discuss the medical aspects. To locate material on this phase of the problem, I talked to Dr. Jonathan Forman, a practicing physician of Columbus, professor emeritus of medical history at The Ohio State University and national chairman of the Committee for the Evaluation of Fluoridation. He stated his position as follows:

> Our Committee has published the following statement: (1) Positive proof of the safety of fluoridation is required and none has been offered; (2) the so-called therapeutic concentration of fluorides arbitrarily established at one part per million in drinking water is within the poison range; (3) dental fluorosis, the first obvious symptom of chronic fluoride poisoning in children, is an inevitable result of fluoridation. The evidence reveals that large numbers may be so afflicted with varying degrees of damage.

Dr. Forman went on to make some more points against fluoridation. He feels the person himself should be the one to decide if he wishes to risk fluoride poisoning. In his opinion, fluoridation of the public water supply is mass medication, and he feels that the function of the public water authority

[5] Abridged and edited from an unpublished manuscript prepared by Brian Jakes and Blaine Hollimon, Ohio University, 1962. Quotations from Dr. Jonathan Forman and Dr. Joseph Hughes reproduced with their permission.

is to provide us with safe, pure water and not to turn water into a vehicle for drugs.

Dr. Forman closed his remarks with a comment on the role and efficiency of fluorides in the prevention of tooth decay:

> The role and efficiency of fluorides in dental caries reduction is a matter of active controversy. Whatever the outcome, there are less hazardous and more efficient ways of obtaining such benefits as the fluorides may offer than putting it in the public water supply.
>
> And I want to add now, not speaking as an official, but as an individual, that this is the first time in the history of medicine that a drug has been offered on the basis of the percentage in the bottle, and not on a dose regulated to the size, age, and sex of the individual who will consume it. But the proponents of fluoridation say, "Drink all you want of this water, and whatever your thirst dictates will be the correct dose for you."

Next I talked to Dr. Joseph Hughes, with whom I discussed the political aspects of the problem. Dr. Hughes, a family physician, was on the board of directors of the recent anti-Communist school held in Columbus. The first question I asked Dr. Hughes was, "Do you think it is the duty of the public authority to provide pure water?" His answer follows:

> It is my contention that it is most emphatically such a duty, namely, to provide pure water to the public rather than to permit the public water supply to become a vehicle for introducing medication into people.

Some persons try to compare the chlorination of water to the fluoridation of water. Dr. Hughes differentiates the two in this manner:

> Chlorine is introduced into water to destroy pathogenic bacteria, that is, to destroy disease-producing germs. The longer the water stands after this process has taken place, the less chlorine will be present. This is due to the fact that chlorine is volatile and evaporates on standing.... On the contrary, the fluoride is not volatile and remains constant after it has been introduced. Consequently, there can be no logical comparison between chlorination and fluoridation of the public water supply. They are two separate and distinct processes—separate and distinct with reference to their differing intentions in that a chlorination is designed to treat the water (to make it potable) and fluoridation is designed to treat the patient or the person.

I then asked him, "If this is the case, is there anything that can be done to take advantage of the principle of fluoridation without using the public water supply?" He answered me with this suggestion:

> It is unwise for the public authority to rush in to perform a function which is not clearly in the public interest, particularly when the fluorides can be introduced into the bodies of those children whose parents desire it if such parents would purchase the fluorides at the drugstore and

would do it themselves. This method permits those who desire it to do so, and it does not force this medication on people against their wishes.

Dr. Hughes summarized his position with this statement:

If we are to train and raise a nation of people who are self-sustaining and self-sufficient rather than dependent, then we must never let the government do for the people what the people can do for themselves. If the people do not or will not fluoridate their own children's water supply, so be it. Such is their choice; and their right to choose, whether wisely or unwisely exercised, is their inalienable right.

In summary, then, from my point of view, it seems that political wisdom dictates against the fluoridation of the public water supply.

In this brief time I have tried to explain to you why I am personally opposed to the fluoridation of the water supply. Now do not misunderstand. I would like to see a way found to guarantee better teeth for you and for me. I wish a way could be found to stop dental problems for everyone for all time. But from my point of view, to turn to the forced fluoridation of the public water is a mistake. Even if it were possible to prove that there are no bad effects from fluorine consumed over an extended period of time, and I hasten to add that research is not yet available to prove such a proposition, I would still oppose adding fluorides to the public water. I do not wish to see the public water used for mass medication. All of us here should be capable of selecting our own medicines. Let us be certain we do not let anyone take that right away from us.

The essay, the diary, and the journal

The authors of the essay, the diary, and the journal seldom compose with any presentiment that their material may be read orally. The interpreter must therefore raise two questions:

Is the essay or diary or journal I am considering suitable for oral reading? If it is suitable, have I taken the necessary steps to overcome a predisposition to silent reading?

A student should be encouraged to conclude that certain materials are not suitable for oral reading, just as he should be encouraged to recognize that some literature is more suitable for oral reading than for silent reading. For example, although a reader should pause long before trying to read aloud Arthur Eddington's essay "The Domain of Physical Science," [6] he should approach much more confidently Eddington's lecture "Man's Place in the Universe." [7] Although both

[6] Arthur S. Eddington, "The Domain of Physical Science," in Joseph Needham (ed.), *Science, Religion and Reality*, George Braziller, Inc., New York, 1955, pp. 193–222.

[7] Arthur S. Eddington, "Man's Place in the Universe," *The Nature of the Physical World*, The Macmillan Company, New York, 1933, pp. 163–178.

are scientific, the style of the latter lends itself much more to oral presentation. Educational television will be making more and more demands on readers to present scientific and cultural materials to an ever-widening adult audience. Readers should train themselves to edit and to offer in an attractive format essays, diaries, and journals which otherwise might remain unknown to a vast audience. However, interpreters must be equally vigilant in rejecting materials which should be read silently for adequate comprehension. Otherwise, they discourage the adult audience and hinder the progress of the contribution of oral reading to adult education.

Once the decision has been made to explore the possibilities of a given essay, diary, or journal, the reader must give critical attention to certain aspects of the preparation of his selection. These aspects, already discussed in general terms in Chapter 5, will be amplified here, and then comments on the analysis of an essay will attempt to crystalize the discussion.

First reading

All literature which is worthwhile improves with association. This point has already been made. But repeated association with the essay, the diary, and the journal is particularly important. These forms, when swallowed whole, seem to enjoy a long digestive process, adding their fuel to the blood slowly. A reader who attempts to interpret for others a diary which he himself has just finished may be disappointed in the result. The assimilation process is far from complete. He is likely to find that the ideas he thought he understood at his first reading are more profound than he had contemplated and, what is even more disturbing, that concepts emerge which he had failed to find in his initial reading. The ideal situation exists when a student can live with an essay for several weeks and then put it away for some time before he reads it aloud to others. Since at times this approach may be impractical, the student may return to essays that he has studied previously. There is nothing more pleasing to a student than to find new meaning and vigor in material which he thought he had mastered. The sensation undoubtedly stems from the exhilaration the student receives upon realizing that his education has improved his powers of perception.

The nature of the selection

The *who* of the essay, the diary, and the journal is usually easy to analyze, but the *what* is more difficult to determine. What is Thoreau saying in *Walden?* Is there a *what* to Dorothy Wordsworth's *The Grasmere Journal?* Can an essay which is as complex as Emerson's "Self-

Reliance" be confined to *a* theme, or should it be permitted to expand itself into a variety of avenues of thought?

There are, of course, no shortcuts to determining the central idea of any selection. But there are several methods which are helpful in approaching the essay, the diary, and the journal. First, the reader should see if the author himself has stated specifically *what* he aimed to say. Thoreau crystallizes his theme several times in his Walden journal. For example, in the essay "Where I Lived, and What I Lived For" Thoreau says:

I went to the woods because I wished to live deliberately, to front only the essential facts of life, and see if I could not learn what it had to teach, and not, when I came to die, discover that I had not lived.[8]

The *what* of *Walden,* therefore, must be a search for deliberate living. Second, the reader should investigate to see if a commentary on the work will clarify the *what.* In her preface to *The Journals of Dorothy Wordsworth,* Helen Darbishire says:

To meet Dorothy Wordsworth we have only to open her journal and enter her world. It is the world which is the world of all of us, the world of man and nature, *her part of it, as she saw it.*[9]

The *what* of Dorothy Wordsworth's journals is therefore the *what* of her world as she saw it, subjectively, yes, but truly drawn. The oral reader can seldom hope to spend as much time with the journals as Miss Darbishire has. Therefore, he is grateful to her for guidance in the interpretation of their spirit. Last, the reader may have to be content with less than a focused purpose of his selection even though he has searched diligently for the core of its thought. It is better for him to conclude on a temporary *what* or to suspend his judgment than it is to reach a false conclusion in haste. False conclusions develop attitudes which are difficult to correct. Moreover, the selection may not have one central idea. Emerson's essay on "Self-Reliance," despite its title, is so profound that it can be said to have many purposes. The often heard quotation "A foolish consistency is the hobgoblin of little minds, adored by little statesmen and philosophers and divines" could be a *what* in itself.

The *to whom* and the *where* are less complex in reading the essay,

---

[8] Henry D. Thoreau, *Walden,* Edwin W. Teale (ed.), Dodd, Mead & Company, Inc., New York, 1946, p. 90. Teale concurs on the purpose of this quotation. See Thoreau, *op. cit.,* p. xiii.

[9] Dorothy Wordsworth, *The Journals of Dorothy Wordsworth,* Helen Darbishire (ed.), Oxford University Press, New York, 1958, p. x.

the diary, or the journal. The reader should consider his audience to see if the selection has purpose for his listeners. However, he should not err by being too orthodox in his tastes. Some students reject all but obviously student-oriented subjects as inappropriate for the college classroom. A reader should not fear to ask his audience to look up, for our reach should exceed our grasp. Henry Thoreau, Dorothy Wordsworth, and Ralph Waldo Emerson all wrote for the college student of today as much as for anyone else.

The *where* is usually pointed out specifically in the diary or journal. It may be relatively unimportant for the essay, but a lack of cause and effect relationship should not be dismissed without research. For example, it strengthens the courage of Emerson's words in his essay on "Self-Reliance" if the reader and his audience know that this work was composed during a period when Emerson had been excluded from most of the pulpits in the New England area and was forced to support his family by the meager income from his books and by his lecturing.

The style of the selection

There is little that is unique in establishing the level of conception and the emotions, mood, and tone of an essay, diary, or journal. The essay may strive for ideas of considerable consequence, as does Emerson in "Self-Reliance," or it may be content with a frivolous or facetious commentary on society, as is James Thurber in many of his essays. The mood is often reflective, particularly with the diary and journal. To meet the contemplative mood, the reader must establish a thought-provoking or a meditating or a homely atmosphere without any obvious efforts to do so. Some guidance in this respect will be offered in the subsequent discussion on delivery.

The imagery, the figures of speech and the composition of these three forms of literature may present no unusual problems to the reader. He should keep in mind, however, that certain figures of speech and elements of composition may add materially to the rhythm. Emerson says: "Trust thyself: every heart vibrates to that iron string." The pithiness of this sentence is largely due to its use of metonymy and metaphor. Notice how much different the rhythm is when the figures of speech are absent: "Trust thyself: every being relies on the strength of its own soul." Anaphora, alliteration, and assonance may not be and perhaps should not be as prominent in these forms as they are in poetry, but their presence does much to establish the *heard rhythm* discussed in Chapter 11. Even the terse style of Thoreau permits an occasional use of anaphora: "Instead of three meals a day, if it be necessary eat but one; instead of a hundred dishes, five; and reduce other things in proportion." Note that Thoreau deliberately breaks his rhythmical sequence at two, and the reader, who is expecting the third "instead of," is jostled back into the attitude of concentration that Thoreau demands. A lesser writer would have been content with completing his anaphoric trilogy. The incomplete sentence in the diary and journal may require the reader to assume a rhythm that emphasizes a "lame beat." Dorothy Wordsworth generally begins her daily notations with an incomplete sentence about the weather. After awhile, the reader begins to look forward to the initial phrase, finding it a refreshing interlude among the complete sentences. Furthermore, the reader should not be surprised to find meter and even rhyme in a format which connotes prose. What elements of poetry does the following Emerson quotation have?

A foolish consistency is the hobgoblin of little minds, adored by little statesmen and philosophers and divines.

The paraphrase. While the paraphrase can be of considerable merit in preparing to read the essay, it varies in its effectiveness as an implement for understanding the journal. The paraphrase is, of course, a clumsy device. It is always unsatisfactory to the reader because he senses his inability to re-create in his words what the author has already said so well. But his very frustration is helpful in enabling the reader to see where he has understood the author and where he has not.

A paraphrase of Emerson's essay on "Self-Reliance" is no little task, but the exercise is instructive. A paraphrase of one of the many essays in Thoreau's *Walden* would be less arduous, but might require more words than the original Thoreau because of the economy of style of the New England naturalist. However, a paraphrase of Dorothy Wordsworth's *The Grasmere Journal* would seem purposeless, for what could one say about the phrase, "Since he has left me at half-past 11 (it is now 2), I have been putting the drawers into order, laid by his clothes which we had thrown here and there and everywhere, filed two months' newspapers and got my dinner, 2 boiled eggs and 2 apple tarts." [10] There would, however, be purpose in forming a chronology of the journals, with a distribution of the dates covered and a record of the places visited.

Therefore, the paraphrase, like all methods of instruction, can be applied with success only where it belongs. In certain instances, it may be used with annoying effectiveness; in others, it may be omitted without hesitation; in still others, it should be amended to adapt itself to the particular materials at hand.

[10] Dorothy Wordsworth, *op. cit.*, p. 126.

Limiting the selection

Literature which was mainly written to be read silently requires careful cutting for oral presentation. The concentration with which Emerson attacks us in his essay "Self-Reliance," may not be so fatiguing in a silent reading where we may put the book down for a moment to get our breath or where we may allow ourselves to skip over some passages until something particularly appeals to us. But the audience for the oral reader must take all that comes its way, and fatigue from the intensity of the essay would be inevitable. For such pithy material, three suggestions are offered:

1. The reader should be content with presenting a minimal amount of material effectively. He will have to be satisfied with less than he would like to read in order that the parts he chooses may be favorably received.
2. The reader should be careful not to eliminate all the examples which the essayist gives, in preference to more premises or statements of philosophy. The examples will permit the audience some relaxation and allow for an absorption of the kernel of thought before another profound idea is offered for consideration. Emerson's illustrations are infrequent, but they should be given preference over new ideas.
3. The reader may wish to pause between major thoughts of an essay to speak informally with the class or the family group about what he has just read or is about to read. Such pauses will permit reflection and allow the audience to get its wind before more stimulating thoughts are offered. The mind works very similar to a muscle which, if permitted to relax for just a moment after hard labor, will resume its ability to function.

Of course, the humorous essay will not require such vigilance and may be read with only the standard precautions for cutting.

The diary and journal present somewhat different problems. Since most keepers of diaries are only speaking to themselves, they may record many personal items which are of interest only to the scholar. Yet it is difficult to make generalizations as to just what should be deleted. Audiences often enjoy the personal bits in a journal, as when Dorothy Wordsworth announces that she baked bread that morning. The following suggestions may be applicable in a limited number of situations:

1. It may be possible to choose a theme from a journal and pursue it, bridging the gaps with summaries of what transpires in between. In Thoreau's *Walden*, a reader might choose the theme of wild life, unusual characters, or comments on fashion; in Dorothy Wordsworth's

journals, the themes of the Wordsworths' association with Coleridge or Dorothy's relationship with William Wordsworth's wife, Mary, offer interesting possibilities.

2. It may be possible to choose a particular sequence in a journal which has historical import or which has a strong personal-interest element. Dorothy Wordsworth's entry of July 27, 1802, has features of historical and personal interest, for not only does Dorothy describe the English countryside as it appeared to her at the beginning of the nineteenth century, but she also reports on the relationship of the Wordsworths to William's natural daughter in France.

The interpreter should remember that diaries and journals are likely to contain many minor plots in the form of the introduction of the names of persons. Such nonessential references should be deleted when possible. Paranthetical thoughts are also frequent in these forms because the authors are free to wander where they will. The elimination of these nonessentials will do much to keep the audience oriented to the more important themes or the central idea which the reader has selected to present.

Voice and bodily movement

When material of an intimate nature is being read, such as a diary or journal, or when the subject matter is complex, as with the essay, the reader may be required to establish that type of rapport which virtually excludes the reader from the conscious consideration of his listeners. A maximum amount of empathy would be established if the members of the class assume for the moment that they could have written the diary, since it seems such a part of what they believe. In such a situation, anything which calls attention to the reader would be resented by his listeners, for the reader represents a second part which was not present when the diary was written. If the members of the class cannot be expected to achieve such a high degree of detachment from self, they may be expected to create an image of Thoreau or Dorothy Wordsworth, living and writing the journal. Although this image will undoubtedly be different for each member of the class, still none of the images will include the figure of an oral interpreter.

Therefore, the reader should consider patterning his delivery to achieve inconspicuousness. For some readers this may mean minimal direct eye contact and conservative vocal variety and bodily movement; for others it may mean adopting a new attitude or concept of reading, such as sitting at a desk or a table or, in a very informal situation, arranging the chairs so that the reader does not face his listeners, as he might well not do in front of a fireplace on a winter evening. Again other readers may be able to achieve the desired detachment without modifying their approach to any appreciable extent. The trial and error method is the only way a reader has to test his success.

The more complex the subject matter, the more easily fatigued the audience may become. Ordinarily, the humorous essay should not tire, unless the demands for laughter are too frequent, resulting from poor material or injudicious cutting. But the serious essay may not wear well, unless the reader is aware of possible audience fatigue and has planned *beforehand* and reacts *during* his reading to combat it. The difficulty seems to be that the very devices which tend to relieve fatigue—variety of voice and bodily movement—also tend to distract an audience which is bent on intellectual concentration. It is for this very reason that many people shy away from reading the more complex of essays aloud, for they feel that the concentration necessary to comprehend an essay such as Emerson's "Self-Reliance" can only be achieved in silent meditation. The relief of fatigue, therefore, must come from elements which support a high level of thought. The reader may consider the following suggestions or add others for his consideration:

1. A tempo which is slower than usual may be helpful. The swiftness of motion of the thought in Emerson's essay on "Self-Reliance" is breathtaking in itself, and the reader may not need to hurry his words along. Students can experiment with reading the Emerson essay at different tempos to gain some concept of how fast the ideas come and how much thought it takes to absorb them.
2. A reader may seek those elements of volume, pitch, and quality which are energetic and yet restful. Any erring toward apathy on the one side or overenthusiasm on the other is likely to be distracting. The general attitude of the reader may be: *There is considerable mental effort to be expended here, but we will approach the opportunity with deliberate speed.*

The introduction. The essay, the diary and the journal propose unique problems in forming an introduction, the most important of which is that the introduction may not be just a preface but may continue from time to time in the reading to keep the audience oriented. Since there will be less emphasis on suspense and plot and more emphasis on thought and continuity, the reader may feel more free to interrupt his reading from time to time to stress a particular point or to establish a transition which the author may have passed over hurriedly. Such a proposal works contrary to the advice previously given that the reader must not call attention to himself. Such are the vagaries of an art. For harmony, the reader must achieve a combination of ingredients which, if mixed in the proper proportion, turns into something palatable, but which, if blended improperly, makes all seem tasteless. The breaks and skips in a diary must often be bridged by personal remarks by the interpreter, and the complex thoughts of some essays may require interpolation by the reader to orient his audience. If such comments are not considered by the audience as interruptions, but rather as smooth contributions to the spirit of the reading, then the reader has achieved the harmony he sought.

There are other items which must be given particular attention in introducing the essay, the diary, and the journal. The reader must decide how much of the *who* saying *what, to whom* and *where* belongs in the introduction. The *who* and the *where* are critical to the diary, whereas the *what* is most important in the essay. Take the phrase from Emerson: "Your goodness must have some edge to it, else it is none." This challenging thought comes in "Self-Reliance" just after Emerson has dismissed the hypocritical abolitionist. What does it mean? It is sufficiently profound so that an audience cannot hope to absorb its meaning completely with one exposure. Naturally, the oral reader hopes that he will encourage his listeners to return to the essay and read it again and again. Nevertheless, he hopes to make as great an impression on his listeners as he can during his reading. If he introduces this phrase in his introduction and prepares his audience for its appearance, it may be received with considerably more understanding than if it came as a surprise.

The introduction to the diary and journal should provide an entrée to the several characters and places that the audience will meet. The *who's* and the *where's* of the material should not be left to chance, unless they are highly familiar. For example, although a reader might expect his audience to be familiar with Coleridge as he appears in Dorothy Wordsworth's journals, he cannot expect the same of the references to Clarkson or Christopher or the Lloyds. Constant reference to places with which the audience is unfamiliar can be annoying. The River Thames, Dover, and Canterbury need no explanation, but Dorothy Wordsworth's references to the City and Charing Cross would establish themselves better in the images of the audience if they were clarified in the introduction.

Summary. There is, of course, much more that can be said about reading aloud the essay, the diary, and the journal. Furthermore, specific attention needs to be given to the letter even though much that applies to the journal and diary also applies to it. The reader should keep in mind that, with these forms of literature, he is probably reading aloud something which was largely intended for silent reading. His efforts to gain rapport with his audience must always be tempered with the knowledge that the listeners are seeking a detachment with which he, the reader, must not interfere. The proper blending of intrusion and exclusion will vary from reader to reader, but the two contrasting forces must achieve for each interpreter their proper balance for maximum effectiveness.

Comments on the analysis of an essay

A cutting of Emerson's essay on "Self-Reliance" [11]

I read the other day some verses written by an eminent painter which were original and not conventional. The soul always hears an admonition in such lines, let the subject be what it may. . . . To believe your own thought, to believe that what is true for you in your private heart is true for all men —that is genius. Speak your latent conviction, and it shall be the universal sense; for the inmost in due time becomes the outmost. . . . Familiar as the voice of the mind is to each, the highest merit we ascribe to Moses, Plato, and Milton is that they set at naught books and traditions and spoke not what men, but what *they* thought. A man should learn to detect and watch that gleam of light which flashes across his mind from within more than the luster of the firmament of bards and sages. Yet he dismisses without notice his thought, because it is his. In every work of genius we recognize our own rejected thoughts; they come back to us with a certain alienated majesty. Great works of art have no more affecting lesson for us than this. They teach us to abide by our spontaneous impression with good-humored inflexibility. . . . Else tomorrow a stranger will say with masterly good sense precisely what we have thought and felt all the time, and we shall be forced to take with shame our own opinion from another. . . .

Trust thyself: every heart vibrates to that iron string. Accept the place the Divine Providence has found for you, the society of your contemporaries, the connection of events. Great men have always done so, and confided themselves childlike to the genius of their age. . . . And we are now men and must accept in the highest mind the same transcendent destiny; and not minors and invalids in a protected corner, not cowards fleeing before a revolution, but guides, redeemers, and benefactors, obeying the Almighty effort and advancing on Chaos and the Dark. . . .

Whoso would be a man must be a nonconformist. He who would gather immortal palms must not be hindered by the name of goodness, but must explore if it be goodness. Nothing is at last sacred but the integrity of your own mind. Absolve you to yourself, and you shall have the suffrage of the world. **I remember an answer which when quite young I was prompted to make to a valued adviser who was wont to importune me with the dear old doctrines of the church. On my saying, "What have I to do with the sacredness of traditions, if I live wholly from within?" my friend suggested, "But these impulses may be from below, not from above." I replied, "They do not seem to me to be such; but if I am the Devil's child, I will live then from**

[11] Certain passages are marked for possible deletion. Others are simply noted with ellipses. The judiciousness of the cutting may be determined by comparing it with any unabridged edition of the essay.

the Devil." [Illustration retained for variety] . . . I am ashamed to think how easily we capitulate to badges and names, to large societies and dead institutions. Every decent and well-spoken individual affects and sways me more than is right. I ought to go upright and vital, and speak the rude truth in all ways. If malice and vanity wear the coat of philanthropy, shall that pass?

If an angry bigot assumes this bountiful cause of Abolition and comes to me with his last news from Barbados, why should I not say to him, "Go love thy infant; love thy wood-chopper; be good-natured and modest; have that grace; and never varnish your hard, uncharitable ambition with this incredible tenderness for black folk a thousand miles off. Thy love afar is spite at home." Rough and graceless would be such greeting, but truth is handsomer than the affectation of love. Your goodness must have some edge to it, else it is none. . . . [Conversational element retained for variety]

The objection to conforming to usages that have become dead to you is that it scatters your force. It loses your time and blurs the impression of your character. If you maintain a dead church, contribute to a dead Bible society, vote with a great party either for the government or against it, spread your table like base housekeepers—under all these screens I have difficulty to detect the precise man you are; and, of course, so much force is withdrawn from your proper life. But do your work, and I shall know you. Do your work, and you shall reinforce yourself. . . .

For nonconformity the world whips you with its displeasure. And therefore a man must know how to estimate a sour face. . . .

The other terror [Transitional clue retained] that scares us from self-trust is our consistency; a reverence for our past act or word because the eyes of others have no other data for computing our orbit than our past acts, and we are loth to disappoint them. . . .

A foolish consistency is the hobgoblin of little minds, adored by little statesmen and philosophers and divines. With consistency a great soul has simply nothing to do. He may as well concern himself with his shadow on the wall. Speak what you think now in hard words and tomorrow speak what tomorrow thinks in hard words again, though it contradict everything you said today.—"Ah, so you shall be sure to be misunderstood."—Is it so bad then to be misunderstood? Pythagoras was misunderstood, and Socrates, and Jesus, and Luther, and Copernicus, and Galileo, and Newton, and every pure and wise spirit that ever took flesh. To be great is to be misunderstood. . . . [Conversational element retained for variety]

[A transition by the reader possible here]

So use all that is called Fortune. Most men gamble with her and gain all and lose all as her wheel rolls. But do thou leave as unlawful these winnings and deal with Cause and Effect, the chancellors of God. In the Will work and acquire, and thou hast chained the wheel of Chance and shall sit hereafter out of fear from her rotations. A political victory, a rise of rents, the recovery of your sick or the return of your absent friend, or some other favorable event raises your spirits, and you think good days are preparing for you. Do not believe it. Nothing can bring you peace but yourself. Nothing can bring you peace but the triumph of principles.

The first readings of the essay

The most important thing that will strike most readers in their first exposures to the essay is its power. So much of the material is *quotable* and has been so often quoted that the interpreter may even be overwhelmed at the task ahead of him. However, the reader must recall that his interpretation of the *what* of the selection can only be as meaningful as the selection itself and that therefore the more powerful the selection, the more powerful his interpretation can be.

During the first readings of the essay, the interpreter may wish to do any of the following:

1. Underline phrases which strike him on the first reading since these may also be the phrases which will have a similar effect on his audience.
2. Encircle the proper names and common nouns with which he is not familiar.
3. Draw brackets around the more relaxing or narrative portions of the essay so that he will not be tempted to cut all of these later on, after he has become more familiar with the selection and perhaps less able to sense its variety in pacing.
4. Read the essay out loud to himself, letting himself hear the words and asking himself what is the significance of such phrases as "With consistency a great soul has simply nothing to do."

The first readings of a complex essay should be strenuous affairs. The student should remember that his later studies, despite their value, will not afford the fresh perspective on the material that come with the first readings and that, therefore, he should not fail to take full advantage of his first impressions.

The nature of the selection. The *who* of the essay is, of course, Emerson. In the interpreter's study of the areas related to the selection, he would have become acquainted with the personal incidents in Emerson's life which make his essay particularly meaningful. Therefore, no detailed comment on Emerson himself will be included here. The *to whom* is everyone, for Emerson is not speaking to any audience in particular but to all audiences. Furthermore, the *where* is relatively unimportant. The conversation could be held anywhere, at any time.

But the *what* requires considerable effort. The whole philosophy of transcendentalism [12] is embodied in this essay. Therefore, it is fool-

---

[12] "... any philosophy, as that of Ralph Waldo Emerson, which asserts the primacy of the spiritual and superindividual as against the material and empirical." By permission. From *Webster's New Collegiate Dictionary*, p. 902. Copyright

hardy to say that an analyst can summarize in a few paragraphs just what Emerson has said. But if he understands the difficulties involved, the analyst can profit from an attempt to draw together what he thinks are some of the things that Emerson is saying. The comments below are, of course, limited to the parts of the essay reproduced in this volume.

Emerson says "Trust thyself: every heart vibrates to that iron string." If there is any one sentence which summarizes the *what* of the essay, this may be it. Emerson is asking his readers to search for the truth and cautions them not to be hindered by a label of goodness, but to see if the label fits the contents. He warns that such a truth seeker who finds what he is seeking within himself will face problems, among which are an inability to prove that he is right (his impulses, Emerson admits, might have come from the Devil), an ever-increasing pressure from his fellows to conform ("For nonconformity the world whips you with its displeasure"), and a fear of being inconsistent and thus losing his own security ("A foolish consistency is the hobgoblin of little minds"). In the end Emerson advises that, although we may look to fortune to save us, we can only save ourselves by obeying the urge to the truth that is within us.

The style of the selection. There can be little doubt about the quality of the thought which Emerson is expressing. He is dealing with the fundamental creed by which man operates. Furthermore, he is approaching his theme (or themes) with considerable fervor and vehemence. Emerson is altogether in earnest. He is not dealing with the petty emotions of jealousy and anger, but the basic emotions of what to fear and what to love. Fear self-betrayal, he says, and love the truth. There is some use of sarcasm, in his imaginary conversations with "a valued adviser," with the abolitionist, and even with the man who reminds us that we shall surely be misunderstood. But the basic tone is one of forthright exposition of the basic problems of the world. The mood is not frivolous or facetious, but earnest and sincere.

One gets the general impression that there are few images in the essay and that the figures of speech are minimal. Such an impression attests to the skill of the author in making his images and figures such an integral part of the selection that they successfully escape notice. For although much of the language is literal, there is no shortage of imagery or figurative language. Man is cautioned to detect the gleam of light which flashes across his mind; he sees the world whip the nonconformist; he gets the vision of the hobgoblins which torture the little minds. Moreover, although the details are few, Emerson gives

1961 by G. & C. Merriam Co., Publishers of the Merriam-Webster Dictionaries, Springfield, Mass.

us the pictures of his conversations with the valued adviser and the abolitionist. Both of these situations are common enough in most men's lives to call to mind memories of similar occasions in which they have participated.

The metaphors far outnumber the similes, and since the comparative words of the simile, such as "like" or "as," call attention to the figure, their absence in Emerson's metaphors permits an inconspicuous use of figurative language. Thoughts have a "majesty"; a heart "vibrates" and it vibrates like an "iron string"; malice and vanity "wear" a "coat of philanthropy." Many of the metaphors are verb metaphors, which are the least conspicuous of all of their kind, and one adjective metaphor, "hard words," is particularly effective. The infrequent similes, such as "like base housekeepers," seem almost too obvious, when compared with the strength of the less showy metaphors. There is an occasional but important use of personification, e.g., "advancing on Chaos and the Dark," and the use of "dead" in "dead institutions" and "usages that have become dead to you."

Images and figures of speech are most effective when they are unobtrusive. One of the outstanding characteristics of Emerson's essay is that his more dramatic elements are submerged successfully in the intensity of his thought and the vehemence of his emotion.

The predominant rhythmical elements in the essay lie in what Chapter 11 refers to as *heard rhythm*. Some would say that the style is flowing; others would say that the sentences go smoothly; still others would express their feeling of the rhythm by saying that the essay *reads well*. To subject such an essay to some of the newer research methods in content analysis would be stimulating. In the absence of such findings, we shall make some subjective comments concerning the elements of heard rhythm in the essay:

1. The topic sentences of paragraphs tend to be of a given length and are often more pithy and terse than what follows. A rhythm is established which forces a slower tempo at the beginning of a paragraph and allows a *slide* until the next paragraph begins.
2. There is an occasional short sentence which breaks the rhythm and adds an element of syncopation.
3. A variety of sentence structure pervades the entire essay. When this variety is broken, the relief is intentional to inject a use of anaphora or to achieve some other rhythmical effect.

There is what appears to be intentional avoidance of the more ostentatious forms of stylized rhythm, such as assonance, alliteration, and onomatopoeia. A diligent search does reveal a few. The "rude truth" is an isolated example of assonance, but the phrase must have been common enough in Emerson's time to allow it to escape notice.

The words "whips" and "sways" are onomatopoetic. The instances of alliteration are limited to such borderline examples as "a great soul has simply nothing to do." There may be a strong poetic element in Emerson's essay, but it is basic and not peripheral.

The author's choice of words is interesting. The vocabulary is not complex or populated with unfamiliar terms, but again, it is not too simple. Both the tumid and the frigid are avoided. The essay is commonly found in high school textbooks, and it seems a wise choice because it offers a sufficient challenge in vocabulary, e.g., "eminent," "manifest," "philanthropy," and "transcendent," without inundating the student with new terms. The several allusions, which might have been discussed under figures of speech, are also provocative. Emerson's citation of the contributions of Moses, Plato, Milton, Socrates, Pythagoras, Jesus, Luther, Copernicus, Galileo, and Newton to upbraid us for our weaknesses is striking. When Emerson turns to the analogy, he uses the homely comparison of reaping the benefits of life by reaping corn, the Biblical antecedents of which are readily apparent.

In summary, Emerson's essay on "Self-Reliance" deserves the place in literature that it has maintained for so long because it fares well on all of the several aspects of style.

A sample paraphrase. Man has within him, in his "private heart," truth, and he is obligated to allow this truth to come out. If he keeps silent when he knows the truth, he shall suffer the chagrin of being superseded in the truth by others. Great works of art help him to understand this principle because they provoke him to express himself, and he is often reluctant to do so.

The very dignity of man requires us to trust our inmost thoughts. This has always been the element of greatness and results in progress. But such an attitude requires nonconformity, because one's inmost thoughts are not always acceptable to society. However, they must be obeyed, even as Emerson obeyed them. Such nonconformity requires rudeness, because the truth is often rude. We must gird ourselves to ward off the conventional aspects of charity when no charity is really intended. A man cannot be really good, unless he makes some harsh decisions on what he wishes to evaluate as goodness.

Abiding by custom absorbs us and keeps us from the truth. Let men know what you stand for and you have nothing to fear.

But there are penalties for such action. First, the nonconformist is persecuted and must be willing to stand persecution. Moreover, we like to conform to ourselves and are loath to depart from our past acts because such departures make us feel insecure. However, we cannot let base consistency rule us. The world is based on change, and we must change with it. If we are persecuted for doing so, we must re-member that the great figures of the past bear us company.

We may rely on Fortune to help us out, but Fortune is fickle. Only inner tranquility resulting from doing what we know we must do will bring us peace.

Exercises

The following exercises refer to the four selections reprinted below.

1. Write a study of the related areas as outlined in Chapter 5 for any one of the selections given below.
2. Write an analysis of any one of the selections given below, using the divisions of Chapter 5 as your main headings.
3. Discuss how you might further limit any one of the selections below. When appropriate, label your deletions as parenthetical thought, descriptive passage, or minor plot.
4. Describe the approach you might use in *introducing* any one of the selections below. Then write an appropriate introduction. If transitory or clarifying comments are to be made internally, give them also, and show where they would occur and why they might be appropriate.

From *The Grasmere Journal* (1802)

Dorothy Wordsworth [13]

July 27th, Tuesday. Market day. Streets dirty, very rainy, did not leave Hull till 4 o'clock, and left Barton at about six; rained all the way almost. A beautiful village at the foot of a hill with trees. A gentleman's house converted into a Lady's Boarding school. We had a woman in bad health in the coach, and took in a Lady and her daughter—supped at Lincoln, Duck and peas, and cream cheese—paid 2/-. We left Lincoln on Wednesday morning, 28th July, at six o'clock. It rained heavily, and we could see nothing but the antientry of some of the Buildings as we passed along. The night before, however, we had seen enough to make us regret this. . . .

On Thursday morning, 29th, we arrived in London. Wm. left me at the Inn. I went to bed, etc. etc. After various troubles and disasters, we left London on Saturday morning at ½-past 5 or 6, the 31st of July. (I have forgot which.) We mounted the Dover Coach at Charing Cross. It was a beautiful morning. The City, St. Paul's, with the river and a multitude of little Boats, made a most beautiful sight as we crossed Westminster Bridge. The houses were not overhung by their cloud of smoke, and they were spread out endlessly, yet the sun shone so brightly, with such a fierce light,

---

[13] Dorothy Wordsworth, *op. cit.*, pp. 193–197. The journey was made so that Wordsworth could spend some time with his natural daughter, Annette, who was the offspring of a liaison Wordsworth had contracted during his stay in France at the time of the French Revolution.

that there was even something like the purity of one of nature's own grand spectacles.

We rode on chearfully, now with the Paris Diligence before us, now behind. We walked up the steep hills, beautiful prospects everywhere, till we even reached Dover. At first the rich, populous, wide-spreading, woody country about London, then the River Thames, ships sailing, chalk cliffs, trees, little villages. Afterwards Canterbury, situated on a plain, rich and woody, but the City and Cathedral disappointed me. Hop grounds on each side of the road some miles from Canterbury. . . . It was a bad hop year. A woman on the top of the coach said to me, "It is a sad thing for the poor people, for the hop-gathering is the women's harvest. . . ."

We saw the castle of Dover, and the sea beyond, 4 or 5 miles before we reached D. . . . It was near dark when we reached Dover. We were told that the packet was about to sail, so we went down to the Custom-house in half-an-hour—had our luggage examined, etc. etc. . . . We arrived at Calais at 4 o'clock on Sunday morning, the 1st of August. We stayed in the vessel till ½-past 7, then Wm. went for letters, at about ½-past 8 or 9 we found out Annette and C. chez Madame Avril dans la Rue de la Tête d'or. We lodged opposite two Ladies, in tolerably decent-sized rooms, but badly furnished and with large store of bad smells and dirt in the yard, and all about. The weather was very hot. We walked by the seashore almost every evening with Annette and Caroline. . . . It was a pretty sight to see, as we walked upon the sands when the tide was low, perhaps a hundred people bathing about a quarter of a mile distant from us, and we had delightful walks after the heat of the day was passed away—seeing far off in the west the Coast of England like a cloud crested with Dover Castle. . . .

On Sunday, the 29th of August, we left Calais at twelve o'clock in the morning, and landed at Dover at one on Monday the 30th.

From *Walden*

Henry David Thoreau [14]

As with our colleges, so with a hundred "modern improvements;" there is an illusion about them; there is not always a positive advance. The devil goes on exacting compound interest to the last for his early share and numerous succeeding investments in them. Our inventions are wont to be pretty toys, which distract our attention from serious things. They are but improved means to an unimproved end, an end which it was already but too easy to arrive at; as railroads lead to Boston or New York. We are in great haste to construct a magnetic telegraph from Maine to Texas; but Maine and Texas, it may be, have nothing important to communicate. Either is in such a predicament as the man who was earnest to be introduced to a distinguished deaf woman, but when he was presented, and one end of her ear trumpet was put into his hand, had nothing to say. As if the main object were to talk fast and not to talk sensibly. We are eager to tunnel under the Atlantic and bring the Old World some weeks nearer to

[14] Henry D. Thoreau, "Economy," *Walden,* Edwin W. Teale (ed.), Dodd, Mead & Company, Inc., New York, 1946, pp. 53–54.

the New; but perchance the first news that will leak through into the broad, flapping American ear will be that Princess Adelaide has the whooping cough. After all, the man whose horse trots a mile in a minute does not carry the most important messages; he is not an evangelist, nor does he come round eating locusts and wild honey. . . .

One says to me, "I wonder that you do not lay up money; you love to travel; you might take the cars and go to Fitchburg to-day and see the country." But I am wiser than that. I have learned that the swiftest traveller is he that goes afoot. I say to my friend, Suppose we try who will get there first. The distance is thirty miles; the fare ninety cents. That is almost a day's wages. I remember when wages were sixty cents a day for laborers on this very road. Well, I start now on foot, and get there before night; I have travelled at that rate by the week together. You will in the meanwhile have earned your fare, and arrive there some time to-morrow, or possibly this evening, if you are lucky enough to get a job in season. Instead of going to Fitchburg, you will be working here the greater part of the day. And so, if the railroad reached round the world, I think that I should keep ahead of you; and as for seeing the country and getting experience of that kind, I should have to cut your acquaintance altogether.

From *Gentlemen Prefer Blondes*

Anita Loos [15]

March 16th:

A gentleman friend and I were dining at the Ritz last evening and he said that if I took a pencil and a paper and put down all of my thoughts it would make a book. This almost made me smile as what it would really make would be a whole row of encyclopediacs. I mean I seem to be thinking practically all of the time. I mean it is my favorite recreation and sometimes I sit for hours and do not seem to do anything else but think. So this gentleman said a girl with brains ought to do something else with them besides think. And he said he ought to know brains when he sees them, because he is in the senate and he spends quite a great deal of time in Washington, d.c., and when he comes into contract with brains he always notices it. So it might have all blown over but this morning he sent me a book. And so when my maid brought it to me, I said to her, "Well, Lulu, here is another book and we have not read half the ones we have got yet." But when I opened it and saw that it was all a blank I remembered what my gentleman acquaintance said, and so then I realized that it was a diary. So here I am writing a book instead of reading one.

But now it is the 16th of March and of course it is to late to begin with January, but it does not matter as my gentleman friend, Mr. Eisman, was in town practically all of January and February, and when he is in town one day seems to be practically the same as the next day.

I mean Mr. Eisman is in the wholesale button profession in Chicago and he is the gentleman who is known practically all over Chicago as Gus

[15] Anita Loos, *Gentlemen Prefer Blondes*, Boni & Liveright, New York, 1925, pp. 11–14. By permission of Liveright, Publishers, New York. Copyright © R-1953, by Anita Loos Emerson.

Eisman the Button King. And he is the gentleman who is interested in educating me, so of course he is always coming down to New York to see how my brains have improved since the last time. But when Mr. Eisman is in New York we always seem to do the same thing and if I wrote down one day in my diary, all I would have to do would be to put quotation marks for all the other days. I mean we always seem to have dinner at the Colony and see a show and go to the Trocadero and then Mr. Eisman shows me to my apartment. So of course when a gentleman is interested in educating a girl, he likes to stay and talk about the topics of the day until quite late, so I am quite fatigued the next day and I do not really get up until it is time to dress for dinner at the Colony.

It would be strange if I turn out to be an authoress. I mean at my home near Little Rock, Arkansas, my family all wanted me to do something about my music. Because all of my friends said I had talent and they all kept after me and kept after me about practising. But some way I never seemed to care so much about practising. I mean I simply could not sit for hours and hours at a time practising just for the sake of a career. So one day I got quite tempermental and threw the old mandolin clear across the room and I have really never touched it since. But writing is different because you do not have to learn or practice and it is more tempermental because practising seems to take all the temperment out of me. So now I really almost have to smile because I have just noticed that I have written clear across two pages onto March 18th, so this will do for today and tomorrow. And it just shows how tempermental I am when I get started.

From *The Letters of Charles Lamb* [16]

8. *To S. T. Coleridge*

[P.M. *27th September 1796*]

My dearest friend—White or some of my friends or the public papers by this time may have informed you of the terrible calamities that have fallen on our family. I will only give you the outlines. My poor dear dearest sister in a fit of insanity has been the death of her own mother. I was at hand only time enough to snatch the knife out of her grasp. She is at present in a mad house, from whence I fear she must be moved to an hospital. God has preserved to me my senses,—I eat and drink and sleep, and have my judgment I believe very sound. My poor father was slightly wounded, and I am left to take care of him and my aunt. . . . Write,—as religious a letter as possible—but no mention of what is gone and done with—with me the former things are passed away, and I have something more to do that [than] to feel—
God almighty

have us all in
his keeping.—

C. Lamb

---

[16] *The Letters of Charles Lamb*—arranged by Guy Pocock from the complete edition edited by E. V. Lucas, Everyman's Library Edition and Guy Pocock, E. V. Lucas, E. P. Dutton & Co., Inc., New York, 1950, vol. 1, pp. 29–36.

9. *To S. T. Coleridge*

[P.M. *3rd October 1796*]

My dearest friend, your letter was an inestimable treasure to me. It will be a comfort to you, I know, to know that our prospects are somewhat brighter. My poor dear dearest sister, the unhappy and unconscious instrument of the Almighty's judgments to our house, is restored to her senses; to a dreadful sense and recollection of what has past, awful to her mind, and impressive (as it must be to the end of life) but temper'd with religious resignation, and the reasonings of a sound judgment, which in this early stage knows how to distinguish between a deed committed in a transient fit of frenzy, and the terrible guilt of a Mother's murther. [sic] I have seen her. I found her this morning calm and serene, far very very far from an indecent forgetful serenity; she has a most affectionate and tender concern for what has happened.... I allow much to other favorable circumstances. I felt that I had something else to do than to regret; on that first evening my Aunt was lying insensible, to all appearance like one dying,—my father, with his poor forehead plaisterd over from a wound he had received from a daughter dearly loved by him, and who loved him no less dearly,—my mother a dead and murder'd corpse in the next room—yet was I wonderful supported. I closed not my eyes in sleep that night, but lay without terrors and without despair. I have lost no sleep since.... One little incident may serve to make you understand my way of managing my mind. Within a day or 2 after the fatal ONE, we drest for dinner a tongue, which we had had salted for some weeks in the house. As I sat down a feeling like remorse struck me,—this tongue poor Mary got for me, and can I partake of it now, when she is far away—a thought occurd [sic] and relieved me,—if I give in to this way of feeling, there is not a chair, a room, an object in our rooms, that will not awaken the keenest griefs, I must rise above such weaknesses....

The Lady at this mad house assures me that I may dismiss immediately both Doctor and apothecary, retaining occasionally an opening draught or so for a while, and there is a less expensive establishment in her house, where she will only not have a room and nurse to herself for £50 or guineas a year.... You know by economy how much more, even, I shall be able to spare for her comforts....

Lamb

Coleridge, continue to write; but do not for ever offend me by talking of sending me cash. Sincerely, and on my soul, we do not want it....

10. *To S. T. Coleridge*

[P.M. *17th October 1796*]

... Mary continues serene and chearful,—I have not by me a little letter she wrote to me, for, tho' I see her almost every day yet we delight to write to one another (for we can scarce see each other but in company with some of the people of the house), I have not the letter by me but will quote from memory what she wrote in it. "I have had no bad terrifying dreams. At midnight when I happen to awake, the nurse sleeping by the side of me, with the noise of the poor mad people around me, I have no fear. The spirit of my mother seems to descend, and smile upon me, and bid me live to enjoy the life and reason which the Almighty has given me— I shall see her again in heaven; she will then understand me better. . . ." . . . At present short letters suit my state of mind best. So take my kindest wishes for your comfort and establishment in life, and for Sara's welfare and comforts with you. God love you; God love us all—

C. Lamb

Prose fiction[1]

9

Poetry and prose fiction have many common elements. The compactness of the emotional quality in poetry is so striking that, to some, prose in contrast seems unemotional. However, such stories as "The Necklace" by Guy de Maupassant or "The Lottery" by Shirley Jackson demonstrate clearly that prose may be intense in mood and tone. It is true that prose does not follow a regular pattern of rhythm to establish emotion as does poetry. The rhythms of prose are seldom based upon so apparent an element as meter or rhyme. But prose may make use of all of the other devices of style to communicate its mood and tone. Further discussion of the differences between poetry and prose will be found in Chapter 11.

Fiction as a semblance of reality

Fiction, perhaps more than any other literary form, comes to us resembling everyday experience. In fiction we see people in certain places, engaging in what appear to be plausible human experiences. As we listen to these people and observe their actions, we begin to think of them as having actual existences. But there is a vast difference between reality and the illusion of reality. Behind each fictional composition there is an artist, the author, who has created in language and in literary form the illusion of a real experience. The artist finds his subjects for fiction in life, but he selects the ones he will treat and puts them in form and order, known as structure. Therefore, when we speak of structure, we do not mean something separate and apart from the author's idea, but rather the conveyance into which the idea is put to achieve the significance the author intends. Structure is not a mechanical device. It involves a vital and functional relationship between idea and the other factors joined by the structure.

The style of prose fiction

The author's style reveals his meaning, for fiction, like other literary forms, is the resultant of the author's idea, his emotional approach to-

[1] A reexamination of the suggestions offered in Chap. 5 is suggested.

ward that idea, his imagery, his diction, and his structure. It is by manipulating these elements that he tells his story.

We are familiar with the old axiom that style makes the man. The statement is also true of authors. Naturally, style reflects the author's personality, for it is the tone of his voice. Style places the writer's indelible stamp on his topic. It is the composition itself and is therefore the means by which we come to understand why the selection ever came into being.

Manner of writing is not to be confused with *mannerism in writing*. Mannerisms are imitated fragments of another's style and therefore may be artificial. The manner of writing is genuine and individual. It does not become so decorative or so trite that it destroys the idea. The reader should know when style tends to become affected, pompous, wordy, or in any other way inferior. When the reader recognizes poor style, he should become suspicious of the quality of his subject matter. Good style will give the semblance of contemporary speech or, when the situation demands, will retain the flavor of the period, adding richness and color not found in contemporary language.

The reader will expect the author to observe decorum in his use of language. Characters will speak in language that is appropriate and true to their surroundings. The choice of words used in descriptive or narrative elements will be in keeping with the object or events described. Appropriateness and decorum are key words for good style.

With this perspective of fiction style in mind, the interpreter must consider in detail the particular problems presented in reading aloud the short story or the novel. Certain of these problems are discussed in the paragraphs below.

The theme in fiction. Fiction revolves around a central idea, known as a *theme*. The theme of the story should not be confused with the *topic*. The theme is the result of what the author makes of his topic. It is what a writer sees in a story, the underlying concept that he wishes to convey. Sometimes the theme is confused with the information that the story contains. A reader of Ernest Hemingway's novel *The Old Man and the Sea* receives valuable information on the catching and reeling in of a big fish, but such items of content are not the theme of the story.

In Chapter 5, attention was called to Shirley Jackson's story "The Lottery." The plot of this story is simple, and we are given little detail about the characters. Nevertheless, the story makes a strong impact by the disconcerting idea it presents. Miss Jackson has been careful not to focus the meaning of her story on typical situations that are likely to parallel the experiences of her readers. On the contrary, she prefers to choose a situation which is far removed from our daily experiences to deal with the psychological aspects involved when people seize a scapegoat to release their own feelings. As we read such fiction, we search to see how the theme unfolds, for we must make it meaningful to us. We may have to ponder or to rearrange some of our previous concepts, making concessions in our own thinking as we proceed. We must be prepared to recognize, if not to accept, the kind of character presented and the type of situation created. In order for these results to be achieved, we must come to grasp the unity and coherence of the story as it amplifies the theme.

When the theme is emphasized, as it is in "The Lottery," the interpreter must concentrate on sustaining the theme without neglecting the other aspects of the story. The dialogue he reads, the description he presents, and the argument he states must not be featured in itself, but must retain its strength as it supports the dominant idea.

Point of view and tone: the emotional cloak of the theme.   An author of prose fiction must establish his *point of view* or the relationship he asks his readers to assume toward the material in time and space; second, he must assume an *attitude* or *tone* toward the theme which he hopes his readers will accept.

On whose authority is the story told? The writer is a guide to show the readers the incidents and characters as he wants them seen. He must therefore choose an angle of vision from which to tell his story. Such is his point of view. Point of view is not to be confused with attitude or opinion. Point of view should be thought of as a type of seeing mind which can shift its position to select the most advantageous glimpse of the theme in time and space to reveal the story.

The point of view is determined by the type of narration employed. There are many different classifications of narrators, but the following four categories are the most inclusive:

1. *The omniscient narrator—the "Godlike" point of view.* This type is perhaps the oldest form employed in story telling. The omniscient narrator knows everything, can move anywhere, any time. He may assume the first person or the third person. When this method is used effectively, it provides the reader with the sense of the vast scope of human life. It has often been compared to a panorama, for it can change from the comprehensive picture to the closeup scene. Thackeray is the omniscient narrator in *Vanity Fair* as is Anton Chekhov in his story "The Lament." [2]

2. *The effaced narrator—third-person objective.* The effaced narrator takes a position opposite to that of the omniscient narrator. He re-

[2] See Cleanth Brooks and Robert Penn Warren, *Fundamentals of Good Writing,* Harcourt, Brace & World, Inc., New York, 1950, pp. 269–273.

sembles the role of the dramatist, for he permits his readers to see his characters only as they might be observed by anyone in action and conversation. The effaced narrator does not tell what his characters think or feel. We may only observe what they say and do. Such a narrator is confined to the immediate scene and therefore has difficulty in indicating the passage of time. Eudora Welty has chosen this point of view for her story "Lily Daw and the Three Ladies." If the reader had been along with Lily and her benefactors, he could have observed the events himself as Miss Welty has set them down.

3. *The first-person narrator—the subjective approach.* The first-person narrator is limited, because he can only tell what he himself sees. But this personalized viewpoint can be very compelling. The first-person narrator is the eye witness, but he need not necessarily tell the events at the time they occur. He may reflect as he chooses. The subjective approach offers the advantage that the narrator can summarize unimportant happenings and develop the more important ones. If the narrator is involved in the situation to the extent that he is an actor as well as an observer, he naturally gives his views of the other characters and action. Truman Capote uses the first person narrator in his story "A Christmas Memory." The character Buddy tells us his experience with an elderly cousin. Capote lets Buddy do the talking, for the theme of "A Christmas Memory" belongs to him. The events between him and his cousin, their plans, talks, and reactions, could be known and told only by Buddy himself.

4. *The roving narrator—"central intelligence."* The roving narrator stands a little above and to one side of his story, using the eyes of the author himself as they move about from scene to scene and from person to person. The roving narrator permits us to reflect upon the state of affairs from any point that the author chooses. We may stand afar and see the totality of the action, or the author may involve us in the roving narrator's immediate concern and thus put before us an intimate scene. The fourth method combines the advantages of the other three and offers the broadest opportunities, but it also requires maturity of judgment and the highest technical skill to control its presentation. Henry James, Joseph Conrad, Jane Austen, and James Joyce are examples of authors who sometimes use this point of view. This method is called central intelligence after Henry James, who believed that all the action of a novel should be evaluated by a single superior mind placed in the center of a main dramatic situation. Thus everything is dramatically rendered. James Joyce's story "The Dead" illustrates the use of central intelligence. In this narrative the reader sees nothing that the character Gabriel Conroy does not see. But through the "evaluation of the superior mind placed in the dramatic situation" the reader is given more of an insight into the story without being consciously aware that he is receiving it.

An author need not be orthodox in his approach. In his novel *The Old Man and the Sea*, Hemingway employs the third-person narrator along with the first person in the form of Santiago himself, for we gain our understanding of the old fisherman through an objective narration of the story and also by a subjective narration of what Santiago tells of himself. The combination, however, does not go so far as to achieve the omniscient point of view. The writer of fiction will have chosen that method which can serve his material and purpose with the fewest limitations. If the author changes his angle of approach, the oral interpreter must be conscious of the shift and by the use of smooth transitions blend the two types of narration into a whole.

In his preparation, the student must ask not only on whose authority the story is told, but also the *attitude* or *tone* that the author encourages the narrator to assume. Browning in his monologue "My Last Duchess" and Eudora Welty in her short story "Lily Daw and the Three Ladies" are both careful to conceal their own personal attitudes toward their characters. However, this form of author objectivity does not prevent the selections from assuming an ironic tone, the duke condemning his most admirable duchess and the three ladies feeling sorry for the blissfully contented Lily.

In his research to discover the attitude of the author toward his theme, the student will attempt to merge his own concepts of what the theme and the tone of the theme are with what the author himself and the critics have said they are. In the selection from *The Light in the Piazza* found at the conclusion of this chapter, what tone does Elizabeth Spencer assume toward Mrs. Johnson's dilemma? The answer is not easily found. She does not aim for pathos, nor is she flippant. There is some irony, but the general approach is not ironic; there is some sympathy, but the attitude is not one of pity. The theme of a demented child of rich parents has been overworked by writers of pulp fiction and could have become tawdry. Miss Spencer escapes such a pitfall largely by the tone she assumes. What is that tone?

Symbolism: an element of diction.   Although every word in a story or novel is used symbolically because it stands for something else, some words will be used to represent not the symbol they *seem* to stand for, but another. For example, when an author uses the word "apple," he is generally using the signs to refer to a particular fruit with which we are all familiar. However, if he intends for us to understand that "apple" as he uses it does not refer to just any apple but to the golden apple which led from the romance of Helen and Paris to the Trojan Wars, then he is using "apple" symbolically.

If we assume that the stones that are thrown in Shirley Jackson's story "The Lottery" are not merely stones, but "the slings and arrows of outrageous fortune," then Miss Jackson is using the word "stone" in a symbolic sense. William Faulkner has created the Snopes family who appear in "Spotted Horses" as well as in many other of his narratives. The Snopeses are not just the Snopeses, for they represent the ignorant, scheming, red-necked poor whites whom Faulkner despised in a patient sort of way.

The interpreter must avoid two pitfalls in working with symbolism in prose. First, he must not ignore symbolism where it exists. In *Anna Karenina*, Tolstoy arranges Anna's first meeting with her lover Vronsky on the Moscow–St. Petersburg express. However, a workman has been killed by the train as it approached the station. Mary McCarthy points out that this incident may be symbolic of the doom which besets Anna because of her ill-fated love, a love which is fulfilled when Anna throws herself in front of a train later in the story.[3] Miss McCarthy proposes that Tolstoy may have made such an association consciously or unconsciously. Nevertheless, the symbolism is there. The train represents not just a train, but the doom that is to come to the heroine. Whether or not the interpreter should point up such mechanics of the author to his audience depends entirely on the circumstances under which he is reading. As long as he understands that there is such a symbolic usage, he can make a calculated risk whether to share such symbolism with his audience. But if he is ignorant of its presence, he cannot make a choice through knowledge, but only by default. Some audiences would profit from knowing of the train symbol; others would not. Some readers could explain the symbol effectively; others could not.

Second, the interpreter must beware of locating symbolism where it does not exist. Some things are just what they seem to be and nothing more. An apple is an apple. A train is a train. Saul Bellow says:

Deep reading has gone very far. It has become dangerous to literature. "Why, sir," the student asks, "does Achilles drag the body of Hector around the walls of Troy?" "That sounds like a stimulating question. Most interesting. I'll bite," says the professor. "Well, you see, sir, the 'Aeneid' is full of circles—shields, chariot wheels and other round figures. And you know what Plato said about circles. The ancients were all mad for geometry." "Bless your crew-cut head," says the professor, "for such a beautiful thought. You have exquisite sensibility. Your approach is both deep and serious. Still I always believed that Achilles did it because he was so angry." [4]

[3] Mary McCarthy, "Settling the Colonel's Hash," *Harper's Magazine*, vol. 208, pp. 72–73, February, 1954.
[4] Saul Bellow, "Deep Readers of the World, Beware!" *The New York Times Book Review*, vol. 64, p. 1, Feb. 15, 1959. Reprinted by permission of the Viking Press and the author. Copyright by The New York Times. Reprinted by permission.

If a circle is a circle and nothing more, the student should leave it as such. An interpreter must learn when things are what they seem and when things are not what they seem. He must do sufficient research to confirm any symbols which seem at all doubtful. If the reader finds symbolism in everything, he is likely to be letting his imagination run away with him and will find that his observations are not confirmed by the critics. Some readers would make Lily Daw the symbol of democracy, and the three ladies, Communist countries trying to put democracy into captivity. The xylophone player would emerge as symbolic of the innocence of Christ who is taking Lily unto himself because Christ said, "Suffer the little children to come unto me." Although no one can prove that Eudora Welty had no such symbols in mind, common sense dictates that she probably did not.

Symbolism is not a requirement of fiction, but it can serve as a strong motivating factor in transmitting the author's theme. The interpreter must read with an awareness of the possibility of symbolism. He must study his selection and its related areas thoroughly and penetrate the surface to see if symbolic meanings can be justified. His study will help him determine how symbolism has assisted the author in conveying the tone of the theme by establishing images with continuity that unite the several elements of the story.

Composition. If the interpreter's purpose is to assist his listeners in understanding a story by telling it as effectively as he can, he needs to examine the elements of composition that the author uses to complete his understanding of the narrative.

1. *Character, action, and plot.* Fiction consists of a sequence of occurrences. One incident provokes another, resulting in a chain of events. This chain, called a story, promotes motion or action going forward. However, a plot is something more than undifferentiated action. It must have a pattern or form to carry on its progression, following a cause and effect relationship between successive events. Such cause and effect configurations may, and often do, change the relationship of one character to another. Therefore, the development of character is the development of plot, and the interpreter should strive to keep the two functioning with unity and coherence.

In delineating character and action, the third-person narrator and the first-person narrator seldom tell us what we are to think about what we see. The characters go about in their relationship to each other in the *world* created by the author. We *hear* the comments made and form a reaction to the people who make them. Since the author does not guide us, we must make our own observations even though the action may be slight.

In addition to being designated as major and minor, characters are often classified as *static,* i.e., flat, or *forceful,* i.e., round. The static or flat characters change very little and often are important in representing stereotypes rather than dynamic individuals. The forceful or round characters change and reveal more clearly the aspects of their personalities. They may be much more active and therefore catch and hold our attention more than the stereotyped characters do. One must be careful not to assume that the static characters are meaningless, for they may contribute significantly to the theme and to the plot by serving as fixed points around which the round characters pivot.

Fiction, like all forms of literature, must have order, but the sequence of events may be artificial. The story does not necessarily begin chronologically. The plot may plunge us into the middle of the action and then step by step take us back to the first incident in the chain. The events, however, do hang together and form an idea with unity. As Brooks and Warren say: "Story is a particular writer's way of saying how you can make sense of human experience." [5] For the writer's use of motivation in the development of his plot brings us closer to the experience as it gives the illusion of reality. Such an illusion is the artistic function of fiction.

Although they may not be in their natural order, the three elements of a unified plot, as Aristotle pointed out, are the beginning, the middle, and the end. In his initial readings and in his paraphrase, the interpreter must seek the point of climax with its maximum emotional impact. The longer set of steps which leads up to this climax and the much shorter set that retreats from it must be located by the student and placed within the framework of the plot. If the climax in "Lily Daw and the Three Ladies" occurs at the point of Mrs. Watts's decisive statement to Lily, "We're taking you to get married," does this announcement conclude the middle or begin the end? Is such an inquiry purely academic? Is there a subclimax which concludes the beginning? How many steps are there in the middle?

There is not a sharp line of demarcation between character, action, and plot. Each must be considered in its relationship to the other elements of fiction. E. M. Forster summarizes the hierarchy of the three when he says: "We have defined a story as a narrative of events arranged in their time sequence. A plot is also a narrative of events, the emphasis falling on causality. 'The king died and then the queen died,' is a story. 'The king died, and then the queen died of grief' is a plot." [6]

[5] Cleanth Brooks and Robert Penn Warren, *Understanding Fiction,* 2d ed., Appleton-Century-Crofts, Inc., New York, 1959, p. 80.
[6] E. M. Forster, *Aspects of the Novel,* Harcourt, Brace and Company, Inc., New York, 1927, p. 130.

2. *Setting.* Setting customarily refers to the time and place of the action. Each event that happens to people in a story or a novel occurs at a certain time and in a particular place. But it will be more meaningful to think of setting as the total atmosphere or environment from which character, action, and plot emerge. A reference to "home" implies a great deal more than a street address. "Home" represents all the influences that have been exerted on us at a particular location. Very much in the same way, the writer of fiction may let the setting of his story or novel give understanding and insight to his characters and the situation. This fact does not mean that the author must use the actual place from which he selected the material for his writing as his setting. Neither is it necessary that the identification be readily recognizable. The value of the setting is not dependent on geographical accuracy, but upon what it does for the story.

The selection of the significant details to make the setting vivid requires a great deal of imagination on the part of the writer. However, when this task is accomplished, it increases the probability of the reader's acceptance of the character, action, and plot. Eudora Welty in "Lily Daw and the Three Ladies" makes an unusually effective use of the setting. The meeting of the three ladies in the post office of Victory, Mississippi, the references to the water tower, the house where Lily lives, the depot, and all landmarks of the town are much more than just names of places where the action occurs. Combined, they create the atmosphere or the local color out of which the story emerges. It is just in such a setting that Mrs. Watts, Mrs. Carson, and Aimee Slocum can live and truly belong. As the story progresses, the action becomes acceptable, for the characters and action have been placed in their proper environment.

Ernest Hemingway permits the element of setting not only to support character, but also to dominate it. In his novel *For Whom the Bell Tolls* the setting of the Spanish Civil War molds the participants, for we observe the characters as they develop during the conflict of the Spanish Loyalists with the Spanish Fascists. If the reader selects a portion of this novel or a similar one, he may be tempted to assume a characteristic voice pattern or an individualized gesture to assist him in conveying the Spanish setting. However, it is better to resist such temptations and seek to impart the setting by the totality of the approach rather than by any gimmick.

The oral interpreter, in his preparation, must be highly conscious of the setting and be able to evaluate its relation to other factors and to the entire story. In order to cut a story or a novel judiciously, the reader must ask, "How much of the material is necessary to fulfill its purpose?" and "Which part can be omitted without harm to the characters, action, plot, and theme of the story?" In "Lily Daw and the

Three Ladies," is the description of Lily's old house essential to the meaning? Reread the story and then reread the suggestions given in Chapter 6 on cutting material for oral presentation. Such a review should assist in determining the role of the setting of a story as it is related to the meaning of the selection.

The interpreter should permit the setting to so contribute to the mood of the story that the audience senses the environment of the selection. He must phrase his introduction appropriately, cut his material wisely, and so blend his voice and body with the setting of the story that his listeners gain the full benefit of the time and place of the events.

3. *The summary: an element of composition.* The author may use the element of summary in many ways. He may summarize in a sentence or two something which has been going on for a much longer period of time, as does Eudora Welty in "Lily Daw and the Three Ladies." Mrs. Carson reviews the happenings leading to the events of the ladies' calling on Lily with their plan to send her to Ellisville:

"We buried Lily's poor defenseless mother. We gave Lily all her food and kindling and every stitch she had on. Sent her to Sunday school to learn the Lord's teachings, had her baptized a Baptist. And when her old father commenced beating her and tried to cut her head off with the butcher knife, why, we went and took her away from him and gave her a place to stay."

In this summary, the writer has allowed Mrs. Carson to give much more than just a recapitulation of what has happened, for she has materially enlarged upon the feelings involved in the story.

The summary is often used for exposition or for tying together more significant moments in the action. In much of fiction, the author vacillates between direct treatment and narrative summary to build his story. Such summaries must be given particular attention by the interpreter, for to omit them all or to include them all will probably result in error. The interpreter may use his introduction, judicious cutting, and internal comments to his audience to provide sufficient summary material to present his story effectively in the time allotted to him.

Selected comments and conclusions

The writing of fiction is an art which presents the interpretation of an experience known as a theme. Each fictionalized account depends upon the creativity of the artist who must select his subject, establish his theme, assume a point of view and an attitude toward the theme, arrange the events, and choose a proper setting for the actions of his characters. With these elements at his command, he begins his narrative, lets it move and build to a climax, and follows through to the conclusion. It is not by the use of any one factor that good fiction is written, but through an understanding of the several aspects which go to make up a short story or novel. A good story is assured when a functional relationship among the various elements exists, resulting in a feeling of unity.

A student of oral interpretation may well ask how a study of style will improve his oral reading of fiction. Perhaps the most significant answer is that such a study will enable the reader to treat each element in its proper perspective. It is easy for the inexperienced reader to present one aspect of a narrative more prominently than its functional purpose requires. Furthermore, oral interpreters have a tendency to neglect descriptions, exposition, or summary to feature dialogue. It is in the dialogue that the reader so often feels he can be most effective. The importance of the conversation of the characters cannot be discredited, but the interpreter must understand that, before a character can speak convincingly, he must emerge from a setting imbued with atmosphere. Through his vocal and bodily reactions, the reader can assist the audience in seeing the place of action, in sensing the mood and feeling of the situation as well as in hearing the characters speak. The unity of the story cannot be maintained if overemphasis is given to one element at the expense of others.

The same cautionary remarks must apply to the transitions used in joining the parts of the narrative. One sentence may change the place, the time, or the mood of the story. In "Lily Daw and the Three Ladies," the sentence "The three women stood at the foot of the water tank" moves the scene from the post office to another part of town. The transition is rather short and could be easily slighted in hurrying on to what the ladies say. If the interpreter is not aware of the importance of this line as it points up the change of place, he may lose the setting for his audience. The reader must say in effect, "Now we have left the post office, and we are following the ladies in their search for Lily. They are now at the outskirts of the town, for here is the water tank. The ladies have been walking and are a little tired as well as annoyed, as we shall soon see when Mrs. Watts says, 'Where in the wide world do you suppose she'd be?'" The oral interpreter can imply all this information in the one sentence that Miss Welty has provided and therefore create the anticipation for the first line of Mrs. Watts's conversation. As we pointed out in Chapter 3, the interpreter's opportunity to assume various roles is one of his unique contributions. He may become the public speaker and talk with his audience, confidentially sharing with his listeners the information that the ladies of Victory may be tired and a little annoyed. And when Mrs. Carson says, "I don't see a sign of her either on this side of the street or on the other side," the interpreter may shift from his role of the public speaker to approximate the role of the actor.

There is no need to prolong the discussion of the difference between acting and interpretation. The closing of this argument is long overdue. It seems rather an easy task to distinguish the actor on the stage, in costume and makeup, creating a character from dramatic literature, from the oral interpreter who is also creating characterization, but with less assistance from the physical aspects of theater. However, the oral interpreter makes use of many of the same methods of the actor in his preparation and presentation. Many have been saying for years, and rightly so: *The oral interpreter has much he can learn from the actor, and the interpreter has a great deal to offer the actor in turn.* The attempt to distinguish between the two and say, "Never the twain shall meet," has been more confusing than illuminating. Often this approach has led to false concepts of what constitutes good oral interpretation. The conclusion is sometimes drawn that anything that is alive and animated, be it good or bad, is acting, and any performance that is dull and dead is interpretation. When occasionally a reader does such extreme movements as crawling on the floor, running around the stage, or tearing at his clothes, we say, "He is overacting." An actor would say that it was not a matter of overacting; it was not acting at all, or certainly not good acting. But it is really a matter of the interpreter's lack of judgment and his use of poor taste.

Consider again Truman Capote's story "A Christmas Memory."

A Christmas Memory [7]

Truman Capote

Of the ingredients that go into our fruitcakes, whiskey is the most expensive, as well as the hardest to obtain: State laws forbid its sale. But everybody knows you can buy a bottle from Mr. Haha Jones. And the next day, having completed our more prosaic shopping, we set out for Mr. Haha's business address, a "sinful" (to quote public opinion) fish-fry and dancing café down by the river. We've been there before, and on the same errand; but in previous years our dealings have been with Haha's wife, an iodine-dark Indian woman with brassy peroxided hair and a dead-tired disposition. Actually, we've never laid eyes on her husband, though we've heard that he's an Indian too. A giant with razor scars across his cheeks. They call him Haha because he's so gloomy, a man who never laughs. As we approach his café (a large log cabin festooned inside and out with chains of garish-gay naked light bulbs and standing by the river's

[7] From Truman Capote, "A Christmas Memory," *Breakfast at Tiffany's*, Random House, New York, 1958, pp. 165–167. © Copyright 1956 by Truman Capote. Reprinted by permission of Random House, Inc.

muddy edge under the shade of river trees where moss drifts through the branches like gray mist) our steps slow down. Even Queenie stops prancing and sticks close by. People have been murdered in Haha's café. Cut to pieces. Hit on the head. There's a case coming up in court next month. Naturally these goings-on happen at night when the colored lights cast crazy patterns and the victrola wails. In the daytime Haha's is shabby and deserted. I knock at the door, Queenie barks, my friend calls: "Mrs. Haha, ma'am? Anyone to home?"

Footsteps. The door opens. Our hearts overturn. It's Mr. Haha Jones himself! And he *is* a giant; he *does* have scars; he *doesn't* smile. No, he glowers at us through Satan-tilted eyes and demands to know: "What you want with Haha?"

For a moment we are too paralyzed to tell. Presently my friend half-finds her voice, a whispery voice at best: "If you please, Mr. Haha, we'd like a quart of your finest whiskey."

His eyes tilt more. Would you believe it? Haha is smiling! Laughing, too. "Which one of you is a drinkin' man?"

"It's for making fruit cakes, Mr. Haha. Cooking."

This sobers him. He frowns. "That's no way to waste good whiskey." Nevertheless, he retreats into the shadowed café and seconds later appears carrying a bottle of daisy yellow unlabeled liquor. He demonstrates its sparkle in the sunlight and says: "Two dollars."

We pay him with nickels and dimes and pennies. Suddenly, jangling the coins in his hand like a fistful of dice, his face softens. "Tell you what," he proposes, pouring the money back into our bead purse, "just send me one of them fruitcakes instead."

"Well," my friend remarks on our way home, "there's a lovely man. We'll put an extra cup of raisins in *his* cake."

The black stove, stoked with coal and firewood, glows like a lighted pumpkin. Eggbeaters whirl, spoons spin round in bowls of butter and sugar, vanilla sweetens the air, ginger spices it; melting, nose-tingling odors saturate the kitchen, suffuse the house, drift out to the world on puffs of chimney smoke. In four days our work is done. Thirty-one cakes, dampened with whiskey, bask on window sills and shelves.

Who would make a hard and fast rule that the interpreter must move or that he must not move, or that he must sit or stand while he reflects on the pleasant memories of Buddy? The concern must rather be that the reader have an understanding and appreciation of the story. The reader should be aware that *Buddy,* as the teller of the experience, is more closely identified with the plot and the theme than is the third person who is telling the action of "Lily Daw and the Three Ladies." The oral reader may decide to be very casual in reading "A Christmas Memory." The tone suggested is that Buddy is reflecting on what has happened in the past. Such reflections do not require a high degree of direct eye contact with the audience. Since Buddy is recalling his experiences with others, the interpreter will want to suggest by his voice and body the characterizations of the other people involved in the story. But the reader should keep in mind that the story belongs to Buddy and not to the others.

The interpreter becomes the narrator for the audience. It is his obligation to present the point of view intended by the author as he understands it, following an intensive study of the related areas and the selection itself. The reader must remember that he is relating the story to someone. It may be to a friend, to a speech class, or to a special audience. Therefore, the interpreter should *tell* the narrative to his listeners. It is not necessary for the reader to use the idea of location of character and place each person in a physical position in the room in which he is reading. However, in some instances, a suggestion of the general location of the characters will assist in making the scene vivid to the audience. A reader may prefer not to use the technique of direct location, but rather to rely on a nondirectional use of his voice and body to create the scene. In either approach, the oral interpreter should establish the scene in the realm of the audience or *offstage*. The reader often feels obligated to bring the scene on stage with him. This feeling is particularly strong in the interpretation of dialogue, for the reader wants to turn to his right or left as if he were speaking to someone at his side. But the interpreter should keep in mind that, as the narrator, he wants to share an experience with his audience. To do this, he must remove the scene from himself and place it in the realm of his audience. Furthermore, there are other techniques than placement, such as tone, pitch, tempo, rhythm, and general bearing and posture that are equally or even more successful in establishing the identity of a character. Such covert approaches do not carry with them the distractions that may occur if a reader turns from side to side or glances first one way and then another. Audiences are often tempted to neglect establishing the location of a character and become fascinated whether such a reader can be consistent in his movements.

Of course, a combination or blending of the overt and covert approaches to the physical location of persons in a story may be used effectively to assist the audience in identifying a character. What one reader may do, another should not even begin to try. What one audience will accept as good taste, another will not. The end result is what is important. The oral reader should at all times maintain flexibility and suggestiveness and never feel bound to one specific technique.

Building and sustaining the action and mood of fiction often present real problems to the oral interpreter. In attempting to solve the difficulties, the suggestion is often made, "You need more variety in your voice." It is true that the reader may lack variety, but he should be told variety for what purpose. It is more meaningful if the student assumes this attitude: *In each work of fiction, I must realize that there is a focal point. From the beginning of the narrative, the events are leading to this turning point and all the happenings following are the consequence of the climax. As an interpreter, I must recognize this process, be aware of building up to the climax, and be prepared to handle the material following the climax. Variety in voice will be necessary to sustain and to communicate the material. Where is it that I have failed to use such variety to the best advantage?*

How can the student prepare and present prose fiction? First, he should know his selection, following the suggestions offered in this discussion plus those he may receive from other studies, and make an analysis of his material. Second, he should prepare himself for the presentation of his material by reexamining the effectiveness of his communicative tools—voice and bodily reaction. He should make sure that his voice is free from any habits that will call attention to themselves and therefore interfere with his communication. He should recognize the need for a flexible voice and a responsive body if he is to share a literary experience with an audience.

Exercises

1. Write a complete analysis of the following selection from the novel *Vanity Fair* by William Makepeace Thackeray.

A very stout, puffy man, in buckskins and Hessian boots, with several immense neckcloths, that rose almost to his nose, with a red striped waistcoat and an apple-green coat with steel buttons . . . was reading the paper by the fire when the two girls entered, and bounced off his arm-chair, and blushed excessively, and hid his entire face almost in his neckcloths at this apparition.

"It's only your sister, Joseph," said Amelia. . . . "I've come home *for good,* you know; and this is my friend, Miss Sharp, whom you have heard me mention."

"No, never, upon my word," said the head under the neckcloth, shaking very much,—"that is, yes,—what abominably cold weather, Miss;"—and herewith he fell to poking the fire with all his might, although it was the middle of June.

"He's very handsome," whispered Rebecca to Amelia, rather loud.

"Do you think so?" said the latter. "I'll tell him."

"Darling! not for worlds," said Miss Sharp, starting back as timid as a fawn. . . .

"Thank you for the beautiful shawls, brother," said Amelia to the fire poker. "Are they not beautiful, Rebecca?"

"O, heavenly!" said Miss Sharp, and her eyes went from the carpet straight to the chandelier.

Joseph still continued a huge clattering at the poker and tongs, puffing and blowing the while, and turning as red as his yellow face would allow him. "I can't make you such handsome presents, Joseph," continued his sister, "but while I was at school, I have embroidered for you a very beautiful pair of braces."

"Good Gad! Amelia," cried the brother, in serious alarm, "what do you mean?" and plunging with all his might at the bell-rope, that article of furniture came away in his hand, and increased the honest fellow's confusion. "For Heaven's sake see if my buggy's at the door . . . I must go."

At this minute, the father of the family walked in, rattling his seals like a true British merchant. "What's the matter, Emmy?" says he.

"Joseph wants me to see if his—his *buggy* is at the door. . . ."

"This young lady is your friend? Miss Sharp, I am very happy to see you. Have you and Emmy been quarreling already with Joseph, that he wants to be off?"

"I promised Bonamy of our service, sir," said Joseph, "to dine with him."

"Oh fie! didn't you tell your mother you would dine here? . . . Come, come, sir, walk down stairs with Miss Sharp, and I will follow with these two young women," said the father, and he took an arm of wife and daughter and walked merrily off.

If Miss Rebecca Sharp had determined in her heart upon making the conquest of this big beau, I don't think, ladies, we have any right to blame her; for though the task of husband-hunting is generally, and with becoming modesty, intrusted by young persons to their mammas, recollect that Miss Sharp had no kind parent to arrange these delicate matters for her, and that if she did not get a husband for herself, there was no one else in the wide world who would take the trouble off her hands. What causes young people to "come *out*," but the noble ambition of matrimony? What sends them trooping to watering-places? What keeps them dancing till five o'clock in the morning through a whole mortal season? What causes them to labor at piano-forte sonatas, and to learn four songs from a fashionable master at a guinea a lesson, and to play the harp if they have handsome arms and neat elbows, and to wear Lincoln Green toxophilite hats and feathers, but that they may bring down some "desirable" young man with those killing bows and arrows of theirs? What causes respectable parents to take up their carpets, set their houses topsy-turvy, and spend a fifth of their year's income in ball suppers and iced champagne? Is it sheer love of their species, and an unadulterated wish to see young people happy and dancing? Psha! they want to marry their daughters; and, as honest Mrs. Sedley has, in the depths of her kind heart, already arranged a score of little schemes for the settlement of her Amelia, so also had our beloved but unprotected Rebecca determined to do her very best to secure the husband, who was even more necessary for her than for her friend.

2. Answer the following questions concerning the selection below, taken from the novel *The Light in the Piazza* by Elizabeth Spencer.

   a. From what point of view is the story approached?
   b. How should a reader solve the problem of Signor Naccarelli's dialect?

c. What is the attitude or tone of Miss Spencer toward her theme?
d. How should the interpreter place his characterizations in the realm of his audience?
e. How does the author give the atmosphere of the setting without using long descriptive passages?

From *The Light in the Piazza* [8]

Elizabeth Spencer

It wasn't that simple, of course. Nobody with a dream should come to Italy. No matter how dead and buried the dream is thought to be, in Italy it will rise and walk again. Margaret Johnson had a dream, though she thought reality had long ago destroyed it. The dream was that Clara would one day be perfectly well. It was here that Italy had attacked her, and it was this that her surrender involved. . . .

Courage, she thought now, . . . riding the train back to Florence. Corraggio. The Italian word came easily to mind. Mrs. Johnson belonged to various clubs, and campaigns to clean up this or raise the standards of that were frequently turned over to committees headed by her. She believed that women in their way could accomplish a great deal. . . . How much did the Naccarellis know? As the train drew into the station, she felt her blood race, her whole being straighten and poise, to the fine alertness of a drawn bow. Whether Florence knew it or not, she invaded it.

As for how much the Naccarelli family knew or didn't know or cared or didn't care, no one not Italian had better undertake to say. It was never clear. Fabrizio threatened suicide when Clara left. The mother of Clara had scorned him because he was Italian. No other reason. Everyone had something to say. The household reeled until nightfall when Fabrizio plunged toward the central open window of the salotto. The serious little maid, who had been in love with him for years, leaped in front of him with a shriek, her arms thrown wide. Deflected, he rushed out of the house and went tearing away through the streets. The Signora Naccarelli collapsed in tears and refused to eat. She retired to her room, where she kept a holy image that she placed a great store by. Signor Naccarelli alone enjoyed his meal. He said that Fabrizio would not commit suicide and that the ladies would probably be back. He had seen Americans take fright before; no one could ever explain why. But in the end, like everyone else, they would serve their own best interests. If he did not have some quiet, he would certainly go out and seek it elsewhere.

He spent the pleasantest sort of afternoon locked in conversation with Mrs. Johnson a few days after her return. It was all an affair for juggling, circling, balancing, very much to his liking. He could not really say she had made a conquest of him: American women were too confident and brisk; but he could not deny that encounters with her had a certain flavor.

The lady had consented to go with him on a drive up to San Miniato, stopping at the casino for a cup of tea and a pastry. Signor Naccarelli managed

[8] From Elizabeth Spencer, *The Light in the Piazza*, pp. 61–69. Copyright (c) 1960 by Elizabeth Spencer. With permission of McGraw-Hill Book Company, Inc., New York.

to get in a drive to Bello Squardo as well, and many a remark about young love and many a glance at his companion's attractive legs and figure. Margaret Johnson achieved a cool but not unfriendly position while folding herself into and out of a car no bigger than an enclosed motorcycle. The management of her skirt alone was enough to occupy her entire attention.

"They are in the time of life," Signor Naccarelli said, darting the car through a narrow space between two motorscooters, "when each touch, each look, each sigh arises from the heart, the heart alone." He removed his hands from the wheel to do his idea homage, flung back his head and closed his eyes. Then he snapped to and shifted gears. "For them love is without thought, as to draw breath, to sleep, to walk. You and I—we have come to another stage. We have known all this before—we think of the hour, of some business—so we lose our purity, who knows how? . . . I do not know if your daughter will be for Fabrizio the first, or will not be. I would say not, but still—he is figlio di mamma, a good boy—I do not know." He frowned. . . .

"There is no question with Clara," Mrs. Johnson murmured. "She has been very carefully brought up."

"Not like other American girls, eh? In Italy we hear strange things. Not only hear. Cara signora, we *see* strange things also. You can imagine. Never mind. The signorina is another thing entirely. My wife has noticed it at once. Her innocence." His eye kept returning to Mrs. Johnson's knee, which in the narrow silk skirt of her dress it was difficult not to expose. . . .

"And her father? How does he feel? An Italian for his daughter? Well, perhaps in America you, too, hear some strange words about us. We are no different from others, except we are more—well, you see me here—we are here together—it is not unpleasant—I look to you like any other man. And yet perhaps I feel a greater—how shall I say? You think I play the Italian when I say there is a greater—"

She did think just that. She had been seriously informed on several occasions recently that Anglo-Saxons knew very little about passion, and now Signor Naccarelli, for whom she had a real liking, was about to work up to the same idea. She pulled down her skirt with a jerk. "There are plenty of American men who appreciate women just as much as you do," she told him.

He burst out laughing. "Of course! We make such a lot of foolishness, signora. But on such an afternoon—" . . . Suddenly he took a notion to start the car. It backed at once, as if a child had it on a string, then leaping forward fairly toppled over the crest of a steep run of hill down into the city, speeding as fast as a roller skate. Mrs. Johnson clutched her hat. . . .

"So you ran away," he said, "upset; you could not bear the thought. You think and you think. You see the signorina's unhappy face. You could not bear her tears. You return. It is wise. There should be a time for thought. This I have said to my wife, to my son. But when you come back, they say to me, 'But if she leaves again—?' But I say, 'The signora is a woman who is without caprice. She will not leave again.'"

"I do not intend to leave again," said Mrs. Johnson, "until Clara and Fabrizio are married."

Drama   **10**

There are several reasons why drama is particularly suitable for oral interpretation. First, with few exceptions, it was written specifically for oral presentation. Even closet dramas were intended to be read aloud.[1] Therefore the reader can be certain that he is offering his selection the medium of presentation for which it was designed. Many plays which are excellent when staged make poor silent reading. Therefore, when a famous Broadway actor says that he is "reading scripts" in his search for a play, he means that he has developed a technique for seeing the words projected on the stage as he reads them to himself. The interpreter likewise must learn to read drama silently, but to hear it as if it were being read aloud.

The second reason why drama is particularly suitable for oral presentation is its compactness. The playwright cannot afford involved descriptions or extraneous expositions. Necessity dictates that he must be terse. The oral reader will find that the drama has already been cut by the trial and error method of production. Such an advantage is also a disadvantage because, as will be pointed out later, the cutting of good drama becomes quite difficult.

Third, drama boasts of the best poetic prose or prose poetry in literature. Although this discussion of drama has been grouped with prose, the student is aware by now that the distinction between prose and poetry is only one of degree, and he already knows, from his study of Shakespeare, that drama can assume verse form and that a given drama can include predominantly prose passages as well as predominantly poetic passages. Dramatic literature contains outstanding examples of conversation written in verse. What better opportunities would an interpreter hope to find than material with all of the advantages of prose and poetry combined? Mark Antony's famous lines to the citizens of Rome are equally effective as a public speech and as poetry. The interpreter has an opportunity to play the role of the public speaker and of the actor at the same time.

The characteristics of the drama

A comparison of the elements of the drama with those given for the novel will assist in pointing up the special characteristics of dramatic

[1] For example, Browning's *Pippa Passes,* Shelley's *Prometheus Unbound,* and Milton's *Samson Agonistes.*

literature. In the drama, little can be known about the characters other than what is acted out, whereas the characters in a novel may be discussed at length using techniques other than conversation. Therefore, the novelist *tells* a story, while the dramatist *presents* a story. In drama, the setting is confined by the realistic limits of production, while the novel can move the reader easily from the past to the future or from one place to another without concerning himself with staging. Furthermore, the dramatist is much more governed by the element of time. He has difficulty in multiplying his number of characters, and he is forced to limit his action to what he can telescope into the time allotted.

Point of view in drama is largely limited to the first person. Variation is provided by the *soliloquy* and the aside, both of which require the particular attention of the interpreter since he must make clear to his audience that the point of view is being shifted. At first glance, the interpreter may conclude that the attitude of the playwright toward his material is inevitably more pronounced than it is in the novel. This is not necessarily true. Shakespeare is renowned for concealing his own feelings toward his characters, as is witnessed by the several legitimate portrayals of Shylock in *The Merchant of Venice*. Aeschylus, Sophocles, and Euripides seldom invaded their legends because they knew that their audiences had established attitudes toward their stories.

A play offers a very challenging and enjoyable experience for the oral interpreter. In his analysis of the drama, the reader comes in contact with exciting situations, unusual conflicts, and colorful characters. Although most dramas are primarily written for the stage, a play can be *produced* by a skillful oral reader in the minds of his audience. Therefore, the oral reader can carry some of the best of dramatic literature to audiences out of contact with the professional or educational theater. Furthermore, many plays which are seldom if ever produced can be effectively presented by the oral interpreter. Classical drama, and in particular Greek tragedy, is very adaptable for reading, providing both an educational and an entertaining medium for the reader.

The selection of a play

There are so many excellent plays from which to choose that an interpreter may flounder in making a choice. His personal tastes and enthusiasms should guide him in part, for he will need to be enthusiastic about his material, but he must also consider the difficulty of the material and the interests of the audience to which he will read. The following suggestions are offered for his assistance:

1. Limit the number of characters to be presented. Either choose a play with few characters, or select material which will permit the deletion of all but a few speaking parts.
2. Select a play that is not altogether dependent upon physical activity or costumes and properties for its effectiveness. Some scenes from the contemporary play *The Miracle Worker* by William Gibson would be inappropriate because they are so dependent upon the scuffling between Helen Keller and her teacher. Musical comedies present many difficulties for the oral reader because of their dependence upon scenery and costume. Shakespearian drama, however, is seldom inappropriate, except for some dueling scenes or situations in which crowds are involved, because Shakespeare wrote for a theater which was largely independent of the technical aspects of drama.
3. Select a scene which has a strong plot and vivid characters. Static drama, such as the plays by Maeterlinck, are difficult enough for the stage because there is so little action. The beginning student of oral interpretation is likely to find it easier to present tragedy than to read the comedy written to cater to the sophisticated audiences of Broadway and London. The plot and characters of tragedy are often more broadly drawn than those of comedy. If an inexperienced reader wishes to attempt comedy, he may do better to choose from the classical repertoire, from Oliver Goldsmith, Molière, Shakespeare, Aristophanes, or George Bernard Shaw, rather than from the more frothy plays of the contemporary theater.

The following plays are recommended for oral reading:

Anderson, Maxwell, *Winterset*
Barrie, James M., *What Every Woman Knows* and *Quality Street*
Chekhov, Anton Pavlovich, *The Cherry Orchard* and *The Three Sisters*
Coffee, Lenore, and W. J. Cowen, *Family Portrait*
Euripides, *Medea* and *Orestes*
Everyman
Fry, Christopher, *The Lady's Not for Burning* and *Venus Observed*
Glaspell, Susan, *Alison's House*
Goldsmith, Oliver, *She Stoops to Conquer*
Hauptmann, Gerhart, *The Weavers*
Hellman, Lillian, *Toys in the Attic*
Ibsen, Henrik, *A Doll's House, Ghosts,* and *Hedda Gabler*
Katayev, Valentin P., *Squaring the Circle*
Kaufman, George S., and Moss Hart, *The Man Who Came to Dinner*
Miller, Arthur, *Death of a Salesman* and *The Crucible*
Molière, Jean Baptiste, *Le Misanthrope* and *The Imaginary Invalid*
Pirandello, Luigi, *Six Characters in Seach of an Author*
Rostand, Edmond, *Cyrano de Bergerac*
Shakespeare, William, *Taming of the Shrew, Julius Caesar,* and *Merchant of Venice*
Shaw, George Bernard, *Candida*

Sheridan, Richard Brinsley, *The School for Scandal* and *The Rivals*
Sophocles, *Antigone* and *Electra*
Van Druten, John, *I Remember Mama*
Wilde, Oscar, *The Importance of Being Earnest* and *Lady Windermere's Fan*
Wilder, Thornton, *Our Town*
Williams, Tennessee, *The Glass Menagerie*

The nature of the selection

The *who* and the *to whom* of drama are not difficult for the oral interpreter to determine for himself, but require special attention to ensure that the listeners remain oriented. A discussion of the location of character aimed to assist the reader in distinguishing characters for his audience has been presented in the discussion of prose fiction.

The *where* of the drama must be dealt with in the introduction since many plays depend upon scenery and costume plus program notes to establish setting.

The *what* of the play will consume most of the interpreter's attention. A play which hopes to attract audiences must be meaningful to those audiences. The theater is an active propaganda agent—preserving tradition, overthrowing tradition; making fun of liberalism, making fun of conservatism; denouncing the nonconformist, applauding the nonconformist. With few exceptions, drama proposes to make itself felt in the society in which it is offered. Its mighty pen is a sword which hacks away at the body politic. It will make itself felt. Therefore, the interpreter must ask himself what motivated the playwright to put these characters into this plot. What is he trying to say? A painter is free to say nothing, for his work of art is still a painting, whether contemporary audiences look at it or not. But a play is not a play while it lies coldly in manuscript form; it only achieves life when it has an audience. Further discussion of the playwright's message will be found under the following discussion of style.

The style of the drama

The dependency of the dramatist upon pleasing his audience is both a serious handicap and a noted advantage. It is a handicap because the level of society to which he offers his material may prefer inferior ideas to superior ones, and therefore the playwright may prostitute his ideas to gain a full house. It is an advantage because, in order to satisfy the demands of a theater audience, the skillful playwright will prune his conceptions of irrelevant ideas which might otherwise cloud his thinking and obscure his thought. The inability to be terse has driven many writers from the theater. Browning found himself unable to write successfully for the stage and eventually turned to the dramatic monologue to satisfy both his poetic urge and his love for the theater. The result has been a happy one, for although Browning's dramas are mediocre at best, his monologues are superior poetry.

Few dramatists are *discovered* after their deaths, as are painters, sculptors, and musicians. If a dramatist is not successful during his life, he is probably destined for obscurity because he has not been able to develop a technique for making his ideas palatable to society. If making the ideas palatable has resulted in too many concessions to the whims of society, then the ideas offered are likely to be inferior. Many plays are of a transient quality which makes them meaningful only to a limited group. The student must avoid being *carried away* with the latest Broadway hit, thereby showing his immaturity of judgment. He is free to read drawing-room comedy or obviously patriotic tragedy, provided he does not offer them for more than they are worth.

No one was more at the mercy of his audience than was Shakespeare. Yet he demonstrates the ability to offer an elevated theme in a highly entertaining format. The plights of Hamlet, Macbeth, Romeo and Juliet, King Lear, and Othello are universal in their application and far reaching in their implications. Othello's dilemma still confronts much of Africa today, whereas the ambition of Macbeth permeates the military juntas of Asia and South America. *Julius Caesar* was performed in modern dress during the 1930s to demonstrate how contemporary were Shakespeare's ideas. The interpreter should avoid overestimating the conceptual level of an inferior drama and be certain to assess correctly the serious implications of a great conception.

The emotion in drama. In order to gain acceptance, a drama must make an almost obvious bid for a sizable emotional reaction. The characters in drama carry their emotions on their sleeves. Nothing is more condemning in a review than to say that a play was "talky" or that it was philosophical. Yet good theater so combines ideas with their supporting emotions that one does not dominate the other.

The interpreter must resist his inclination to lean on the emotional elements of a play at the expense of its theme. If he finds it necessary to let the emotion subjugate the ideas, he should reexamine his selection to see if it is worth his consideration. "Hamming" is as much to be avoided in oral reading as it is in theater.

The soliloquy and the aside afford good illustrations of the necessity for restraint on the part of the oral reader. Shakespeare was hesitant to offer a soliloquy until his audience had become well accustomed to his characters. An audience can better enjoy what a character is thinking if it has been properly prepared, for talking out loud to oneself is not acceptable in society and occurs only when someone is sufficiently aroused to break convention. Therefore, when Hamlet says: "O, what a rogue and peasant slave am I!" it is Act II, Scene 2. Sufficient action has preceded to prepare the audience for Hamlet's outburst. If a student chooses to omit the preceding action and begin with the soliloquy, he must underplay his role to avoid taking his audience by surprise with a too vehement emotional attack. When Shakespeare does open his play with a soliloquy, as he does in *Richard III*, the emotional element is subdued.

The abrupt change in point of view offered by the aside can break aesthetic distance unless it is properly handled. The aside is similar to the soliloquy in that the character lets us know not only what he says to others but what he is actually thinking. The role of the narrator, in such contemporary plays as *Our Town* by Thornton Wilder, consists of nothing more than extended asides. The prologues and epilogues of classical drama are also similar to the aside, using direct address to interpret indirect address. A too noticeable change in voice or bodily action may destroy the effect. Much of the strength of the aside lies in its slyness. The character who delivers the aside or acts the part of the narrator or gives the prologue or epilogue is, in a way, a traitor to the other characters, for he is telling the audience more than it deserves to know. Furthermore, he often has an exclusive opportunity of presenting his point of view. Therefore, he should offer his comments unobtrusively rather than flaunt his superior position.

Hamlet says: "Nor do not saw the air too much with your hand, thus, but use all gently; for in the very torrent, tempest, and, as I may say, the whirlwind of passion, you must acquire and beget a temperance that may give it smoothness." Tearing passions to tatters to split the ears of the groundlings is both poor theater and poor oral interpretation.

Imagery in the drama.   The pictorial aspects of drama are as prominent as are its emotions. The dramatist carefully builds each scene so that the eye can grasp the action. Every effort is made to focus attention on one scene at a time. Obscurity is avoided. Furthermore, the imagery is predominantly literal in prose drama, for ordinary conversation seldom contains figurative language. Only in verse drama is there much emphasis on the figurative image.

Diction.   Prose drama may be literal, but it is also economical. If it cannot risk amplifying its meaning by a terse metaphor or simile, it must locate the exact word which will briefly convey the meaning. Prose drama appears to be continually in battle with the inherent wastefulness of ordinary conversation. So much of what man says is meaningless or redundant, and such inaptitudes are discouraging when dialogue is staged. Therefore, the dramatist gives his dialogue the semblance of reality, but provides it with the economy he requires to get on with his theme. The interpreter must realize how much every word in drama counts and project the lines sufficiently so that they can be easily grasped. A member of a theater audience who interrupts his companion to supply a missed line has not only lost that line but the next several which follow.

Poetic drama is equally economical in its literal aspects, but can make freer use of figurative language to amplify its meaning tersely. The search for figures of speech in verse drama can be overdone. James Thurber points this out in discussing his former English teacher, Miss Groby.

"Night after night, for homework, Miss Groby set us to searching in ... 'Julius Caesar' for metaphors, similes, metonymies, apostrophes, personification, and all the rest. It got so that figures of speech jumped out of the pages at you, obscuring the sense and pattern of the ... play you were trying to read. 'Friends, Romans, countrymen, lend me your ears.' Take that, for instance. There is an unusual but perfect example of Container for the Thing Contained. If you read the funeral oration unwarily—that is to say, for its meaning—you might easily miss the C.F.T.T.C. Antony is, of course, not asking for their ears in the sense that he wants them cut off and handed over; he is asking for the function of those ears, for their power to hear, for, in a word, the thing they contain." [2]

As facetious as Thurber's comments may be, they are truthful enough to make us reflect. Obviously, Miss Groby was not interested in the way figures of speech supported the meaning, but only in locating the figures themselves. The interpreters role may be compared to that of the surgeon. He must continually keep his perspective on the over-all progress of his work, while, at the same time, he must be able to identify each of the elements which will contribute to that progress. The doctor's patient may or may not care which nerve or which muscle has been adjusted or which organ has been removed. He is only interested in the general effect of the operation. The interpreter who understands that *ear* is a use of metonymy which permits Shakespeare to speak colloquially and at the same time to avoid calling for something as revealing of intent as the mind, the heart, or the conscience, knows how important the opening line is. Then he can reinstate the figure into its context and concentrate on conveying the meaning in its full significance.

[2] James Thurber, "Here Lies Miss Groby," *My World and Welcome to It,* Harcourt, Brace and Co., New York, 1942, p. 169. Reprinted by permission; Copr. © 1942. The New Yorker Magazine, Inc.

Composition. The major divisions of the plot of a drama are usually indicated by the acts and scenes into which the play is divided. The subclimaxes which occur at the conclusion of acts and scenes are usually more pronounced than are the preliminary periods of suspense generated at the end of a chapter in a novel. If the student chooses to read to the class excerpts from the second act of a three-act play, he should remember that a minor climax has preceded and a major climax is yet to come.

Even though it may be necessary to omit some descriptive and narrative directions offered by the playwright, the interpreter should not conclude that such elements are unimportant and can be automatically de-emphasized. In the scene from *Summer and Smoke* given at the conclusion of this chapter, the description of John provided by Tennessee Williams is essential to an understanding of what follows. The language provided by the author here is so effective that it can be read as is. Such passages are often as important as the dialogue itself in creating an image for the listener. If the interpreter has seen a production of the play, he may wish to add details that he has gleaned there, provided he does not overdo it.

Other mechanics of the author's script are important. When the interpreter is reading or extemporizing on the setting, he should remember that he is "ringing up the curtain and turning on the lights" for his listeners. By his voice and physical actions, he creates the mood and sets the stage in the imagination of the audience. He is often at an advantage over the theatrical production, for he can create Shakespeare's battlefields much more effectively in the minds of his audience than a producer can ever do on stage.

Very special attention must be given to the transitional lines that change the place, time, or situation. Such lines as "John steps in" or "John has risen abruptly" are pivotal, and their absence will obscure subsequent action. Often a reader, in his eagerness to get on with the dialogue, will slight these comments, which Lee refers to as "pegs" on which to hang the story.[3] At times, the reader can so clarify his remarks in his introduction that he can omit these interpositions; elsewhere, he can infer their meaning by a change of voice or a slight movement of the body; other passages must be inserted as they are or put into the words of the interpreter.

The suggestions offered in the preparation and presentation of characterization for the novel and short story are equally applicable to the drama. However, the interpreter usually feels freer in creating the character in a play than he does in other literary forms. The chief con-

[3] Charlotte Lee, *Oral Interpretation,* 2d ed., Houghton Mifflin Company, Boston, 1959, p. 307.

cern of the oral interpreter is not how much or how little characterization he should develop, but rather how can he best present the
author's theme with its supporting emotions and images. The play is
composed of characters, setting, and plot. Summary, exposition, and
description occur within the scenes. The oral interpreter should recognize these various factors and study each as it relates to the other.
He must give proper emphasis to each, but maintain unity at the same
time. DeWitt Parker calls such balance "equilibrium or impartiality."
He explains: "It demands, despite the subordination among the elements, that none be neglected. Each, no matter how minor its part
in the whole, must have some unique value of its own. . . ." [4]

Limiting the selection

The principles used for cutting and arranging the drama are largely
the same as those used in other types of literature. However, there are
elements that have special significance in preparing the play. Each
line devoted to stage direction or stage setting must be analyzed to
see, first, if it is expendable. If the explanatory material must be retained, it may be read as the playwright has presented it or rephrased
in the interpreter's own language. Some readers will find it convenient
to use more direct eye contact during the expository passages than
during the dialogue and will thus prefer to express these directions in
their own terms. Other readers will develop a reverse technique, purposely limiting direct eye contact during stage directions to signify a
change in point of view and will therefore retain what the playwright
has written. A combination of these approaches is also functional.

Minor characters, such as maids, delivery boys, and butlers, may
be omitted altogether if possible. If not, their lines can be absorbed
into the explanatory passages. Whenever possible, the dialogue itself
should be preserved for the featured characters. Since the listeners to
an oral reading do not have movement, costumes, scenery, and lighting to help them identify characters, they can become easily confused
if there are too many persons with speaking parts.

The short scene from *Summer and Smoke* provided at the conclusion of this chapter can be cut, if necessary. How much of the comments on the setting is necessary to create the mood? Are such phrases
as "She drops the papers" or "There is another ripple of laughter"
expendable?

The first part of the scene presents an interesting problem for the
interpreter. The dialogue consists of only one or two words for each

[4] DeWitt Parker, *The Principles of Aesthetics*, Appleton-Century-Crofts, Inc., New
York, 1946, p. 78. 2nd edition. Copyright, 1920, 1946, F. S. Crofts & Company,
Inc. Reprinted by permission of Appleton–Century–Crofts, Inc.

character, offering a difficult conversation for oral interpretation. Assuming that a verbatim reading is rejected, there are several approaches for cutting out the difficulty. Some bits of the conversation may simply be omitted, while others may be combined to reduce the number of characters, giving additional lines to those who are retained. For example, to delete the initial remarks on Bastille Day, the reader might say:

ALMA (reading): [At] our last meeting . . . it was debated whether or not we ought to suspend operations. . . .

If the reader chose to omit the poem, he might give its title and indicate that following Miss Alma's presentation of the poem, the stage directions call for "various effusions and enthusiastic applause."

Summary and conclusions

The interpreter who is presenting only a portion of a play should, of course, read the entire script, studying each character thoroughly and examining his position each time he makes an appearance. In *Summer and Smoke*, the reader has learned from earlier scenes that Miss Alma is in love with John. Her confusion is only accentuated by the caustic remarks of Mrs. Bassett and the apathy of the other people who surround her. In the excerpt provided in this chapter the action must be swift. The dialogue must proceed rapidly, with the reader picking up his cues with alacrity. Such speed may be broken occasionally by a reflective pause, but in general, the reader causes one line to follow quickly upon another. The interpreter must learn to interrupt himself to provide the illusion of conversation. One of the most difficult and challenging aspects of drama for the reader is the maintenance of proper tempo. The emotional tension of the scene regulates the speed. If a reader proceeds too fast and permits one character to snatch the words from another's mouth, the effect is fatiguing; if the reader proceeds too slowly so that a lag occurs between comments, the result is equally tiring. A change in idea or mood usually calls for a change in tempo. Keeping the tempo in harmony with the pace of the play furnishes the much needed variety and keeps any scene from bogging down.

Review the material in Chapters 4 to 6. Remember that the play is dramatic literature, demanding motion and progress. The interpreter must deal with a theme highly imbued with mood and atmosphere. He must be thoroughly prepared and must not hesitate to make the reading a dramatic experience for his listeners.

Exercises

1. Select three reviews of the play *Summer and Smoke,* and show how each agrees or disagrees with the other.
2. Prepare a bibliography of fifteen critical articles on Tennessee Williams, using the *International Index to Periodicals,* the *Reader's Guide to Periodical Literature,* and the *Book Review Digest.* Follow the bibliographical form established in Chapter 5.
3. How similar are the problems in interpreting the Shakespearian soliloquy and the Browning monologue? Illustrate your comments with references to the paired selections which follow.
4. Choose an act from any play by Richard Brinsley Sheridan, and cut it for presentation. Reproduce the entire act, encircling the portions you would delete. Write in the margin the justification for each omission.
5. Write a detailed analysis of any one of Shakespeare's comedies.
6. Write an essay explaining how you would prepare the class to listen to Macbeth's soliloquy in Act III, Scene 1, beginning, "To be thus is nothing; but to be safely thus."

Summer and Smoke [5]

Tennessee Williams

Scene 3

Inside the Rectory.
The meeting is in progress, having just opened with the reading of the minutes by Alma. She stands before the green plush sofa and the others. This group includes Mr. Doremus, Vernon, a willowy younger man with an open collar and Bryonic locks, the widow Bassett, and a wistful older girl with a long neck and thick-lensed glasses.

Alma [*reading*]: Our last meeting which fell on July fourteenth...
Mrs. Bassett: Bastille Day!
Alma: Pardon me?
Mrs. Bassett: It fell on Bastille Day! But, honey, that was the meeting before last.
Alma: You're perfectly right. I seem to be on the wrong page... [*She drops the papers.*]
Mrs. Bassett: Butterfingers!
Alma: Here we are! July twenty-fifth! Correct?
Mrs. Bassett: Correct! [*A little ripple of laughter goes about the circle.*]
Alma [*continuing*]: It was debated whether or not we ought to suspend operations for the remainder of the summer as the departure of several

members engaged in the teaching profession for their summer vacations . . .

Mrs. Bassett: Lucky people!

Alma: . . . had substantially contracted our little circle.

Mrs. Basset: Decimated our ranks! [*There is another ripple of laughter.*]

[*John appears outside the door-frame and rings the bell.*]

Alma [*with agitation*]: Is that—is that—the doorbell?

Mrs. Bassett: It sure did sound like it to me.

Alma: Excuse me a moment. I think it may be . . . [*She crosses to the door-frame and makes the gesture of opening the door. John steps in, immaculately groomed and shining, his white linen coat over his arm and a white Panama hat in his hand. He is a startling contrast to the other male company, who seem to be outcasts of a state in which he is a prominent citizen.*]

Alma [*shrilly*]: Yes, it is—our guest of honor! Everybody, this is Dr. John Buchanan, Jr.

John [*easily glancing about the assemblage*]: Hello, everybody.

Mrs. Bassett: I never thought he'd show up. Congratulations, Miss Alma.

John: Did I miss much?

Alma: Not a thing! Just the minutes—I'll put you on the sofa. Next to me. [*She laughs breathlessly and makes an uncertain gesture. He settles gingerly on the sofa. They all stare at him with a curious sort of greediness.*] Well, now! we are completely assembled!

Mrs. Bassett [*eagerly*]: Vernon has his verse play with him tonight!

Alma [*uneasily*]: Is that right, Vernon? [*Obviously, it is. Vernon has a pile of papers eight inches thick on his knees. He raises them timidly with downcast eyes.*]

Roger [*quickly*]: We decided to put that off till cooler weather. Miss Rosemary is supposed to read us a paper tonight on William Blake.

Mrs. Bassett: Those dead poets can keep! [*John laughs.*]

Alma [*excitedly jumping up*]: Mrs. Bassett, everybody! This is the way I feel about the verse play. It's too important a thing to read under any but ideal circumstances. Not only atmospheric—on some cool evening with music planned to go with it!—but everyone present so that nobody will miss it! Why don't we . . .

Roger: Why don't we take a standing vote on the matter?

Alma: Good, good, perfect!

Roger: All in favor of putting the verse play off till cooler weather, stand up! [*Everybody rises but Rosemary and Mrs. Bassett. Rosemary starts vaguely to rise, but Mrs. Bassett jerks her arm.*]

Rosemary: Was this a vote?

Roger: Now, Mrs. Bassett, no rough tactics, please!

Alma: Has everybody got fans? John, you haven't got one! [*She looks about for a fan for him. Not seeing one, she takes Roger's out of his hand and gives it to John. Roger is non-plussed. Rosemary gets up with her paper.*]

Rosemary: The poet—William Blake.

Mrs. Bassett: Insane, insane, that man was a mad fanatic! [*She squints her eyes tight shut and thrusts her thumbs into her ears. The reactions range from indignant to conciliatory.*]

Roger: Now, Mrs. Bassett!

Mrs. Bassett: This is a free country. I can speak my opinion. And I have *read up* on him. Go on, Rosemary. I wasn't criticizing your paper. [*But Rosemary sits down, hurt.*]

Alma: Mrs. Bassett is only joking, Rosemary.

Rosemary: No, I don't want to read it if she feels that strongly about it.

Mrs. Bassett: Not a bit, don't be silly! I just don't see why we should encourage the writings of people like that who have already gone into a drunkard's grave!

Various voices [*exclaiming*]: Did he? I never heard that about him. Is that true?

Alma: Mrs. Bassett is mistaken about that. Mrs. Bassett, you have confused Blake with someone else.

Mrs. Bassett [*positively*]: Oh, no, don't tell me. I've read up on him and know what I'm talking about. He traveled around with that Frenchman who took a shot at him and landed them both in jail! Brussels, Brussels!

Roger [*gaily*]: Brussels sprouts!

Mrs. Bassett: That's where it happened, fired a gun at him in a drunken stupor, and later one of them died of T.B. in the gutter! All right. I'm finished. I won't say anything more. Go on with your paper, Rosemary. There's nothing like contact with culture! [*Alma gets up.*]

Alma: Before Rosemary reads her paper on Blake, I think it would be a good idea, since some of us aren't acquainted with his work, to preface the critical and biographical comments with a reading of one of his loveliest lyric poems.

Rosemary: I'm not going to read anything at all! Not I!

Alma: Then let me read it then. [*She takes a paper from Rosemary*] . . . This is called "Love's Secret." [*She clears her throat and waits for a hush to settle. Rosemary looks stonily at the carpet. Mrs. Bassett looks at the ceiling. John coughs.*]

Never seek to tell thy love,
Love that never told can be,
For the gentle wind doth move
Silently, invisibly.
I told my love, I told my love,
I told him all my heart.
Trembling, cold in ghastly fear
Did my love depart.

No sooner had he gone from me
Than a stranger passing by,
Silently, invisibly,
Took him with a sigh!

[*There are various effusions and enthusiastic applause.*]

Mrs. Bassett: Honey, you're right. That isn't the man I meant. I was thinking about the one who wrote about "the bought red lips." Who was it that wrote about the "bought red lips"? [*John has risen abruptly. He signals to Alma and points to his watch. He starts to leave.*]

Alma [*springing up*]: John!

John [*calling back*]: I have to call on a patient!

Alma: Oh, John! [*She calls after him so sharply that the group is startled into silence.*]

Rosemary [*interpreting this as a cue to read her paper*]: "The poet, William Blake, was born in 1757 . . ." [*Alma suddenly rushes to the door and goes out after John.*]

Roger: Of poor but honest parents.

Mrs. Bassett: No supercilious comments out of you, sir. Go on, Rosemary. [*She speaks loudly.*] She has such a beautiful *voice!* [*Alma returns inside, looking stunned.*]

Alma: Please excuse the interruption, Rosemary. Dr. Buchanan had to call on a patient.

Mrs. Bassett [*archly*]: I bet I know who the patient was. Ha-ha! That Gonzales girl whose father owns Moon Lake Casino and goes everywhere with two pistols strapped on his belt. Johnny Buchanan will get himself shot in that crowd!

Alma: Why, Mrs. Bassett, what gave you such an idea? I don't think that John even knows that Gonzales girl!

Mrs. Bassett: He knows her, all right. In the Biblical sense of the word, if you'll excuse me!

Alma: No, I will not excuse you! A thing like that is inexcusable!

Mrs. Bassett: Have you fallen for him, Miss Alma? Miss Alma has fallen for the young doctor! They tell me he has lots of new lady patients!

Alma: Stop it! [*She stamps her foot furiously and crushes the palm leaf fan between her clenched hands.*] I won't have malicious talk here! You drove him away from the meeting after I'd bragged so much about how bright and interesting you all were! You put your worst foot forward and simpered and chattered and carried on like idiots, idiots! What am I saying? I—I—please excuse me! [*She rushes out the inner door.*]

Roger: I move that the meeting adjourn.

Mrs. Bassett: I second the motion.

Rosemary: I don't understand. What happened?

Mrs. Bassett: Poor Miss Alma!

Roger: She hasn't been herself lately. . . . [*They all go out. After a moment Alma reenters with a tray of refreshments, looks about the deserted interior and bursts into hysterical laughter. The light dims out.*]

Soliloquy of the Spanish Cloister	*Richard III*
GR-R-R—there go, my heart's abhorrence!	Act I, Scene 1
Water your damned flower-pots, do!	
If hate killed men, Brother Lawrence,	Gloucester: Now is the winter of our discontent
God's blood, would not mine kill you!	Made glorious summer by this sun of York;
What? your myrtle-bush wants trimming?	And all the clouds that lour'd upon our house
Oh, that rose has prior claims—	In the deep bosom of the ocean buried.
Needs its leaden vase filled brimming?	Now are our brows bound with victorious wreaths;
Hell dry you up with its flames!	

Soliloquy of the Spanish Cloister (cont.)

At the meal we sit together:
  Salve tibi! I must hear
Wise talk of the kind of weather,
  Sort of season, time of year:
Not a plenteous cork-crop: scarcely
  Dare we hope oak-galls, I doubt:
What's the Latin name for 'parsley'?
  What's the Greek name for Swine's
  Snout?

Whew! We'll have our platter bur-
  nished,
  Laid with care on our own shelf!
With a fire-new spoon we're furnished,
  And a goblet for ourself,
Rinsed like something sacrificial
  Ere 'tis fit to touch our chaps—
Marked with L, for our initial!
  (He-he! There his lily snaps!)

Saint, forsooth! While brown Dolores
  Squats outside the Convent bank,
With Sanchicha, telling stories,
  Steeping tresses in the tank,
Blue-black, lustrous, thick like horse-
  hairs,
  —Can't I see his dead eye glow,
Bright as 'twere a Barbary's corsair's?
  (That is, if he'd let it show!)

When he finishes refection,
  Knife and fork he never lays
Cross-wise, to my recollection,
  As I do, in Jesu's praise.
I, the Trinity illustrate,
  Drinking watered orange-pulp—
In three sips the Arian frustrate;
  While he drains his at one gulp!

Oh, those melons! If he's able
  We're to have a feast; so nice!
One goes to the Abbot's table,
  All of us get each a slice.
How go on your flowers? None double?
  Not one fruit-sort can you spy?
Strange!—And I, too, at such trouble,
  Keep them close-nipped on the sly!

There's a great text in Galatians,
  Once you trip on it, entails
Twenty-nine distinct damnations,
  One sure, if another fails:

Richard III (continued)

Our bruised arms hung up for monu-
  ments;
Our stern alarums changed to merry
  meetings,
Our dreadful marches to delightful
  measures.
Grim-visaged war hath smooth'd his
  wrinkled front;
And now, instead of mounting barbed
  steeds
To fright the souls of fearful adver-
  saries,
He capers nimbly in a lady's chamber
To the lascivious pleasing of a lute.
But I, that am not shaped for sportive
  tricks,
Nor made to court an amorous looking-
  glass;
I, that am rudely stamp'd, and want
  love's majesty
To strut before a wanton ambling
  nymph;
I, that am curtail'd of this fair propor-
  tion,
Cheated of feature by dissembling na-
  ture,
Deform'd, unfinish'd, sent before my
  time
Into this breathing world, scarce half
  made up,
And that so lamely and unfashionable
That dogs bark at me as I halt by them;
Why, I, in this weak piping time of
  peace,
Have no delight to pass away the time,
Unless to spy my shadow in the sun
And descant on mine own deformity:
And therefore, since I cannot prove a
  lover,
To entertain these fair well-spoken
  days,
I am determined to prove a villain
And hate the idle pleasures of these
  days.
Plots have I laid, inductions danger-
  ous,
By drunken prophecies, libels and
  dreams,
To set my brother Clarence and the
  king
In deadly hate the one against the
  other:

Soliloquy of the Spanish Cloister (cont.)

If I trip him just a-dying,
  Sure of Heaven as sure as can be,
Spin him round and send him flying
  Off to Hell, a Manichee?

Or, my scrofulous French novel
  On grey paper with blunt type!
Simply glance at it, you grovel
  Hand and foot in Belial's gripe:
If I double down its pages
  At the woeful sixteenth print,
When he gathers his greengages,
  Ope a sieve and slip it in't?

Or, there's Satan!—one might venture
  Pledge one's soul to him, yet leave
Such a flaw in the indenture
  As he'd miss till, past retrieve,
Blasted lay that rose-acacia
  We're so proud of! *Hy, Zy, Hine* ...
'St, there's Vespers! *Plena gratiâ*
  Ave, Virgo! Gr-r-r—you swine!

Robert Browning

Richard III (continued)

And if King Edward be as true and
  just
As I am subtle, false and treacherous,
This day should Clarence closely be
  mew'd up,
About a prophecy, which says that G
  of Edward's heirs the murderer
  shall be.
Dive, thoughts, down to my soul: here
  Clarence comes.

William Shakespeare

Poetry 11

In previous chapters, we have discussed the preparation of a selection for oral interpretation. The suggestions offered are applicable to prose and poetry. However, there are certain elements which, although not peculiar to the study of poetry, are by emphasis significantly important to its understanding.

A definition of poetry could be selected from any one of those formulated by the authorities from Aristotle to the many critics and poets of today. In the final analysis, however, poetry cannot be defined. It is too intricate, too complex to be explained in a single definition. It is more important that the oral reader focus his attention on the *nature* of poetry. In order to understand its nature, we must know something of its elements.

It is natural to begin an investigation of the elements of poetry by comparing poetry to prose. It is not easy to distinguish between the two. The difference is only one of degree. In the broader sense, poetry makes its appeal to emotion and thus to the imagination. Prose has an emotional element, but such an element is often subordinate to reason. A selection which is on the borderline between prose and poetry is sometimes called poetic prose or prose poetry. Throughout this chapter, references will be made to the two types of literature, with the understanding that the difference between the two is largely a matter of degree. (In this connection, the student should review the discussion of meter in Chapter 5.)

It is well to keep in mind from the very beginning just what can be expected of poetry and what cannot be expected of poetry. If the reader has a misconception of the purposes of poetry, it is easy for him to be disappointed and confused. One of the most common false conceptions is that all poetry must teach a lesson, must contain a moral, or, as is often said, "must have a message." The reader may get a worthy or noble idea from a poem, but such a result alone does not make for poetry. As moral teaching is not the intent of poetic literature, it cannot be evaluated or appreciated on that basis alone. The reader who is always looking for the *lesson* may slight a very important element that the poet has used to create his poem. The concept of *lesson searching* can further hamper the student in his evaluation and judgment of poetry. It can cause him to cast aside a very good poem and hold onto some inferior jingle because the jingle represents a moral or lesson that parallels his thinking at the time. Lesson searching may seriously affect the growth and development of literary taste.

Another false conception is that the subject matter of poetry is synonymous with beauty. Yet the experience of literature encompasses not only the beautiful, but also the ugly, the average, and the nondescript. However, the question that must be answered here is "What *is* beauty?" To the poet Robinson Jeffers, the hawk is an artistic being, worthy of poetic treatment.[1] But the common conception of a hawk with a broken wing, returning to its home to die, would not encompass the beautiful. William Faulkner is often criticized because he illuminates what many term the *ugly*. People say, "Why doesn't Faulkner tell about the nice things in Mississippi?" as if his failure to describe what is commonly considered as beautiful condemns him to literary oblivion.

Still others have the false conception that poetry is a means of emotional escape. A young man who had just received a "Dear John" letter from his girl back home found great solace in Longfellow's poem "The Rainy Day." No one would deny the depressed young man assistance, but his particular emotional problem should not become his sole basis for understanding and appreciating poetry.

It is true that at times poetry may serve in each of these situations. However, the appreciation and evaluation of poetry do not rest on any one of the concepts. In order to inquire intelligently what we may expect of poetry, let us examine in detail some of its elements. The student must keep in mind that, although for the purpose of study and clarity we may discuss an element in isolation, we must consider each element in its relationship to the other elements. We do not want to think of the association as a mechanical one, the separate elements to be assembled as one would a jigsaw puzzle. We would rather think that poetry is a gestalt, the separate aspects of which may be examined only in their relationship to the whole.

The compactness and concentration of poetry calls for a special use of language. The very nature of poetry makes it more difficult to communicate than informative material. Poetry deals with an emotionalized experience. The experience encompasses moods, feelings, and attitudes. This does not mean that special words are reserved for poetry. Any word rightly used may contribute to a poem. No one facet of language is the exclusive property of poetry, but all are of significance in giving intensity to poetry. It is through language that the poet is able to turn his experiences into an aesthetic form, i.e., into a poem.

---

[1] See "Hurt Hawks," *The Selected Poetry of Robinson Jeffers*, Random House, Inc., New York, 1938, pp. 198–199.

The style of poetry

The poet chooses an idea, assumes an attitude toward that idea, and selects the images that he feels will convey his attitude toward the idea. Then he chooses his words (diction) and arranges them (composition) to convey the images that in turn convey the attitude toward the idea. Not that a poet goes through such steps deliberately, for he is caught up in a wave of creativity that engulfs him.[2] But he is subject to their order, nevertheless. Therefore, to convey the images of his emotionalized idea, the poet must choose and arrange his words with care. In his arrangement, the artist is of course free to use the same word for more than one meaning. The fact that a word can have a threefold or even a tenfold meaning serves as a valuable resource for the poet. He is not always troubled by the equivocal property of symbols, for he is willing to permit his readers to enrich and intensify the meaning of his poem by their own associations with his words. But the predominantly factual or informative writer finds that the multiplicity of meaning of words confuses the sense, if not destroys it, and he is continually waging an unsuccessful war against the equivocal property of symbols.

The poet selects the proper words to give the intellectual, emotional, and imaginative aspects of the poetic experience. Whereas a prose writer may go to great lengths to gather many details for his presentation, the poet may rely on a few, but well-selected sharp details. He deliberately chooses words which offer flexibility. He never restricts himself to exacting dictionary meanings. When the poet sees that the literal meaning of a word will not reflect his intent, he turns to figurative language.

Let us discuss here certain phrases of each of the facets of style which are particularly important to poetry.

The idea or meaning of a poem

The total meaning of a poem is the totality of the experience it represents. When we speak of meaning, we do not mean the *kernel* that we can take out and put in a prose paraphrase. Robert Frost once said that a poem is that which is lost in a paraphrase. Although the paraphrase may be used to help clarify the meaning, it is never the poem.

In the dramatic monologue "My Last Duchess," is there a single,

[2] William Faulkner refers to his inspiration as a "demon" (see "Forward," *The Faulkner Reader*, Vintage Books, Random House, Inc., New York, 1959); Housman refers to his inspiration as a "continuous excitement" (see "Preface to the First Edition," *Last Poems*, Richards Press Ltd., London, 1937).

dominant idea? No, for the ideas, although they are many, are only a part of the poem. They must be supported by the other elements of style, and the value of the monologue must be judged on the ideas as they are illuminated, not just on the ideas themselves. As Brooks and Warren state: ". . . the real poet in presenting his theme never depends *merely* on general statement. The poem itself is the dramatizing of the theme in terms of situation, character, imagery, rhythm, tone, etc." [3]

John Donne's sonnet "Death" illustrates how a poem can present one dominant idea. But Donne uses the other elements of style to achieve the complete work of art he seeks. The personification of Death and Fate, as well as paradox and variation in meter, are utilized to vivify the theme. All these elements are a part of the total poem. Note how the form of the sonnet itself, by its compactness, contributes to the idea.

In the poem "Dover Beach," there is a prevailing idea, but Matthew Arnold also uses a variety of the aspects of style to create the poem. There is a narrative element, for a situation is given and a person is speaking. The use of imagery and rhythm contribute to the mood, feeling, and total impact of the poem.

By its very nature, a sonnet presents a thought or statement of an idea. Therefore, in analyzing the nature of a sonnet, the student must seek the dominant theme, but he must not stop there, for he will not understand the theme in its entirety until he has appreciated the other elements of style that complete the sonnet's idea. Read the selection below by the master poet William Shakespeare, and note the poetic devices used to enhance the idea of the sonnet:

Let me not to the marriage of true minds
Admit impediments. Love is not love
Which alters when it alteration finds,
Or bends with the remover to remove.
O no! it is an ever-fixed mark
That looks on tempests and is never shaken;
It is the star to every wandering bark,
Whose worth's unknown, although his height be taken.
Love's not Time's fool, though rosy lips and cheeks
Within his bending sickle's compass come;
Love alters not with his brief hours and weeks,
But bears it out even to the edge of doom.
   If this be error and upon me proved,
   I never writ, nor no man ever loved.

[3] Cleanth Brooks and Robert Penn Warren, *Understanding Poetry*, rev. ed., p. 363. Copyright 1950 by Holt, Rinehart and Winston, Inc., New York.

We would emphasize that there are elements of poetry which serve as the tools by which the artist creates his work. The idea of the poem serves as a point of departure and is developed by emotion. Emotion, in turn, is revealed by imagery, diction, and composition. Therefore, let us consider the other devices that a poet uses to develop his idea.

The emotionalized response of the author: tone

In relating the experience in a poem, the poet reveals his attitude toward that experience. In so doing, the poet expresses *tone*. *Tone* is defined as the attitude of the writer toward his material and his audience. Therefore, an analysis of the tone of a selection will lead the student to the emotions that the poet has used to surround his ideas. There is no limit to the shadings of tone that an author may choose from. Gorrell and Laird say: "The writer may approach his material and his audience seriously, or he may adopt a joking or whimsical manner toward both. He may promote confidence with a judicial calm, or he may stimulate action with exaggerated enthusiasm. He may be objective, formal, informal, ironic, jovial, confidential, flattering, wheedling, belligerent, conciliating, or what not." [4] Tone may also be spoken of in the terminology used to classify emotions, for the poet may be angry, sad, joyful, hateful, proud, and the like.

We are continually taking attitudes toward what we say in our daily conversation, thereby imparting shades of meaning to what we say by our *tone* of voice. There is a common expression, "It is not what you say but how you say it." In our everyday speech, we vary the meaning of "yes" and "no" by the inflection in our voice, by the expression on our face, or by a twinkle in our eye. Usually the poet does not have these visual tools to clarify his tone. He must rely upon the use of mute symbols to convey his meaning. Yet tone is very important to the poet, and he must achieve his tone by the symbols he chooses to arrange on the printed page. Tone is equally important to the oral reader of poetry, for he must translate the mute symbols into an oral response. The oral reader will find that tone is more easily determined in dramatic poetry than in lyrical poetry, for a dramatic poem labels its speakers and clarifies their attitudes. But in a highly subjective lyric, the tone is so integrated into the totality of the poem that it may escape notice. Therefore the lyrical poem, by its subtle approach, may create emotion without seeming to do so. Although it may be enough for the audience to grasp the total impact of the lyric, the reader must be astute enough to know how that impact is achieved.

[4] R. M. Gorrell and C. Laird, *Modern English Handbook*, 2d ed., pp. 125–126. © 1956 by Prentice-Hall, Inc., Englewood Cliffs, N.J.

For it is through the use of tone that a writer can take a hackneyed, trite idea and make of it something fresh and new. The use of the correct words is again important in supporting the tone. A conversational quality created by the carefully selected word can give a casual tone which assists in circumventing the overly serious implications of an idea. Thus the *light touch* obviates the maudlin and permits Emily Dickinson to deal effectively with subjects whose treatment might otherwise become sentimental, tawdry, or distasteful.

Tone is not delineated by any set of rules or a formula. Its appreciation requires careful reading, a keen sensitivity, and an awareness of words and word relationships. The tone of each of the poems in the Prefatory Readings for Chapters 5 and 6 is easily recognizable. Reread the poems and see how obvious is the tone in each. Compare the tone in the more dramatic poem "My Last Duchess" to the tone of the less dramatic "Stopping by Woods on a Snowy Evening." How does the poet prepare for the mood, and what did the poet use to create the tone? Is there any variation in the tone?

Read the following poems to determine the tone. Keep in mind that the poet will choose and arrange his words to develop an emotional component.

Come Not, When I Am Dead

Come not, when I am dead,
   To drop thy foolish tears upon my grave,
To trample round my fallen head,
   And vex the unhappy dust thou wouldst not save
There let the wind sweep and the plover cry;
      But thou, go by.

Child, if it were thine error or thy crime
   I care no longer, being all unblest:
Wed whom thou wilt, but I am sick of Time,
   And desire to rest.
Pass on, weak heart, and leave me where I lie:
      Go by, go by.

Alfred, Lord Tennyson

Why So Pale and Wan?

Why so pale and wan, fond lover?
   Prithee, why so pale?
Will, when looking well can't move her,
   Looking ill prevail?
Prithee, why so pale?

Why so dull and mute, young sinner?
  Prithee, why so mute?
Will, when speaking well can't win her,
  Saying nothing do't?
  Prithee, why so mute?

Quit, quit for shame! This will not move;
  This cannot take her.
If of herself she will not love,
  Nothing can make her:
  The devil take her!

Sir John Suckling

The Bustle in a House [5]

The bustle in a house
The morning after death
Is solemnest of industries
Enacted upon earth,—

The sweeping up the heart,
And putting love away
We shall not want to use again
Until eternity.

Emily Dickinson

Imagery

The poet seeks to vivify his emotionalized idea through imagery. If extrasensory perceptions are excluded as irrelevant to this discussion, sensory perceptions form the basis for conveying experience. Because the poet is generally limited to communicating his experience by sight through the use of words, he employs language to arouse the entire spectrum of sensory perception. The poet's use of words to stimulate our senses is referred to as *imagery*, perhaps because the reader tends to *see* all sensations in his imagination. But as has been pointed out in Chapter 5, an image may stimulate not only sight but also any of the other senses.

An awareness of the way in which the poet uses imagery is very important to the oral reader, for he must re-create these images for his audiences. The images of the poet are effective only to the degree that they recall or evoke vivid experience in the reader. An image ef-

[5] Emily Dickinson, "The Bustle in a House," from *The Complete Poems of Emily Dickinson*, edited by Thomas H. Johnson, Little, Brown and Company, Publishers.

fectively interpreted can intensify the meaning of a poem by arousing all the forces that the reader associates with the image. The descriptive aspect of imagery often generates symbolic overtones. Matthew Arnold's poem "Dover Beach" illustrates how complex imagery may further meaning. Note how Arnold's image of the sea utilizes a variety of sensations. The calm of the water sets the noise level; the flickering of the moon dominates the sight; the sweetness of the night air fills the nostrils. In place of the tactile sense, Arnold inserts kinesthesia; for the fullness of the tide, the weight of the moon on the straits, and the standing of the cliffs all act on us inwardly, forcing our body to tense and to relax with the pressures put upon us by the setting of the poem. Arnold keeps up this pressure with "a bright girdle," "naked shingles," and "nor help for pain."

Kinetic imagery is likewise present in "Dover Beach," for although the sea is calm, the following phrases connote movement:

The tide is full

the light gleams, and is gone

the cliffs of England stand, glimmering

Come to the window

pebbles which the waves suck back, and fling.

And all of these from the first stanza alone! It is possible to imagine that Arnold deliberately plans to keep his lovers static, to demonstrate their helplessness, while all of the rest of the world is in movement against them.

The thermal sense makes its contribution. The coolness of the sea pervades the whole poem, and we grasp the refreshing sensation of the night air and the spray on our skin. The breath of the night wind affects our nakedness, depriving us of the soothing sensation of the sea air.

Students often ask whether Arnold *planned* to include such a variety of images or whether they arose unconsciously in his moment of creativity. Arnold himself could not be trusted to answer this question definitively. As was pointed out earlier, Poe claims a premeditated formula for the successful composition of a poem, but his essay seems facetious. Actually, the inquiry is academic, for the images are present regardless of how they made their appearance.[6] The oral interpreter

---

[*] Von Abele says: "The rightful answer is that the only 'intention' with which we, as readers, have any business is what might be called 'intention realized,' or the work as it exists in its presumably final form, not the work as it might have been had its author done other things than those he in fact did do." See

must be aware of the use of imagery and develop a sense of the use of descriptive language if he is to share his understanding of poetry with his listeners.

Figurative language: a choice of words

If the poet cannot create the imagery he seeks for in his emotionalized idea by employing language in its conventionalized form, he turns to figurative usage. Yelland, Jones, and Easton say: "In literal language we mean exactly and completely what we say, in figurative language we do not." [7] This indirect route to the senses has been discussed in Chapter 5, but it is particularly important to the compact and concentrated style of poetry. A metaphor or simile can say much in a few words. This possibility suggests to the oral reader that he must carefully study how the poet has used his words *when he is not meaning exactly and completely what he is saying*. Although figurative language can add intensity to the emotionalized idea, it can also be misunderstood and misinterpreted and therefore subtract rather than add. A careless reader can slip over a simile or a metaphor and fail to grasp the comparison. A superficial reader can easily miss the significance of personification or allegory and thus fail to convey the basic meaning of the poem.

Most poetry tends to be evocative, that is, it calls up various experiences and feelings, offering the reader imaginative pleasure in seeing likeness in unlike things. A poem may begin with the known or real experience, but increases its sense appeal by the imaginative experience offered by the image. Using figures of speech intensifies the emotional reaction to a poem, not by duplication, but by suggestion and comparison. The value of a poem is never dependent solely upon the quantity of ideas, but rather upon the degree to which the poet can let the reader participate in the depths of his exploration and his insights. Again, it is by the figure of speech that he can communicate his subjectivity to his readers.

The symbol. The simile and the metaphor are always useful, but the poet often finds a need to go to more complex figures. The *symbol* serves as an important element to the creative author in his efforts to intensify the imagery. To distinguish between a symbol and its cousins, the *image* and the *metaphor*, is a task equal to the best of the

---

Rudolph von Abele, "Symbolism and the Student," *College English*, vol. 16, p. 428, April, 1955. Reprinted with the permission of the National Council of Teachers of English.

[7] H. L. Yelland, S. C. J. Jones, and K. S. W. Easton, *A Handbook of Literary Terms*, Philosophical Library, Inc., New York, 1950, p. 74.

critics,[8] and not all will consider the effort worthwhile. Perrine says: "Imagery, metaphor, and symbol shade into each other, and are sometimes difficult to distinguish. In general, however, an image means only what it is; a metaphor means something else than what it is; and a symbol means what it is and something more too." [9] Of course, literally, a symbol means something which stands for something else, and in this sense all words are symbols. However in a literary sense, the meaning is more confined. Abrams says: "As commonly used in criticism . . . 'symbol' is applied only to a word or phrase signifying an object which itself has significance; that is, the object referred to has a range of meaning beyond itself." [10] For example, in Frost's poem "Wild Grapes" the image of the poem is its referent in the empirical world and is what it is—a boy and a girl in a birch tree. Frost uses a metaphor when he says that the top of the white birch tree is a headdress, but Frost means something else than what he says because he knows, and he knows that the reader knows, that the top of a birch tree is not a headdress. Furthermore, the word "headdress" itself is used literally and has no symbolic quality. It is merely a headdress. However, in his conclusion, when Frost speaks of what he has and has not learned with his "hands" and his "heart," the poet is using these parts of the body symbolically, for these have a range of meaning beyond themselves, and they refer to hands and hearts and yet to something more. The symbol is perhaps the most potent and the most difficult of the three cousins to understand. It has at least two meanings: the literal meaning, which is fairly easy to grasp; and the symbolic meaning, which is offered in such a way that it suggests a variety of special meanings.

The complexity of the symbol is shown in the poem "Stopping by Woods on a Snowy Evening." Much controversy has arisen about the last two lines. What symbolism *is* implied? The general frame of reference is usually agreed upon, but within that frame there could be several different meanings. Are the miles symbolic of all the tasks that Frost must perform before he is entitled to sleep, which, in turn, is symbolic of death? Or is the sleep symbolic of the reward that comes to a man who does his duty rather than lingering on to enjoy the pleasures of life? The same controversy has arisen over Frost's poem "The Road Not Taken." What choice does the author mean? There is

[8] For distinguishing definitions, see William F. Thrall, Addison Hibbard, and C. Hugh Holman (eds.), *A Handbook to Literature*, The Odyssey Press, Inc., New York, 1960, p. 478.
[9] Laurence Perrine, *Sound and Sense*, Harcourt, Brace & World, Inc., New York, 1956, p. 63.
[10] M. H. Abrams, *A Glossary of Literary Terms*, p. 95. Copyright 1957 by Holt, Rinehart and Winston, Inc., New York.

agreement that the poem was not written about the choice a man made on two paths in a wood. What is the significance of the choice? [11]

The stock symbols are familiar, but the poet is not obligated to use conventional associations. The *lamb* may be traditionally used to symbolize weakness, as it is in Blake's poem "The Tiger." However, Blake makes some departure from convention by using the *tiger* symbol in an almost personal way, asking the tiger, "Did he who made the Lamb make thee?" A complete break with conventional symbolism occurs in T. S. Eliot's poem "Gerontion"; Eliot compares Christ, who is traditionally spoken of as a *lamb,* with the lamb's archenemy, the *tiger,* when he says, "In the juvescence of the year came Christ the tiger...." [12] Note that Eliot's departure from tradition would not be effective unless the reader was familiar with the conventional response to the symbol *lamb* as it was used by Blake.

The oral interpreter may well ask what symbolism means to interpretation. He will find that the use of symbolism requires much study, a broad knowledge of literature, and a sensitivity for the delicate or possibly the prescient in order that he may reach an accurate interpretation. In attempting to understand symbolism, the reader must be cautious to use restraint with his imagination. It is easy to see symbolism in everything. One student became so carried away with Robert Frost's "Stopping by Woods on a Snowy Evening" that he saw symbolism everywhere. To him the woods was the world he was about to enter, the darkness was symbolic of the evil, and the snow was the light of education. A reader may not read anything he chooses into a poem. There must be a legitimate basis for the symbolic interpretation.

Irony. Another figure of speech which requires special consideration in interpreting poetry is *irony,* wherein the intended meaning is opposite to that expressed. As Thrall, Hibbard, and Holman point out, irony is more easily detected in speech than in writing because of the added property of vocal intonation. [13] Therefore, the interpreter is doubly obligated to use irony effectively.

At its best, irony is subtle. Its use presumes a very special understanding between the author and the reader, as if they were good

---

[11] Frost himself may have had this poem in mind when he spoke of the roads open to the Presidency of the United States in his essay "The Constant Symbol." See *The Poems of Robert Frost,* Vintage Books, Random House, Inc., New York, 1946, pp. xvi–xvii.

[12] T. S. Eliot, *The Complete Poems and Plays 1909–1950,* Harcourt, Brace & World, Inc., New York, 1958, p. 21.

[13] Thrall, Hibbard, and Holman, *op. cit.,* p. 248.

enough friends to say one thing and mean the opposite. When irony is grasped by the oral reader and used effectively, it can portray the attitude and mood of the selection in its entirety.

As with other figures of speech, irony can be misunderstood. It should not be confused with sarcasm and satire, which involve ridicule, pain, derision, and bitter language. Satire may have a higher motive than sarcasm, but it is still ridicule. Irony, a figure of literary speech, may or may not be used for ridicule.[14] A misunderstanding of its application can give the very opposite meaning from that which was intended. For example, in the poem "My Last Duchess" a misreading of the duke's line, "Even had you skill in speech—(which I have not)" could distort Browning's intent, for the author means for the duke to call attention to the nobleman's fluency by a false gesture toward humility. This type of irony is called *verbal irony*. A second type, which Laurence Perrine calls *dramatic irony*,[15] allows the speaker to say what he means, but the author means for the reader to know that the author does not believe what the speaker is saying. If, for example, the duke had been sincere in his apology, but Browning intended the reader to assume that the apology was inappropriate, then dramatic irony would be employed.

The modern poet E. A. Robinson seems to cultivate the ironic, as is clearly seen in his poem "Captain Craig": [16]

> She gives enough,
> You say; but what is giving like hers worth?
> What is a gift without the soul to guide it?
> "Poor dears, and they have cancers?—Oh!" she says;
> And away she works at the new altar-cloth
> For the Reverend Hieronymus Mackintosh—
> Third person, Jerry. "Jerry," she says, "can say
> Such lovely things, and make life seem so sweet!"
> Jerry can drink, also.—And there she goes,
> Like a whirlwind through an orchard in the springtime—
> Throwing herself away as if she thought
> The world and the whole planetary circus
> Were a flourish of apple blossoms. Look at her!

Notice the suggested irony of the possible but unrealized service that existed for the shallow heroine. What ironic suggestion did Robinson intend in the rush and hurry of the woman's activity?

In the phrase "the world and the whole planetary circus," Robinson uses irony to reinforce his diction. This technique is illustrated in one

---

[14] Perrine, *op. cit.*, p. 88.
[15] *Ibid.*, p. 90.
[16] Edwin Arlington Robinson, *Collected Poems*, The Macmillan Company, New York, 1937, pp. 127–128. Reprinted with permission of The Macmillan Company.

of the earlier poems "Zola," in which Robinson joins adjectives with a noun of opposite meaning in the phrase "squeamish and emasculate crusade." The tone of irony may be found in many of Robinson's poems of character such as "Richard Cory," "Miniver Cheevy," and "Mr. Flood's Party."

The poets Ezra Pound, T. S. Eliot, and W. H. Auden also make wide use of irony. One of Auden's poems, "As I Walked Out One Evening," will be analyzed at the close of the chapter and comments on its use of irony are found there. Browning uses irony in "My Last Duchess" very interestingly, for the duke's description of himself is quite different from the way he is described in the remainder of the poem. Ironically, although the duke intends to describe the duchess, the duke has described himself.

Allusion. The special use of language by which the poet brings historical or literary material into his selection from sources outside his own work is known as *allusion*.[17] The use of the allusion lets the poet say much in very few words, often in only one word. If recognized by the reader, this figure of speech can add much to the understanding and appreciation of poetry. Therefore, it is the well-read and informed interpreter who can respond to the poet's allusions. Frost has his heroine in "Wild Grapes" say that she "was come after like Eurydice." With only two words, "like Eurydice," Frost is able to add for the knowledgeable reader the entire story of Orpheus and Eurydice and their experiences in Hades. Keats makes use of allusion throughout the poem "Ode to a Nightingale":

Perhaps the self-same song that found a path
Through the sad heart of Ruth, when sick for home
She stood in tears amid the alien corn.

The reference to the familiar Biblical story, with the one word "Ruth," brings the image and the emotion of the traditional story to intensify the feeling of forlornness.

The allusion can be used in many different ways. It can make its references to places, situations, events, and characters in literary or historical or Biblical material. The oral reader may find the poet's reference beyond his range of knowledge. If this is true, the interpreter will need to discover the background of the allusion. He must keep in mind the importance of allowing the listener to share the

[17] It may come as a surprise to some that allusion is considered a figure of speech rather than a literal comparison or simply the use of inductive reasoning by example. However, if figurative language is defined as an "intentional departure from the normal order ... to create a pictorial effect ..." the allusion is a figure of speech. See Thrall, Hibbard, and Holman, *op. cit.*, p. 202.

same experience. If the reader feels that the majority of his listeners will be unfamiliar with an allusion, he may wish to call attention to it in his introduction. Furthermore, when he approaches the passage in which the allusion occurs, he may wish to read more slowly so that the audience will have time to recall the allusion and/or to reflect on its significance. A review of the discussion on timing in Chapter 6 would be helpful here.

The composition of the poem

The fifth component of style, arrangement, is crucial, for it serves "to hold all the others in union." [18] Composition is highly important to poetry because its structure is graphically presented by its verse form. A short story or a novel may wander without running the risk of immediate detection, but a poem must preserve its unity or be immediately unmasked. Several of the elements of arrangement which are strategically important in the composition of a poem are discussed below.

Sound. The musical quality of sound is so strong in poetry that DeWitt Parker says that poetry is closer to music than is any other art.[19] Many poems make their strongest appeal through sound and therefore the reader of poetry must have a sensitive ear. It is difficult to discuss sound and musical language separately from the other elements of poetry. We may enjoy musical sound in poetry for its own sake, but we must remember that our enjoyment will be intensified if we enjoy the rhythm as it supports the emotionalized idea.

The poet may reinforce or intensify meaning through sound by his choice of words, not just the obviously onomatopoetic words, but the ones that suggest sound by their connotations. This point is illustrated by the phrase "put a bullet through his head," taken from the last line of the poem "Richard Cory" by Edwin Arlington Robinson, referred to in a previous chapter. These words are not obviously onomatopoetic, but the phrase "put a bullet" suggests the sounds of violence. Such a phrase is much more intense than the words in the remainder of the poem, producing a quick, surpriselike effect.

The parallel of sound and meaning through choice of words is also shown in William Carlos Williams' poem "The Jungle": [20]

[18] Allan H. Gilbert, *Literary Criticism,* American Book Company, New York, 1940, p. 153.
[19] See DeWitt Parker, *The Principles of Aesthetics,* Appleton-Century-Crofts, Inc., New York, 1946, chap. 8.
[20] From *The Complete Collected Poems of William Carlos Williams,* p. 170. Copyright 1938 by New Directions. Reprinted by permission of New Directions, Publishers, Norfolk, Conn.

It is not the still weight
of the trees, the
breathless interior of the wood,
tangled with wrist-thick

vines, the flies, reptiles,
the forever fearful monkeys
screaming and running
in the branches—

          but
a girl waiting
shy, brown, soft-eyed—
to guide you
        Upstairs, sir.

The early English poets made widespread use of the various forms of repeating sound and of associating meaning with sound, a brief discussion of which occurs in Chapter 5 under Alliteration, Assonance and Onomatopoeia. Later English and American poets have made more sparing use of these devices. The way in which alliteration conveys an image or a sudden action and therefore helps to convey the meaning of a poem is often mystical and defies analysis. In the W. H. Auden poem "O Where Are You Going?" Auden uses alliteration profusely. Yet the result is a most happy one. The antithesis of "reader" and "rider" seems to sharpen the image and demonstrate how the concepts are related. Just how this comes about is not easy to explain by simply saying that the two words begin with the same sound. Yet the effect is achieved. When alliteration is used for ornamentation rather than as one facet of a unified composition, it may become monotonous or even ludicrous.

Assonance may escape notice when used boldly because the repetition of the medial sound is more camouflaged than the repetition of the initial consonant in alliteration or the final sound in rhyme or consonance. The phrase "on your path to the pass" from "O Where Are You Going?" seems less forced than does "said horror to hearer." It is interesting to note that some oral interpreters miss opportunities for assonance because they do not pronounce their words as the author had intended. Many English-speaking persons do not use the same vowel sound in "path" that they use in "pass." If the vowel sounds change, the repetitive effect is lost. The reader must examine his poem to see what were the intentions of the author and should, under most circumstances, be willing to make his pronunciation conform to the poet's intent. What other possibilities besides "path" and "pass" might some interpreters speaking American English be likely to miss?

A dilemma occurs when the interpreter must either pronounce a word artificially or in an archaic manner to complete a rhyme or must sacrifice the rhyme to give a word its accustomed sound. The adverb "again" is frequently made to rhyme with "pain" or "rain" or other words featuring the [eɪ] glide or diphthong. If the reader feels that the rhyme needs punctuating, he may risk artificiality; if the reader feels that the audience will sense the rhyme sufficiently by employing the accustomed pronunciation, then he may risk the conventional sounds. In many instances, there may be no completely satisfactory solution, for the author has built the dilemma into the selection itself.

The use of repetition of sound in alliteration, assonance, consonance, chiasmus, and other lesser known antithetical forms can give the effect of binding together the isolated elements of a poem. Such an effect has a tendency to shape the poem. Note how much of the composition of W. H. Auden's "O Where Are You Going?" is dependent upon his repetition of sounds.

In working with devices of repetition, the interpreter must be doubly aware that his audience is receiving from him only an audible stimulus. Any visuality of the words must be an invention of the listeners themselves. Not only can the silent reader *see* the symbols which represent the parallel sounds, but he can also see them *in their context* and therefore suppress to the proper extent the rhythmical elements of the repetition that tend, when dominant, to absorb the meaning. The extent to which alliteration pervades the poem "O Where Are You Going?" would require careful planning by the reader to assist his audience in maintaining a proper balance between the idea that the poem conveys and the rhythm that it uses to reinforce the idea.

Onomatopoeia is listed along with alliteration and assonance because it is a device of sound. It could, however, be listed under diction, for it definitely involves a choice of one word over another. It is also, in a sense, repetitive because the sound of the word echoes its meaning, setting up an instantaneous oscillation between symbol and thing symbolized in the ears of the listener. The "lowing" of the herd in the first stanza of Thomas Gray's famous poem adds emphasis to the image of the end of the day to anyone who has heard the cattle bellow as they begin their way home at dusk. The interpreter should refrain from pushing such a word vocally in order not to appear imitating the cattle. The thrill of association must belong to the audience, for onomatopoeia gains its effect when the listener recognizes the double effect of lowing, in the same manner that an audience responds to a pun or a play on words. Nor can the word be slighted. It must be given just the correct pronunciation so that it prods the audience to make its own associations.

Sound devices in poetry should not be used for decorative purposes. When the experience of the poem can be enhanced by the devices of sound, then such devices are legitimate technique. The oral interpreter must be aware of these implements available to the poet and feel their effects for they are meant to be pleasing to the ear. It is the obligation of the reader, therefore, to encourage his listeners to put the devices of sound in their proper places to assist in achieving the total experience of the poetry.

The following poems have been chosen because their sound patterns are evident. Read them carefully, listening for the sound as it supports the meaning. In the first poem, "God's Grandeur," note the use of alliteration and assonance. How does the use of these two devices of sound contribute to the meaning of the poem. How would an oral reader communicate these effects to his audience.

"O Where Are You Going?" also illustrates assonance. Does its usage assist in forming and shaping the poem? In addition to the use of assonance, are there other sound techniques in this selection? In reading the poem aloud, did it require extra effort in enunciation and pronunciation to communicate the sound effects?

The last selection makes use of onomatopoeia, but what other sound patterns are used? How does the word "toll" contribute to the totality of the poem?

God's Grandeur [21]

The world is charged with the grandeur of God.
    It will flame out, like shining from shook foil;
    It gathers to a greatness, like the ooze of oil
Crushed. Why do men then now not reck his rod?
Generations have trod, have trod, have trod;
    And all is seared with trade; bleared, smeared with toil;
    And wears man's smudge and shares man's smell: the soil
Is bare now, nor can foot feel, being shod.

And for all this, nature is never spent;
    There lives the dearest freshness deep down things;
And though the last lights off the black West went
    Oh, morning, at the brown brink eastward, springs—
Because the Holy Ghost over the bent
    World broods with warm breast and with ah! bright wings.

Gerard Manley Hopkins

[21] Gerard Manley Hopkins, *Poems of Gerard Manley Hopkins*, 3rd. ed., W. H. Gardner, ed., 1948, p. 70. Reprinted by permission of the Oxford University Press, New York.

O Where Are You Going? [22]

'O where are you going?' said reader to rider,
'That vallye is fatal when furnaces burn,
Yonder's the midden whose odours will madden,
That gap is the grave where the tall return.'

'O do you imagine,' said fearer to farer,
'That dusk will delay on your path to the pass,
Your diligent looking discover the lacking
Your footsteps feel from granite to grass?'

'O what was that bird,' said horror to hearer,
'Did you see that shape in the twisted trees?
Behind you swiftly the figure come softly,
The spot on your skin is a shocking disease?'

'Out of this house'—said rider to reader,
'Yours never will'—said farer to fearer,
'They're looking for you'—said hearer to horror,
As he left them there, as he left them there.

W. H. Auden

From *Elegy Written in a Country Churchyard*

The curfew tolls the knell of parting day,
    The lowing herd winds slowly o'er the lea,
The plowman homeward plods his weary way,
    And leaves the world to darkness and to me.

Thomas Gray

In conclusion, various sound devices are used to help communicate mood and attitude. Yet as Main and Seng point out, "Words are pleasant according to their meaning just as much as according to their sound." [23] Osborne says: "The beauty of sound exists only in relationship to meaning and emerges as an intensification of meanings or of the relations among fused meaning." [24] The interpreter is therefore encouraged to keep sound in its proper perspective.

[22] W. H. Auden, *Collected Shorter Poems 1930–1944*, Faber and Faber, Ltd., London, 1950, p. 253. Copyright 1934 and renewed 1961 by W. H. Auden. Reprinted from *The Collected Poetry of W. H. Auden*, by permission of Random House, Inc., and from *Collected Shorter Poems 1930–1944*, Faber and Faber, Ltd.
[23] C. F. Main and P. J. Seng (eds.), *Poems: Wadsworth Handbook and Anthology*, Wadsworth Publishing Company, Inc., Belmont, Calif., 1961, p. 197.
[24] Harold Osborne, *Aesthetics and Criticism*, Routledge & Kegan Paul, Ltd., London, 1955, p. 277.

Structure. Poetry, like all art, must have form. Poetry is more intricately organized than prose. The skillful poet carefully selects his details which he then places in the proper relationship to the intention of the poem. In discussing form, we do not want to think of structure as something that *holds* the content. Rather, it shapes and gives force to defining the meaning.

1. *Rhythm.* Rhythm is one of the most distinguishing qualities in the structure of poetry. It is usually emphasized in any discussion of poetic structure that rhythm is a very natural part of the world in which we live.[25] All of nature has a pulse or a beat. The very seasons themselves are rhythmical and demonstrate by their irregularity that rhythm may be achieved by variation from a pattern as well as by strict adherence to a pattern. Although rhythm is difficult to define, it is not so difficult to understand. The small child soon becomes conscious of rhythm through running and playing, pulling a small toy, or bouncing a ball. As he enters school, this natural rhythm is encouraged through play, rhythm bands, and folk dances. This close contact with rhythm is maintained by all of us throughout our daily lives.

All language is to some degree rhythmical, for it involves some kind of alternation between accented and unaccented syllables. There should not be a mystery about the use of rhythm in language. In our daily conversation we give more prominence to some words than to others. The student can use his already existing knowledge of rhythm to help him understand the more complex rhythms of the poet.

Rhythm, rather than meter or rhyme, is the comprehensive term for describing the various elements that affect the flow of poetry. Its comprehensiveness, however, is perplexing, and therefore definitions tend to become awkward because a definition of rhythm approximates a definition of the life itself that poetry contains. Therefore, three brief discussions are offered which may serve the student in developing his own concept of rhythm.

Bacon and Breen say: "Rhythm is the tension in the prosodic surface of a poem produced by the recurrence of a pattern of sound interrupted or varied by substitutions in the meter, by pauses, by inflections—indeed, by any aspect of sound other than the simple recurrence of the basic metrical unit. Rhythm in poetry is a kind of counterpoint." [26] This definition is distinctive in that it makes the *interruption* of a regular pattern indigenous to rhythm. In other words, rhythm is basically irregular. The rhythm of a line of poetry would therefore be determined by factors other than the formal metrical

[25] See also Chap. 5.
[26] Wallace A. Bacon and Robert S. Breen, *Literature as Experience*, p. 201. Copyright 1959 McGraw-Hill Book Company, Inc., New York. Used by permission.

scheme. Thrall, Hibbard, and Holman allow for irregular rhythm and permit the inclusion of an uninterrupted pattern: "The passage of regular or approximately equivalent time intervals between definite events or the recurrence of specific sounds or kinds of sounds is called rhythm." [27] Yelland, Jones, and Easton, although they are less specific, also allow rhythm to be defined in terms of regularity or irregularity, saying that rhythm is "the musical flow of language, produced mainly by a recurrence of pauses and accents." [28]

Therefore, the interpreter must watch for a regular rhythm, one that will occur again and again throughout the poem. But he must also listen for a second rhythm that will not conform, that will not repeat, but will vary within the regular pattern. Laurence Perrine calls this *heard rhythm*.[29] For example, in the first stanza of the Auden poem "As I Walked Out One Evening" the regular rhythm is dominant, but the heard rhythm enters in the second line, for instead of the flow following the pattern "walk-ING down BRIS-tol STREET," the reader must say, "WALK-ing down BRIS-tol STREET," giving what amounts to syncopation. The oral interpreter, in his preparation, should be very sensitive to this heard rhythm, for it will give meaning and feeling to the poem. He must be careful not to let the regular rhythm, the tapping out of a beat, block out the heard rhythm.

2. *Meter.* Although much that can be construed as poetry achieves its rhythm by an irregularity of pattern (just as a statue has rhythm without a mechanical repetition of features), much of poetry has an accent so arranged as to occur at regular intervals. In other words, the rhythm has been determined by the metrical unit, meter.

If rhythm is measured motion or recurrence in time, meter is accent and time interval within the recurrences. The meter of a poem is developed in terms of the line within the poem. The unit of measure is called a foot. The foot is composed of a group of syllables arranged according to a definite pattern. The four principal feet are:

Iambic—two syllables with accent on the second:
"He prayeth best who loveth best." Coleridge, "The Rime of the Ancient Mariner"

Trochaic—two syllables, with accent on the first:
"Once upon a midnight dreary, while I pondered weak and weary." Edgar Allen Poe, "The Raven"

[27] Thrall, Hibbard, and Holman, *op. cit.*, p. 416.
[28] Yelland, Jones, and Easton, *op. cit.*, p. 172.
[29] Perrine, *op. cit.*, p. 153.

Anapestic—three syllables, with the accent on the third:

"Or the least little delicate acquiline curve in a sensitive nose." Alfred, Lord Tennyson, "Maud"

Dactylic—three syllables with accent on the first:

"Just for a handful of silver he left us." Robert Browning, "The Lost Leader"

A line is classified according to its prevalent foot and the number of feet it contains, as one foot to a line (monometer), two feet to a line (dimeter), three feet (trimeter), four feet (tetrameter), five feet (pentameter), six feet (hexameter), and so forth.

In a poem the poet does not necessarily adhere to a single type of foot. He may change the established pattern to focus on a particular image, to intensify an emotion, or to show a change in thought. The poet is using meter as only one factor of composition; he may use it in its regular pattern or he may depart from the regular pattern to achieve his intent.

The oral interpreter must be aware of the poet's purpose and be sensitive to the poet's method of achieving it. And the interpreter must keep constantly in mind that his own purpose is to interpret the whole poem, not just the meter of the poem.

It is often asked whether it is necessary to have a knowledge of meter in order to appreciate poetry. Such knowledge may not be a prerequisite for appreciation, but it is of value in enlarging appreciation. A knowledge of meter can assist the student in his probing of the poem to see how the poet achieved the total effect. An interpreter who was unaware of the meter in Frost's poem "Stopping by Woods on a Snowy Evening" might be tempted to read the poem in a singsong manner, not even realizing why it was that his reading became monotonous.

The question is also raised as to the value of scanning as a means of studying poetry. It is true that few readers will deliberately scan a poem before reading it aloud for the first time, marking each foot as short or long. However, the student of poetry must learn to crawl before he can walk. If he has practiced scansion, he will learn to respond to the meter of a poem subconsciously and will defer to its rhythm without premeditation. Yet even though he is not conscious of what foot is being employed, he could label it correctly were it called to his attention.

The interpreter who can scan correctly can attend to elements in poetry that are sometimes neglected. If the reader overemphasizes the accent and *beats out* the measure of feet, he can easily distort the over-all flow of the rhythm and therefore misinterpret the poem. An experienced scanner would be much less likely to make this error. Although we do recommend the study of scanning to the student of oral interpretation, we caution against the overstressing of its use. When scanning is overemphasized, the student tends to beat out smooth and perfectly regular meter. Reading strictly according to meter will produce a very monotonous quality, but the student who uses meter to enhance the understanding of the rhythm of poetry will not only make a pleasing sound, but will also prick the sensitiveness of the reader and make him aware of the total impact of the poem.

3. *Rhyme.* The presence of rhyme is one of the most distinguishing factors of poetry. It serves the poet as a highly important melodic element, for it is very pleasing to the listener. He hears a sound and then anticipates the repetition of the same sound. Such anticipation is associated with what is perhaps the greatest contribution of rhyme, its unifying and organizing of the lines and stanzas of poetry. To the oral interpreter, rhyme is another means to assist him in grasping the total creative experience, for he can see by the way the poet has grouped his rhymes into stanzas how the poet has grouped his thoughts. A stanza can be defined as a group of lines arranged as a melodic unit according to a definite pattern. It may be described by its type of meter and its rhyme scheme. Letters of the alphabet are customarily used to signify the pattern of rhyme:

a—denotes the first line and all lines thereafter in the same stanza which rhyme with it
b—denotes the next line after the first line which employs a different rhyming word
c—denotes the third line containing a different rhyming word, and so on

This method of designating rhyme is illustrated by the first stanza of "The Hound of Heaven" by Francis Thompson:

I fled Him, down the nights and down the days;	*a*
I fled Him down the arches of the years;	*b*
I fled Him, down the labyrinthine ways	*a*
Of my own mind; and in the mist of tears	*b*
I hid from Him, and under running laughter.	*c*
Up vistaed hopes I sped;	*d*
And shot, precipitated,	*d*
Adown Titanic glooms of chasmèd fears,	*b*
From those strong Feet that followed,	
followed after.	*c*
But with unhurrying chase,	*e*
And unperturbèd pace,	*e*
Deliberate speed, majestic instancy,	*f*
They beat—and a Voice beat	*g*

> More instant than the Feet—   *g*
> "All things betray thee, who betrayest Me."   *f*

Generally the stanza is composed of groups of the same number of lines held together by a meter and rhyme scheme, and appears on the printed page as a unit. However, some poems do not follow this pattern, but are broken into verse paragraphs based upon a unit of thought, e.g., "Dover Beach."

Summary

The praise that Samuel Johnson gives to Shakespeare as "the poet of nature" must be equally sought by the interpreter of poetry. The interpreter should seek to unify the theme with its supporting elements of emotion, imagery, diction, and composition so that he holds up to his readers "a faithful mirrour of manners and of life." The narrators of poetry should represent "the genuine progeny of common humanity," not an atypical product but a natural consequence of the experiences of men. His persons should "act and speak by the influence of those general passions and principles by which all minds are agitated" so that the poetry is not artificial but real. Such is the goal of the oral interpreter of poetry. That the goal is elusive should make it more worthwhile to seek.

The roles of the poet [30]

For many years, poetry was categorized as lyric, dramatic, epic, or narrative. Recent critics have departed from these categories in a variety of ways in order to discuss poetry to better purpose. However, no divisional scheme can be entirely satisfactory because the poet is usually eclectic and uses lyrical passages in his dramatic poetry or employs the story element in his lyrics.

Lyrical poetry has been given considerable attention in the earlier portions of this chapter; and a lyrical poem, although it has a narrative element, has been chosen for the detailed comments which conclude this chapter. The dramatic monologue "My Last Duchess" is discussed in Chapter 5, and separate sections are provided for drama and the staged reading, both of which consider the poet as *singer*. Therefore, the following discussion will devote particular attention to the poet as *story teller* and the poet as *painter*. The intention here is not to discuss the roles of the poet comprehensively, but only to supplement by presenting materials not found elsewhere.

[30] For the inspiration for the subtitles in this section, the authors are indebted to J. Hooper Wise, J. E. Congleton, Alton C. Morris, and John C. Hodges, *College English: The First Year*, Harcourt, Brace & World, Inc., New York, 1952.

The poet as story teller

The story is a popular element in poetry. It may predominate or it may remain relatively unimportant, for the poet may combine narration with other elements to produce his objective, the poem itself. In the narrative poem, we are interested in the process used to reach the conclusion, but we are not concerned with all of the detail involved in the process. Such a focus of attention is often one of the differences between narrative poetry and narrative prose. In poetry we want only enough detail to make us grasp the meaning of the events. The poem itself is the experience. We, as readers, want to be a part of the experience; we want an intellectual and an emotional response. The poet may take just a few essential facts and treat them in ways that give the reader or listener the desired reaction. The poet wants the reader not only to understand the feelings, but also to share in the feelings. In some poems the narration is implied. The details are chosen carefully to give a particular effect, and the development of the action is often given in terms of narration. The poet is more interested in provoking a reaction toward a story than he is in telling the story. He must provide, however, enough detail to make clear the situation so as to evoke the mood of the poem.

Just as a clear line of distinction cannot be drawn between poetry and prose, a sharp division between narrative poetry and lyrical poetry is not functional. There is an overlapping and blending of the two types. For example, the folk ballad is narrative poetry. There is a story in the ballads, and in some, even a complex plot is developed. However, in the popular folk ballad "Frankie and Johnny" the story is strong, but the lyrical aspect is also an important part of the poem. The narrative is often of primary importance in the literary ballad, the long narrative poem, and the epic. Yet it may also play a subordinate role, as it does in Coleridge's poem "The Rime of the Ancient Mariner" in which the story element is slight and not *the* experience but only another facet of the total impact of the selection.

A narrative element is present in many of the predominantly lyrical poems, e.g., "I Wandered Lonely as a Cloud" by William Wordsworth. The speaker is telling the listener that he was out walking, what he saw, what his reactions were, and what the experience meant to him on his return home.

Where the story is predominant, there are also other elements working together to create the narrative. Just as the lyric poem often has narrative or dramatic elements, so may the narrative have descriptive passages. It is the manner in which the author uses the element of narration that provides a distinction between narrative prose and narrative poetry. As Brooks and Warren point out: "In general, it may be said that the writer of prose fiction tries to convince his reader by the accumulation of detail, and that the poet tries to convince his reader by the sharpness of selected detail." [31] The narrative element is strong in "My Last Duchess," but even in this dramatic monologue, where the story plays such a prominent part, the descriptive elements are noticeable:

> The dropping of the daylight in the West,
> The bough of cherries some officious fool
> Broke in the orchard for her. . . .

The narrative is relatively easy to follow in Frost's "Wild Grapes," even though it is not as predominant as it is in "My Last Duchess." If we ask why the little girl was dangling in the air holding tenaciously to the limb of a tree, we may naturally inquire as to how she got down. But in the last part of the poem, where Frost has the little girl say, "It was not my weighing anything," is Frost still telling us a story or is he letting the little girl, now turned woman, reflect and become philosophical?

The story of "Dover Beach" could be told in a few sentences. The narrative element is there, but the descriptive and the emotional elements are more important. "Stopping by Woods on a Snowy Evening" tells us that a man is out driving and that he does stop to watch the snow before he drives on. But the lyrical element in the poem is more dominant than is the narrative.

We have emphasized that labeling poems lyrical or descriptive can be misleading. Each of these terms describe a tool in the hands of the artist. He may use one, two, or all to create his work of art. As oral interpreters, we wish to approach the study of the poem by understanding how the various roles of the poet relate one to the other.

The poet as painter: descriptive poetry

Another label often used to categorize poetry is *descriptive*. However, just as we pointed out that the narrative poem does more than tell a story, the descriptive poem does more than describe. The poet must select the details of his description just as he must select details of the story in a narrative poem. If he wishes to describe a hill or a mountain, he presents sharp details in one part of the poem and allows these to serve as the foundation for his approach.

A clear-cut presentation of images is an important factor to the poet.

[31] Cleanth Brooks and Robert Penn Warren, *Understanding Poetry*, rev. ed., p. 71. Copyright 1950 by Holt, Rinehart and Winston, Inc., New York.

If we are to understand the selectivity and arrangement of his descriptive details, we must always consider the writer's purpose, which may center on the development of vivid imagery. The poet may choose to use descriptive detail to focus attention on a particular aspect of the poem. He may not comment directly on the point of focus, but indirectly, by an accumulation of imagery, he calls it to our attention, thereby accentuating the idea or the effect the poet desires the reader to achieve. It is true that some shorter poems have no story to tell. Their only intention is to give a single image, to create a single mood. Elsewhere, the descriptive element of poetry is interwoven within the narration, the idea, and the emotion of the composition. Yet again, the element of description is predominant in many poems, such as "The Great Lover" by Rupert Brooke, "To a Waterfowl" by William Cullen Bryant, and "Ode to the West Wind" by Shelley.

The descriptive element lends itself to the tone, sound, and attitude found in a poem. These elements have been discussed previously.

Summary

We have attempted to discuss very briefly the various elements in poetic literature. We have not attempted to give a comprehensive discussion of any one of the aspects of the creative process of poetry. For further reading, consult the references listed in the bibliography. In our rather limited and brief discussion, we have tried to emphasize the necessity of understanding the various aspects of poetry as they relate to each other and to the whole. We believe this is of utmost importance to the reader; therefore, our focus has been on the total experience.

Comments on the analysis of a poem

The interpreter who is asked to write an analysis of a poem has been given considerable assistance in Chapter 5 and in this chapter. Still he must decide how to organize his analysis, how detailed he should be, and what elements he should include and omit. The discussion below is intended to clarify these points. The comments on the analysis of an essay found in Chapter 8 use as their structure the major headings of Chapter 5. However, for reasons pointed out later, the organization of the comments on poetry are more pragmatic. Thus the interpreter will have two methods of approach for consultation. An exposition of the related areas has also been omitted from this analysis since the coverage in Chapter 5 is sufficiently detailed.

The comments below are not intended as a definitive example of how the analysis of a poem should be written. The point of view shifts from the type of exposition the student himself might write to instructional comments on how he may proceed on his own. It is hoped that the student will be sufficiently instructed without being coached and that he will find in the comments in Chapters 5, 8, and 11 the motivation to develop the critical sense so necessary to the successful oral reader.

We have chosen for the basis of our comments on analysis a poem by a contemporary writer, W. H. Auden, whose place of distinction in the literary world of today makes him worthy of consideration. As was suggested in Chapter 5, in approaching the study of a poem, the student should read his selection several times and let it *talk* to him. When the reader feels that he has a preliminary, over-all impression of the selection, he is ready to begin his analysis. Continued references to the poem itself as it is analyzed are important. It is helpful to re-read the entire poem several times while the analysis is underway.

As I Walked Out One Evening [32]

As I walked out one evening,
  Walking down Bristol Street,
The crowds upon the pavement
  Were fields of harvest wheat.

And down by the brimming river
  I heard a lover sing
Under an arch of the railway:
  "Love has no ending.

"I'll love you, dear, I'll love you
  Till China and Africa meet,
And the river jumps over the mountain
  And the salmon sing in the street.

"I'll love you till the ocean
  Is folded and hung up to dry,
And the seven stars go squawking
  Like geese about the sky.

"The years shall run like rabbits,
  For in my arms I hold
The Flower of the Ages.
  And the first love of the world."

But all the clocks in the city
　　Began to whirr and chime:
"O let not Time deceive you,
　　You cannot conquer Time.

"In the burrows of the Nightmare
　　Where Justice naked is,
Time watches from the shadow
　　And coughs when you would kiss.

"In headaches and in worry
　　Vaguely life leaks away,
And Time will have his fancy
　　Tomorrow or today.

"Into many a green valley
　　Drifts the appalling snow;
Time breaks the threaded dances
　　And the diver's brilliant bow.

"O plunge your hands in water,
　　Plunge them in up to the wrist;
Stare, stare in the basin
　　And wonder what you've missed.

"The glacier knocks in the cupboard,
　　The desert sighs in the bed,
And the crack in the tea-cup opens
　　A lane to the land of the dead.

"Where the beggars raffle the banknotes
　　The Giant is enchanting to Jack,
And the Lily-white Boy is a Roarer,
　　And Jill goes down on her back.

"O look, look in the mirror,
　　O look in your distress;
Life remains a blessing
　　Although you cannot bless.

"O stand, stand at the window
　　As the tears scald and start;
You shall love your crooked neighbor
　　With your crooked heart."

It was late, late in the evening,
　　The lovers they were gone;

The clocks had ceased their chiming,
And the deep river ran on.

As the analysis develops, it is valuable for the reader to establish *who* is speaking, *what* he is saying, *to whom* he is talking, and *where* the experience is taking place. The following discussion reveals these factors of analysis by placing them in the sequence of events that forms the narrative of the poem.

The first line of the poem gives an important clue to the understanding of the selection. By saying "As I walked out one evening," Auden identifies the speaker and gives the setting. Moreover, by the use of the subordinate conjunction "as," the poet suggests further action, anticipating for us something more than an ordinary walk.

The situation suggested by the first line is developed in the remainder of the first stanza. We are told that the first person "I" is to be the observer as he walks out, and we are told the vicinity of his stroll. In the second stanza, the scene shifts from Bristol Street to the river, where the remainder of the action takes place. Although the speaker "I" continues to hold the center of attention, he begins to share the scene with the lovers in the last two lines of the second stanza. The interest for the next three stanzas is focused on the ardently proclaimed vows given in song by the lovers.

The mood of the love song continues until stanza 6. However, the phrase "but all the clocks" begins abruptly a different theme with a different mood, for we become aware of the attitude of Auden toward his material. The oral interpreter must recognize this change and offer it to his listeners in such a way that they can also share the shift of mood and attitude. In the following eight stanzas, we hear, see, and otherwise experience the opposite ideas and emotions of the lovers' vows as given by the clocks. A strong warning supported by vivid realistic description is offered in reply to the lovers' song. Here the realistic picture is pitted against the idealistic illusion.

The last stanza completes the circle of the experience. Although the speaker is not directly mentioned, we assume that it is he who is making the summary and the observation. The concluding stanza relates the final act of each element involved: The lovers had gone, "the clocks had ceased," and "the deep river ran on." The experience "As I walked out one evening" is complete. The attitude of the poet is definitely established for the reader.

The preceding paragraphs fulfill the obligation of a paraphrase. As has been said earlier, a paraphrase is not *the* poem. However, it is a means by which the reader can express his reaction to poetry and therefore, despite its limitations, it is of value to the interpreter. The paraphrase of this analysis began by establishing *who* is speaking. Since the poem begins with the speaker saying, "As I walked out one evening," we can assume that he was not speaking directly to anyone present at the time of the action. It could be, however, that the *to whom* is a friend who, at some later time, is being invited to share the experiences of the speaker. But the *what* that he is communicating is of as much interest to a universal audience as it is to any particular individual.

The transitions of time, mood, and idea are pointed out as the poem develops, with the concluding stanza being given special attention. As the paraphrase progresses, attention is focused on the degree of the feeling, the sensation, and the mood of the selection.

Again the student should remember that the paraphrase is no substitute for the poem. But if the interpreter can articulate his response by rewording it, he will discover a simple but excellent adjunct to understanding the experience embodied in the selection.

The over-all tempo of the poem is moderate, but there are periods of effective variation throughout. The opening situation has an easy, casual tempo. The reader can visualize a man walking out as he ordinarily might. Then the mood moves into a higher tension and a quicker tempo to respond to the love song. Subsequently, the poet changes the tempo again to a much calmer, more deliberate speed in keeping with the mood of the clocks. A somewhat more somber but strong urgency in tempo results, e.g., "O, look, look" and "O, stand, stand." A rather slow tempo concludes the poem.

Chapter 5 pointed out that imagery has many different functions and must be evaluated as it is related to its purpose. In this particular poem, W. H. Auden uses the element of imagery in its various aspects to convey the very meaning of the poem. Basically, the theme of the poem is a simple one. Two lovers are making extravagant vows to each other. But, as is rather characteristic of the poetry of Auden, the images create the tone and the tone plays a very important part in creating the total poetic experience.

Imagery, tone, and sound are all brought together and blended into a single unit. In analyzing this selection, it is necessary, therefore, to be aware always of the overlapping and the fusing of the various poetic elements. Therefore, this analysis will not treat each element of style separately, but will consider them collectively.

For example, Auden makes use of figurative language to intensify his theme and his tone throughout the poem. The metaphor is used to provide a vivid image, e.g., "The crowds ... were fields of harvest wheat." The simile is employed to point up the image and at the same time to add to the sound pattern. Notice two examples in particular:

Like geese about the sky

years shall run like rabbits

Personification can deepen or lighten the emotional overtones by just one word. Auden personifies Time as a unifying force, as well as a symbol of his theme. When it is first used in "O let not Time deceive you," the personification evokes the *stock* response. We are accustomed to various clichés such as "Time will take care of that." In the seventh stanza, however, Time takes on more meaning; it is more intense and once again suggests the tone of the poem. The oral interpreter must note this increase in intensity in the phrase "Time watches from the shadow," and by his vocal and bodily reaction, communicate the acceleration or *build* of mood to his audience. In the eighth stanza, in the line ". . . time will have his fancy," personification continues, but with a slight modification of mood. As the poem proceeds, the symbol of Time forces itself more and more to the center of attention until it dominates the poem.

In the third stanza, the allusion "Till China and Africa meet" contributes to the ironical mood of the poem. Although these two geographical terms are well known, the physical distance between them accentuates the extravagance of the statements of the lovers.

Irony in literature requires the special attention of the reader. It is easy for the student to overemphasize or "to play it so broadly" that the subtleties are lost. On the other hand, if the interpreter *races* the tempo, the ironic effect may also be forgotten. Recognition of word grouping, effective use of the pause, and sensitiveness to the attitude of the author are all useful techniques for the student to help him interpret ironic poetry. Sometimes a lifted eyebrow, a slight shrug of the shoulder, or a faint smile can reveal irony most effectively.

The ironical reference to the familiar character, the Giant, as being enchanting to Jack, is in contradiction to the old story and points once again to the poet's attitude toward his material. The ironical touch is also evidenced in "The Lily-White Boy is a Roarer," and "Jill goes down on her back." W. H. Auden uses irony to create the basic tone or emotional atmosphere which is so important to this poem. The dialogue between the lover and the clocks enhances and intensifies the irony. Each participant uses extravagant statements in bartering with the other. In the dialogue, when the lover sings:

"I'll love you till the ocean
  Is folded and hung up to dry,
And the seven stars go squawking
  Like geese about the sky."

the clocks answer with equal exaggeration:

"The glacier knocks in the cupboard,
  The desert sighs in the bed,
And the crack in the tea-cup opens
  A lane to the land of the dead."

The broader humor of the poem as well as its irony is intensified
by the choice of images. The lovers talk in terms such as "the Ocean
is folded" and "the seven stars go squawking" while the clocks refer
to common domestic items such as cupboards, bed, and teacups. Follow the dialogue and compare the way the answers and counteran-
swers are given. Notice that the interest is intensified by the contrast
made throughout the dialogue.

The interpreter will need not only to be aware of the contrasting
dialogue, but also to consider how to make this contrast evident to
his audience. There are, of course, many ways such an effect can be
achieved, and therefore it would be improper to prescribe one particular method. The student might use a change of tempo, a slight
modification in pitch, or a variation in emphasis in any other form to
point up the small changes of the rhythmic pattern. However, a word
of caution is necessary. In creating such a contrast, the interpreter
must make a smooth transition from the conversational element to the
expository element that follows.

Of course, each student's response to the poem will be affected by
his connotative meanings of the symbols and by his attitude toward
the ironical situation. Most of us are willing to stand aside and over-
hear the lovers' declarations. Our reaction varies from a mildly amused
response to an ironic one. But few are totally unsympathetic to the
lovers. When the clocks answer, the listeners will vary more widely
in their repsonses. There will be agreement that the theme is effectively presented, but some listeners will smile, others will laugh, while
still others will register a slight frown. Such varied reactions are in
keeping with the attitude of the poet.

The choice of words in "As I Walked Out One Evening" would be
an interesting study in itself. The symbols used by Auden contribute
not only to the creation of the imagery but also to the sound of the
poem and thus to its composition. But perhaps more important to the
study of the selection is an awareness of the manner in which the
poet weaves the individual word into the rhythm of the poem. Notice
the descriptive words "brimming river." To some, this image has a
strong appeal to the sense of sight, to others the appeal may be
stronger through the auditory sense. Then read the phrase "And down
by the brimming river," and attempt to capture how the image fits the

rhythm. How does the choice of certain words contribute to that rhythm?

What are the images in the alliterative lines "And the river jumps over the mountain and the salmon sing in the street." Which image predominates? Is the alliteration prominent or does it have to be pointed out? How does the repetition of the initial consonant contribute to the rhythm of the poem? Reread the entire poem, observing how the use of alliteration contributes to the total experience of the poem.

In the tenth stanza, we notice a change in sound, tone, and rhythm:

"O plunge your hands in water,
Plunge them in up to the wrist. . . ."

Which words are particularly well chosen to give the contrast between the boldness of this stanza and the sound, tone, and rhythm that precede? What do the above lines have to contribute to the general impact of the poem?

The mood and tone continue to build with the lines "O, stand, stand at the window." It is not until the last stanza that the mood and the tempo become quieter, very much as the tone in the first stanza, not as casual as at first, for something has happened to intervene, but in a concluding, sober manner, beginning with the line "It was late, late in the evening."

By now it is clear that there is a narrative element in the poem and a touch of the dramatic; however, the lyrical aspect is predominant. Auden uses irony very effectively to fulfill his purpose, continuing his figure of speech into the last stanza which completes the *story* and crystallizes the tone of the poem. Perhaps we could say that this poem is more predominantly poetic and varies far less from poetry to prose than many we could have selected. Although the poem begins in a rather factual manner, it quickly assumes the texture of poetry by its figurative language and the pattern of its rhythm. We do not claim that the poem is among the great, but we do believe that, because of the skillful way in which Auden has blended the various components of figurative language with the theme he selected and with the tone or emotional aspect he chose to amplify the theme, the poem "As I Walked Out One Evening" is worthy of careful consideration and study.

Summary and Conclusions

In oral interpretation, there is no line of demarcation between preparation and performance. We have used the word "performance" as a generalization. Whether an interpreter be reading to his roommate, to a class, or to a public gathering, each step of preparation is a part of the performance. The oral interpreter should always be aware of the different elements of the poem as he studies and explores the selection, responding to the discoveries he makes. When the poet reveals the situation or creates the mood in the opening lines of a poem, the oral interpreter must respond to these cues as a part of his preparation.

The oral reader must be cautioned not to overemphasize any one element of poetry to the neglect of another. A student may be so impressed with the imagery in the selection that he stresses it, but fails in presenting other contributing parts of the poem and thereby presents a distorted interpretation. A reader in his eagerness to *read out* the rhythm often neglects the other elements. There are some poems, such as "The Congo" or "The Bells," in which the rhythm *is* the dominant experience, and it must therefore be given prominence. But in most poetry the rhythm is only a supporting element.

Another common mistake of the interpreter lies in concentrating on *what* the poem says without realizing that this *what* cannot be separated from its supporting elements. If an interpreter neglects the elements of tone, figurative language, rhythm, or form of any sort, he will be giving only a partial interpretation or a misinterpretation.

The reader of poetry will wish to avoid two extremes that often tempt the beginning reader. To avoid the monotony of overemphasizing the form, the student may read the poem in a straightforward manner. In his eagerness and determination to be certain of *reading out* the meaning, the rhythm and the sound may be neglected. Remember that the interpreter is reading poetry. The writer has chosen a form and an order that harmonizes with what he is saying. Therefore the student should not try to read a poem as if it were prose. The other extreme lies in an overaccentuation of the beat, which has been discussed previously. The inexperienced reader may feel that he must choose between *straight prose* or *singsong* reading. This is not true. The interpreter should concentrate on reading the *poem*, not just the thought or just the image or just the rhythm, but the total experience.

Inexperienced readers tend to begin a line of a poem, read it through, and at the end of the line, let it go, pick up another line, and repeat the same attack. To them, each line is read as a separate unit. This type of reading will be choppy and lacking in meaning. The end of a line in a poem is not necessarily the end of a clause, phrase, or sentence. A line is seldom complete within itself, but depends upon its relationship to all elements. A drop of the voice is not necessarily required at the end of a line. A reader may wish to give a slight recognition of the fact that he has reached the conclusion of a poetic line, but he should also take care to suggest, when appropriate, that the rest of the thought or feeling is to come. The reader's holding on slightly to the word at the end of a line as he continues with the thought may keep the rhythmical flow of the line and maintain the over-all rhythmical flow of the poem. This procedure results in a completeness rather than in a piecing line by line.

In his first readings, the interpreter should review the poem slowly to get the full impact of sound and feeling in the poem. He should become aware of a pattern by which he adds something distinctively personal each time he reads the poem. In the oral presentation, the student must allow time for the listener to receive and to respond to the total experience. The response of the reader may be different from that of his audience, but if the listener is to appreciate the selection, he must be permitted to react, even independently, if need be.

It is often a temptation for a reader, when interpreting a lyrical poem, to "take flight" from the audience and revel alone in the feeling. An oral interpreter should be aware of the sensitive feeling of the poem, but only to the extent that the mood and tone are communicated and shared with the listeners. A beautiful scene may be very delicate, and in his analysis, the interpreter should have sensed this delicateness. But the interpreter must remember his listeners are of primary importance. The most lyrical of poems will require special attention in matters such as direct or indirect eye contact and the like, but the emphasis must still be on communicating the poem to the audience.

In summary, we suggest rereading Chapters 5 and 6. The suggestions offered in these two chapters are applicable to the interpretation of all types of literature. With a knowledge and an appreciation of the total poem, the interpreter should examine the skills available to him. Is the voice free from habits that will distract from the reading? Is the diction clear but not too precise? Has the ability to project been tested? All is lost if it cannot be heard. In other words, are the voice and body in tune to respond to an understanding of the selection?

The interpreter's role is not an easy one, but it is a challenging and rewarding one. It calls for keen intellectual study and a sensitiveness to the material. It demands an awareness of the response of the audience. When he steps into the shoes of the artist to share a work of art, i.e., poetry, with an audience, the oral interpreter must have a prudent temperament and a well-balanced judgment.

Exercises

1. Write a complete analysis of the style of any one of the following four poems:

Centennial [33]

Shaft poised above his faceless foe,
The soldier, in another sudden guise,
Feels panic turn to primary awareness,
And, motionless, begins to realize
A separate entity: this was the form
Of one upon whom sunshine smiled,
Whose arms enscribed a throbbing
Of the seasons; eyes mild,
But hot with summer; shoulders curved
To start the plowing.
Inside this structure dwelt
Unbounded warmth, allowing
For the arbitrary future.
The color of reality is blurred, until
He understands the southern enemy
As one impossible to kill.
Impression slides away, lost
In subjectivity, to join an endless file
Of undescribables. His hands tense

To finalize the action. Meanwhile,
A flourish, in mute warning
Breaks the soundlessness of fear,
And voices from another time
Scream into silence in his ear.

R. B. Sherman

Lady Selecting Her Christmas Cards [34]

Fastidiously, with gloved and careful fingers,
    Through the marked samples she pursues her search
Which shall it be: the snowscape's wintry languors
    Complete with church,

An urban skyline, children sweetly pretty
    Sledding downhill, the chaste, ubiquitous wreath,
Schooner or candle or the simple Scottie
    With verses underneath?

Perhaps it might be better to emblazon
    With words alone the stiff, punctilious square.
(Oh, not Victorian, certainly. This season
    One meets it everywhere.)

[33] "Centennial" is reproduced by permission of the author.
[34] From Phyllis McGinley, *Times Three*. Copyright 1943 by Phyllis McGinley. Reprinted by permission of the Viking Press, Inc., New York.

She has a duty proper to the weather—
A Birth she must announce, a rumor to spread,
Wherefore the very spheres once sang together
And a star shone overhead.

Here are the Tidings which the shepherds panted
One to another, kneeling by their flocks.
And they will bear her name (engraved, not printed),
Ten-fifty for the box.

Phyllis McGinley

Upon Julia's Clothes

When as in silks my Julia goes,
Then, then, methinks, how sweetly flows
The liquefaction of her clothes.
Next, when I cast my eyes and see
That brave vibration each way free
Oh, how that glittering taketh me!

Robert Herrick

Could Man Be Drunk For Ever [35]

Could man be drunk for ever
With liquor, love, or fights,
Lief should I rouse at morning
And lief lie down of nights.

But men at whiles are sober
And think by fits and starts,
And if they think, they fasten
Their hands upon their hearts.

A. E. Housman

2. Contrast the use of rhythm, meter, and rhyme in the four selections above, remembering the widely divergent dates of the four poets: Robert Herrick (1591–1604), A. E. Housman (1859–1936), Phyllis McGinley (1905–   ), R. B. Sherman (1919–   ).

3. Write an introduction to any one of the four selections above. Review the comments offered in Chapter 6.

4. In order to gauge the effectiveness of the poet's technique, try writing a paraphrase of either the poem by Herrick or the poem by Housman. Can you complete your paraphrase in the same number of words used by the poet or must you use more words?

[35] From A. E. Housman, *Complete Poems.* Copyright 1922 by Holt, Rinehart and Winston, Inc. Copyright renewed 1950 by Barclays Bank Ltd. Reprinted by permission of Holt, Rinehart and Winston, Inc., New York.

5. Give the *who, what, to whom,* and *where* for the poem "Centennial."
6. Write an analysis of the related areas for either Herrick or Housman.
7. How should an interpreter communicate the irony in the poem "Lady Selecting Her Christmas Cards"?
8. The rhyme patterns of the Herrick and Housman poems are pronounced. How should the interpreter read these poems to convey the assistance that rhyme contributes to the total experience of these poems without letting the rhyme absorb the experience?
9. Choose any one of the four poems and discuss in detail how each of the following factors assists in the composition: assonance, consonance, alliteration, and onomatopoeia.
10. Discuss in detail the relationship between the mood, tone, and emotions in the McGinley poem.

The staged reading

For the past several years there has been an accelerated interest in a new approach to oral interpretation, called by some the *staged reading,* by others *experimental reading.* Some directors use the term *theater reading* to designate the staged reading of drama, and *chamber theater* to indicate the presentation of other forms of literature.[1] Although there are many variations in the methods used to present the staged reading, it is generally agreed that the purpose of the approach is to present good literature in a lively, dramatic manner.

However, the staged reading should not be confused with play reading, dramatization, or choral reading. A group of theater lovers, sitting around in their host's living room, reading a play with each person taking a part, is an enjoyable experience, but it is not theater reading. A short story can be effectively dramatized for the stage, but such a dramatization is not chamber reading. Although choral reading is often used as a form of support in theater reading (e.g., to supply the part of the chorus in Euripides' *Medea*), the choral reading in itself is not the medium under consideration in this chapter.

The staged reading, as its name implies, is a compromise between drama and oral interpretation, in which readers adopt a limited amount of the technique of the theater without making any pretense of "giving a play." It encourages more movement on the part of the readers than is generally found in oral interpretation, but not necessarily so. It is characterized by the simultaneous appearance of two or more readers before the audience, using scripts, seated or standing in a variety of arrangements. The use of stools and lecterns is a fairly common practice. The readers may create different stage levels by having part of the group sit and part of the group stand. For example,

---

[1] Robert Breen defined chamber theater as a method of preparing and presenting undramatized fiction for the stage.

in one production of Truman Capote's "A Christmas Memory," four readers were used. The central character of the story, Buddy, was seated on a high stool slightly to stage left. Buddy's friend, the elderly woman, was seated on a stool on the same level, in the center and a little upstage. The remaining two readers occupied chairs on a lower level on stage right, somewhat downstage. The readers who sat on stools used lecterns, while the ones who sat on chairs held their manuscripts in folders.

In a production of *Pale Horse, Pale Rider* by Katherine Anne Porter, five readers sat on stools on the same level. The narrator, the observing third person, sat a little apart from the other four readers.[2] A second staged reading of *Pale Horse, Pale Rider* featured only two readers who alternated their positions between stools placed relatively far downstage and a small flat-topped platform with a bench on center stage.[3]

The director of a staged reading can, through experimentation, find the best stage arrangement for each production. He should keep in mind maintaining the unity of the material while at the same time creating the best pictorial effects on stage.

The exits and entrances of the several characters may be indicated in several different ways. In some situations it may be effective for a reader to make a literal exit or to suggest his departure by turning to one side or by turning his back to the audience. The lowering of the head is another way to indicate the exit of a character. It would follow that the entrance of a character could be achieved by the reader returning to his original position.

In a production of theater reading, one interpreter may assume the lines of several different characters. The change from one character to another can be suggested by the same techniques used to indicate exits and entrances. In addition, the reader may change position on stage to show a change of role. If the reader is seated on a stool, he may change to stand by it or take a few steps away to show that he is now interpreting the lines of a different character. A minimum amount of motivated action, well executed, can be most effective, but excessive action can distract from the unity of the performance. The same principle applies to the use of properties and sound effects. They may be used occasionally, but only with care and good taste, or they will detract.

There are many different answers as to where the interpreter should look during the staged reading. In general, as in all interpretation, the scene should be kept "offstage." However, the interpreter may

[2] "A Christmas Memory" and *Pale Horse, Pale Rider* were both presented as part of a series at Baylor University, Waco, Texas, in 1961.

[3] Presented as part of a series at Ohio University, Athens, Ohio, in 1961.

glance toward the character to whom he is speaking, creating a sense of conversation without bringing the scene onstage.

It is most important in this form of group oral interpretation to present a unified performance. Although each interpreter is an individual with given roles to play, he does not try to be the star of the show. Group interpretation is not a variety program, but a production where each person is making his contribution to the whole. Each interpreter should be aware of how he fits into the total situation at all times. As he enters a scene, he immediately becomes a part of it and should make his role conform to what has preceded and what will follow. Throughout the staged reading, each interpreter, when in scene, must be attentive to all lines, reacting to what is said. If any one of the interpreters appears aloof or seems to be just waiting to read his lines, the unity of the production is lost.

The technique of employing one reader as a narrator can help hold the unity of the production and, at the same time, accelerate action. As in all forms of interpretation, the literature must be analyzed into its several components. At times, one narrator will read all of the exposition while a second narrator will read all of the description and any other material not included in the dialogue. In Archibald Mac-Leish's play "*J.B.*," all narration and descriptive material are presented in the form of dialogue between the two characters, Mr. Zuss and Nickles, as they watch Job in his struggles, making an interesting variation in the role of the narrator.

The same principles of characterization discussed in Chapter 6 are applicable for interpreters of the staged reading. As in all good oral interpretation, a successful staged reading is the result of a careful selection of material, an understanding of the material, and a group of interpreters who can communicate the literature to their listeners.

Advantages of the staged reading

What are the advantages of the staged reading? As has been pointed out in Chapter 4, one of the contributions of the oral interpreter is his wide range in the selection of his material. Such an advantage is particularly operative in the staged reading, for there are many plays which, because of their unusually large casts, elaborate setting, and expensive costumes, are seldom produced on stage. But through the technique of theater reading, these plays can come alive to many audiences. The novel, the short novel, and the short story also offer a full repertoire for chamber theater. A long narrative poem that is seldom read silently can become a dramatic experience through the medium of the staged reading.

The following is a list of selections that have been used effectively for theater reading:

Short stories and novels

Charles Dickens, *A Christmas Carol*
Truman Capote, "A Christmas Memory"
Robert Peter Tristram Coffin, "Christmas in Maine"
Eudora Welty, "Lily Daw and the Three Ladies"
Katherine Anne Porter, *Noon Wine*
Katherine Anne Porter, *Pale Horse, Pale Rider*
Katherine Mansfield, "The Garden Party"
Henry van Dyke, *The Story of the Other Wise Man*
Henry James, *The Turn of the Screw*
Ray Bradbury, "There Will Come Soft Rains"

Plays

Arthur Laurents, *A Clearing in the Woods*
Sophocles, *Antigone*
Edna St. Vincent Millay, *Conversation at Midnight*
George Bernard Shaw, *Don Juan in Hell*
Henrik Ibsen, *Hedda Gabler*
Archibald MacLeish, "*J.B.*"
Robinson Jeffers, *Medea*
Tennessee Williams, *Summer and Smoke*
William Shakespeare, *A Winter's Tale*
Dylan Thomas, *Under Milk Wood*

Poems

W. H. Auden, "The Age of Anxiety"
John Masefield, "Enslaved"
Robert Frost, *In the Clearing*
Stephen Vincent Benét, *John Brown's Body*
Edgar Lee Masters, *Spoon River Anthology*
Robert Frost, "The Death of the Hired Man"
Dante Gabriel Rossetti, *The Blessed Damozel*
Edwin Arlington Robinson, *Tristram*
Stephen Vincent Benét, "Western Star"

The second advantage of the staged reading is that the technique employed in story telling brings the audience close to the literature. Such an advantage is particularly apparent when a narrator is used who guides the point of view throughout the presentation and therefore permits the audience to see the scenes and meet the characters through his eyes. His presence gives the listeners the opportunity to watch the situation much as the author first saw it in his own imagination, bringing the author, the interpreter, and the audience into a close relationship for a dramatic experience.

A third advantage stems from the time element, for by careful cutting and arranging, a full-length novel or a three-act play can be presented in approximately an hour.

Fourth, a group of oral interpreters can learn much from each other in their preparation for staged reading. A beginning actor has much to gain from being in productions with experienced personnel. He learns to *play with* and to *play to* the veteran, gaining a sense of timing from his exchange of lines. The novice oral interpreter can do likewise. It is very gratifying to see an inexperienced oral reader suddenly get an entirely new perspective on interpretation by participating with others in a staged reading.

There are no set rules for selecting material for oral interpretation. However, the following suggestions are appropriate. As a matter of expediency, plays which are not frequently given on stage should be given preference for the staged reading, for such a selection will increase the experiences of both the participants and the audience. There are many good college, university, and community theater productions of the popular plays. Why repeat these selections for theater reading? Moreover, certain plays are particularly adaptable to the staged reading approach, e.g., *Under Milk Wood* by Dylan Thomas and *A Clearing in the Woods* by Arthur Laurents. Such long poems as "The Age of Anxiety" by W. H. Auden or Edwin Arlington Robinson's *Tristram* seem designed for the staged reading.

Summary

Because of its experimental nature, there are no exact rules for the staged reading. These few suggestions have been offered in the hope that they may be helpful to those who are exploring this medium in an effort to make literature an exciting experience for those who participate and those who listen.

The oral interpretation *appendix* B
of Biblical literature

The majority of people will agree with Bishop Horace W. B. Danegan when he says: "It is essential that people should read the Bible itself. But it is equally important that they should know how to read it." [1] Oral interpretation offers one approach to *know how to read* scripture. Oral reading places the Bible in its natural habitat, for the historical and biographical portions of the Bible were told and retold and circulated from country to country long before they were written down. Furthermore, canon law was communicated to the people by having one person read it to an assembled group. The Psalms are songs composed to be read in unison, chanted, or sung. The prophets for the most part were not concerned with writing down their pronouncements, and it was left to others to record their words, retaining for the most part the oral style of the prophet. The letters of the New Testament were directed to be read aloud to small groups of Christians resembling family groups more than a church audience. One of the best known of the epistles is the thirteenth chapter of First Corinthians, in which Paul makes a strong plea to his followers to come together in an atmosphere of love.

Though I speak with the tongues of men and of angels
and have not charity, I am become as sounding brass
or a tinkling cymbal.

[1] Frederick C. Grant, *How to Read the Bible*, Morehouse-Gorham Company, Inc., New York, 1956, pp. 7–8. See also Julian Price Love, *How to Read the Bible*, rev. ed., The Macmillan Company, New York, 1959; J. Edward Lantz, *Reading the Bible Aloud*, The Macmillan Company, New York, 1959; and Edgar J. Goodspeed, *How to Read the Bible*, Holt, Rinehart and Winston, Inc., New York, 1946.

He closes his letter with these words: "And now abideth faith, hope, charity, these three: but the greatest of these is charity." Paul knew that much of the effectiveness of his message would depend on the success of its oral style. Is it not therefore reasonable to believe that he wrote it with that viewpoint in mind?

At present, when so much emphasis is put on speeded reading, we forget that the ancients read their philosophy aloud, taking time even in their private study to form each word, to pronounce it, and to hear how it sounded. This is why so much of the Bible has such a strong poetic element, and therefore an oral reading of Biblical literature permits a free expression of the poetic style.

Just as the ancient Jewish and early Christian leaders read the Bible orally in their synagogues and churches, so today the oral reading of scripture is still an important part of our church services. It would be difficult to estimate how many of us hear the Bible read aloud more than we read it silently. For the past several years, there has been an increasing interest in a study of the oral interpretation of Biblical literature, manifested in the establishment of special courses in colleges and universities and in adult seminars for laymen and clergy held in conjunction with church conferences. Such an interest has arisen from two conclusions: first, that the quality of oral reading from scripture is in need of improvement, and second, that an investigation needs to be undertaken as to why the quality is substandard.

There are several factors which have assisted us in reaching these conclusions. First, there is often a lack of proper preparation for the oral reading of the Bible, both in understanding the material to be read and in understanding *how* the material should be read. Chapters 5 and 6 pointed out how much preparation would be necessary to read from Shakespeare, Browning, Keats, Eliot, or any other author worthy of study. Does the Bible deserve less consideration?

To understand the books of the Bible, we must know who wrote them, to whom the remarks were addressed, and why the author phrased his message. Furthermore, if we are to get the universal message of scripture, we must study it in the light of the times in which it was written. The books were written to meet problems and conditions confronting the people of the time who followed a religion that was much more social and communal than most of our religions of today. The oral interpreter of such religious experiences must see each book as it is related to the times in which the material was written. What do we know of the Hebrew people, their way of life, their poetry, their folk lore?

The material in the Bible was written to real people, living in real places, facing real situations. If the interpreter is to communicate scripture to his audience, he must picture the characters as moving in a society which had its own characteristics. Such an approach does not take away from the inspiration and universality of the Bible. It only offers a fuller appreciation of the material and therefore a greater inspiration to read.

It would be very helpful for the interpreter to be able to read Hebrew, Aramaic, and the colloquial Greek in which the scriptures originally appeared. Unfortunately, this knowledge is beyond the grasp of most of us. However, we can read the several translations of the Bible which are easily available and consult the commentaries by Biblical scholars. Note how different is the language in these three versions:

King James version:
> For God so loved the world, that he gave his only begotten Son, that whosoever believeth in him should not perish, but have everlasting life. For God sent not his Son into the world to condemn the world; but that the world through him might be saved.

Goodspeed version:
> For God loved the world so much that he gave his only Son, so that no one who believes in him should be lost, but that they should all have eternal life. For God did not send his Son into the world to pass judgment upon the world, but that through him the world might be saved.[2]

The New English Bible version:
> God loved the world so much that he gave his only Son, that everyone who has faith in him may not die but have eternal life. It was not to judge the world that God sent his Son into the world, but that through him the world might be saved.[3]

The following references will serve as a starting point for the interpreter in his quest to gain a sufficient comprehension of the Bible to interpret it properly:

Colwell, Ernest: *The Study of the Bible*, The University of Chicago Press, Chicago, 1937.

Denton, Robert C.: *The Holy Scriptures—A Survey*, The Seabury Press, Greenwich, Conn., 1949.

Fosdick, Harry Emerson: *The Modern Use of the Bible*, The Macmillan Company, New York, 1947.

---

[2] J. M. Powis Smith and Edgar J. Goodspeed (trans.), "The Gospel according to John," *The Bible: An American Translation*, The University of Chicago Press, Chicago, p. 87. Copyright 1935 by the University of Chicago.

[3] The Joint Committee on the New Translation of the Bible, Alwyn Winton, Chairman, *The New English Bible, New Testament*, Oxford University Press, New York, 1961, p. 154. © The Delegates at the Oxford University Press and The Syndics of the Cambridge University Press, 1961. Reprinted by permission.

Wright, G. Ernest, and Reginald H. Fuller: *The Book of the Acts of God,* Gerald Duckworth & Co., Ltd., London, 1960.

The following is a scene fairly familiar to all of us. A group has assembled for a Sunday school class, a chapel program at school, or a meeting of a social or civic organization. The chairman decides that a short devotional is appropriate and calls on one of the members to read from the Bible. Without advance notice or preparation, the chosen delegate turns to a chapter and reads—or at least stumbles along. Would the same delegate have attempted to read from one of the classics without any advance preparation? It is imperative that the Bible be read only after thorough study, using the available sources for preparation. To attempt reading without such background information is unfair to the listener, to the reader, and, most of all, to the book being interpreted—the Bible.

A second reason for concluding that the quality of oral reading of scripture is sufficiently substandard to deserve searching study is that readers of the Bible fail to recognize the scripture as literature. As we have already pointed out, much of the Bible is poetry. Note the meter and rhythm of the Twenty-third Psalm:

The Lord is my shepherd; I shall not want.
He maketh me to lie down in green pastures: he leadeth me beside the still waters.
He restoreth my soul: he leadeth me in the paths of righteousness for his name's sake.
Yea, though I walk through the valley of the shadow of death, I will fear no evil: for thou *art* with me; thy rod and thy staff they comfort me.
Thou preparest a table before me in the presence of mine enemies: thou anointest my head with oil; my cup runneth over.
Surely goodness and mercy shall follow me all the days of my life: and I will dwell in the house of the *Lord* for ever.

In addition to the reassuring theme of the psalm and its comforting emotional quality, what are the images that contribute to the consoling idea and mood? How figurative is the language? What sounds do the words connote? Into what form of composition has the song been placed? A homiletical analysis of the psalm would not be complete until its literary style had been clarified. It is a lyrical poem, and it must be studied as such.

Similarly, an interpreter must understand the Book of Ruth for its qualities as a short story. The same narrative elements are used in the Books of Esther and Job that are found in other stories. The study of Biblical literature should be approached as would the study of any great literature, providing a broad insight into its spiritual values.

Considerable study can contribute much to answering the question of why the quality of Biblical reading is substandard and what steps can be taken to raise the level of reading. A study completed in 1951 by Paul Hunsinger made a major contribution in this area [4] and has been followed by the work of Elizabeth Cunningham [5] and others. Further study to clarify attitudes toward oral reading of the Bible and methods of upgrading its presentation should be encouraged.

Selected comments on the oral presentation of scripture

It is often asked whether a reader should be *dramatic* in interpreting the Bible. The question undoubtedly arises from the nature of scripture which requires more than ever that the material and not the reader be dominant. The answer to the inquiry lies in the nature of the Biblical literature being read. Paul's plea to Agrippa in the twenty-sixth chapter of the Book of Acts is intense and dramatic. Therefore, it should be read in a manner which will communicate such deep feeling to the audience. Naturally, the reader should use restraint and good taste in reading any dramatic literature. However, the reader who receives adverse criticism for being too dramatic in reading Paul's plea to Agrippa should examine the type of dramatics he is using. He has probably violated in some manner the aesthetic distance which the listeners expect, a distance which screens out the reader and transfers the audience into the images of the Bible.

In some instances, the oral interpreter, in his eagerness to get the *message* of the scripture across, gets between the material and his audience. He may have made appropriate intellectual preparation, but the theme of his material is so close to him and he feels so strongly about it that he *pushes* too hard. He seems to be forcing an idea rather than sharing it. The interpreter should remember that, particularly in reading the Bible, the *message* will speak for itself if given the opportunity. It needs only an interpreter who will explore all the avenues to understanding and then who will step outside the material to communicate it to his audience.

While Paul's plea to Agrippa is dramatic, the Book of Proverbs is much more conversational. Note the directness of style in the excerpt below:

[4] Paul Hunsinger, "A Study of the Oral Interpretation of the King James Version of the Bible as the Scripture Lesson in the Sunday Morning Worship Services of the Protestant Churches," unpublished doctoral dissertation, Northwestern University, 1951, abstracted in *Speech Monographs*, vol. 19, no. 2, pp. 130–131, June, 1952.

[5] Elizabeth T. Cunningham, "Suggestions and Audio-visual Aids for Reading the Bible Aloud," unpublished master's thesis, The University of Michigan, Ann Arbor, Mich., 1954.

Proverbs 4:1–13

1. Hear, ye children, the instruction of a father, and attend to know understanding.
2. For I give you good doctrine, forsake ye not my law.
3. For I was my father's son, tender and only *beloved* in the sight of my mother.
4. He taught me also, and said unto me, Let thine heart retain my words: keep my commandments, and live.
5. Get wisdom, get understanding: forget *it* not; neither decline from the words of my mouth.
6. Forsake her not, and she shall preserve thee: love her, and she shall keep thee.
7. Wisdom *is* the principal thing; *therefore* get wisdom: and with all thy getting get understanding.
8. Exalt her, and she shall promote thee: she shall bring thee to honour, when thou dost embrace her.
9. She shall give to thine head an ornament of grace: a crown of glory shall she deliver to thee.
10. Hear, O my son, and receive my sayings; and the years of thy life shall be many.
11. I have taught thee in the way of wisdom; I have led thee in right paths.
12. When thou goest, thy steps shall not be straitened; and when thou runnest, thou shalt not stumble.
13. Take fast hold of instruction; let *her* not go: keep her; for she *is* thy life.

Here the author is teaching and counseling. To communicate such didactic material, the oral reader needs to assume some of the role of the public speaker and be more direct with his audience than he would in Paul's plea to Agrippa.

Parts of the Book of Revelation cannot be read with directness. Note the opening verse of chapter twenty-one: "And I saw a new heaven and a new earth: for the first heaven and the first earth were passed away; and there was no more sea." John is telling of his revelation, what he saw and what he heard. Such material is subjective, featuring the use of imagery and figurative language very effectively to recount the experience. The oral reader must suggest a mood which will appropriately re-create John's revelation.[6]

The Bible presents difficulties to the interpreter because it includes unfamiliar words in an unusual format. A part of these problems may be obviated by a careful selection of the translation employed. However, these elements do present a challenge to the reader in any

---

[6] See the comments in Chaps. 5 and 6 on mood.

version he chooses, and he must do research to understand the meaning of the Biblical language used. To read Chaucer, Spenser, and Shakespeare requires study, research, and practice. Some of the contemporary writers such as Dylan Thomas and E. E. Cummings employ unfamiliar words and a most unusual form. Great literature is not passed by because it is difficult to understand. The interpreter must investigate the language and the structure until he feels he has mastered their significance.

An anthology by Mary Ellen Chase entitled *Readings from the Bible*,[7] formerly used in conjunction with the course at Smith College entitled the Literature of the Bible, can serve as a guide in choosing selections from the scriptures which are suitable for classroom reading. The chief limitation of the collection is that it confines itself to the King James or Authorized Version. The student may wish to compare the excerpts in the Chase anthology to their appropriate counterparts in other versions.

Summary

There are no special techniques for reading the Bible. The same principles discussed throughout the text are applicable to the oral interpretation of Biblical literature.

[7] Mary Ellen Chase, *Readings from the Bible*, The Macmillan Company, New York, 1952.

Chapter notes

Note on objective measures of empathy

There are two approaches to an objective measurement of empathy, which apply equally well to both the ability of the speaker to empathize and to the ability of the audience to empathize.

Measurement of the theoretical capacity to respond

At least two tests have been devised which purport to predict empathic ability. If these tests are sufficiently valid and reliable, they will permit a measurement of the capacity of a reader and his audience to empathize. Even though the tests will not tell how to improve empathic talent, they will permit a measurement of any increases in empathic ability. Continued research is in order, not only to improve on empathy tests, but also to offer structured procedures for expanding one's empathic abilities.[1]

In 1949, Dymond proposed a scale for the measurement of empathic ability.[2] Defining empathy as "the imaginative transposing of oneself into the thinking, feeling and acting of another and so structuring the world as he does," [3] Dymond pursued the qualities clinicians term *insight* by an application of role playing. Fifty-three subjects made evaluations of small groups of students with whom they had been working intimately on class projects:

[1] Luchins says: "Research is . . . needed to discover factors which increase or decrease an individual's empathic behavior." Abraham S. Luchins, "A Variational Approach to Empathy," *Journal of Social Psychology*, vol. 45, p. 15, 1957.
[2] Rosaline F. Dymond, "A Scale for the Measurement of Empathic Ability," *Journal of Consulting Psychology*, vol. 13, no. 2, pp. 127–133, April, 1949.
[3] *Ibid.*, p. 127.

Subject A rated himself on a five-point scale on his self-confidence—superior–inferior, selfish–unselfish, friendly–unfriendly, leader–follower, and sense of humor.

Subject A rated B, C, D, E, etc., on how A thinks B, C, D, E, etc., rate on the above characteristics, using the same scale.

Subject A rated B, etc., on how he thinks B would rate himself.

Subject A rates himself (A) on how he thinks B would rate him (A).

Since B has done the same for A, Dymond could compare the accuracy with which A could predict B's ratings *and* the accuracy with which B could predict A's ratings. In other words, Dymond measured A's potential to empathize by his ability to predict how B would rate B and how B would rate A.

Although there are distinct limitations to this test,[4] it has the advantages of being easily administered and easily scored. It makes no pretense of measuring aesthetic empathic responses, except perhaps in the case of the sense of humor. But in the absence of research which shows the relationships between conscious empathic abilities and unconscious empathic abilities, its effectiveness in measuring the latter is unknown. However, it should be of probative value until more data is known.

In 1955, Kerr and Speroff released a standardized test based on the assumption that "individuals who are superior in empathic ability are persons who are above average in understanding and anticipating the reactions of other people."[5] The authors secured data in three areas: first, the preference of nonoffice factory workers for types of music while they are working; second, the total paid circulation of leading magazines; and third, the severity of certain annoying habits, such as "a person slapped me on the back" or "seeing a person's nose running." Subjects are simply asked to rank the types of music as they would be preferred by nonoffice factory workers at work, the magazines according to total paid circulation, and the annoying habits as the average person would rank them. In other words, subjects are asked to put themselves into the place of the factory worker, the average American, and the average person aged 25 to 39. Scoring is simple and time involved in completing the test is minimal.

Again, the Kerr and Speroff test aims to measure a conscious effort at empathy. This text assumes that the aesthetic empathic response is

---

[4] Since Dymond could locate no other test of empathic ability in 1949 with which to validate her results, she compared her scores with a previous technique which she had developed and reported. See R. Dymond, "A Preliminary Investigation of the Relation of Insight and Empathy," *Journal of Consulting Psychology*, vol. 12, no. 4, pp. 228–233, July–August, 1948.

[5] W. A. Kerr and B. J. Speroff, "Manual of Instructions," *The Empathy Test,* Psychometric Affiliates, Chicago, 1955, p. 1.

largely unconscious. Still this test, like the Dymond test, if it is valid,[6] could show the interpreter his improvement in developing empathy and might even point out to him the possibility that unconscious reactions cannot be improved without conscious effort.

Measurement of capacity to respond in context. As was pointed out earlier, the difficulties in measuring empathic responses while they occur are numerous. It seems imperative that the subject not know he is being evaluated in order that his empathic responses may remain unconscious. Such a requirement rules out the conventional types of audience analyzers and indeed most of the methods of measurement now commonly employed.

However, at least three possibilities for measuring aesthetic empathic responses deserve immediate investigation. First, the semantic differential, because it purports to avoid direct measurement, has considerable potential as a measuring device for empathy.[7] If we can assume that the semantic differential for theater concepts developed in 1961 [8] can measure factors also operating during oral reading, we need not even wait for the development of a semantic differential for oral interpretation before beginning investigation. A reader who modifies his responses on the semantic differential after studying a selection and intensifies this modification after presenting the selection to the class is undergoing an experience. If the reader's certification of his changed behavior on the semantic differential can be found to correlate with certification of his changed behavior on either the Dymond or the Kerr and Speroff tests, he may be registering on the semantic differential a reaction equivalent to his empathic responses. This appears to be only one of the many possibilities which the semantic differential offers as a contextual measure of empathy.

Second, noise level appears highly indicative of the presence of empathy.[9] A very quiet audience may indicate one which is free of its conscious bodily needs; a very noisy audience may indicate one which has freed itself of ordinary social restraints and is responding without inhibitions. During World War II, as long as the blackouts were on, the streets of English cities were often noisy at night with singing

[6] Kerr and Speroff discuss the validity of their test in some detail in their manual of instructions. See also *The Fifth Mental Measurements Yearbook*, O. K. Buros (ed.), Gryphon Press, Highland Park, N.J., 1959, p. 120 for references and an analysis by R. L. Thorndike.
[7] See Charles E. Osgood, George J. Suci, and Percy Tannenbaum, *The Measurement of Meaning*, The University of Illinois Press, Urbana, Ill., 1957.
[8] Raymond G. Smith, "A Semantic Differential for Theatre Concepts," *Speech Monographs*, vol. 29, no. 1, pp. 1–8, March, 1961.
[9] Elwood A. Kretzinger, "Gross Bodily Movement as an Index of Audience Interest," *Speech Monographs*, vol. 19, no. 4, pp. 244–248, November, 1952.

and joking, but when the lights came back on, the English became self-conscious and the boisterousness disappeared. Therefore, an audience which is sympathetically quiet or noisy may well be an audience which is empathizing. A tape recording of a reading synchronized with any of the common types of noise meters would seem an elemental method of investigating the relationship between noise level and empathic responses.

Third, appearance may be indicative of the degree of empathy in operation. Hidden motion-picture cameras or trained observers operating behind one-way vision mirrors may furnish data which can be interpreted as indicating the degree of empathy present.

Naturally, combinations of these objective methods, particularly the second and third, are in order.

Just as there are many tests in medicine which are only indicative and which take their place along with the subjective observations of the trained physician, so the objective tests of aesthetic empathy will probably only form one of many indications of the presence of aesthetic empathy. Yet indicative results can be very helpful, and experimentation in the area of the objective measurement of empathy during oral reading should be encouraged.

Summary

Only through evaluation can the oral interpreter hope to improve. Evaluation is a painful and often wasteful process. All of us like to think that we are capable of pointing out to ourselves how we can improve, because when we are criticized by others, we tend to accept such advice as an indication that we are not strong enough to help ourselves. It is only by the careful development of objectivity that man can secure the proper blend of self-help with outside help. Furthermore, much time can be consumed in the evaluation process, some of which must inevitably be lost pursuing fruitless goals. We cannot expect all of our subjective and others' objective comments to ring true. Some spurious directions will be given. Needless to say, the interpreter must accept such blind roads with as much grace as he can muster, turn around, and seek a more successful method of improvement.

At present, oral interpreters are judged largely on a subjective basis. There appear to be several channels, the exploration of which may offer worthwhile indications to assist these subjective interpretations. The future holds improved methods of evaluating oral reading not only subjectively, but also objectively. An appropriate combination of the two should enable students of oral interpretation to accelerate their learning processes.

Note on empathy

Early in the twentieth century, Theodor Lipps attempted to clarify some of the confusion and controversy surrounding the term *Einfühlung* by publishing a series of essays discussing the concept from a variety of points of view. Although Lipps states that he is not seeking a definitive definition of *Einfühlung*, he does distinguish a primary and a secondary type, making the primary use of *Einfühlung* that power by which man experiences an object outside of himself. In other words, unless man actively appreciates an object by sharing part of himself with it, the object has no meaning for him.[10] Heidbreder interprets Lipps as saying that an observer "tends to 'feel himself into' the object he is contemplating and that the slight and almost unnoticed muscular responses he makes in doing so form the basis of the esthetic experience."[11]

Einfühlung, which literally means *sympathic understanding*, was translated by Titchener as *empathy*, saying:

The various visual images, which I have referred to as possible vehicles of logical meaning, oftentimes share their task with kinaesthesis. Not only do I see gravity and modesty and pride and courtesy and stateliness, but I feel or act them in the mind's muscles. This is, I suppose, a simple case of empathy, if we may coin that term as a rendering of *Einfühlung;* there is nothing curious or idiosyncratic about it; but it is a fact that must be mentioned.[12]

Definitions of empathy are varied in their scope and purpose. As early as 1899, Groos referred to *Einfühlung* as "inner mimicry."[13] In 1948, Dymond defined empathy as "the imaginative transposing of oneself into the thinking, feeling and acting of another and so structuring the world as he does."[14] Recently, Berlo proposed that empathy is "the ability to project ourselves into other people's personalities."[15] However, there seems no reason to limit the project to "other people" at the expense of places and things.[16] Empathy may be defined, there-

---

[10] Theodor Lipps, *Zur Einfühlung*, W. Engelmann, Leipzig, 1913, pp. 481–482.
[11] Edna Heidbreder, *Seven Psychologies*, Century Company, New York, 1933, p. 101. Copyright, 1933, Century Company. Reprinted by permission of Appleton–Century–Crofts, Inc.
[12] E. B. Titchener, *Lectures on the Experimental Psychology of the Thought-processes*, The Macmillan Company, New York, 1909, pp. 21–22.
[13] Karl Groos, *Die Spiele der Menschen*, Gustav Fischer, Jena, 1899, p. 500.
[14] Dymond, *op. cit.*, p. 127.
[15] D. K. Berlo, *The Process of Communication*, p. 119. Copyright 1960 by Holt, Rinehart and Winston, Inc., New York.
[16] See Luchins, *op. cit.*, p. 11.

fore, as *that phenomenon wherein the receiver of a stimulus sympa-thizes sufficiently with the stimulus so that he reacts mentally and physically to what he experiences.*[17]

Note on the relationship between oral and silent reading

During the last decade, there has been an accelerated interest in quantitive research designed to compare the effectiveness of oral read-ing, silent reading, and oral reading reinforced by silent reading. Needless to say, the research is far from complete, but the results to date are interesting.

A series of studies has compared the effects of listening to a poem with and without textual reinforcement. In 1949, Beardsley reported a gain in the *appreciation* of poetry when listeners read as well as heard a poem, but reported no results in which listening was superior to listening and reading.[18] In 1952, Bernard Goldstein published simi-lar results for comprehension, following a study in which respondents listened to poems while looking at the text.[19] Silvestri concluded in 1959: "There must be a combination of oral presentation and silent study of a given poem to achieve maximum learning experience."[20]

Another series of studies has measured the effect of oral reading versus silent reading. In 1953, Young compared a group which read five stories orally with two groups, one of which read the same stories silently and the other of which listened to the five stories on tape. In light of the findings of Beardsley, Goldstein, and Silvestri, Young's findings are complimentary to oral reading, for he reported that, al-though all three groups gained significantly in vocabulary growth, the group which read the five stories orally showed a significantly higher gain in vocabulary scores over the listeners to the tape recordings and

[17] In order to sympathize, the receiver of the stimulus need not feel *sympathetic* in the sense that he has compassion. To sympathize here means to derive a re-sponse which can be directly attributed to a given stimulus.

For further information, see Herbert S. Langfeld, *The Aesthetic Attitude*, Har-court, Brace and Company, Inc., New York, 1920, pp. 109–142; Kerr and Sper-off, *op. cit.*, p. 1; and Berlo, *op. cit.*, pp. 116–129. The discussion above is in-debted to all three of these references.

[18] Paul Wesley Beardsley, "Listening versus Listening and Reading: A Study in the Appreciation of Poetry," unpublished master's thesis, University of Oklahoma, Norman, Okla., 1949.

[19] Bernard J. Goldstein, "The Comprehension of Poetry from Recordings," un-published doctoral dissertation, Columbia University, New York, 1952.

[20] Vito N. Silvestri, "An Experimental Examination to Determine Whether the Goal to Interpret a Poem Orally Increases Retention and General Understanding as Compared to Silent Study," unpublished master's thesis, Emerson College, Boston, 1959, p. 109.

a gain, though not significant, over the silent readers.[21] It is not known what would have been the results had Young added a fourth group which read the poem silently and orally, permitting a comparison of his research with that of Beardsley, Goldstein, and Silverstri. In 1958, Gray reported on significant differences in "over-all understanding, response to central meaning, response to central images, response to metaphorical images, or appropriate critical comments on the poem" when comparing tape recordings of poems with silent reading of poems.[22] Again, in light of the previous findings, the results are complimentary to the oral interpretation of poetry, particularly when tape recordings rather than live interpreters were used. Three subsequent studies, two performed at the University of Southern California and one at Emerson College, likewise testify to the effectiveness of oral reading. Campbell selected three audiences: a group of trained oral interpreters, a group of trained silent readers, and a group untrained in either oral or silent reading. All three groups heard six poems orally and read the same poems silently. A comparison of results showed that the interpreters were as successful as were the trained silent readers in comprehension, but less successful in retention.[23] In 1959, Collins exposed two matched groups to seven prose selections, ranging in difficulty from "very easy" to "very difficult." One group read the prose silently, while another listened to it orally. Collins reports significant differences in comprehension in favor of oral reading for the "very easy," the "easy," and the "fairly difficult" selection. In the other four instances, subjects who read the prose orally made higher scores than the silent readers, but the results did not reach significance. The main (or summary) effect of the oral readers was significantly greater than that of the silent readers.[24] In the same year, Silvestri used a three-dimensional design to compare the interactions of silent and oral reading with levels in college and with groups matched and unmatched in reading skills. He reports that the group which prepared to read orally had a higher mean score in re-

[21] James D. Young, "An Experimental Comparison of Vocabulary Growth by Means of Oral Reading, Silent Reading, and Listening," *Speech Monographs,* vol. 20, no. 4, pp. 273–276, November, 1953.

[22] Wallace Allison Gray, "Listeners' and Readers' Responses to Poetry," unpublished doctoral dissertation, Columbia University, New York, 1958.

[23] Paul Newell Campbell, "An Experimental Study of the Retention and Comprehension of Poetry Resulting from Silent Reading and from Oral Interpretation," unpublished doctoral dissertation, University of Southern California, Los Angeles, 1959. Reported in *Speech Monographs,* vol. 27, no. 2, pp. 146–147, June, 1960.

[24] Raymond E. Collins, "An Experimental Investigation of the Comprehension of Prose Materials When Read Silently and When Read Aloud," unpublished doctoral dissertation, University of Southern California, Los Angeles, 1959. Reported in *Speech Monographs,* vol. 27, no. 2, p. 147, June, 1960.

tention and general understanding than did the group which read the poem silently, when the two groups were matched on reading abilities. The means, however, were not significantly different.[25]

The studies reported thus far exposed subjects to varying stimuli for a relatively short period of time. In 1950, however, Gilbert asked: "What effect, if any, does training in oral reading (as now taught by speech teachers) have on the silent reading skills of students in junior high school, senior high school, and college?"[26] Standardized tests measuring vocabulary, reading speed, and reading comprehension were administered at the conclusion of a semester's instruction in oral reading or voice and diction at all three levels. The control for Groups I, II, and IV of experiment III which pertained to the college level was selected from the general college population, while the controls for the high school and junior high school groups (seventh and ninth grades) usually took English, except for one ninth grade control group which was a class in speech. Gilbert reports that, although the college experimental sections for Groups I, II, III, and IV of experiment III made greater gains in silent reading skills, except in speed, than did the general college population, "... none of the differences in gains obtained was statistically significant enough to warrant generalization...."[27] The control group for the senior high school, an English class which studied mostly literature, had higher means on silent reading skills than did the experimental group, reaching significance at the .01 level on vocabulary and total score, but the probability of error was considerably greater for comprehension and speed. At the end of a semester, the seventh grade control group showed significant improvement at the .01 level in reading speed, vocabulary, and total score when compared with the experimental group, but not in comprehension.[28] The comprehension score was the only one on which the seventh-grade experimental group showed improvement, and that gain was considered no more than normal.

The Gilbert study raises several questions. By definition, the nature of the instruction in oral reading was largely uncontrolled. Will a difference in method of teaching oral interpretation affect the measures of criterion used by Gilbert? Second, oral interpretation may well slow the speed of reading rather than accelerate it since instruction in oral interpretation often stresses a critical analysis of literature, causing the student to approach cautiously what he is reading.

[25] Silvestri, *op. cit.*
[26] Edna Gilbert, "An Experimental Study of the Effects of Training in Oral Readings on Silent Reading Skills," unpublished doctoral dissertation, University of Wisconsin, Madison, Wis., 1950, p. 1.
[27] *Ibid.*, p. 80.
[28] *Ibid.*, p. 161.

Furthermore, a standard English class seems likely to read far more literature in a semester than does a class in oral interpretation, and therefore vocabulary gains would be less in the oral interpretation class than in the English class. Should oral reading make any pretense of increasing vocabulary or reading speed more than would occur in a course in English literature? What methods of teaching oral interpretation would serve to accelerate the gains in comprehension noted in several phases of the Gilbert study?

Summary

Two hypotheses may be drawn from these studies. First, oral reading and silent reading appear to be complementary studies. One is not intended as a substitute for the other. Students of oral interpretation must do the appropriate amount of research on their selections before reading them in public. Such research includes a critical analysis of the literature. Furthermore, students of oral interpretation should be expected to absorb the content of the literature read orally to an equal degree as do their fellow students in classes which stress silent reading. The ready availability of paperback editions makes this procedure now feasible.

Second, instruction in and exposure to oral reading cannot be substituted for instruction in and exposure to silent reading, particularly if a class in oral reading seeks improvement in skills which conventional instruction in oral interpretation does not stress.

The unique contribution of oral interpretation to reading skills remains as yet undefined. Beardsley's efforts to measure particular components of language such as rhythm needs to be given more consideration. Studies replicating controlled methods of instruction are needed, e.g., an experimental group which requires comprehension of the literature equal to that demanded in standard classes in English needs to be compared with control groups in conventional instruction in oral interpretation and literature. The next decade should produce research which will further clarify the unique contribution of oral reading to silent reading skills.

Supplementary bibliography

Anderson, Irving H., and Donald E. Swanson: "Common Factors in Eye-Movements in Silent and Oral Reading," *Psychological Monographs*, vol. 48, no. 3, pp. 61–69, 1937.

Bond, Guy L.: "The Auditory and Speech Characteristics of Poor Readers," *Contributions to Education* 657, Teachers College, Columbia University, New York, 1935.

Eames, Thomas H.: "The Relationship of Reading and Speech Difficulties," *Journal of Educational Psychology,* vol. 41, no. 1, pp. 51–55, January, 1950.

Ewers, Dorothea: "Relations between Auditory Abilities and Reading Abilities: A Problem in Psychometrics," *Journal of Experimental Education,* vol. 18, no. 3, pp. 239–262, March, 1950.

Goldstein, Harry: "Reading and Listening Comprehension at Various Controlled Rates," *Contributions to Education* 821, Teachers College, Columbia University, New York, 1940.

Hildreth, Gertrude: "Interrelationships among the Language Arts," *Elementary School Journal,* vol. 48, no. 10, pp. 538–549, June, 1948.

Loge, Dennis R.: "An Experimental Study of the Comparative Effectiveness of the Oral and Traditional Methods of Teaching High School Literature," unpublished master's thesis, University of North Dakota, Grand Forks, N.D., 1957.

Maynard, Norma: "Poor Reading, Handmaiden of Poor Speech," *The Speech Teacher,* vol. 5, no. 1, pp. 40–46, January, 1956.

Pintner, J., and A. R. Gilliland: "Oral and Silent Reading," *Journal of Educational Psychology,* vol. 7, no. 1, pp. 201–212, January, 1916.

Rossignal, Lois J.: "The Relationship among Hearing Acuity, Speech Production, and Reading Performance in Grades 1A, 1B, and 2A," *Contributions to Education* 936, Teachers College, Columbia University, New York, 1948.

Swandon, Donald E.: "Common Elements in Silent and Oral Reading," *Psychological Monographs,* vol. 48, no. 3, pp. 36–60, 1937.

Note on the relationship between speech and personality

Only a limited amount of research is available on the degree to which the speech of an individual molds his personality traits and vice versa. Little or no attention has been given to the degree to which improvement in oral reading is associated with improvement in personality. Correlations between the improvement in the several phases of oral reading on the one hand, and self-evaluations, standardized test scores, and audience evaluations of personality traits on the other hand may indicate the degree to which the speech activity known as oral interpretation interacts with personality.

The following bibliography includes a variety of studies on the interaction of speech and personality.

Allport, G. W., and H. Cantril: "Judging Personality from Voice," *Journal of Social Psychology,* vol. 5, pp. 37–55, 1934.

Barbara, Dominick A.: *Your Speech Reveals Your Personality,* Charles C Thomas, Publisher, Springfield, Ill., 1958.

Black, A. Duane: "An Investigation of Judgments of Intelligence and Personality Based on Voice, Appearance, and Speaking before a Group," unpublished master's thesis, University of Hawaii, Honolulu, 1958.

Dow, Clyde W.: "The Personality Traits of Effective Public Speakers," *Quarterly Journal of Speech,* vol. 27, no. 4, pp. 525–532, December, 1941.

Duncan, Melba Hurd: "An Experimental Study of Some of the Relationships between Voice and Personality among Students of Speech," *Speech Monographs,* vol. 12, pp. 47–60, 1945.

Eckert, R. G., and N. Keyes: "Public Speaking as a Cue to Personality Adjustment," *Journal of Applied Psychology,* vol. 24, pp. 144–153, 1940.

Eisenberg, P., and E. Zalowitz: "Judging Expressive Movement: III. Judgments of Dominance-Feeling from Phonographic Records of Voice," *Journal of Applied Psychology,* vol. 22, pp. 620–631, 1938.

Fay, P. J., and W. C. Middleton: "The Ability to Judge Sociability from the Voice as Transmitted over a Public Address System," *Journal of Social Psychology,* vol. 13, pp. 303–309, 1941.

———: "Judgment of Introversion from the Transcribed Voice," *Quarterly Journal of Speech,* vol. 28, no. 2, pp. 226–228, April, 1942.

———: "Judgment of Occupation from the Voice as Transmitted over a Public Address System and over a Radio," *Journal of Applied Psychology,* vol. 23, pp. 586–601, 1939.

———: "Judgment of Spranger Personality Types from the Voice as Transmitted over a Public Address System," *Character and Personality,* vol. 8, pp. 144–155, 1939–1940.

Gilkinson, Howard, and Franklin H. Knower: "A Study of Standardized Personality Tests and Skills in Speech," *Journal of Educational Psychology,* vol. 32, no. 3, pp. 161–175, March, 1941.

Kelly, E. L.: "Personality as Revealed by Voice and Conversation without Face to Face Acquaintance," *Psychological Bulletin,* vol. 35, p. 710, 1938. (Abstract.)

Mallory, Edith B., and Virginia R. Miller: "A Possible Basis for the Association of Voice Characteristics and Personality Traits," *Speech Monographs,* vol. 25, no. 4, pp. 255–260, November, 1958.

Michael, W., and C. C. Crawford: "An Experiment in Judging Intelligence by the Voice," *Journal of Educational Psychology,* vol. 18, no. 2, pp. 107–114, February, 1927.

Moore, Wilbur E.: "Personality Traits and Voice Quality Deficiencies," *Journal of Speech Disorders,* vol. 4, no. 1, pp. 33–36, March, 1939.

Murray, Elwood: *The Speech Personality,* J. B. Lippincott Company, Philadelphia, 1937.

Pear, T. H.: *Voice and Personality,* Chapman & Hall, Ltd., London, 1931.

Remsberg, Anna Jane: "An Investigation of the Question: Do People Associate Certain Voice Types with Particular Combinations of Body Shape and Heights?" unpublished master's thesis, Miami University, Oxford, Ohio, 1959.

Sanford, F. H.: "Speech and Personality: A Comparative Case Study," *Character and Personality,* vol. 10, pp. 169–198, 1941–1942.

———: "Speech and Personality," *Psychological Bulletin,* vol. 39, no. 10, pp. 811–845, December, 1942.

Sapir, E. A.: "Speech as a Personality Trait," *American Journal of Sociology,* vol. 32, no. 6, pp. 892–905, May, 1927.

Stagner, R.: "Judgments of Voice and Personality," *Journal of Educational Psychology,* vol. 27, no. 4, pp. 272–277, April, 1936.

Taylor, H. C.: "Social Agreement on Personality Traits as Judged from Speech," *Journal of Social Psychology,* vol. 5, pp. 244–248, 1934.

Turner, Daniel: "A Study of Speech Effectiveness and Personal and Social Adjustment among Ninth Grade Pupils," unpublished doctoral dissertation, Boston University, Boston, 1957. Reported in *Speech Monographs,* vol. 25, no. 2, p. 97, June, 1958.

Note on the contribution of oral interpretation to communication theory

Learning and its corollary, attitude change, have been receiving renewed emphasis among philosophers, semanticists, and social psychologists. The provoking questions of how man learns and how learning can be accelerated have always been important in education, but the recent publications of Skinner,[29] Miller,[30] Hovland,[31] Shannon and Weaver,[32] and others have opened new vistas in learning theory and attitude change. For example, in areas of interest closely allied to oral interpretation, there have been a series of studies comparing the readability of material with the listenability of material.[33]

It will not be possible here to explore the many ways in which the theories of communication may be amplified by research in oral interpretation. The discussion will be limited to three concepts which deserve immediate comment.

First, spokesmen for oral interpretation have always been interested in establishing rapport with their listeners. Such an interest is es-

[29] B. F. Skinner, *Verbal Behavior,* Appleton-Century-Crofts, Inc., New York, 1957; B. F. Skinner, "A Quantitative Estimate of Certain Types of Sound-patterning in Poetry," *American Journal of Psychology,* vol. 54, pp. 64–79, 1941.

[30] G. A. Miller, "Speech and Language," in S. S. Stevens (ed.), *Handbook of Experimental Psychology,* John Wiley & Sons, Inc., New York, 1951; G. A. Miller, *Language and Communication,* McGraw-Hill Book Company, Inc., New York, 1951.

[31] Carl I. Hovland, Irving L. Janis, and Harold H. Kelley, *Communication and Persuasion,* Yale University Press, New Haven, Conn., 1953. Four additional volumes have appeared to supplement this progress report.

[32] C. E. Shannon and W. Weaver, *The Mathematical Theory of Communication,* The University of Illinois Press, Urbana, Ill., 1949.

[33] Harry Goldstein, "Reading and Listening Comprehension at Various Controlled Rates," *Contributions to Education* 821, Teachers College, Columbia University, New York, 1940; Kenneth A. Harwood, "Listenability and Rate of Presentation," *Speech Monographs,* vol. 22, no. 1, pp. 57–59, March, 1955; and Kenneth A. Harwood, "Listenability and Readability," *Speech Monographs,* vol. 22, no. 1, pp. 49–53, March, 1955.

sential because the interpreter is partially dependent upon audience reaction to guide him in the establishment of mood. Communication theorists have measured the results of this rapport in terms of *feedback*. Since the cyclical response is important to both disciplines, the oral interpreter is interested in exploring the following:

What are the relationships between reading at a particular time of day and the creation of mood?

To what extent is mood dependent upon key emotional words in contrast to general thought content?

What adjustments on the part of the reader will dissipate a hostile feedback to classical literature?

Under what conditions will college men respond favorably to lyric poetry?

The list could be extended indefinitely. As early as 1941, Skinner was interested in sound patterning in poetry. The interrelationships of rhyme, meter, and rhythm deserve study. The reactions to material which has been labeled *verse* in contrast to identical material which has been labeled *prose* would involve experimentation in both semantic and communication theory. Although the controlling of variables in quantitive study is complex, the obstacles are not insurmountable.

Not only can oral interpretation make a contribution to communication theory by clarifying certain of the complexities of feedback, but it is at present training readers whose skills are needed in existing communication research. The two studies footnoted earlier comparing listenability with readability presumes an effective oral reading of the material designed for listening. Otherwise, meaningful comparisons may not be made with effective silent-reading performances. Research in reading has been much concerned with the appearance of printed material—whether it is to be arranged in one or two columns, what type of print should be used, what punctuation should be involved. Research in listening must be equally concerned with the properties of oral presentation.

Third, oral interpretation is much concerned with the reaction between retention and appreciation. Initially, the extent to which oral reading conveys content must be established in detail.[34] Subsequently, the correlation between retention of content and acceleration in ap-

[34] A study of the effect of choral reading on learning done at Mississippi Southern College in 1958 indicated that historical facts can be taught by group exercises in reading aloud. Twenty-five high school students participating in a choral reading of the life of George Rogers Clark made impressive scores on an immediate and a delayed posttest for retention. Rehearsals of from twenty to thirty minutes were held once a day for two weeks. Subjects did not know they were to be posttested. The open-ended short-answer test question was used to measure retention.

preciation will show the extent to which the communication of the content of a selection contributes to its sympathetic reception.

The discipline of oral interpretation provides to researchers in communication trained personnel who know the nuances of aural learning and who can offer a variety of readings for investigation, all of which are delivered with the effectiveness that should be expected of research in communication.

A supplement of selected references on communication theory and attitude research

Berlo, David K.: *The Process of Communication*, Holt, Rinehart and Winston, Inc., New York, 1960.

Cofer, Charles N. (ed.): *Verbal Learning and Verbal Behavior*, McGraw-Hill Book Company, Inc., New York, 1961.

Fairbanks, Grant: "The Relation between Eye-movements and Voice in the Oral Reading of Good and Poor Silent Readers," *Psychological Monographs*, vol. 48, no. 3, pp. 78–107, 1937.

Grigsby, O. J.: "An Experimental Study of the Development of Concepts of Relationship in Pre-school Children as Evidenced by Their Expressive Ability," *Journal of Experimental Education*, vol. 1, pp. 144–162, December, 1932.

Kantor, J. R.: *An Objective Psychology of Grammar*, Indiana University Press, Bloomington, Ind., 1936.

Lazarsfeld, P. F.: "Communication Research and the Social Psychologist," in W. Dennis (ed.), *Current Trends in Social Psychology*, The University of Pittsburgh Press, Pittsburgh, Pa., 1948.

Osgood, Charles E., George J. Suci, and Percy Tannenbaum: *The Measurement of Meaning*, The University of Illinois Press, Urbana, Ill., 1957.

Skinner, B. F.: "The Alliteration in Shakespeare's Sonnets: A Study in Literary Behavior," *Psychological Record*, vol. 3, pp. 186–192, 1939.

Underwood, Benton J., and Rudolph W. Schulz: *Meaningfulness and Verbal Learning*, J. B. Lippincott Company, Philadelphia, 1960.

Wiener, Norbert: *The Human Use of Human Beings*, Doubleday & Company, Inc., Garden City, N.Y., 1956.

Yule, G. Udny: *The Statistical Study of Literary Vocabulary*, The University Press, Cambridge, England, 1944.

Zipf, G. K.: *Human Behavior and the Principle of Least Effort*, Addison-Wesley Publishing Company, Inc., Reading, Mass., 1949.

Bibliography[1]

Abrams, M. H.: *A Glossary of Literary Terms*, Holt, Rinehart and Winston, Inc., New York, 1957.

Aggertt, Otis J., and Elbert R. Bowen: *Communicative Reading*, The Macmillan Company, New York, 1956.

Aristotle: *Rhetoric*, Lane Cooper (trans.), D. Appleton-Century Company, Inc., New York, 1932.

Arnold, Matthew: "Introduction" to *The English Poets*, T. H. Ward (ed.), The Macmillan Company, New York, 1880, vol. 1, pp. xvii–xlvii.

Auden, W. H.: *Collected Shorter Poems: 1930–1944*, Faber & Faber, Ltd., London, 1950.

Bacon, Wallace A., and Robert S. Breen: *Literature as Experience*, McGraw-Hill Book Company, Inc., New York, 1959.

——— and ———: *Literature for Interpretation*, Holt, Rinehart and Winston, Inc., New York, 1961.

Baldwin, Charles Sears: *Ancient Rhetoric and Poetic*, The Macmillan Company, New York, 1924.

Bates, Gladys Graham: "Two Southerners," *Saturday Review*, vol. 24, no. 31, p. 10, Nov. 22, 1941.

Beardsley, Paul Wesley: "Listening versus Listening and Reading: A Study in the Appreciation of Poetry," unpublished master's thesis, University of Oklahoma, Norman, Okla., 1949.

Bedard, George T.: "An Analysis of the Statements of Purpose in Teaching Oral Interpretation," unpublished master's thesis, Indiana University, Bloomington, 1959.

Beebe, Maurice (ed.): *Literary Symbolism*, Wadsworth Publishing Company, Inc., Belmont, Calif., 1960.

Bellow, Saul: "Deep Readers of the World, Beware!" *The New York Times Book Review*, vol. 64, no. 7, p. 1, Feb. 15, 1959.

Bentley, Phyllis: *Some Observations on the Art of Narrative*, The Macmillan Company, New York, 1947.

---

[1] This bibliography includes all works cited in the text plus selected materials suitable for supplementary reading.

Bergson, Henri: "Laughter" in Wylie Sypher (ed.), *Comedy*, Doubleday & Company, Inc., Garden City, N.Y., 1956.

Berlo, David K.: *The Process of Communication*, Holt, Rinehart and Winston, Inc., New York, 1960.

Blackmur, R. P.: *Form and Value in Modern Poetry*, Anchor Books, Doubleday & Company, Inc., Garden City, N.Y., 1957. (Cf. R. P. Blackmur, *Language as Gesture*, Harcourt, Brace & World, Inc., New York, 1952.)

Bloom, Edward A., Charles H. Philbrick, and Elmer M. Blistein: *The Order of Poetry: An Introduction*, The Odyssey Press, Inc., New York, 1961.

Brigance, William N., and Florence M. Henderson: *A Drill Manual for Improving Speech*, 3d ed., rev., J. B. Lippincott Company, Philadelphia, 1955.

Brooks, Cleanth: *The Well Wrought Urn*, Reynal & Hitchcock, Inc., New York, 1947.

————, John T. Purser, and Robert Penn Warren: *An Approach to Literature*, Appleton-Century-Crofts, Inc., New York, 1938.

———— and Robert Penn Warren: *Fundamentals of Good Writing*, Harcourt, Brace & World, Inc., New York, 1950.

———— and ————: *Understanding Fiction*, 2d ed., Appleton-Century-Crofts, Inc., New York, 1959.

———— and ————: *Understanding Poetry*, rev., Holt, Rinehart and Winston, Inc., New York, 1950.

————, ————, and Robert B. Heilman (eds.): *Understanding Drama*, Appleton-Century-Crofts, Inc., New York, 1945.

Bryngelson, Bryng, and Elaine Mikalson: *Speech Correction through Listening*, Scott, Foresman and Company, Chicago, 1959.

Burke, Kenneth A.: *The Philosophy of Literary Form*, rev. and ab., Vintage Books, Inc., Random House, Inc., New York, 1957.

Buros, O. K. (ed.): *The Fifth Mental Measurements Yearbook*, Gryphon Press, Highland Park, N.J., 1959.

Campbell, Paul Newell: "An Experimental Study of the Retention and Comprehension of Poetry Resulting from Silent Reading and from Oral Interpretation," unpublished doctoral dissertation, University of Southern California, Los Angeles, 1959.

Capote, Truman: *Breakfast at Tiffany's*, Random House, Inc., New York, 1958.

Ciardi, John: "Robert Frost: The Way to the Poem," *Saturday Review*, vol. 41, no. 15, pp. 13–15, Apr. 12, 1958.

Cobin, Martin: *Theory and Techniques of Interpretation*, Prentice-Hall, Inc., Englewood Cliffs, N.J., 1959.

Collins, Raymond E.: "An Experimental Investigation of the Comprehension of Prose Materials When Read Silently and When Read Aloud," unpublished doctoral dissertation, University of Southern California, Los Angeles, 1959.

Crane, R. S. (ed.): *Critics and Criticism*, ab., Phoenix Books, The University of Chicago Press, Chicago, 1957.

Cunningham, Cornelius Carman: *Literature as a Fine Art*, The Ronald Press Company, New York, 1941.

317   *Bibliography*

Daiches, David: *Critical Approaches to Literature,* Prentice-Hall, Inc., Englewood Cliffs, N.J., 1956.
————: *Poetry and the Modern World,* The University of Chicago Press, Chicago, 1940.
————: *The Present Age in British Literature,* Indiana University Press, Bloomington, Ind., 1958.
————: *A Study of Literature,* Cornell University Press, Ithaca, N.Y., 1948.
Davidson, Donald: *American Composition and Rhetoric,* 3d ed., Charles Scribner's Sons, New York, 1939.
de la Mare, Walter: *Peacock Pie,* Faber & Faber Ltd., London, 1946.
DeVane, William Clyde: *A Browning Handbook,* 2d ed., Appleton-Century-Crofts, Inc., New York, 1955.
Dewey, John: *Art as Experience,* Minton, Balch & Co., New York, 1934.
Dickinson, Emily: *Bolts of Melody,* Mabel Loomis Todd and Millicent Todd Bingham (eds.), Harper & Row, Publishers, Inc., New York, 1945.
————: *The Complete Poems of Emily Dickinson,* Thomas H. Johnson (ed.), Little, Brown and Company, Publishers.
Drew, Elizabeth: *Discovering Drama,* W. W. Norton & Company, Inc., New York, 1937.
Dymond, Rosaline F.: "A Preliminary Investigation of the Relation of Insight and Empathy," *Journal of Consulting Psychology,* vol. 12, no. 4, pp. 228–233, July–August, 1948.
————: "A Scale for the Measurement of Empathic Ability," *Journal of Consulting Psychology,* vol. 13, no. 2, pp. 127–133, April, 1949.
Eddington, Arthur S.: "The Domain of Physical Science," in Joseph Needham (ed.), *Science, Religion and Reality,* George Braziller, Inc., New York, 1955.
————: "Man's Place in the Universe," *The Nature of the Physical World,* The Macmillan Company, New York, 1933.
Eisenson, Jon: *The Improvement of Voice and Diction,* The Macmillan Company, New York, 1958.
Eliot, T. S.: *The Complete Poems and Plays: 1909–1950,* Harcourt, Brace & World, Inc., New York, 1958.
————: "On Teaching the Appreciation of Poetry," *Teachers College Record,* vol. 62, no. 3, pp. 215–221, December, 1960.
————: *Selected Essays, 1917–1932,* new ed., enlarged, Harcourt, Brace & World, Inc., New York, 1950.
————: *The Use of Poetry and the Use of Criticism,* Harvard University Press, Cambridge, Mass., 1933.
Ellison, Ralph: "As the Spirit Moves Mahalia," *Saturday Review,* vol. 41, no. 39, p. 41, Sept. 27, 1958.
Emerson, Ralph Waldo: *Letters and Social Aims,* Houghton Mifflin Company, Boston, 1876.
Fairbanks, Grant: *Voice and Articulation Drillbook,* Harper & Row Publishers, Incorporated, New York, 1960.
Faulkner, William: "Barn Burning," *Harper's Magazine,* vol. 179, pp. 86–96, June, 1939.

————: "Spotted Horses," *Scribner's Magazine,* vol. 86, no. 6, pp. 585–597, June, 1931.

Forster, E. M.: *Aspects of the Novel,* Harcourt, Brace and Company, Inc., New York, 1927.

Frost, Robert: *Mountain Interval,* Henry Holt and Company, Inc., New York, 1916.

————: *New Hampshire,* Henry Holt and Company, Inc., New York, 1923.

Geiger, Don: *Oral Interpretation and Literary Study,* Scott, Foresman and Company, Chicago, 1958.

Gilbert, Allan H.: *Literary Criticism,* American Book Company, New York, 1940.

Gilbert, Edna: "An Experimental Study of the Effects of Training in Oral Reading on Silent Reading Skills," unpublished doctoral dissertation, University of Wisconsin, Madison, Wis., 1950.

————: "Oral Interpretation at Speech Festivals," *The Speech Teacher,* vol. 5, no. 2, pp. 117–120, March, 1956.

Goldstein, Bernard J.: "The Comprehension of Poetry from Recordings," unpublished doctoral dissertation, Columbia University, New York, 1952.

Goldstein, Harry: "Reading and Listening Comprehension at Various Controlled Rates," *Contributions to Education* 821, Teachers College, Columbia University, New York, 1940.

Gorrell, Robert M., and Charlton Laird: *Modern English Handbook,* 2d ed., Prentice-Hall, Inc., Englewood Cliffs, N.J., 1956.

Grant, Frederick C.: *How to Read the Bible,* Morehouse-Gorham Company, Inc., New York, 1956.

Granville-Barker, Harley: *The Study of Drama,* Cambridge University Press, New York, 1934.

Grasham, John A., and Glenn G. Gooder, *Improving Your Speech,* Harcourt, Brace & World, Inc., New York, 1960.

Gray, Wallace Allison: "Listeners' and Readers' Responses to Poetry," unpublished doctoral dissertation, Columbia University, New York, 1958.

Green, A. W., Dudley R. Hutcherson, William B. Leake, and Pete Kyle McCarter: *Complete College Composition,* Appleton-Century-Crofts, Inc., New York, 1945.

Grimes, Wilma H., and Alethea Smith Mattingly: *Interpretation: Writer-Reader-Audience,* Wadsworth Publishing Company, Inc., Belmont, Calif., 1961.

Groos, Karl: *Die Spiele der Menschen,* Gustav Fischer, Jena, 1899.

Guest, Edgar A.: *A Heap O' Livin',* Reilly & Lee Company, Chicago, 1916.

Hardy, J. E.: "Delta Wedding as Region and Symbol," *Sewanee Review,* vol. 60, no. 3, pp. 397–417, July, 1952.

Harwood, Kenneth A.: "Listenability and Rate of Presentation," *Speech Monographs,* vol. 22, no. 1, pp. 57–59, March, 1955.

————: "Listenability and Readability," *Speech Monographs,* vol. 22, no. 1, pp. 49–53, March, 1955.

Hedges, Fay L.: "Selecting, Abridging, and Arranging Humorous Prose for Oral Interpretation by High School Students," unpublished master's thesis, State University of Iowa, Iowa City, Iowa, 1959.

Heidbreder, Edna.: *Seven Psychologies*, Century Company, New York, 1933.

Honan, Park: *Browning's Characters*, Yale University Press, New Haven, Conn., 1961.

Hopkins, Gerard Manley: *Poems of Gerard Manley Hopkins*, W. H. Gardner (ed.), 3d ed., Oxford University Press, New York, 1948.

Horace: "Epistle to the Pisos" in *The Great Critics*, J. H. Smith and E. W. Parks (eds.), W. W. Norton & Company, Inc., New York, 1939.

Housman, A. E.: *Last Poems*, Richards Press, Ltd., London, 1937.

Hovland, Carl I., Irving L. Janis, and Harold H. Kelley: *Communication and Persuasion*, Yale University Press, New Haven, Conn., 1953.

Jackson, Shirley: "The Lottery," *New Yorker*, vol. 24, no. 18, pp. 25–28, June 26, 1948.

James, Henry: *The Art of the Novel: Critical Prefaces*, Charles Scribner's Sons, New York, 1934.

Jeffers, Robinson: *The Selected Poetry of Robinson Jeffers*, Random House, Inc., New York, 1938.

Johnson, Samuel: "Preface" to *The Plays of William Shakespeare*, London, 1765.

The Joint Committee on the New Translation of the Bible, Alwyn Winton, Chairman: *The New English Bible, New Testament*, Oxford University Press, Fair Lawn, N.J., 1961.

Jones, W. M.: "Eudora Welty's Use of the Myth in 'Death of a Traveling Salesman,'" *Journal of American Folklore*, vol. 73, pp. 18–23, January, 1960.

————: "Growth of a Symbol: the Sun in Lawrence and Eudora Welty," *University of Kansas City Review*, vol. 26, no. 1, pp. 68–73, October, 1959.

Kennedy, John F.: "The Inaugural Address," delivered January 20, 1961, *New York Times*, p. 8, col. 2, Jan. 21, 1961.

————: "The Inaugural Address," delivered January 20, 1961, in *Public Papers of the Presidents of the United States, John F. Kennedy*, U.S. Government Printing Office, 1962, pp. 1–3.

Kerr, W. A., and B. J. Speroff: "Manual of Instructions," *The Empathy Test*, Psychometric Affiliates, Chicago, 1955.

Kipling, Rudyard: *Rudyard Kipling's Verse, Inclusive Edition, 1885–1926*, Doubleday & Company, Inc., Garden City, N.Y., 1931.

Kretzinger, Elwood A.: "Gross Bodily Movement as an Index of Audience Interest," *Speech Monographs*, vol. 19, no. 4, pp. 244–248, November, 1952.

Lamb, Charles: *Letters*, E. V. Lucas (ed.), arr. Guy Pocock, 2 vols., E. P. Dutton & Co., Inc., New York, 1950.

Langfeld, Herbert S.: *The Aesthetic Attitude*, Harcourt, Brace and Company, Inc., New York, 1920.

Lee, Charlotte I.: *Oral Interpretation*, 2d ed., Houghton Mifflin Company, Boston, 1959.

Leonardo, M. M.: "The Teaching of Imagery in Selected Books Dealing with Oral Interpretation Published from 1757–1956," unpublished master's thesis, Louisiana State University, Baton Rouge, 1958.

Lipps, Theodor: *Zur Einfühlung*, W. Engelmann, Leipzig, 1913.

Longinus: "On the Sublime," W. Rhys Roberts (trans.), in *The Great Critics*, W. W. Norton & Company, Inc., New York, 1939.

Loos, Anita: *Gentlemen Prefer Blondes*, Boni & Liveright, New York, 1925.

Lowes, John Livingston: *The Road to Xanadu*, Houghton Mifflin Company, Boston, 1927.

Lowrey, Sara: "Interpretative Reading as an Aid to Speech Correction, Acting, and Radio," *The Quarterly Journal of Speech*, vol. 31, no. 4, pp. 459–464, December, 1945.

————, and Gertrude E. Johnson: *Interpretative Reading*, rev. ed., Appleton-Century-Crofts, Inc. New York, 1953.

Luchins, Abraham S.: "A Variational Approach to Empathy," *Journal of Social Psychology*, vol. 45, pp. 11–18, February, 1957.

McCarthy, Mary: "Settling the Colonel's Hash," *Harper's Magazine*, vol. 208, pp. 68–75, February, 1954.

McGinley, Phyllis: *Stones from a Glass House*, The Viking Press, Inc., New York, 1943.

Mack, Maynard (ed.): *Twentieth Century Views*, Prentice-Hall, Inc., Englewood Cliffs, N.J., 1962.

Main, C. F., and Peter J. Seng (eds.): *Poems: Wadsworth Handbook and Anthology*, Wadsworth Publishing Company, Inc., Belmont, Calif., 1961.

Michener, James: *Tales of the South Pacific*, The Macmillan Company, New York, 1952.

Miller, G. A.: *Language and Communication*, McGraw-Hill Book Company, Inc., New York, 1951.

————: "Speech and Language," in S. S. Stevens (ed.), *Handbook of Experimental Psychology*, John Wiley & Sons, Inc., New York, 1951.

National Broadcasting System: "They Knew Bernard Shaw," a Biography in Sound, broadcast on March 27, 1955.

Nicholson, Harold: *Tennyson*, Houghton Mifflin Company, Boston, 1923.

Norman, Richard A.: "Reading Aloud and Extemporaneous Speaking on the Radio," unpublished doctoral dissertation, Columbia University, New York, 1957.

Noyes, Alfred: *Collected Poems*, Frederick A. Stokes Company, Philadelphia, 1913.

Oldsey, Bernard S.: "The Movies in the Rye," *College English*, vol. 23, no. 3, pp. 209–215, December, 1961.

Ong, Walter J.: *Ramus: Method, and the Decay of Dialogue: from the Art of Discourse to the Art of Reason*, Harvard University Press, Cambridge, Mass., 1958.

Osborne, Harold: *Aesthetics and Criticism*, Routledge & Kegan Paul Ltd., London, 1955.

Osgood, Charles E., George J. Suci, and Percy Tannenbaum: *The Measurement of Meaning*, The University of Illinois Press, Urbana, Ill., 1957.

Parker, DeWitt H.: *The Principles of Aesthetics*, 2d ed., Appleton-Century Crofts, Inc., New York, 1947.

Parrish, Wayland M.: *Reading Aloud*, 3d ed., The Ronald Press Company, New York, 1953.

Pepper, Stephen: *The Work of Art,* Indiana University Press, Bloomington, Ind., 1955.

Perrine, Laurence: *Sound and Sense,* Harcourt, Brace & World, Inc., New York, 1956.

Poe, Edgar Allan: "The Philosophy of Composition," *Graham's Magazine,* vol. 28, no. 4, pp. 163–167, April, 1846.

Porter, Katherine Anne: "Introduction," in Eudora Welty's *A Curtain of Green and Other Stories,* Harcourt, Brace & World, Inc., New York, 1941.

Read, Herbert: *The Nature of Literature,* Grove Press, Inc., New York, 1958.

Richards, I. A.: *Principles of Literary Criticism,* 5th ed., Harcourt, Brace and Company, Inc., New York, 1934.

Robinson, Edwin Arlington: *Collected Poems,* The Macmillan Company, New York, 1937.

Rosenthal, M. L., and A. J. M. Smith: *Exploring Poetry,* The Macmillan Company, New York, 1955.

Russell, Bertrand: *The Impact of America on European Culture,* Beacon Press, Boston, 1951.

Saintsbury, George: *Historical Manual of English Prosody,* The Macmillan Company, New York, 1930.

Sandburg, Carl: *Complete Poems,* Harcourt, Brace & World, Inc., New York, 1950.

Schrodes, Caroline, and Justin Van Gundy: *Approaches to Prose,* The Macmillan Company, New York, 1959.

Service, Robert: *Complete Poems,* Dodd, Mead & Company, Inc., New York, 1950.

Sewell, Elizabeth: *The Structure of Poetry,* Routledge & Kegan Paul, Ltd., London, 1951.

Shannon, C. E., and W. Weaver: *The Mathematical Theory of Communication,* The University of Illinois Press, Urbana, Ill., 1949.

Shepardson, Marie, and Paul D. Brandes, "The Effect of the Introduction on a Literary Communication," unpublished study completed at Ohio University, Athens, Ohio, 1960.

Sill, John Thomas: "Oral Interpretation of the Letters of Abraham Lincoln with Production Notes on a Group Reading of Lincoln's Letters," unpublished master's thesis, Southern Illinois University, Carbondale, Ill., 1958.

Silvestri, Vito: "An Experimental Examination to Determine Whether the Goal to Interpret a Poem Orally Increases Retention and General Understanding as Compared to Silent Study," unpublished master's thesis, Emerson College, Boston, 1959.

Simon, Clarence T.: "Appreciation in Reading," in Gertrude Johnson (ed.), *Studies in the Art of Interpretation,* Appleton-Century-Crofts, Inc., New York, 1940.

Skinner, B. F.: "The Alliteration in Shakespeare's Sonnets: A Study in Literary Behavior," *Psychological Record,* vol. 3, pp. 186–192, 1939.

———: "A Quantitative Estimate of Certain Types of Sound-patterning in Poetry," *American Journal of Psychology,* vol. 54, no. 1, pp. 64–79, January, 1941.

————: *Verbal Behavior*, Appleton-Century-Crofts, Inc., New York, 1957.

Smith, Joseph F., and James R. Linn: *Skill in Reading Aloud*, Harper & Brothers, New York, 1960.

Smith, J. M. Powis, and Edgar J. Goodspeed (trans.): *The Bible: An American Translation*, The University of Chicago Press, Chicago, 1935.

Smith, Raymond G.: "A Semantic Differential for Theatre Concepts," *Speech Monographs*, vol. 29, no. 1, pp. 1–8, March, 1961.

Spencer, Elizabeth: *The Light in the Piazza*, McGraw-Hill Book Company, Inc., New York, 1960.

Swetman, Glen: "The Effect of the Introduction on the Comprehension of a Complicated Literary Communication," unpublished study performed at Mississippi Southern College, Hattiesburg, Miss., 1957.

Tate, Allen (ed.): *The Language of Poetry*, Princeton University Press, Princeton, N.J., 1942.

Tate, Allen: *The Man of Letters in the Modern World*, Meridian Books, Inc., New York, 1960.

Thoreau, Henry D.: *Walden*, Edwin W. Teale (ed.), Dodd, Mead & Company, Inc., New York, 1946.

Thrall, William F., Addison Hibbard, and C. Hugh Holman (eds.), *A Handbook to Literature*, The Odyssey Press, Inc., New York, 1960.

Thurber, James: *The Middle-Aged Man on the Flying Trapeze*, Harper & Brothers, New York, 1935.

————: *My World and Welcome to It*, Harcourt, Brace & World, Inc., New York, 1942.

Titchener, E. B.: *Lectures on the Experimental Psychology of the Thought-process*, The Macmillan Company, New York, 1909.

Tresidder, Argus: *Reading to Others*, Scott, Foresman and Company, Chicago, 1940.

Twain, Mark: *The Adventures of Huckleberry Finn*, Harper & Brothers, New York, 1923.

Von Abele, Rudolph: "Symbolism and the Student," *College English*, vol. 16, no. 7, pp. 424–429, April, 1955.

Wellek, René, and Austin Warren: *The Theory of Literature*, Harcourt, Brace & World, Inc., New York, 1949.

Welty, Eudora: *A Curtain of Green and Other Stories*, Harcourt, Brace & World, Inc., New York, 1941.

————: "How I Write," *Virginia Quarterly Review*, vol. 31, pp. 240–251, Spring, 1955.

Wilcox, Ella Wheeler: *Poems of Sentiment*, W. B. Conkey Company, Chicago, 1892.

Williams, Tennessee: *Summer and Smoke*, New Directions, Norfolk, Conn., 1948.

Williams, William Carlos: *Complete Collected Poems*, New Directions, Norfolk, Conn., 1938.

Wise, J. Hooper, J. F. Congleton, Alton C. Morris, and John C. Hodges: *College English: The First Year*, Harcourt, Brace & World, Inc., New York, 1952.

Woolbert, Charles H., and Severina E. Nelson: *The Art of Interpretative Speech*, 4th ed., Appleton-Century-Crofts, Inc., New York, 1956.

Wordsworth, Dorothy: *The Journals of Dorothy Wordsworth*, Helen Darbishire (ed.), Oxford University Press, Fair Lawn, N.J., 1958.

Wordsworth, William: "Preface" to *Lyrical Ballads*. The preface first appeared in the edition of 1800 and was subject to revision through 1845.

Yelland, H. L., S. C. J. Jones, and K. S. W. Easton: *A Handbook of Literary Terms*, Philosophical Library, Inc., New York, 1950.

Young, James D.: "An Experimental Comparison of Vocabulary Growth by Means of Oral Reading, Silent Reading, and Listening," *Speech Monographs*, vol. 20, no. 4, pp. 273–276, November, 1953.

Index ,